Contemporary Issues
in Canadian Policing

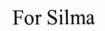

For Silma

Contemporary Issues in Canadian Policing

Edited by
Stephen E. Nancoo

Canadian Educators' Press
Mississauga   Ontario

Contemporary Issues in Canadian Policing
Edited by Stephen E. Nancoo

For information address:
Canadian Educators' Press
100 City Centre Drive
Box 2094
Mississauga, Ontario
Canada, L5B 3C6
Telephone/Fax 905-826-0578
E-mail: cepress@sympatico.ca

National Library of Canada Cataloguing in Publication Data

Nancoo, Stephen E. (Stephen Emmanuel)
Contemporary Issues in Canadian Policing/Stephen E. Nancoo.

Includes bibliographical references.
ISBN 1-896191-09-6

    1. Police-Canada.   I. Title.

HV8157.N35 2004   363.2'0971   C2003-901671-4

Printed and bound in Canada

CONTENTS

Part 111. Culture, Ethics and Technology

Part 1V. Human Resources Issues

Part V. Operational Issues

Part V1.   The Future

PREFACE

Contemporary Issues in Canadian Policing stems from an abiding academic and personal interest in Canadian Policing. In reflecting on policing over the last decade as a social scientist, I am impressed with the numerous changes in policing and police research and writing. The nineteen chapters in this book reflect some of those significant changes and controversies that have taken place.

While there are many classic studies in policing generally, they are somewhat dated. Consequently the timely need for a book like *Contemporary Issues in Canadian Policing* which examines current realities. In compiling this anthology, therefore, a commitment was made to focus on excellent scholarship that is also very recent. This anthology is the most contemporary collection of articles on Canadian policing.

Another significantly compelling factor in the publishing of *Contemporary Issues in Canadian Policing* is the paucity of literature in Canadian policing. The articles in this book are primarily related to Canadian policing and they are written mainly by Canadian scholars and practitioners. It is a modest attempt at providing distinctively Canadian perspectives to *Contemporary Issues in Canadian Policing*. Notwithstanding the recent progress in publishing material on Canadian policing, there is still an urgent need for more research and writing that record the unique experiences and practices of policing in Canada. This is especially important given the increasing number of courses in policing that are being offered at universities and colleges.

In 1993, I co-edited the pioneering book *Community Policing in Canada*. Over the last 13 years, I have trained thousands of Canadian police leaders and managers from all levels

Preface

of policing. The personal motivation stems from the thousands of hours spent teaching, observing and interacting with these police leaders.

Contemporary Issues in Canadian Policing is written for three main groups. The first consists of students and academics of policing. Courses in policing are being offered increasingly in universities and colleges as well as professional police colleges. This book offers participants in these courses a useful blend of theory and practice. The second major audience is police practitioners and administrators in the many police services across the country. A third audience consists of elected and appointed policy makers and decision-makers who play an important role in police governance. Others who will find this book interesting are the many citizens and groups who have an interest in policing and in the continuous improvement of public safety and security of the communities in which they live.

Contemporary Issues in Canadian Policing includes articles that are being published for the first time and a few contributions from academic journals. The authors of articles included in this book are: Ken Menzies, Leanne J. Fitch, David MacAlister, David Sunahara, Marcel-Eugène LeBeuf, Peter J. Carrington, Jennifer L. Schulenberg, Willem de Lint, Alan Hall, J. W. Williams, Tammy Landau, Lori A. Cooke-Scott, Harish C. Jain, Parbudyal Singh, Carol Agocs, Julia McLean, Richard B. Parent, Simon Verdun-Jones, James Sheptycki, Matt Torigian and Stephen E. Nancoo.

For permission to reprint articles, our thanks are due to: *Canadian Journal of Criminology, Canadian Review of Sociology and Anthropology, Canadian Public Administration, the Police Journal, International Journal of the Sociology of Law* and the *Revue Internationale de criminology et de police technique et scientifique.*

For their intellectual support over the years, I am grateful to Jean Havel, Subhas Ramcharan, James Chacko, V. Subramaniam and John Samuel. I also want to thank Steven Reesor, John Girvan, Keith Gregory, Tom Cameron, Brent Stitt, Joseph Mlacak and Spiro Misevski. For her assistance in formatting *Contemporary Issues in Canadian Policing,* my thanks are due to Carla Onoroto. We wish to acknowledge Robert Nancoo, Denese Ramadar and Canadian Educators' Pres for their editorial advice and assistance.

I must thank my wife, Silma and my sons Steve and Robert for their encouragement and support. For their unfailing assistance through the years, my sincere appreciation to Stella Jebodh, Ruth Babwah, Grace Ramjuss, Florence Achong and Myrtle Lynch; as well as, James, Joseph, Kenneth, Kelvin, Victor, Mervyn, Anna, Franklyn, and most of all Dorothy and Nathan Emmanuel Nancoo. Thanks are also due to Parbatee, Shirley, Kelvin, Kenrick and Ronald Deonarine; and Julia and Denese Ramadar.

I am indeed grateful to the many individuals who have contributed directly or indirectly to the publishing of this book. As editor, however, I accept full responsibility for the final output.

Stephen E. Nancoo
Mississauga, Ontario
September 19, 2004

PART 1

SETTING THE STAGE

Introduction

Two concepts of public policing

1

Introduction

Stephen E. Nancoo

General Plan of the Book

This book, **Contemporary Issues in Canadian Policing** is organized into six parts. Part 1 sets the stage with the introductory chapter, by Stephen Nancoo, which gives an overview of the general plan and content of the book. In Chapter 2, Ken Menzies broad-based article promotes the idea of Policing as non-negotiable Force and Policing as Risk minimization. He argues that these two conceptions of policing are linked to traditional and community policing. The nature of community policing, he indicates, is clarified further by distinguishing a neo-liberal version which is based on steering local cooperation from a neo-conservative version which is based on zero-tolerance for minor offences.

Part 11 of the book focuses on the Issue of Community Policing. Beginning with Chapter 3, Ontario Community Policing: An Integrated Approach to Policing, Stephen Nancoo reviews an attempt at modeling through the formulation of a distinctively Canadian model of Community Policing. In this chapter, he delineates the components of the Ontario Community Policing Model, outlines the views of senior police leaders on the application of the model by their organizations in Ontario and proposes future directions in terms of the re-conceptualization and application of the model. There are five components of the model – Police Service Reengineering, Community Development, Enforcement, Police Learning and Community/Police Partnerships. Each component is inter-related and must exist simultaneously for community policing to exist.

In Chapter 4, Lori A. Cooke-Scott outlines the lessons to be learned from the Halton Regional Police Service experience in community based policing. She notes that community policing has faced some fundamental problems in implementation, both internal and external. The changes in Halton indicate that community policing cannot be merely a set of programs; it must be built on a vision of what a police service should be, and that vision must be communicated throughout the police organization. Implementation requires patience, constancy, and commitment: the organizers in Halton gradually recognized that lasting results should not be expected overnight, that changing the entire organization would take a long time and that setbacks and obstacles would occur.

Leanne Fitch, in Chapter 5, examines Organizational Change and Community Policing in Fredericton Police Force. She traces the movement from the formative stages in community policing to its present status as a proactive community centered organization. Change is explored in terms of a social system tapestry, which theoretically explains the reciprocal relationships between the external environment, being the community, and the formal and informal cultures within the police organization. Central to the successful implementation of organizational change is the cooperation and involvement of all three groups.

In Chapter 6, Tammy Landau looks at the issue of Policing and security in four remote aboriginal communities: a challenge to coercive models of police work. In Landau's article abstract, she notes: "most of the academic literature on the nature and function of the uniformed public police has emerged from a framework in which the essential nature of police work has been conceptualized in terms of the powers to use coercive force. There exists a small body of policing literature which identifies a social service role for the police. While this literature has been similarly limited by traditional frameworks which emphasize coercion and control, it suggests that people from lower socioeconomic classes rely more heavily on the police to provide a broader range of services than do socially more advantaged people. This includes "primary" security – the protection of one's physical well-being (from violence, accident, illness, and death) in the immediate situation. The particular role played by the public police within the broader context of a community's social service and security needs and the ability of the existing network of resources to meet those needs. The particular situation of Indian reserves in which risk is high while accessibility to social services is low, provides the specific context. Interviews with community members, community leaders and service providers in four remote aboriginal communities in northern Ontario reveal that alcohol is seen as the most serious social problem in three out of four of the communities, and is perceived to be at the root of most other community problems. At the same time, the public police are seen as the social agency which is best at dealing with either social problems, or problems related to alcohol use. Most other social agencies in the community are viewed as limited in their ability to deal effectively with these kinds of problems. Police occurrence data indicate that the police in each community react to calls involving domestic and non-domestic disputes, problems of order, and request for a broad range of services. The vast majority of situations to which the police in each community respond involve alcohol use. The particular position of the police in the broader network of social services questions conventional views about the extent to which their coercive powers define their social involvement, or whether it is more their ability to provide primary security that other social agencies cannot. The results have theoretical and policy implications for addressing the over-representation of aboriginal people in correctional institutions, the trend toward the "indigenization" of policing services and the development of community-based or problem-oriented policing."

Part 111 focuses on Police Culture, Police Ethics and Information Technology in Policing. David MacAlister takes a penetrating look at Canadian Police Subculture in Chapter 7. He observes that while American and British policing academics have an active research agenda in place that continues to investigate police subculture, Canada has been lacking in this regard as of late. He poses a number of questions that could form an agenda for research by asking how police handle internal conflicts and contradictions in the sub-cultural normative order. Sporadic research efforts have only scratched the surface of the topic in this country. Does the subculture differ in the RCMP compared to municipal departments? Is there variation within the RCMP, or within various units in different police agencies? He notes that American research has found rural policing reflects the same subcultural themes found in urban policing, however only fieldwork will determine if this holds true for the police in Canada's remote regions. Despite the difficulties in carrying out sound, ethical observational research on the police, this still appears to be the best avenue for uncovering the mysteries of police subculture.

In Chapter 8, A Social-Psychological Model of Unethical and Unprofessional Behaviour, David Sunahara proposes a model that differs from much of the existing literature on police ethics in several important ways. Most importantly, it is not prescriptive, i.e., it does not talk about the values that police officers should have. Rather, the emphasis is upon the processes that translate external conditions into attitudes, emotions, beliefs and values which in turn cause some officers to act unethically or unprofessionally. The model of unethical and unprofessional behaviour also differs from the existing literature in terms of scope, and its attempt to be causal rather than philosophical.

In Chapter 9, Marcel-Eugène LeBeuf looks at Policing and Information Technology in Canada. He suggests that not only must police departments prepare themselves to understand the major changes that will be caused by the introduction of high performance technological tools, they must also prepare themselves to integrate these tools, to handle them properly, so that they do not lag behind when it comes to dealing either with new forms of crime that derive from such technology, or with more traditional criminal behaviour. The industry brings together a number of technologies that used to be separated. In order to be efficient in using this technology the police must first and foremost understand the issues at stake. If it may be fairly easy to understand that combating e-crime requires up-to-date skills and specialized knowledge one must also realize that crime control is also dependent on new connected tools and that these tools have to

5

be available to duty police officers and understood by coherent executives.

Part 1V examines Human Resources Issues in such key areas as the contemporary issue of managing diversity in police organizations, the recruitment, selection and promotion of visible minority and aboriginal police officers, and the status of women in policing. With the changing face and fabric of police organizations, Stephen Nancoo explores in Chapter 10 the challenging new dimensions of Managing Diversity in Police Services. He observes that there are significant changes in terms of age, education, gender, culture, ethnicity, race, values and the physically challenged. The organization of the future is also changing in terms of our understanding, the structure and culture of organizations. Given these changes, it is necessary for police organizations to recognize the advantages of diversity and to create and nourish a culture of diversity within organizations so that the full potential of the diverse workforce can be harnessed to the advantage of police organizations as well as Canadian society. Linkages were also made between diversity and contemporary leadership practices. A model of strategic planning, leadership and organizational change was developed with a view of assisting police organizations to adapt to and benefit from the changes and challenges that are an inherent part of the internationalization of the organization culture and the realities of a diverse workforce.

In Chapter 11, Harish Jain, Parbudyal Singh and Carol Agocs examine recruitment, selection and promotion of visible-minority and aboriginal police officers in selected Canadian Police Services. They argue that "the demographic composition of the Canadian police services in major cities generally does not reflect the diversity of the communities they serve, especially with respect to the representation of visible minorities and aboriginal peoples. As many commissions and inquiries on race relations issues in policing have reported, this lack of representation may be a factor that is hindering the effectiveness of police work in major urban centres across Canada. Hence, many commentators have called for increased representation of visible minorities and aboriginal people in the police services through effective recruitment, selection and promotion strategies. Through the use of both quantitative and qualitative research methodologies, the authors identify and assess the various staffing and promotional polices and practices of thirteen police services across Canada. Results suggest that there has been some progress in the representation of visible minorities and aboriginal people in policing over the fifteen-year period of this study. However, there is still room for considerable improvement in the policies, practices and culture of police services if they are to become more representative of the diversity of the community they serve."

In Chapter 12, Marcel-Eugène LeBeuf and Julia McLean reviews the status of Women in Policing in Canada. Their article highlights some of the major issues which concern female officers but also for male officers and more globally for police organizations. Even if we agree on the fact that women have joined the police field and are here to stay, it suffices to acknowledge and reflect on the role and status of women who still constitute a minority in a male universe such as the police milieu in Canada. However, LeBeuf and McLean wish to pursue this reflection by a concrete hold on reality which would entail establishing policies that favour not only recruiting women but maintaining their standing by a more apparent affirmation of the specificity of women within the police.

Part V focuses on operational issues in such critical areas as public order, police interrogation, use of force, the important emerging issues of transnational policing and police discretion. In Chapter 13, Willem de Lint and Alan Hall look at Making the Pickets Responsible: Policing Labour at a Distance in Windsor, Ontario. They examine "the 1987 introduction of a policy for policing labour disputes in Windsor, Ontario. The policy emphasizes the explicit use of consensus-building tactics over coercion in strike situations. Events leading to this policy are traced to the local politics of policing and to changing economic and industrial conditions representing the general decline in Fordist industrial relations. Changes within the police, such as the adoption of community policing, are also considered as important explanations. Both the labour-dispute policy and broader police changes are understood as reflecting the decline of Keynesian state and the movement toward neo-liberalism."

James W. Williams focuses on Interrogating Justice: A critical analysis of the police interrogation and its role in the criminal justice process in Chapter 14. He observes that "in recent years the Canadian criminal justice system has been plagued by a number of high profile wrongful convictions. While each of these cases has raised serious questions concerning the justice process as a whole, particular attention has been directed towards the police and their ability to satisfy their dual mandate of investigating crime while protecting the interests, rights and freedoms of the accused. One notable aspect of police operations that has come under increasing scrutiny in this regard is the police interrogation, a practice which is both upheld by police officers as a crucial means of gathering information and disposing of cases, and denounced by civil rights advocates as a serious threat to the standards of fairness and due process. In adopting the police interrogation as its object of study, he argues that each of these characterizations are severely limited, and ultimately misrepresentative of the more subtle functions of interrogative practices. Specifically, drawing upon the research literature in Britain, the United States, and Canada, the police interrogation will be conceptualized as an interactional medium in which commitments are fashioned to particular criminal identities and renditions of events in a manner that seeks to confirm and legitimize official police narratives. The implications of this constitutive rather than merely coercive function of the interrogation will be examined with particular attention to the issues of police accountability, and the limits of legislative reform."

In Chapter 15, Richard Parent and Simon Verdun-Jones analyze When Police Kill: The aftermath. They examine the use of force and potentially deadly force in the Province of British Columbia, Canada, during the period from 1980 to 1994. The analysis is based on a total of 58 separate, documented incidents involving potentially lethal threats to municipal and Royal Canadian Mounted Police Officers within the Province of British Columbia. In 27 of these incidents, the police responded by discharging their firearms and killing a total of 28 people. The remaining 31 cases that were examined concerned incidents in which the police responded with less lethal force. The study reveals that enormous psychological and emotional stresses that police officers experience during a lethal threat. In many instances these stressors continue to affect the officers long after the lethal threat has been resolved.

In Chapter 16, James Sheptycki offers some Reflections on the transnationalization of policing: the case of the RCMP and serial killers. The article is concerned with the way in which police agencies have reacted to the phenomena of serial killers. It gives an account of how police have gone about being seen to respond to this type of crime and of the technological and organizational innovations that have sprung up as a result. His special focus is on the role that the Royal Canadian Mounted Police are playing in the transnationalization of policing responses to this type of crime.

Peter J. Carrington and Jennifer L. Schulenberg look at Police Discretion with Young Offenders in Chapter 17. They discuss the main areas of police work with young offenders in which discretion is exercised: the detection of youth crime, clearing youth-related incidents by informal action, referring to alternative measures, or laying a charge, and procedures used to compel the attendance at court of youth who are charged.

Part V1 deals with the future. In Chapter 18, Stephen Nancoo reflects on the Police and the Diverse Canadian Society: Trends and Prospects in the 21st Century. In Chapter 19, Nancoo and Matt Torigian address some additional challenges facing Canadian policing today. The current issues they focused on are globalization and transnational policing, terrorism and national security, racial profiling, public policing-private security, and organizational performance measurement.

2

Policing as Force and Policing as Risk Minimization: Two Concepts of Public Policing[1]

Ken Menzies

What is public policing? This chapter clarifies two possible definitions: non-negotiable force and risk minimization. These two conceptions of policing are linked to traditional and community policing. The nature of community policing is clarified further by distinguishing a neo-liberal version which is based on steering local cooperation from a neo-conservative version which is based on zero-tolerance for minor offences. Conceptual clarity helps us understand the realities of modern Canadian policing. I argue that Canadian police mostly apply non-negotiable force to do emergency repairs to the social order. In applying this force they are guided increasingly by understandings with other institutions. Neo-liberal community policing embeds the police substantially further into the local social structure than neo-conservative community policing.

For philosophical realists, good definitions pick out the key features of what is being defined (Bhaskar, 1978). Good definitions are not arbitrary choices about how to use words. A good definition is one whose terms are essential to the causal impact of what is being defined. For instance, if we define policing as risk minimization, then we are saying this is the core of policing. Risk minimization provides policing with its causal efficacy. Disputes about definitions are about what is central to understanding a topic. This chapter shows how accepting particular definitions of policing implies accepting particular theoretical understandings of police activity.

Definitions of Policing

Public policing can be defined by whom it serves. Conflict theorists see police as maintaining the status quo for the benefit of the powerful (e.g. Cain, 1979, p.158). Consensus theorists see the police as serving everybody by regulating relationships among people for the benefit of society as a whole (e.g. Bailey, 1985, p.7). Policing also can be defined in terms of the nature of police activity. The Ontario Police Services Act (Section 4.2) requires the police to prevent crime, enforce the law, provide assistance to victims of crime, maintain public order and respond to emergencies. Theorists seek the underlying unity in these diverse activities.

Bittner defines the police as "a mechanism for the distribution of non-negotiably coercive force employed in accord with the intuitive grasp of situational exigencies" (1970, p.46). His conception of public policing highlights police using their own judgement to handle situations which threaten to become more disorderly. Their capacity to act decisively rests on their authorization to use force if required. Thus this definition of public policing identifies the key characteristic of public policing as the means police use, non-negotiable force, not the ends which they seek. Illustrations of this definition include police arresting a robber or police threatening to charge people partying if another noise complaint is received. Another example is a Guelph police officer who brought an eight year old boy to the police station. The boy's parents had just died in a car crash. To distract and entertain the boy until his relatives arrived, the officer let him play with police equipment. Force in this situation is unlikely, but if the boy had tried to leave then he would have been restrained.

This approach views force, arrest and the law as police resources (Ericson, 1982). The presence of a resource does not imply its use. Much of the craft of policing lies in using the authority of the office and the officer's skills in handling people to avoid using physical force (Bittner, 1983). Whether force is used or not, this view sees policing as oppositional: somebody is being policed against. The central ethical concerns when policing is identified as non-negotiable force are: Who is being policed against? and Is it legally and morally justified for these people to be coerced? In summary, the police are canny folk who decide what they want and get their way with deceptive ease.

The risk minimization approach to policing draws on the risk society perspective. This sees our society as changing from a simple modern society with a focus on industrial production to an advanced modern or risk society (Beck, 1992). Risk societies with their large service sectors attempt to manage adverse events as accidents. Accidents are normal and their incidence predictable. Thus insurance is the appropriate response. In addition, society seeks to cost effectively minimize accidents by ensuring compliance with safety routines rather than responding to adverse events as injustices whose perpetrators should be punished.

Ontario's brief experiment with photo radar exemplifies this risk approach. To reduce speeding, cameras in vans took photographs of speeding vehicles. License plate numbers identified vehicle owners who were fined. As the driver was not identified, no demerit points were deducted from a license. Speeding was treated as a normal accident to be managed. The concern was to cost effectively reduce speeding, not to target and blame offenders. While the Progressive Conservatives cancelled photo radar on coming to power in 1995 (Montgomery, 2002, pp.123-4), a preliminary evaluation showed it successfully reduced speeding (Safety Research Office, 1995).

In the risk society approach, public policing is activities which are intended to minimize risk from crime or the immediate adverse effects of social disorder. The key characteristic of public policing is the security ends being pursued, not the means used to pursue these ends. Risk is a wider category than crime and disorder. For instance, Vancouver's needle exchanges provide illegal drug users with clean needles to reduce the risk of AIDS and Hepatitis C. For needle exchanges to work, the police must avoid policing drugs near the facility. Vancouver's harm minimization approach to drug use requires tacit police cooperation. Law enforcement is neglected in order to minimize risk (O'Malley, 2001). Recently, Vancouver police have stepped up law enforcement and thereby reduced the effectiveness of the needle exchanges (Cohen, 2003).

This approach identifies public police as problem solvers who minimize crime and disorder risks. A variety of incidents must be grouped together, and a solution found that is based on police work alone, or the police working with other institutions. For instance, the Edmonton police discovered that one gas service center chain had 27% of all city robberies. Some appeared to be inside jobs. To tackle this problem, a detective went to all service stations and put basic security precautions in place: limited money in the cash register and cigarettes behind the counter. The police also worked with the company to introduce a security check which required all employees to be cleared by the Edmonton Police Service. The problem solving approach worked: robbery rates at this service station chain dropped to the level of other Edmonton service stations (Hawkins, 2000).

Ericson and Haggerty present an analysis of what they call risk communication policing. They define policing as consisting "of the public police coordinating their activities with policing agents in all other institutions to provide a society-wide basis for risk management (governance) and security (guarantees against loss)" (1997, p.3). Their analysis shows public policing involves communication with other institutions such as credit card companies and public health offices. The central theme of *Policing the Risk Society* is that the classification schemes of other institutions fundamentally influence how the public police operate (1997 p.17). Their analysis focuses on the planning and aftermath of policing and neglects actual policing. Risk minimization defines public policing more inclusively. It includes the entire range of police activities from planning, to police-citizen encounters, ("the sharp end of policing"), to the communication of these encounters to others.

Ericson and Haggerty illustrate their central themes by discussing police reports after a drunk driving accident. Not only do the police prepare a report for the crown attorney, they also send reports to the provincial motor vehicle registry, insurance companies, the health system, authorities concerned with traffic management, and car companies to improve car safety. Finally, they report to themselves: to their own CPIC record system, to account for property seized and to manage police time (1997, pp.23-4). This example also shows that how police operate on the street is not just a response to their own hierarchy and sub-culture, it is also controlled by the forms, many now electronic, which police must file. Police mobilization must be understood in terms of the demands of other institutions, not just 911 calls and the police's internal concerns. The police are knowledge workers engaged in communications at the hub of governmental processes to classify the population and suppress risk (Loader and Walker, 2001). In short, the public police are armed actuaries whose forms type populations.

The risk minimization approach to policing raises different ethical issues than the policing as non-negotiable force approach. As policing is centrally a service reducing risks, the central ethical questions are: "Who benefits?" and "Should everybody pay through their taxes for these benefits or should the beneficiaries of public policing pay?" For instance, while owners of burglar alarms pay the public police for answering false alarms, they gain the benefit of a police response to correct alarms as they have been able to afford an alarm system. Should a tax be added to alarm systems to cover this benefit? Another way of raising the ethical issues of risk minimization policing is by asking: "To what extent should public policing be treated as a commodity to be paid for by its direct beneficiaries?" Some Canadian police knowledge now is commodified. For instance, insurance companies pay for occurrence reports and for police time spent with an insurance adjustor (Ericson and Haggerty, 1997, p.30).

Traditional and Community Policing

Much has been written in this book and elsewhere (eg. Chacko and Nancoo, 1993; Griffiths, Parent and Whitelaw, 2001) about traditional and community policing in Canada. Consequently, my objectives in this section are to highlight key features of each type of policing and relate them to policing as non-negotiable force and as risk minimization, in a preliminary way.

Traditional policing is based on an ideology of police professionalism. Police professionalism asserts that police have expert knowledge about fighting crime and that they should be allowed to go about their central task of crime fighting without political interference (Seagrave, 1997, pp.56-8). Crime is fought best through the 3 Rs: Random patrol, Rapid response and Reactive investigation. Random patrols deter criminals by making the police visible. Rapid responses to calls from citizens allows the police to react by investigating each crime occurrence as soon as possible. This "tradition" arose in Canada in the immediate post-World War Two period to take advantage of the possibilities which arose from two way radios, cars and widespread public ownership of telephones to call police. Its professional ideology was part of the growing competence and administrative independence of municipal, provincial and federal government bureaucracies in the post war period.

The professional policing ideology identifies policing with crime fighting. This identification ensured a limited police role in society. It also masked substantial police discretion and order maintenance work. For instance, a study of calls to police dispatchers in Toronto in 1971 found that only one quarter was crime related. Other calls were for order maintenance and service work such as accidents, collapses and illnesses (16%) or traffic problems (9%) (Shearing, 1984, pp.20-22).

Bittner's definition of policing (1970) was based on his observations of the police using a wide range of techniques with considerable discretion in their policing of skid row in the 1960's (1967). Thus, not surprisingly, his definition fits traditional policing activity. Traditional policing is police controlled or police-centric. This fits Bittner's emphasis on non-negotiable force being applied in accord with an officer's own intuitive grasp of the situation. The non-negotiable force definition implies a limited police role: crime fighting, emergency order maintenance and service activities which are linked closely to order maintenance such as directing traffic and organizing searches for missing people.

Police, politicians and policy analysts began moving away from traditional policing in the late seventies in the United States and in the early eighties in Canada. More random police patrols, faster police response times and reacting to crimes individually, more of the 3 Rs, came to be seen as poor ways of improving the fight against crime (Bayley, 1994, pp.3-12). A community policing ideology gradually replaced the professional policing ideology throughout Canadian public police forces (Murphy, 1993). In many cases, the shift can be dated by when a police department renames itself a police service. For instance, the Edmonton Police Department became the Edmonton Police Service in 1990 after introducing several community policing innovations (Hawkins, 2000). While people knew what they wanted to move away from, they were uncertain as to what the solution to traditional policing problems should be. However, they knew the solution should be called "community policing". Experimentation with a wide variety of solutions to the problems of traditional policing led the term to be applied to numerous police practices. In 1994 the United States federal government made money available to hire one hundred thousand community policing officers (Cordner, 2000, p.45). Political considerations required that the money and police officers be spread among America's 17,000 police departments. This ensured that the term "community policing" would apply to a great diversity of police practices.

The definition of community policing as "a diverse set of practices united by the general idea that the police and the public need to become better partners in order to control crime, disorder and a host of other problems" (Weisel and Eck, 1994, p.53) captures its broad scope. A community policing "ideology inevitably means accepting a widely expanded definition of what the police are responsible for" (Skogan and Hartnett, 1997, p.14). Community policing is based on the 3Ps: Partnership with the community, Problem solving and Prevention. Only in partnership with the community can the police effectively act to solve the problems which generate crime and thus prevent crime. For example, in response to numerous offences by youths in a park, the Ontario Provincial Police approached the park supervisor to argue for three more lights. They also established a committee to look into recreational facilities, particularly two tennis courts and a baseball diamond. They wrote letters of support to the town council for lights and the recreational facilities (Griffiths, Parent and Whitelaw, 2001, pp.98-103).

Ericson and Haggerty conclude, "Community policing turns out to be risk communication policing" (1997, p.5). Risk minimization, or as they call it, risk communication policing, fits community policing in several ways. Community policing commits the police to being proactive in grouping incidents together into soluble crime and disorder problems. Grouping incidents involves considering them in relation to a variety of factors which can be tackled in a risk minimization way. For instance fights near a bar might be reduced by working with the licensing authority to ensure that the bar does not serve inebriated customers and stepped up police patrols. How far the public police penetrate towards the root causes of crime and disorder is left open. Community policing's expansive view of the police mandate fits risk minimization policing.

Neo-liberal and Neo-conservative Community Policing

In order to explore fully the relationship between traditional and community policing with non-negotiable force and risk minimization policing, it is necessary to distinguish two different approaches to community policing. Community policing has been defined as "a philosophy, management style, and organizational strategy" (Griffiths, Parent and Whitelaw, 2001, p.38). This implies community policing is future-oriented. Expectations about the future must be based on explicit or implicit theories about the consequences of police actions. Two main theories, neo-liberalism and neo-conservativism underlie community policing. These underlying theories shape what the police identify as community priorities. The term "community policing" suggests implicitly a consensus among an area's people. For instance, the RCMP commissioner advocates "establishing as operational priorities those problems which disturb a community most" (as cited, Bayley, 1993, p.39). While police like to give examples where consensus is probable such as stolen bicycles being of greater concern than bank robberies, they ignore conflicting demands from different groups. In a multi-cultural, multi-racial, multi-class, multi-sexual orientation city, in short, in a normal Canadian city, public police face conflicting demands for enforcement about drugs, illegal immigrants, disorderly conduct and much more. Police choose which demands to call the community priorities on the basis of their values, the overall political climate and their theories about what constitutes effective policing.

Neo-liberal Community Policing

Classic nineteenth century liberalism asserted individual

17

freedom in a market society against aristocratic privilege. Discovering the stunting impact on people's potential of inequalities flowing from a market society, twentieth century welfare liberalism argued that people could only develop their potential if society provided basic services such as health care and a social safety net. Neo-liberal governments recognise that governments cannot deliver all the services which citizens want. The government's role is to provide some services and to steer other institutions to provide the services which are needed to compliment government services (Rose, 1996). Neo-liberal community policing is based on the public police providing some services and steering other institutions into coordinated actions to reduce crime and disorder. The more closely an activity is linked to the causes or consequences of disorder, the more prominent the police's steering role. Neo-liberal approaches stress police arrangements (formal or informal partnerships) with local institutions such as mall security forces, hotel bouncers, sexual assault centers and community mental health groups. While still delivering key services, the police recognise that coordination and oversight of others, particularly private security, is the way to provide low crime and disorder (De Lint and Hall, 2002; O'Malley and Palmer, 1996). Neo-liberal community police help create community by overcoming the limitations of the market and public institutions which focus on their mandate interpreted narrowly, by encouraging all institutions to include more security and to act in coordination with the public police.

Windsor Police's current approach to labour disputes illustrates neo-liberal policing. In 1989, the police adopted a formal labour liaison policy and appointed labour liaison officers. These officers try to maintain order by teaching labour and management their legal rights and helping them agree on how to regulate themselves. For instance, they would seek an agreement on how long a vehicle could be delayed before being allowed to pass through a picket line. By making both sides more responsible for their behaviour, the public police have raised the threshold for coercive intervention. Nevertheless, coercive intervention remains as a backup for order maintenance (de Lint and Hall, 2002).

Neo-liberal approaches provide little guidance as to how extensive a role the public police should play in ensuring low crime and disorder. This poses potential ethical problems (Loader and Walker, 2001). If the public police role is highly restricted, then some people, particularly those with limited resources, receive inadequate security (Murphy 1998). On the other hand, if the public police role is extensive, if they penetrate to the root causes of crime and disorder, then we have the horrors of a police state. How extensive a role the police have now in Canada is determined largely by police budgets, not a reasoned analysis of how extensive a role they should play in security provision.

Neo-conservative community policing

The "broken windows" theory underpins neo-conservative community policing. Its logic is appealing. If somebody breaks a factory window and nobody repairs the window, then people feel that nobody is in charge and nobody cares. Vandals smash more windows. Similarly, if there are visible signs of disorder, if minor incivilities are allowed to flourish in an area, then people feel that nobody is in charge. As the authority of a neighbourhood over its space declines, disorder grows and crime flourishes. Thus the police should do quality of life policing based on zero-tolerance for minor offences (Wilson and Kelling, 1982; Kelling and Coles, 1997).

Neo-conservative policing moves aggressively against visible minor offences such as illegal drug use, aggressive begging and street prostitution. It seeks to create defensible space. Defensible space is an area which people who use the space see it as their own space and therefore seek to control it (Newman, 1972). By enabling people to feel safe in asserting control of their neighbourhoods, people will be able to maintain order and low crime themselves. The police help create community. This indicates the key difference between conservatism and neo-conservatism. Conservatives see community as natural, while neo-conservatives believe that now it must be created. The focus of neo-conservative policing is enabling citizens, not working with institutions. The police role in society is limited: focus on reducing crime and disorder, with particular emphasis on visible minor crime and disorder. The preceding is the public media face of neo-conservative policing. The actual practice is usually more complex, for instance, using minor offenders as intelligence sources about major offences (Johnson and Shearing 2003, ch.6).

This approach raises several ethical concerns. First, should police target the people such as youth and homeless whose offences are visible, rather than people whose offences are less visible? The problem becomes particularly acute if the visible offenders are more likely to be from some minority group. This problem is particularly troubling as the evidence in favour of the effectiveness of neo-conservative zero-order policing is ambiguous. For instance, while Skogan (1990) found a link between visible disorder and major crime, a reanalysis of his data provide arguments for and against the link between visible disorder and major crime. Harcourt (1998) discusses problems caused by how missing data was handled and shows that if five extreme cases which were all from Newark, New Jersey are removed from the data set, that statistical significance disappears in Skogan's data for the visible disorder-major crime link. On the other hand, Eck and Maguire (2000) argue that if Skogan had removed some dubious cases from his data, his conclusion on the visible disorder-major crime link would be statistically stronger. Targeting minor offenders to reduce serious crime has successes and failures. For instance, when New York Transit police targeted fare dodgers, they found that one in ten of those arrested either was carrying a concealed illegal weapon or was wanted on an outstanding warrant (Kelling and Coles, 1997, ch.4). On the other hand, in Chandler, Arizona, a police crack down on minor offences and disorder, reduced these, but had no effect on more serious crime (Katz, Webb and Schaffer, 2001). The safe conclusion is that neo-conservative policing works only under some limited, and at present unclearly identified, circumstances. The second ethical concern with neo-conservative policing is how to ensure that the police do not overstep their legal authority. Offences such as creating a disturbance or threatening behaviour are difficult to define clearly. After New York city adopted a zero-tolerance approach to minor offences, civilian complaints against the police increased by 60% between 1993 and 1996 (Greene, 1999). While police abuse is not inherent in neo-conservative community policing, it appears to be more difficult to avoid than with neo-liberal community policing.

Some analysts (eg. Forcese, 1999, p.232) present community policing as based on a broken windows theory. The failure to distinguish neo-liberal from neo-conservative variants of community policing obscures that police use two different strategies for crime and disorder control. All Canadian police forces incorporate some elements of both neo-liberal and neo-conservative community policing models. At the provincial and national level, the neo-liberal approach is dominant. Institutional cooperation and information sharing is encapsulated in police reporting forms.

At the local level, major differences exist between neo-conservative and neo-liberal police forces. The differences depend both on the police and other local institutions. For instance, in the early 1990s, "Toronto's orientation to street youth had many features of a social welfare model" (Hagan and McCarthy, 1998, p.108), such as several youth hostels to which police could take street youth. At this time in Vancouver, there were no such facilities (Hagan and McCarthy, 1998, pp.105-34). Vancouver police adopted a law and order neo-conservative approach to street youths using "constant vigilance and charging practices" (O'Grady and Bright, 2002, p.38). In 1995, Ontario elected a Progressive Conservative government on a neo-conservative platform. Welfare for youths aged 16 and 17 who wanted to live away from their parents was curtailed drastically. By 1999, Toronto had shifted from a neo-liberal to a neo-conservative approach to street youth with their Community Action Policing Program. For instance even before the Safe Streets Act came into force in January 2000, they were targeting squeegee cleaning and other forms of begging in what they identified as Toronto's crime spots (O'Grady and Bright, 2002).

Current Realities

Many contend that community policing is a fundamental break from the past. A typical assertion is: "Community Policing represents a fundamental change in the basic role of the police officer, including his or her skills, motivations, and opportunities to engage in problem-solving activities and to develop new partnerships with key elements of the community." (Wilkinson and Rosenbaum, 1994, p.110). When we contrast current Canadian policing realities with those of thirty years ago major continuities and changes appear:

21

1. Police-citizen encounters remain the application of non-negotiable force: Community policing books abound with examples of police problem solving. Their pages are littered with acronyms such as SARA (Scanning, Analysis, Response, Assessment) or PARE (Problem Identification, Analysis, Response, Evaluation which is used by the Ontario Provincial Police) (Griffiths, Parent and Whitelaw, 2001, pp.87-130). While problem solving forms part of the overall pattern of community policing, it is misleading to identify it as the key characteristic of community oriented policing. Policing, like most jobs, largely is doing the work, not planning the work. While more planning goes into community policing than traditional policing, most front-line policing work remains applying non-negotiably coercive force. After this work is done, what has been accomplished is communicated.

An American time use study suggests that police continue to do much of what they have been doing (Parks et al., 1999). This study of front-line police compared patrol generalists who did traditional policing focussed on answering 911 calls with community policing specialists. The data were gathered in Indianapolis which had adopted a neo-conservative community policing approach and St Petersburg which had adopted a neo-liberal community policing approach. Results were similar for both cites. In an organizational arrangement aimed at maximizing the difference between community oriented police officers and traditional police, 75% of police time in each city is spent the same ways. When problem-directed and information activities are examined, the activities which we might expect the largest differences between the two types of policing, the results remain similar. For the two cities combined, in an eight hour shift, community policing specialists spend 90.5 minutes in these activities, while traditional police spend 73 minutes. Stated alternatively, community-oriented police spend a little more time than traditional police learning about their area, so that they can apply non-negotiable force in a more sophisticated manner. More generally, as traditional police officers normally knew their area well, the difference between community policing and traditional policing is that this learning about an area has become acknowledged, systematized and formally shared, not tacit, ad hoc and casually communicated.

2. Police focus remains crime and emergency order repair:

Community police "seek holistic solutions" (Loader and Walker, 2001, p.16) to "all sorts of community problems" (Lab, 2000, p. 164). For instance an RCMP management document asserts community policing members "routinely engage in problem solving activities and work closely with other agencies to address the root causes of crime and disorder" (as cited Laing and Hickman, 2003, p.35). While police occasionally do make input into how society tackles root causes of crime, these actions are peripheral to their central concerns. The routine of policing is responding to crime and disorder and conditions directly linked to emergency social order repair. Community groups and people are seen as information sources, support groups - resources to help the police accomplish their security goals - not partners in changing the root causes of crime (Murphy, 1993). Canadian police have a strong tradition of wanting to stay apart from political matters, so this situation is unlikely to change soon. Many police, especially those with a neo-conservative approach to policing recognise and endorse this. For instance, Police Chief Fantino, a leading advocate of neo-conservative policing said "It is ludicrous to relegate to the police the role, responsibility and accountability for urban renewal and social reform." (As cited Griffiths, Whilelaw and Parent, 2001, p.44).

3. Policing is less police-centric: Police have become increasingly concerned with coordinating their responses to situations with other institutions. In police-citizen encounters, a central concern now, unlike previously, often is to gather the information which their reporting forms demand. These forms incorporate the agendas and concerns of numerous other agencies. Police form part of wider crime reduction strategies. A possible police slogan is: "Act regionally, display locally."

4. Neo-liberal community policing is less police-centric than neo-conservative: All modern policing is less police-centric, than traditional policing as we have just noted. However, there is substantial variation with neo-conservative community policing being much more police-centric than neo-liberal community policing. Neo-conservative police forces do zero-tolerance policing and implement provincial and national agreements contained in their forms. They also implement forms of community policing which can be done with citizens rather than organized groups with whom power would have to be shared. For instance, they are likely to implement Neighbourhood Watch programs as these involve the police encouraging individuals to form organizations oriented to providing the police with information. Neo-conservative police will have fewer and less developed arrangements than neo-liberal police with organizations such as community mental health, shelters for homeless youth and private security firms. An interesting hypothesis to test is: The better the relationship with the local sexual assault center, the more neo-liberal the police force. The logic is that forming a good relationship with a sexual assault center requires the police to make substantial accommodations to their focus on arresting an offender. While the sexual assault center accepts this concern, its agenda has other concerns as well.

Differences between neo-liberal and neo-conservative community policing exist at objective and subjective levels. Objectively, neo-liberal community policing exists when police are embedded strongly in the security concerns of local institutions. Agreements made by police administrators can produce this result. Subjectively, neo-liberal policing requires front line public police get to know people throughout an area and to form informal links with citizens, particularly those working in security such as hotel bouncers or university police force members. Neo-liberal front line police officers see themselves as part of society-wide approach to security concerns not standing alone to defend society as the thin blue line. Analysts of Canadian policing suggest considerable resistance by the police subculture to community policing (eg. Seagrave, 1997, pp. 240-2; Stansfield, 1996, pp. 199-201). RCMP internal surveys have found many officers sceptical or hostile to community policing (Forcese, 1999, p.233). Thus the objective and subjective dimensions of neo-liberal community policing often diverge.

Conclusion

Good definitions identify the core features of phenomena. Thus clarity about what different definitions of policing and different types of community policing imply and a discussion of traditional and community policing helps us specify the current realities of Canadian policing. Throughout the post-war period, at the point of contact with civilians, policing has been the application of non-negotiable force to arrest offenders, to effect emergency social order repair, or to deal with conditions directly linked to crime and disorder. Behind the front lines, policing has changed. Policing is no longer guided largely by an officer's intuitive grasp of a situation. Police are guided by their reporting forms. These embed the police in the information demands and security concerns of many provincial and national institutions. Police forces which adopt a neo-liberal approach to community policing are also embedded in local institutions' security concerns. Neo-conservative police forces are more police-centric. Their policing is based on zero-tolerance and policing initiatives which are focussed on individuals.

Endnote

1. I would like to thank Ron Hinch, Bill O'Grady, Anne-Marie Singh and Ron Stansfield for helpful comments on previous drafts of this chapter.

References

Bayley, D. (1985). *Patterns of policing: A comparative international Analysis*. New Brunswick, NJ. Rutgers University Press.

Bayley, D. (1993). Strategy in J. Chacko, and S. Nancoo (Eds.), *Community Policing in Canada* (pp. 39-46). Toronto: Canadian Scholar's Press.

Bayley, D. (1994). *Police for the future*. New York: Oxford University Press.

Beck, U. (1992). *Risk society: Towards a new modernity*. Trans. M. Ritter, London: Sage.

Bhaskar, R. (1978). *A realist theory of science*. Hassocks, Sussex: Harvester.

Bittner, E. (1967). The police on skid row: A study of peacekeeping. *American Sociological Review* 32, 699-715.

Bittner, E. (1970). *The functions of the police in modern society*. Chevy Chase, Maryland: National Institute of Mental Health

Bittner, E. (1983). Legality and workmanship: Introduction to control in the police organization in M. Punch (Ed.), *Control in the*

police organization (pp.1-11). Cambridge: Massachusetts
Institute of Technology Press.

Cain, M. (1979). Trends in the sociology of police work.
International Journal of the Sociology of Law 7, 143-67.

Chacko, J., and Nancoo, S. (Eds.). (1993). *Community policing in
Canada.* Toronto: Canadian Scholar's Press.

Cohen, J. (2003, May 8) Collateral damage of a drug war. *Globe and
Mail* A19.

Cordner, G. (2000). Community policing: Elements and effects in G.
Alpert, and A Piquero (Eds.) *Community policing:
Contemporary readings* 2nd ed. (pp. 45-62) .Prospect Heights,
IL.: Waveland.

Eck, J., and Maguire, E. (2000). Have changes in policing reduced
violent crime: An assessment of the evidence in A. Blumstein
and J. Wallman (Eds.) *The crime drop* (pp. 207-265)
Cambridge: Cambridge University Press.

Ericson, R. (1982). *Reproducing order: A study of police patrol work.*
Toronto: University of Toronto Press.

Ericson, R., and Haggerty, K. (1997). *Policing the risk society.*
Toronto: University of Toronto Press.

Forcese, D. (1999). *Policing Canadian society* (2nd ed.). Scarborough:
Prentice Hall Allyn and Bacon, Canada.

Greene, J. (1999) Zero tolerance: A case study of police policies and
practices in New York City. *Crime and Delinquency,* 45,171.

Griffiths, C., Parent, R. and Whitelaw, B. (2001). *Community
policing in Canada.* Scarborough: Thompson Canada.

Hagan, J., and McCarthy, B., (1998). *Mean streets: Youth crime and
Homelessness.* Cambridge: Cambridge University Press.

Harcourt, B. Reflecting on the subject: A critique of the social
influence conception of deterrence, broken windows theory
and order-maintenance policing New York style. *Michigan
Law Review* 97, 291-389.

Hawkins, C. (2000). Ready, fire aim: a look at community policing in
Edmonton Alberta, Canada in G. Alpert and A. Piquero
(Eds.) *Community policing: Contemporary Readings* 2nd ed
(pp. 291-304). Prospect Heights, Il.: Waveland.

Johnson, L., Shearing, C. (2003). *Governing security: Explorations in
policing and justice.* London: Routledge.

Katz, C., Webb, V., and Schaffer D. (2001). An assessment of quality-of-life policing on crime and disorder. *Justice Quarterly* 18, 826-76.

Kelling, G., and Coles, C. (1997). *Fixing broken windows: restoring order and reducing crime in our communities.* New York: Simon and Schuster.

Lab, S. (2000). *Crime prevention: Approaches, practices and Evaluations.* 4th ed. Cincinnati: Anderson.

Laing, R., and Hickman, L. (2003). Community policing in the Royal Canadian Mounted Police: From preventive policing to a national strategy for crime prevention in S. Lab and D., Das (Eds.), *International perspectives on community policing and crime prevention* (pp.28-41). Upper Saddle River, New Jersey: Prentice Hall.

Lint, W. de, and Hall, A. (2002). Making the pickets responsible: Policing labour at a distance in Windsor, Ontario. *Canadian Review of Sociology and Anthropology* 39,1-27.

Loader, I., and Walker, N. (2001). Policing as a public good: Reconstituting the connection between policing and the state. *Theoretical Criminology* 5, 9-35.

Montgomery, B. (2002). *The common (non)sense revolution: The decline of progress and democracy in Ontario.* Creemore: Mad River Publishing.

Murphy, C. (1993). The development impact and implications of community policing in Canada. In J. Chacko and S. Nancoo (Eds.), *Community policing in Canada* (pp.13-26). Toronto: Canadian Scholars' Press.

Murphy, C. (1998). Policing postmodern Canada. *Canadian Journal Of Law and Society* 13, 1-25.

Newman, O. (1972). *Defensible space: Crime prevention through urban design.* New York: Macmillan.

O'Grady, B., and Bright, R. (2002). Squeezed to the point of exclusion: The case of Toronto squeegee cleaners. In J. Hermer and J. Mosher (Eds.), *Disorderly people: Law and the politics of exclusion in Ontario* (pp. 23-39). Halifax: Fernwood.

O'Malley, P. (2001). Risk crime and prudentialism revisited. In K. Stinson and R.Sullivan (Eds.), *Crime, risk and justice: The*

politics of crime control in liberal democracies (pp. 89-103).
Portland Oregon: Willan.

O'Malley, P., and Palmer, D. (1996). Post-Keynesian policing.
Economy and Society 25,137-155.

Parks, R., Mastrofski, S., Dejong, C., and Gray, M. (1999). How
officers spend their time with the community *Justice
Quarterly* 16,483-518.

Rose, N. (1996). Governing advanced liberal democracies in A.Barry,
T. Osbourne, and N. Rose (Eds.), *Foucault and political
reason: Liberalism, neo-liberalism and rationalities of
government* (pp. 37-64). Chicago: University of Chicago Press

Safety Research Office. (1995). *Photo radar safety evaluation:
Preliminary 4 month speed results.* Toronto: Ontario Ministry
of Transport.

Seagrave, J. (1997). *Introduction to policing in Canada.* Scarborough:
Prentice Hall Canada.

Skogan, W. (1990). *Disorder and Decline: The spiral of urban decay
in American neighbourhoods.* New York: Free Press.

Skogan, W. and Hartnett, S. (1997). *Community policing: Chicago
Style.* New York: Oxford University Press.

Stansfield, R. (1996). *Issues in policing: A Canadian perspective.*
Toronto: Thompson Educational Press.

Shearing, C. (1984). *Dial-a-cop: A study of police mobilization.*
Toronto: Centre of Criminology, University of Toronto.

Weisel, D., and Eck, J. (1994). Toward a practical approach to organ-
izational change: community policing initiatives in six cities.
In D. Rosenbaum (Ed.), *The challenge of community policing:
Testing the premises* (pp.53-72). Thousand Oaks, CA.: Sage.

Wilkinson, D., and Rosenbaum, D. (1994). The effects of organizational structure on community policing: A comparison of two
cities. In D. Rosenbaum (Ed.), *The challenge of community
policing: Testing the promises* (pp.110-126). Thousand Oaks,
CA.: Sage.

Wilson, J., and Kelling, G. (1982 March). Broken windows. *Atlantic
Monthly* 29-38.

PART 11

COMMUNITY POLICING ISSUES

Ontario Community Policing Model

Lessons Learned from Halton Regional Police

Organizational Change and Community Policing in Fredericton

Policing and Security in four Aboriginal Communities

3

Ontario Community Policing Model:
An Integrated Approach to Policing

Stephen E. Nancoo

Introduction

In policing services and in communities across Canada, significant changes are being made under the umbrella of community policing. What is evident, however, is that there are many disparate approaches and programs to police service delivery and addressing issues of crime and disorder. The new paradigm of community policing has not been without its critics. Among the criticisms leveled against community policing are that there is a focus on programs rather than a holistic approach to policing; that it is concentrated in a few areas in the police department rather than the whole organization.

Inspite of these criticisms, the future of community policing looks positive. Senior police officials and police organizations in Canada are searching for new and innovative ways of institutionalizing community policing. Indeed, there will come a time when the term community policing will become redundant because all policing will be premised on the profound imperative that the community has a seminal role in the prevention and solving of crime and disorder problems. In this regard a progressive step was made in the Province of Ontario, Canada with the development of an integrated approach to policing through the formulation of the Ontario Community Policing Model (OCPM).

The purpose of this chapter is three-fold: (1) To delineate the components of the Ontario Community Policing Model; (2) To outline the views of senior police officers on the application of the model by their police organizations in communities in Ontario; (3) To outline some future directions in terms of the reconceptualization and application of the model.

The Ontario Community Policing Model

The Ontario Community Policing Model was developed jointly by the Ontario Association of Chiefs of Police sub-committee on Community Policing and the Ontario Ministry of Public Safety and Security. As depicted in Figure 1, there are five components - Police Service Re-engineering, Community Development, Enforcement, Police Learning and Community/Police Partnerships - to the Ontario Community Policing Model. Each component is inter-related and must exist simultaneously for community policing to exist.

According to the Model's definition, Community Policing can be defined as a means of police service delivery which recognizes that the maintenance of order, the prevention of crime and the resolution of crime and order problems are the shared concerns and responsibilities of the community and the police. Working in partnership, the community and the police participate jointly in decision-making and problem solving. This includes: the identification and analysis of crime and order problems, the determination of policing priorities and needs; and the development and implementation of strategies for dealing with crime and order problems identified. Elaborating on the five components, the Ontario Community Policing Model provides for:

Figure 1:Ontario Community Policing Model

POLICE LEARNING

Development of systems both within a police services and provincially to ensure continuous learning for members of police services.

Education for police leaders in strategic planning, change management, & organizational reengineering.

Delivery of problem-oriented policing training for frontline officers

Community Development

Programs initiated & led by the community that contribute to crime prevention, public education & other community policing goals.

Encouraging communities to become full partners in policing.

Initiatives intended to identify & address some of the root causes of crime.

COMMUNITY/POLICE PARTNERSHIPS

Full & equal partnership between the police and community.

Maintenance of public order, the prevention of crime, & the response to crime, are shared concerns & responsibilities of the community & the police.

Permanent mechanisms to permit meaningful community input into all aspects of policing in a

ENFORCEMENT

Enforcement activities that optimize services to the community.

Focused enforcement in response to community safety concerns.

Involvement of communities in determining objectives and priorities.

POLICE SERVICES RE-ENGINEERING

Change management to revise police service structures, human resources and administration processes, and operational policies. Strategic planning for effective police service.

Technology enhancement and streamlining of administrative processes.

1. **Police Service Re-engineering**: affecting organizational change to support contemporary management styles and processes. Change management to revise police service structures, human resources and administration processes, and operational policies. Strategic planning for effective Police service. Technology enhancement and streamlining of administrative processes.

2. **Enforcement**: focusing on community safety concerns and serious violent crime. Enforcement activities that optimize services to the community. Focused enforcement in response to community safety concerns. Involvement of communities in determining objectives and priorities.

3. **Community Development**: community led initiatives that contribute to solving crime and public order problems. Programs initiated and led by the community that contributes to crime prevention, public education and other community policing goals. Encouraging communities to become full partners in policing. Initiatives intended to identify and address some of the root causes of crime.

4. **Police Learning**: supporting continuous learning. Development of systems both within a police service and provincially to ensure continuous learning for members of police services. Education for police leaders in strategic planning, change management and organizational re-engineering. Delivery of problem-oriented policing training for frontline officers.

5. **Community/Police Partnerships**: develop and maintain partnerships in the community at both the front-line and corporate level, permitting meaningful community input into all aspects of policing. Full and equal partnership between the police and community. Maintenance of public order, the prevention of crime, and the response to crime, are the shared concerns and responsibilities of the community and the police. Permanent mechanisms to permit meaningful community input into all aspects of policing in a community.

Applying the Ontario Community Policing

In this section, we would describe applications of the five components of the Ontario Community Policing Model by police services in Ontario. Senior police leaders - Chief Ken Robertson of Hamilton Police, Deputy Chief Mike Boyd of Toronto Police, Deputy Chief Ron Bain and Staff Superintendent Dan Parkinson of Peel Regional Police, Chief Larry Gravill and Superintendent Kevin Chalk of Waterloo Regional Police, Superintendent Chris Wyatt of the Ontario Provincial Police, Superintendent Keith Gregory of Halton Regional Police and Deputy Chief Steven Reesor of Toronto Police Service – have articulated examples in the application of the Ontario Community Policing Model within six policing jurisdictions in Ontario. Much of the literature on Community Policing has been written by academics and researchers. The approach taken in this Chapter is refreshing as it outlines the views, analyses and police service delivery activities of the above-mentioned practitioners who are on the front-line of experiments to create better and safer communities through community policing.

Police Service Re-Engineering

Chief Kenneth Robertson of Hamilton Police said in the case of Hamilton, police service reengineering involved a fundamental redesign of the organization's structure, process and service delivery. Strategic/business planning initiatives were critical to transformation of the police service. In reviewing the planning process, the four key dimensions forming the focus of Hamilton's attention were: organizational culture, the change process, outcomes and the future.

Robertson (2002) believes that organizational change is the catalyst that transforms the culture. Between 1992-1999 a transformational journey had to be made at Hamilton in relation to the two strategically important areas of organizational culture and quality of life:

34

Organizational Culture

Prior to 1992	Transition	1999
Command and Control	Re-engineering	Value-based
Policy driven	(change process)	Community
		driven

Quality of Life

1992	1999
Police responsibility	Shared Police /Community
Reactive-closed organization	Proactive-Open Organization

Robertson notes that the Hamilton Police Service focused on the transformation of its culture from one that was traditional, command and control and policy driven to one that is strategic, value based and community driven. This transformation is premised on the profound view that quality of life issues are the shared responsibility for the police, community and elected officials.

The Change Process

The key to inaugurating a regime of fundamental change was the strategic/business planning process – which envisioned the transformation of the organization through the formulation of a compelling vision, an identifiable mission and values that drive the organization. Hamilton's Strategic Plan 1991-1995 identified the need to change the way police services were delivered. The organization recognized that the re-engineering efforts and processes must be keyed to the vision, mission and values (Robertson, 2002).

A high performing organization needs to have an explicit vision. Transformational leaders need to develop a shared vision that clearly articulates what the organization can become. In the case of Hamilton, the Vision is "to be recognized by our communities and our members as the best and most progressive police service." A clearly defined purpose or mission must also animate high performing organizations, and in the case of Hamilton its mission is "to serve, protect and support in partnership with our communities." In its pursuit to become an excellent organization, Robertson observed, Hamilton must have a commitment to a system of values that guide the practices of the people in the organization.

Enforcement

Deputy Chief Mike Boyd (2000) of Toronto Police Service employed a Strategic Crime Management process to outline the Enforcement component of the Ontario Community Policing Model. In Toronto's overall Strategic Crime Management program, there are four elements to the formula for community policing: (1) contact between the police and the community; (2) communication with the community; (3) the building of trust with the community and (4) working with the community.

Working with the community involves partnerships with:
* the residential and business community
* the social and government agencies
* the politicians from our municipal, provincial and federal levels
* the media, because of the power of communications
* the police.

Boyd (2000) observed that the end result they were trying to achieve was to improve the quality of life, and a very major component of quality of life in any community is the element of safety. Further, when you reduce fear you also elevate the level of safety. One of the tasks faced by the organization was to move along the continuum from traditional policing to community policing. Traditional policing is reactive, the focus is on responding to calls for service, there is little collaboration with the big five partners, and it is primarily incident driven. On the other hand, community policing is both proactive and reactive, it involves problem solving and it is results-oriented; there are partnerships with the community; and there should be a focus on reducing and preventing crime along with the collaboration of the partners, because the police cannot do it by themselves.

Boyd explained that in piloting Toronto's Strategic Crime Management Process it was important for all members to understand that their target involved improving the quality of life in the community through enhancing public safety, reducing crime and reducing disorder. One need to recognize that disorder is an important variable because there is a relationship between disorder and crime, and a relationship between crime and urban decay. Because of inadequate resources, there needs to be a process where problems can be identified and then prioritized so that the important things can be tackled. Some of the inputs that can guide in identifying problems are calls for service, reported crime, community input, officer input, letters of complaint, newspaper articles. The Strategic Crime Management Process (Boyd, 2000: 54) is a cyclical process which begins with the gathering of information resources. Given the structure of Toronto Police Service it is a process which begins with Divisional Planners and Divisional Crime Analysts, who are at the centre of the strategic crime management process. In the Toronto Police Divisions, crime management committees have been formed to discuss the information gathered. At the committee discussions there would be the divisional planner, crime analyst, crime prevention officer, divisional detectives, primary response officers, community response officers, alternate response officers, detectives, non-uniform personnel and the crime manager. Once the committee discusses the issues and decides what issues need to be worked on and who should be involved, the next step is communicating the decision and getting the involvement of sub-units within the station that can take action to address the problem. For example, if a division decides that break and enter of houses is one of the crime management issues, one would find that the detectives in the major crime unit see their contribution as addressing that problem. One might also recognize that the crime prevention officer is involved in addressing the problem with a view of diminishing the problem of housebreaking. Similarly, the uniform response officers on patrol will direct their patrol towards assisting in the diminishing of the house-breaking problem. Finally, one needs to move out into the community and start working with the partners to decide who else can help address the problem. Because the process is cyclical, it also involves monitoring the outcomes to determine whether the various strategies and police tactics are working.

Boyd (2000:55) identifies the individual steps of the process as follows: the analysts and divisional planners retrieve the data and analyze the data to arrive at some conclusions. The crime management meeting takes a problem solving approach and looks at strategy development, accountability, task assignments that are required, evaluating their success, and issues of communication and measurement. The last main step in the process is what is referred to as action steps. This is the stage where police officers and community members are actively involved at doing something which will address the problem.

Providing focus to the Toronto approach is the crime prevention model, which is made up of the elements of apprehension, deterrence and suppression (Boyd, 2000:56). While we need enforcement and apprehension, the crime prevention model also guides the organization to the things that need to be done in addition to apprehension. The other two significant steps are deterrents (things that can be done that will have a deterrent effect on somebody thinking about committing crime) or tactics and strategies that can be used to suppress the opportunity for crime to be committed.

Two organizational arrangements supporting the strategic crime management process in Toronto are:
i. The Crime Conference which, brings together the various police participants, provides a forum for demonstrating leadership, ensuring information sharing, discussing crime trends, strategies and tactics, and addressing issues of accountability.
ii. Information Technology Service which provides the technological tools to analyze crime and the information that would be received from the data bases.

Intelligence-led Policing

Another approach to Enforcement within the Ontario Community Policing Model is that of Intelligence-led policing, which involves the collection and analysis of information to produce an intelligence end product designed to inform police decision-making at both tactical and strategic levels. It is a model of policing in which intelligence serves as a guide to operations, rather than the reverse. It is innovative and by some standards even radical, but it is predicated on the notion that an important task of the police is to prevent and detect crime rather than simply to react to it (Parkinson, 2002:29).

Clark and Felson (1979) postulate that when crime occurs three elements come together: a motivated offender, a suitable victim and the absence of a capable guardian. Crime will flourish in a community if these three elements are present. On the basis of this analysis, Staff Superintendent Dan Parkinson (2002: 31) suggests that in order to address crime successfully one or more of these elements must be the focus of police and community attention. A sound strategy to address crime should encompass a complementary application of approaches. Targeting offenders should not be done at the exclusion of proven crime prevention techniques, or vice versa. The absence of capable guardianship can be viewed as a bi-product of the modern family consisting of dual income earners, lack of a sense of community, feeling of helplessness, ineffective design, fear of crime, etc. This situation creates an environment in which dwellings are left unoccupied for prolonged periods of time and present themselves as an easy target (suitable victim) for a break and enter. Crime Prevention through Environmental Design (CPTED), and Crime Prevention through Physical Design (CPTPD) can play significant roles in alleviating the element of lack of capable guardianship. Other measures to address the lack of capable guardianship could also include discriminate use of alarms (while recognizing the inherent weakness in relying on them exclusively), closed circuit television, a Neighbourhood Watch program in which residents are motivated and actually watching and community revitalization. The reduction of suitable victims is a matter for police to consider through the delivery of a sound prevention strategy. Crime prevention, when incorporated into the culture of a police organization, can be very effective in proactively preventing crime from occurring or to safeguard against repeat victimization.

Parkinson (2002:32) indicates that an initial step in changing the culture of policing from reaction to reason is to have front-line officers, when attending all incidents, apply the intelligence profile model by asking three fundamental questions: Why have the police been called here? Have the police been called here before? Is there anything the police can do to ensure that the police would not have to attend here again for the same reason?

By applying the intelligence profile model (Parkinson, 2000: 32) the front line officer will start to consider critical issues, such as: the underlying cause of the call for service (i.e. victim/culprit profile, type of premises, location, strategic crime prevention); and issues of re-victimization: the delivery of sound prevention advice (tactical crime prevention). Intelligent policing targets resources to known offenders and to locations where crime is likely to occur. In making the case for an intelligent approach to developing crime strategies, Parkinson argues that an effective crime strategy will clearly set out its objectives; define what is meant by reactivity, pro-activity and prevention. It will target patterns of crime, offenders, and underlying causes of crime and disorder. At its foundation will be intelligence. Good intelligence results in a clear understanding of crime and criminality. It defines which crimes are active, which crimes are linked, where to target resources to counter increased crime levels, where problems occur and are likely to occur, current challenges posed by criminal activity, emerging trends and future issues.

Parkinson (2002:33) believes that the clear identification of problems allows teams to unite and partnerships to be formed, both internally between police managers and staff, and externally between the police and community agencies in appropriate circumstances. Valuable internal partnerships are reflected in a multi-faceted, multi-bureau, multi-unit approach to dealing with crime that is strongly based on the analysis of crime, crime patterns, and offenders' modus operandi. Examples of such partnerships would be the integration of front line officers into a unified, divisional approach to crime reduction. This can reasonably be achieved through targeting offenders (who are they; where do they live; what crimes are they likely to commit) or by identifying where 'hotspots' of crimes are – or are likely to occur. By providing this information to uniform patrol and directing their activities, invaluable information (intelligence) from front line officers is in turn made available to those with the responsibility of developing strategies to combat crime within a geographic jurisdiction. Partnerships with other units within the division, such as Neighbourhood Policing Unit, Bicycle Patrol, for example, are essential to the success of an intelligent approach to crime. By identifying the specific crime patterns, locations or hot spots of crime or activities of known offenders who continue to commit crime, it is logical to devote as much available resources to those areas or individuals in order to reap the most benefit.

Deputy Chief Ron Bain of Peel Regional Police (2002:3) noted that based on current literature, intelligence-led policing is about being able to:

- describe, understand and map criminality and the criminal processes
- make informed choices about decisions;
- engage the most appropriate tactics
- allow the targeting of resources
- disrupt prolific criminals, and
- articulate a case to the public and in court.

To retool, to implement intelligence-led policing, a strategically directed police effort must be based on analysis. It is only by focusing on intelligence work performed by a specialized workforce that police organizations can be released from the predominantly reactive cycle of policing (Bain: 2002).

Brantingham (1993:264) hypothesized that crimes are patterned; decisions to commit crime are patterned and the process of committing crime is patterned. Assistant Chief Constable of Kent County Constabulary in England, Jim Barker-McCardle (2002) noted that if most offences are committed by very few offenders and if incidents can often be analyzed to establish patterns, considered law enforcement activity should be able to impact on the aggregate level of crime. Bain concluded that criminal hot spots need to be identified, sites at risk for crime based on intelligence gathered. Police personnel in a branch would be organized into two units – one for prevention of crime and the other for reaction to crime. The prevention teams work at selected sites, targeted as result of the Intelligence gathered by the Branch. The reaction unit responds to crimes against persons, despite very good intelligence, this part of policing will always be with the police. The goal is to move as much of the business to the preventive side as possible (Bain, 2002:5).

A Pilot Project on intelligence led policing was initiated in Peel Regional Police. Within a four-month period since this project was initiated there was an overall reduction in property crimes of

21.8%. It includes a 15.7% reduction in residential break-ins; an 11.8% reduction in thefts under $500,000; a 13.3% reduction in thefts from motor vehicle; and a 15.9% reduction in thefts of motor vehicles.

Community Development

In addressing the Community Development component of the Ontario Community Policing Model, Chief Larry Gravill (2000:19) said that Waterloo Regional Police Service is aligned organizationally in such a way that there is a strong commitment to the wellness of the organization and the community. This, in itself is a transformation from traditional policing directives.

Community Development

Gravill (2000:10) described how in the Cedar Hills community in downtown Kitchener the police experienced a problem with crack houses in and around the fall of 1992 and the spring of 1993. They were surfacing literally overnight and before too long the neighbourhood had a problem of almost epidemic proportions. A group of citizens in the area herded together and decided to form patrol teams. Armed with nothing more than flashlights, pen and paper, a cell phone, but more notably the courage to care, they came to the police for support. They wanted the police blessing and to make sure their neighbourhood, their community, and their backyards were safe again. These citizens were prepared to go it alone. They wanted to have a relationship with their police service whereby they could pass on information and be certain that it would be acted upon. That information would enable police officers to clean up their neighbourhood and restore it to where it once was. This highly visible and publicly lauded group of citizens might in itself have discouraged criminal activity through its own vigilance, but these community members were asking for traditional enforcement-style policing as a solution to their problems. The community members wanted to become part of that enforcement. A serious problem existed. The risk was very high and the Cedar Hills community would experience a significant change in its quality of life. Fortunately the community members were very well organized and very much determined. They needed assistance in establishing the processes and some direction in training. Hence the birth of Citizens on Patrol. Police commanders in Kitchener established a patrol unit tasked solely with exercising traditional enforcement strategies. The community members would gather intelligence and pass the information on to the patrol unit. Over time, the problem subsided. The success of Citizens on Patrol is directly proportionate to the citizens who participate. Citizens have dedicated hundreds of hours to make this program successful.

Community Mobilization

In terms of an agenda for the 21st century, Gravill (2002:20) suggested that as members of police agencies and as community leaders they must direct their efforts into a community mobilization model and all that it encompasses. To illustrate, he cited the Waterloo Regional Police initiative in Sunnydale Place, a relatively small neighbourhood in the middle of a larger area of upper-middle class neighbourhoods. The Sunnydale Place initiative was embarked upon by the police as an experiment in helping this high-risk community mobilize in order to deal more effectively with their problems of crime and disorder. Unlike Cedar Hills, Sunnydale is comprised of disproportionate large numbers of unemployed and underemployed people; single parents, persons with physical, mental and emotional disabilities; new immigrants; a diversity of languages, religions and cultures; and transient residents who fail to make a personal contribution towards community-building. Since the early 1990s, an average of one call for service every day of the year was being made. The trend was upward. This was not unlike the Cedar Hills experience which was occurring at around the same time. In Sunnydale most of the complaints related to minor events, many of which were never recorded as occurrences, and most of which never resulted in charges laid or other enforcement activities, but the quality of life was suffering. Interestingly enough in Sunnydale, fewer than 15% of the calls for service led to enforcement activity It appeared that if police officers did the "right thing" in Sunnydale, then there would be some change that residents could begin to deal more effectively with their own issues.

In Sunndydale, (Gravill 2000: 22) the police had to overcome a number of obstacles. One was a decade of denial, avoidance and inappropriate response of public and private agencies in the community. Stereotyping within the community depicted a neighbourhood that harboured misfortune – thereby justifying law enforcement and a police presence – perhaps even in the form of programs and initiatives. Further examination of the underlying roots of crime and social dysfunction discovered that the cause of disturbances and abuses in the neighbourhood related to systemic and situational circumstances, over which the residents had little or no control, but simply reacted. More importantly, the police discovered that Sunnydale was the home to a wealth of human motivation, skills and energies. In Sunnydale, it was observed that the police have a vital and unique role in identifying, acknowledging and mobilizing the capacities of community residents.

In the experiment with community mobilization, Gravill (2000:23) noted that the police wanted to figure out how to help the community gain more control over the conditions of life that affected them so adversely. One wanted to figure out how to help residents work together, support each other, on behalf of the whole community. The Police sought to discover what its role and capacities in this work could and should be. The goals for mobilizing the community in Sunnydale were: increase public safety; reduce incidence of anti-social behaviour; prevent crime; reduce incidence of calls-for-service. Police officers want so badly "to do", "to help", or "to solve". But taking control is opposite to what the police organization wanted to do in community mobilization. If the police were to take charge, the community will remain in a co-dependant relationship with the social service net – never learning to solve things for themselves. So it is important to help the community recognize its own assets and capacities for solving it own problems; and supporting them to implement those solutions. Communities like Sunnydale or Cedar Hill cannot go it alone. They need inputs from outside, businesses, social agencies, schools, municipal officers, retailers, churches, clubs and individuals must all play a role. Imaginative and properly trained police officers have the capacity to help the community find those external partners and hook-up in a constructive way. The philosophy of community policing must encompass the notion that a policing member in this context is a facilitator. As a first responder, police have a unique opportunity to observe the problem. Fortunately the response that many police members are employing is to engage partners that will collectively make a long term difference in the community. One of the things learnt about community mobilization is that if you do your part well, then the community puts in the hard work. That simply leaves the police to provide the support the community needs, as and when it needs it.

Gravill (2000: 24) identified three steps in the Community Mobilization approach. These are: In the first step, the police have to take the lead in community mobilization; balancing problem-oriented policing with enforcement to remove social predators. There are public safety and security issues that take the police into a high-risk community. However, in responding to these opportunities for community mobilization, one has to recognize that something more than enforcement is needed. The police have to manage a delicate balance between problem-oriented policing and enforcement, to remove social predators. In the second step of the model, the police help to link the community to external partners; and encourage integration of services. The police would use its special knowledge and working relationships to gain access to a wide range of social service agencies and organizations throughout the municipality in order to link the mobilizing community to external resources. Further, the police can take the lead in bringing such external partners together to share disclosure of their separate operations in the community. Partners discuss how they can support each other in providing amore integrated and holistic support to the mobilizing community. In the third step of the model, residents learn self-sufficiency and self-determination with the support of the police and others. With the emerging leadership in the community and a family of external partners working together to support community mobilization, the police agency can fulfill its role of support and ongoing public safety and security. As residents of the community learn self-sufficiency and self-determination, there will be far less demand for enforcement in the community, and many opportunities for preventing crime.

Proactive efforts are undergoing a transformation in policing from development to mobilization. The organizational implementation of this is vital to community growth and subsequently, organizational and community wellness (Gravill, 2000: 25). .

In explaining how community mobilization works at Waterloo Regional Police Service, Superintendent Kevin Chalk (2002: 44) said the police organization applies a standard planning model in four phases of activity for which the police share responsibilities with citizens, other social agencies, and departments of government. The planning model involves: Police scan the nature and extent of threats to community safety and security; analysis is made to determine the root of the problem and plan appropriate interventions; police respond to some problems with enforcement and also support citizens and other community members respond to the problems in ways that not only reduce its impact but also help prevents it from occurring again; and during assessment, police and community partners share responsibility for determining whether community mobilization has its desired effects.

Chalk (2002:45) observes that a community mobilization initiative entails four distinct phases of activity: in the readiness phase, a determination is made on whether conditions in the neighbourhood are ripe for an effective action. Then a number of actions are initiated. When neighbours are feeling better about working together on their mutual concerns, the police help connect them to other community agencies and offices that can help address specific problems. Finally, the police do not significantly reduce its inputs to any community mobilization initiative until community participants show significant capacities to sustain their efforts.

Police Learning

Another component of the OCPM is Police Learning. The Ontario Police College and the Canadian Police College are the two principal providers of training and education to police leaders in Ontario. In addition, the Ontario Provincial Police has a training Academy, while Toronto has its C.O.Bick College. Within the last decade many police organizations have expanded their role in the design and delivery of training and education programs for their officers. Some police organizations have formed alliances with community colleges. This is the case with Durham Police and Durham College, Niagara Police and Niagara College, the Ontario Provincial Police and Georgian College, Ottawa Police and Algonquin College. Some police organizations absorb the costs of their officers pursuing post-secondary education. Peel Police has also provided members with three-month sabbaticals to conduct research into topics or issues of their choice. The Ontario Association of Chiefs of Police and the Rotman School of Management of the University of Toronto are partners in the design and delivery of a Police Chiefs Leadership Program, an intensive residential program that provides experienced officers with opportunities to learn the leadership and management skills required for leading a police service. The Strategic Planning Committee on Police Training and Education in Ontario (1992) emphasized in its report the need for police services to make a commitment to continuous learning. Some police organizations have as one of their core values the notion of continuous learning; and in a number of police organizations we find promotional opportunities, performance appraisals and personal development plans emphasizing the value of continuous learning. In short, organizational and individual learning are high priorities for police organizations in Ontario.

Problem solving and problem-oriented policing are important aspects of the Police Learning component in the integrated Ontario Community Policing model. According to Parkinson (2000:33) problem-oriented policing can be defined as a strategy aimed at solving persistent community problems. Police identify, analyze, and respond to the underlying circumstances that create problems in an effort to eradicate or diminish the circumstances that create problems in an effort to eradicate or diminish the circumstances.

Two approaches to Problem Oriented Policing that are being used by the Peel Regional Police to address various types of crimes are Crime Prevention through Environmental Design (CPTED) and Crime Prevention Through Physical Design (CPTPD). The key principle in CPTED is the belief that proper design and effective use of built environment can lead to a reduction in the incidence and fear of crime as well as improvement in the quality of life. It relies on three concepts involving (1) natural surveillance (lines of sight), (2) natural access control (how many points of access to a particular property exist) and (3) territorial reinforcement (is it obvious if CPTED begins with a space assessment which clarifies the three following issues: designation – how well does the space support its current use? definition – is it clear who owns it? design – does the physical design conflict with or impede the function of the space?

A case in the application of CPTED (Parkinson, 2000:40) involved dealing with recurring problems at a secondary school complex in Peel. On any given day from 20 to 25 trespassers parked their cars in a remote area of the school parking lot next to some basketball courts and from there entered the school buildings unchallenged. While on school property trespassers would loiter and frequently engage in criminal activity such as brandishing a handgun during the playing of a basketball game. For example in 1995, approximately 62 incidents, including assault, thefts, property damage, weapons possession, and armed robbery had occurred on campus during the previous school year. This type of behaviour combined with the students' own incidents of vandalism and loitering, had resulted in the school having a reputation of being unsafe. As a result of changes as part of an environmental design program to the school and its environs, the average annual incidents dropped from 62 incicidents to seven incidents per year. Another approach to problem solving is Crime Prevention through Physical Design (CPTPD). This problem solving approach seeks to integrate the use of physical design concepts and security technology within the environment in response to specific threats while not detracting from the quality of life. Peel Regional Police offers courses in both CPTED and CPTPD.

The Ontario Provincial Police (OPP) (1997) created its own problem solving approach, PARE – an acronym for Problem identification, Analysis, Response and Evaluation.

Problem identification includes a listing of the perceptions and symptoms of the problem and a clear identification of the perceived problem.

Analysis relates to an examination of the problem to determine answers to the questions who, what, when, where and why. Information must be gathered and consideration given to the victim, the offender, and the situation. A determination of the impact, seriousness, complexity and solvability of the problem is made. Also, along with some prioritization of the problems an identification of the problem and goals are made.

Response includes the identification of an appropriate response strategy and the development of an action plan, including tasks and an evaluation mechanism.

Evaluation signifies the actual conduct of a plan evaluation, analyzing the plan results, and documenting and sharing of the results.

Superintendent Chris Wyatt (2003) indicated that training of OPP officers in the PARE approach is done at the recruit, patrol and supervisory training levels. These officers' problem solving abilities are assessed in their performance evaluations. In elaborating how problem oriented policing works in the OPP. Wyatt cites as an example the case of the Duffferin Detachment where an environmental scan indicated youth related mischief and disorder incidents were on the increase in the Grandvalley area. Community consultations were held through a town hall meeting with 151 residents. The problem was identified as youth skateboarding and congregating in the downtown area that led to mischief and intimidation of some citizens. A committee was established which included the OPP detachment commander, police sergeants, constables, parents, representatives of the municipality, the Business Improvement Association and service clubs to explore possible solutions to the problem. A facility was constructed to allow for skateboarding and other sports. Tracking of mischief incidents through crime statistics continued to ensure that the problem was eliminated. Wyatt explained that the business planning process at the OPP provide a structured framework for problem solving policing and police learning.

Some police organizations engaged in problem solving and problem oriented policing use an approach called SARA, an acronym which stands for Scanning, Analysis, Response and Assessment. It was the American academic, Herman Goldstein (1979, 1990) who laid the groundwork for problem oriented policing. This was followed by Eck and Spelman (1988) who outlined the SARA model as the process to be used for solving problems. SARA represents four stages of problem-solving. They are as follows: Scanning begins the problem solving process. It involves identification of the problem and scanning the nature and extent of threats to community safety and security. Analysis is the second step. It involves the information gathering and data collecting stage and determines the root of the problem and plan appropriate interventions. The analysis phase asks the questions of who, what, how, when, where and why. Response is the third step. In this stage an attempt is made to develop, select and implement the most appropriate responses or options. Assessment is the final stage of the problem solving process and involves the evaluation of the effectiveness of the responses that were implemented.

Halton Regional Police, one of the leaders in community policing in Canada, employs the SARA approach. Superintendent Keith Gregory (2000:56) pointed to the organization's business plan which indicates that utilizing the concept of teams, members of the Service work in partnership with the community to respond to problems. Scanning is an integral part of Halton's planning process. The problem solving process involves a comprehensive analysis to ensure the actual problem is identified, not just the symptoms. Once the problem is articulated, the response is developed recognizing the role of various partners in this response. As the plan is implemented, it is monitored on an ongoing basis and is adapted as required. At the completion of the project, a thorough assessment/evaluation is undertaken to ensure the problem has been addressed. This process is supported by a written policy in Halton Regional Police. A number of Ontario police organizations provide their officers training in problem oriented policing using the SARA approach.

Community/Police Partnerships

In outlining the pivotal role of community/police partnerships in the Ontario Community Policing Model, Deputy Chief Steven Reesor (2000:8-18) explained that Toronto Police Service believes that community involvement is important for solving crime and disorder problems. The police organization does not have the staffing or expertise to solve all community crime and disorder problems. Partnering with individuals and groups from across the community gives the organization access to resources, information, and most importantly the creativity of about three million people as all work towards the improvement of the quality of life in the city.

There are seven priorities for the Toronto Police Service: Youth Violence and Victimization of Youths, Organized Crime, Drug Enforcement and Education, Human Resource Development, Service Infrastructure, Community Safety and Satisfaction. The priorities would be meaningless without community partnerships and a strong community focus.

Elaborating on the extent of community partnerships, Reesor (2000:11) indicated that there are partnerships that are ongoing, that are there a continuing relationship with these partners. There are other partnerships that are created to deal with specific short term issues. Among the key corporate relationships identified by Reesor are:

Chief's Advisory Council and Chief's Youth Advisory Council. They provide a voice for ethnic and community groups and youth on a range of issues.

Advisory Committees: They consist of community members representing the diversity of the community in Toronto. The groups and senior police officers address issues that impact on cultural, ethnic and other related matters.

Walkabouts: Intended to build bridges and open lines of communication between the police and specific groups.

Civilian Police College: Every year about 100 members of the community enroll for an eleven-week course that gives them insights into the world of policing.

Auxiliary Police: about 400 uniformed volunteers who work under the authority of the Police Services Act to support regular officers at major events such as Caribana and Santa Claus Parade.

Crime Stoppers: In 2001, Toronto's Crime Stoppers received 2,979 tips that led to 273 arrests and 889 charges. This information led to 219 cases cleared, $537,916 in property and $2,382,835 in drugs seized, and $34,325. rewards paid.

Corporate Youth Initiatives: Reesor (2002:13) pointed out that solving problems in which young people are either victims or suspects is a high priority for the service. To support this priority, a Youth Crime Coordinator position has been established to assist field units and the community members working with them. The Youth Crime Coordinator administers a number of important partnerships designed to address all aspects of youth crime. These partnerships include the Catholic and Public School Boards, Earlscourt Child and Family Services, Operation Springboard (a youth-serving agency that addresses causes of youth crime through social services and group homes), and Central Toronto Youth Services (which provides supportive services and mentoring to high risk youths). The partnerships address strategic corporate initiatives that advance the service priority focusing on youth crime. These initiatives include the Toronto Police Service Youth Referral Program and the Serious Teen Offender Program. These programs give police officers a reliable social agency network that can help youths to overcome personal problems that contribute to delinquent behaviour, and contribute to the many school-based education programs designed to help young people stay out of trouble and avoid being victims of crime.

Funding Initiatives. Toronto Police Service works closely with all three levels of government with respect to funding; federal and provincial ministries and the foundations connected with them are important resources for special initiatives. The Toronto Police Services Board has approved the establishment of an arms-length Police Foundation to fund initiatives that do not receive funding approval from city council.

ProAction: Since 1992, Proaction is a charitable foundation that funds activities involving members of the Toronto Police Service and the city's youths. ProAction works to build a strong relationship between the police and youth, and to prevent high-risk youth from turning to crime. Since 1992, ProAction has funded over $1m. in police programs for kids.

Community Response Unit: Directed by a staff sergeant, the CRUs are consistent, accessible groups that are specifically mandated to support field-level partnerships and co-operatively solve the problems they identify.

Examples of divisional partnerships are:

Community Policing Liaison Committees (CPLC) are mandated to provide guidance and support to divisional and traffic management, to give advice on how to prioritize police activity, and to help to create additional partnerships as required. CPLC membership is drawn from neighbourhod-based local community organizations such as ratepayer associations, tenant associations and business interests.

Citizens on Phone Patrol (COPP): A program in which carefully screened volunteers are trained to observe and report suspicious activities on cellular phones. The program provides crime information to the police and also helps members of the community to take ownership of solutions in their neighbourhoods.

Youth Issues. All divisions work closely with the community to address youth issues through both enforcement and education. These partnerships allow communication between police and other agencies concerned with youth and youth violence, to identify issues of concern related to youth and develop solutions, to create and endorse positive youth programs, deterrence, intervention, education, promotion of safety, and to foster and enhance relationships between the police and youth. At least 187 such relationships existed.

Traffic Safety. More than a hundred formal relationships with partners exist to enhance traffic safety and to support the Police education and enforcement efforts.

Private security: Private security officers significantly outnumber police officers and they are a valuable resource to front line police officers.

Specialty units have developed partnerships in projects such as:

Operation Strike Force was created in response to the proliferation of guns and violence in Toronto streets. The partnership was also mandated to deal with drug use and trafficking, gang membership and gang activity. This productive partnership evolved into *Operation Gun Stop* which included police and response agencies, city and provincial departments and politicians. Toronto Raptors basketball team offered free tickets in exchange for turning in targeted firearms during a gun amnesty.

Parking Enforcement: The Parking Enforcement Unit meets with outside agencies to help ensure balanced parking enforcement, address the misuse of disabled parking permits, and support the Parent School Safety Program.

Toronto Transit Security, University of Toronto Police, and Toronto Housing Authority Police: Toronto Police Service officers work in partnership with special constables from these three agencies in providing services on and about their properties.

Traffic partnerships: As well as partnering with the Ontario Provincial Police and other Greater Toronto Area police services for traffic safety, the Service partners with about 24 community and specialist groups as well as public agencies to enhance safety within the city.

Reesor (2002:17) pointed out that specific rules and accountabilities are in place to ensure that the consultative structure of the Toronto Police Service remains accountable and effective. *Mandate*: The Service's consultative committees have been developed to provide advice to the police on community concerns, and help through partnerships, formulate long-term solutions. They also work proactively with all stakeholders to plan and implement ongoing activities to improve the quality of life in their communities. *Accountability*: The Chief, Command Officers and Unit Commanders are personally responsible for the establishment and effective operation of consultative groups that are appropriate to their areas of command. This includes the creation of a clear, accountable fundraising policy to support each group. Police management does not take direction from the groups; formal accountability remains with the chain of command and the Police Services Board. *Representation*: Each consultation committee must reflect the demographics of the community, diverse groups, various interest and youths.

Reesor (2002:18) noted that the Toronto Police Service has devoted a great deal of time and effort in creating and maintaining constructive relationships with people and groups across the community. These relationships exist to advise, support and assist the organization and its members as they strive to accomplish the mission and priorities. The organization is committed to the reality of community policing, and the relationships developed over the years have allowed the organization to gain insights into community issues, to access resources and to benefit from the expertise of thousands of people. Through these partnerships, one can see – and implement – the best practices of other businesses and organizations across society. Engaging the community and benefiting from their ideas and practices helps the organization to make better decisions, which leads to greater community satisfaction? Community partnerships also provide access to the skills, abilities and hard work of many people, including experts in many fields which can be leveraged to help in a practical sense to achieve the organization's goals.

Toronto Police, according to Reesor, places great value on the many effective partnerships which are so integral to what has world-wide become the dominant police service delivery model – community policing. Partnerships help define the police organization and add value to the policing services delivered to a diverse community.

Future Directions

There are examples of Ontario police organizations systematically attempting to apply all components of the Ontario Community Policing Model. For example, the Ontario Community Policing Model was the basis for the development of Niagara Regional Police Service "Community Policing Strategic Action Plan. Similarly, York Regional Police classroom instruction on the OCPM to all officers forms part of its annual mandatory re-qualification training program.

Police leaders need to look at developing an integrated approach addressing all components of the model as part of their strategic/business planning processes. This could be the lever for organizational change and the pursuit of excellence within police organizations. They also need to incorporate training so that all police officers are socialized into using the model. The learning and socialization aspects are important for long term sustained commitment and action given the pockets of resistance within policing to notions of change, community policing and partnerships with stakeholders. It is especially important for police training organizations to have competent and qualified instructors to communicate both the theory and practice of the components of the model.

The empirical realities of contemporary policing in Ontario suggest that there should be some minor changes to the conceptual components of the model. Such changes would lend greater application and efficacy to the model and blunt the traditional debate between the rhetoric and reality of community policing.

Two of the components of the model that are amenable to such realistic changes are:

1. **The component of Community Development should be retitled Community Development and Mobilization.** This would give formal recognition to the work being done in this area by Waterloo Regional Police. To reinforce the validity of this change, it should also be noted that at the national level Community Mobilization is also being promoted. As part of its National Strategy on Community Safety and Crime Prevention, the Government of Canada has a Community Mobilization Program which is designed to help groups across the country develop strategies to prevent crime and victimization by addressing their root causes.

2. **The component Police Learning should be renamed Police Learning and Problem Solving**. Mention is made of problem-oriented policing within the current Police learning component of the model. However, because it is widely recognized that problem solving informs much of what the police does, the highlighting and explicit recognition of problem solving as one of the important components of the community policing model would add to the comprehensiveness, logic and greater feasibility of the Ontario Community Policing Model. This recognition and visibility would be easily obtained through the renaming of the Police Learning Component as Police Learning and Problem solving.

In the United States of America some academics, researchers and police practitioners consider community policing as a separate entity from problem oriented policing. Perhaps this has to do with the historical evolution of policing in the United States of America. In the 21st Century, from a conceptual and practical perspective, this view of the separation of community policing and problem oriented policing need to be revisited.

In Ontario, however, this is not the case. It was pointed out sometime ago, (Nancoo, 2000:172) that unlike the United States with its continuing debate on differences between community policing and problem oriented policing, in the Canadian environment problem solving and problem oriented policing are conceptually and operationally considered an integral part of community policing. Certainly in Ontario, problem solving and problem oriented policing are merely aspects – albeit very significant aspects – of community policing. As such while there is mention of problem-oriented policing within the model, the more generic concept of problem solving should be fully anchored and given greater visibility and emphasis within the overall Ontario Community Policing Model. Further justification for such a change could be found in the fact that Section 29 of the Adequacy Standards Regulation of the Ontario Police Services Act requires a police service board to have a policy on problem-oriented policing. In addition Section 3 requires the Chief of Police to establish procedures and processes on problem oriented policing. It is therefore imperative that focused attention be given to problem solving and problem oriented policing by renaming Police Learning component as Police Learning and Problem Solving. Once the notion of Problem Solving is fully established as an important component within the Ontario Community Policing Model, individual police organizations would then determine what is the most appropriate method of problem solving – whether it is the Herman Goldstein's version of problem-oriented policing, the SARA model, the OPP's PARE model or the Royal Canadian Mounted Police (R.C.M.P.) CAPRA[1] model – that is best suited to a police service's overall strategy of community policing.

A re-conceptualized Ontario Community Policing Model would therefore include:
1. Police Service Re-engineering
2. Community Development and Community Mobilization
3. Police Learning and Problem Solving
4. Enforcement
5. Community/Police Partnerships

It was argued (Nancoo: 1993, 359), that there are aspects of policing that have always been the subject of change. The rise of community policing represents today one of those significant change – a paradigm shift...We have also expressed the view that

that while we continue to tackle the teething problems and fundamental concerns that have been expressed by some, the philosophy of community policing should nevertheless be embraced and that the efforts and energies of police leaders should be focused on overcoming the problems that stand in the way of its effective implementation in democratic societies. In doing so, it is worthwhile to remember that with community policing, even though the means might be different, the ends are essentially the same. In the final analysis, highly successful organizations are innovators. Organizational innovation and change depend on creative leadership. The whole question of a successful, continuous and acceptable paradigm shift to community policing resides in great measure on the long term, sustained commitment to innovation and change by our police leadership.

Endnotes

[1]CAPRA is the R.C.M.P problem solving model. The acronym CAPRA stands for: **C** represents Clients. Police assess and define problems through understanding the needs and expectations of the clients. **A** stands for Acquiring and Analyzing information. **P** is for Partnership. Complex police problems require partnerships with multidisciplinary teams as well community groups and their representatives. **R** represents Response. Enforcement, providing service, crime prevention and protection are among a wide range of responses available. **A**=Assessment for Continuous Improvement. Effective policing requires approaches and techniques for ongoing assessments that promote continuous improvement and learning. (Himelfarb 1997, 34-37)

References

Bain, R. (2002). The dynamics of retooling and staffing: excellence and innovation in police management. Presentation delivered at *Canadian Police College Symposium for Council for Investigative Excellence.*
Barker-McCardle, J. (2002). Intelligence-led Policing. In

S. Nancoo (Ed.), *Organizational Performance Measurement.* Aylmer: Issues and Themes in Police Leadership. Occasional Papers.

Boyd, M. (2000). Enforcement. In S.E. Nancoo (Ed.), Perspect-*ives in Policing.* Aylmer: Issues and Themes in Police Leadership. Occasional Papers.

Brantingham, P.L and Brantingham, P.J. (1993). Environment, Routine, and Situation: Toward a Pattern Theory of Crime. In R.V.Clarke, and M. Felson (Eds.), *Routine Activity and Rational Choice, Advances in Criminological Theory,* Vol. 5, pp.259-287. London: Transaction Publishers.

Chalk, K. (2002). Community Mobilization. In S.E. Nancoo (Ed.), *Community Policing in Ontario.* Aylmer: Issues and Themes in Police Leadership. Occasional Papers.

Clark, L. and Felson, M. (1979). Social Change and Crime Rate Trends: A Routine Activity Approach. *American Sociological Review,* Vol. 44, pp. 588-608.

Eck, J.E and Spellman W. (1988). *Problem solving: Problem oriented policing in Newport News.* Washington, DC: National Institute of Justice

Goldstein, H. (1979). Improving policing: A problem-oriented approach. *Crime and Delinquency 25, no.2:238-241*

Goldstein, H. (1990). *Problem-oriented policing.* New York: McGraw-Hill.

Government of Canada, *Community Mobilization Program, Access Guide.*

Gravill, L. (2000). Community Development. In S.E. Nancoo (Ed.), *Perspectives in Policing.* Aylmer: Issues and Themes in Police Leadership. Occasional Papers.

Himelfarb, F. (1997). RCMP learning and renewal: Building on strengths. In Q. Thurman and E. McGarrel (Eds.), *Community policing in a rural setting.* Cincinnati OH: Anderson.

Nancoo, S. E. (1993). The Future. In *Community Policing in Canada.* Toronto: Canadian Scholars Press.

Nancoo, S. E. (2000). The Police and the Diverse Society: Trends and Prospects in the 21st Century. In *21st Century Canadian Diversity.* Mississauga: Canadian Educators' Press.

Ontario Ministry of the Solicitor General. (2000). *Problem*

Oriented Policing & Crime Analysis Resource Package.

Ontario Ministry of the Solicitor *General Policing Standards Manual*

Ontario. Police Services Act. Revised Statutes of Ontario. Queen's Printer of Ontario.

Ontario Provincial Police Community Policing Development Centre. (1997). *Community Policing Manual: How Do We Do It.*

Parkinson, D. (2000). Police Learning and Problem Solving. *In* S.E. Nancoo (Ed.), *Perspectives in Policing.* Aylmer: Issues and Themes in Police Leadership Conference. Occasional Papers.

Parkinson, D. (2002). Intelligence-led Policing. In S.E. Nancoo (Ed.)*, Community Policing in Ontario.* Aylmer: Issues and Themes in Police Police Leadership Occasional Papers.

Reesor, S. (2002). Community Police Partnerships. In S.E, Nancoo (Ed.), *Community Policing in Ontario.* Aylmer: Issues and Themes in Police Leadership Occasional Papers.

Robertson, K. (2002). Police Service Re-engineering, In S. Nancoo (Ed.), *Community Policing in Ontario.* Aylmer: Issues and Themes in Police Leadership Occasional Papers.

Wyatt, C. (2002). *Problem solving in the Ontario Provincial Police.* Presentation at the Issues and Themes in Policing and Police Leadership Conference.

4

Community-based policing
in Ontario: Lessons from the
Halton Regional Police Service*

Lori A. Cooke-Scott

Abstract: Community policing represents a fundamental shift in police-services management and has replaced the military model as the dominant service-delivery model in Western countries. But this so-called "community policing" model has faced some fundamental problems in implementation, both internal and external. This article examines some of the more striking internal challenges faced by a Canadian example of community-based policing (CBP) – one that is based in a fairly "generic," or unexceptional, crime region, the region of Halton in Ontario, where CBP has been implemented on a comprehensive basis over the past fifteen years. As one of the earliest regions to institute CBP in Canada, the history of the Halton organization can provide some valuable lessons as to "how" the implementation should work.

During the past decade, the administration of police service in the United States, Canada and other industrialized countries has undergone significant changes. A growing demand for police accountability, responsiveness to the community and new responsibilities has been well documented, as has the move towards a more community-oriented approach to policing as the dominant administrative paradigm. Community policing represents a fundamental shift in police-services management and has replaced the military model as the dominant service-delivery model in Western countries. But this so-called "community policing" model has faced some fundamental problems in implementation, both internal and external.

Many case studies of community policing have been conducted, but mostly in major urban areas (with highly specific crime problems relating to the inner city), and most in the U.S.[1] Many of these have been analyses of individual programs, and researchers have noted that the effects of community-based policing (CBP) programs tend to be very difficult to evaluate when they are implemented only piecemeal, rather than comprehensively This article examines a Canadian example of CBP based in a more "generic", or unexceptional, crime region with both urban and rural components and without some of the highly specific crime problems related to individual urban centres. This makes the region of Halton in Ontario particularly valuable as a case study, since the origins of its CBP policy were not based on a reaction to a geographically specific "crisis" situation, making its experiences more universally applicable to other organizations. Halton's experience with CBP also represents the implementation of a comprehensive change in philosophy, as opposed to a series of add-ons or piecemeal programs that have taken place fairly consistently over the past fifteen years.

The Halton Regional Police Service (HRPS) was one of the earliest and most comprehensive community-policing programs to be implemented in North America.[2] If you want to "do" community policing, you have to "do it" the hard way. That is clearly the lesson to be learned from the Halton Regional Police Service's experiences with community-based policing over the past fifteen years. For many in police administration today, the question is not *whether* to implement a more community-based approach, but *how* to do it. As crime rates and dissatisfaction with police grow, few have found a basis to argue for a continuation of the status quo. In Halton, the question has never been whether to follow the path of a more community-based approach; leaders there headed in that direction long before it was widely considered a viable option and have not wavered from the philosophy of it since. Understandably, then, the history of this organization can provide some valuable lessons as to "how" the implementation should work.

Recently, the HRPS conducted a lengthy internal review involving just about everyone in the organization, from the governing body to street-level constables. Then it began to implement a revised approach to community policing that represented years of trial and error, rigorous self-examination, and learning from its mistakes. The change does not represent a radical transformation but rather a series of adjustments that shows recognition of what has worked in the past and what has not. These adjustments are important, because they offer some lessons that should be of relevance to many other communities considering CBP.

The changes in Halton reflect some important conclusions. Community policing cannot be merely a set of programs; it must be built on a vision of what a police service should be, and that vision must be communicated throughout the organization. Implementation requires patience, constancy, and commitment: organizers in Halton gradually recognized that lasting results should not be expected overnight, that changing the entire organization would take a long time, and that setbacks and obstacles would occur. They also learned the importance of admitting past errors and using mistakes to lessen obstacles in the future, of allowing for a structure that encourages innovation from within, and of initiating changes from the bottom up rather from the top down. In all, the experience of the Halton Regional Police Service proves that community policing is not a panacea and that there is no "magic pill" program. In short, "doing" community policing is hard work.

This case study will evaluate and draw some lessons pertaining to the internal administration and organization that derive from the implementation of the HRPS's community-policing policy, which began in the early 1980s and continues today. The article begins by reviewing the background of community policing. It then examines the implementation of CBP, beginning with early steps taken in the 1970s and culminating in a fundamental review conducted in 1994 that led to some new changes implemented thereafter. The third section of the article presents some of the key problems that emerged in Halton and that should be relevant to other communities. The article concludes with a broad set of lessons that emerges from the Halton program.

The research is based on archival information obtained both from the HRPS and the Burlington Public Library. These sources include newspaper accounts from Halton publications over the past 20 years and information prepared within the HRPS, some of it distributed internally and some of it publicity material dealing with the organization's community-policing program. These include mission statements, annual reports (including crime statistics), statements of community-policing principles, "strategic plans," committee or task force reports, and material used for in-service training. These documents are supplemented by interviews with key police leaders and with others at various levels with the police service.[3]

Community policing: background

The concept of modern community policing in the U.S. and Canada can be traced to Britain, specifically to Robert Peel's "nine principles of policing" implemented by the London Metropolitan Police Force in 1829.[4] Peel's ideas stressed accountability through public acceptance, responsibility through an "impartial service to law", and responsiveness through the focus on the public's "acceptance" and "cooperation" as necessary elements in effective policing. In short, Peel stated that "the police are the public and the public are the police."[5]

These principles show that relating the role of police to public acceptance is not a brand new idea. A big part of the problem with Peel's "public" paradigm was that the police got *too close* to the public. In the first decades of this century, police corruption became an increasing problem and was thought to have been brought about by the "close ties that police established with their local communities, which were understood to have facilitated the widespread, systemic corruption of police agencies by local political party organizations."[6] In responding to this problem, B.N. Leighton argues that leaders of urban North American police forces, "intentionally distanced themselves from the community they served. Tactics were developed to ensure this distancing occurred, assisted by technological developments such as the telephone, then the patrol car and two-way radio, followed by on-board computers."[7]

Thus, Peel's public-policing paradigm gradually gave way to what is called the "professional policing" or "military" paradigm. As Leighton wrote in 1991, new technologies permitted tighter control over individual police-officer behaviour. In addition, two new policing strategies were "even more powerful influences in distancing the police from the local community, random motorized patrol as a presumed deterrent to potential criminals, and the invention of rapid response as the uniform response to all calls to police from the public."[8] A focus on efficiency and a rapid response to calls for service fit well within an organizational structure emphasizing a strict chain of command hierarchy, close supervision, and a narrow span of control, very much like a military organization.

Distinct from Peel's approach, which emphasized relations with a community, the professional approach focuses on individual incidents rather than on community trends, reaction rather than "proaction", and on organizational efficiency rather than on the broader goal of community effectiveness. There is a strict division of labour in the crime-fighting functions (front-line officers have very limited investigative duties), and officers' scope of responsibility is strictly limited by standard operating procedures, meaning there is very little focus on the "big picture", the underlying causes of crime, and the broader trends.

More recent pressure to back away from the distant, militaristic style of policing has been well documented in North America. J.E. McElroy finds much research reflecting a "great degree of consensus about the deficiencies of conventional urban policing."[9] Some basic points of agreement on the need for change include the following:

1. A recognition that reliance on the traditional tactics of preventive patrol, rapid response to citizen calls, and increasingly sophisticated investigative techniques *offers little hope of improving crime-control performance;*

2. A recognition that *fear of crime is a serious matter in its own right* and that it is largely a product of perceived incivilities and signs of disorder on the neighbourhood level; and

3. A recognition that the police have not focused attention on such "quality of life" or "order maintenance" problems because of their preoccupation with serious street crime and because their resources are largely consumed by mobile response to apparently disparate incidents. Whatever their merits, these tactics leave patrol officers *relatively ignorant of the community's quality of life and order maintenance concerns* and largely anonymous to community residents.[10]

Researchers have noted that the pressures for change have been both internal and external. D. Clairmont points to the internal pressures of "the demand for input by better educated officers, the morale problems associated with limited promotion opportunities in a hierarchical, rank-emphasizing organization." He also notes the external pressures of various race controversies concerning the police in Britain, the U.S. and Canada.[11]

Resurgence of community-oriented policing as a model also reflects a response to increases in crimes committed in fears about crime in the community. Consequently, police departments have been prime targets of public criticism. Public frustration has intensified with the lack of police effectiveness in solving the problems of crime and with the distant, unresponsive, even biased and repressive manner in which police work has been carried out. The resulting public pressure, often led by organized anti-crime and minority interest groups, has forced police departments to move away from the military paradigm to a community-based approach.

A shift from the professional model to a community model presents complex administrative challenges. The change entails at least three fundamental changes in the way policing is carried out: 1) an expansion of the role of police in the community, with more individual responsibility for officers; 2) an organizational change from the paramilitary hierarchical style to a decentralized, more open, democratic management style; and 3) the establishment of close ties with the community (responsiveness, accountability). In practice, such changes imply more decentralized decision-making and job enrichment in the police organization; more proactive, problem-solving policing; more involvement of "community" influences in police planning and accountability; and more status in the police organization for the uniformed officer, often renamed the "constable generalist" to underscore his or her more expansive police role.[12]

Not surprisingly, the term "community policing" has been used to refer to everything from specific local government programs to a vague effort to bring police departments closer to the people. For our purposes, we follow the statement provided by the commissioner of the RCMP in his Directional Statement of 1990:

> Community policing is not a self-contained program but a method and a style of delivering most police services ... This broad responsibility is fulfilled by demonstrating local accountability and treating the community not as a passive recipient of police services but as an active agent and partner in promoting security. It requires establishing as operational priorities those problems that disturb the community most, adopting a proactive, problem-solving approach and measuring effectiveness by the degree of public co-operation received and by the absence of crime and disorder in a community. It is a generalist rather than a specialist style of policing and it is built on community consensus rather than the unilateral view of the police.[13]

In short, community policing entails changes in philosophy, structural changes in the organization of police departments, and new strategies. Some of these include community mini-stations, or "storefronts," bike and foot patrols, school anti-crime education (e.g.DARE) programs, officer-led neighbourhood watch programs programs, citizens' review boards, more accessible complaint procedures, and stricter restrictions on the use of force.

Community Policing in Halton Region
Phase 1: 1975-1994

Halton Regional Municipality is a combination of rural areas and suburban cities in southern Ontario. It is bordered by the Regional Municipality of Peel (Mississauga, Brampton) on the east; the Regional Municipality of Wellington (rural) on the north; Hamilton-Wentworth (City of Hamilton) on the west; and Lake Ontario on the south. It includes the cities of Burlington (pop. approx. 140,000) and Oakville (pop. approx. 130,000), as well as a large rural area including the towns of Milton (pop. approx. 33,000) and Halton Hills (Acton and Georgetown, pop. approx. 38,000). These geographical distinctions mark the four administrative divisions of the Halton Regional Police Service. The organization is governed by the Halton Regional Police Services Board, made up of seven members appointed by various municipal, regional and provincial governing authorities.

Community policing in Halton can be dated to 1975, when the newly amalgamated Halton Regional Police Department began a "team policing" program in Burlington. According to a newspaper account, police administrators claimed this experiment showed "this system gets police closer to the people they serve" by giving constables more of a chance to "leave their cars and mingle with the public, getting to know them and their problems on a less formal basis."[14] Then Police Chief Kenneth Skerrett had been quoted as early as 1971 as being committed to the policing philosophy of "halt a crime before it's committed"[15] and made news by heading up the first Canadian police department to hire a full-time social worker for "crisis intervention."[16] These events indicate the willingness of the organization to break new ground by trying community-based techniques before they became "trendy". A review of the literature (in scholarly and popular publications) shows that such departures from the "military model" were hardly reported at all until around 1980 and were not commonplace until the mid-1980s.

Community policing in Halton began in earnest in 1982, when administrators created a "pro-active" policing squad in Aldershot, the zone in Burlington with the highest crime rate. Officials were quoted at the time as saying that the plan was to build up a "good rapport" between officers and the public. The stated philosophy involved "preventing crimes, by making conditions such that an illegal act is less likely to occur." It was noted at the time that this effort was "the opposite of reactive policing, where a response is made after a crime occurs."[17] A year later, it was announced that the "proactive policing" program was being implemented city-wide in Burlington.[18] Again, the idea of discouraging crime or "be[ing] on the scene when it happens instead of chasing criminals after the deed has been done" was stressed, along with the idea that police would be "getting out of their cruisers more to meet the public."[19]

In the next two to three years, other programs were phased in, including "community conference committees" administered by constables and designed to give community members an opportunity to meet with each other and their local constable to air complaints and discuss community problems. Some structural changes were made in this period in the way the traditional patrol "platoons" were deployed. First, as part of the "proactive policing" effort, patrol officers were instructed to spend one-half of their work-time on proactive, or "community", policing. This step replaced the "team policing" program that had been implemented almost six years earlier. Problems with administering the split-time proactive-reactive approach led to the division of the platoons themselves into proactive and reactive officers. Additional problems with this effort eventually led to the creation of a separate deployment division, "Community Directed Patrol." Some patrol constables were reassigned as "village constables," who were assigned to specific areas, including the Warwick Court (low-income) housing complex, Burlington Mall, and the downtown core. It also included the deployment of two "community directed" officers in the northern regions of Halton, a program dubbed "project visibility." A bike-patrol program has been implemented more recently, utilized mainly by the rural officers and village constables.

In addition to structural changes in deployment, administrators from the outset recognized the importance of setting out a mission or vision statement that reflected the new philosophy. In 1982, the Halton Regional Police Force (later changed to "Service") adopted this "policing philosophy": Halton Regional Police Force will respond to community needs through a combined strategy of preventative, proactive and reactive policing programs, using the concept of the Constable Generalist,[20] the whole of which will be supported by a participatory management environment.[21] Within the same internal document, these definitions were provided:

Preventative policing: the recognition, anticipation and appraisal of a crime risk and initiating the necessary action to remove or reduce it.

Proactive policing: the specifically planned response to a particular pattern of crime or situation of concern that may develop in specific areas at certain times.

Reactive policing: the capability of responding to calls for service relating to crime, traffic and social-order complaints.

This same brief statement with only the one word, "force," changed, was the official mission statement of the HRPS through the 1980s and until very recently (1995). In 1991, the HRPS board hired a consultant from the Institute of Environmental Research to facilitate the development of a new "strategic plan." Once this process, carried out by "selected senior management and the Police Services Board," was complete, a document was produced and distributed. The mission statement was retained and "goals, objectives and action steps" were developed for five key-issue areas: changes in community demographics and cultural makeup; accountability and community involvement; employment equity; career enrichment and personnel development; and changes in technology. Some of the specific goals that relate most closely to the community-policing philosophy were in the "accountability and community involvement" area. They included:

- increasing the understanding of the community's needs and issues as they relate to the service;
- increasing the public's understanding of policing; and
- operating the service so that it is responsive to the community's needs and concerns.

Specific objectives under this heading included

- reducing the number of community complaints about the HRPS by twenty-five per cent by 31 December 1994;
- developing a "service excellence" attitude by January 1993;

-   establishing community consultation committees in each policing community by January 1993 and ensuring that each committee meets a minimum of four times per year;
-   surveying the general public to obtain information of perceptions of our policing service, commencing in October 1992; and
-   assessing annually the number of village constables required to respond to community needs.[22]

Though this plan was scheduled to serve as the "strategic planning" map to "guide the Halton Regional Police Service into the next decade," it was decided less than three years later (1994) that a complete reassessment of the service's community-policing approach was necessary.

Phase 2: 1994

In early 1994, a complete overhaul of the organization's entire structure, including its community-policing policy, was undertaken. The Halton Regional Police Service Organizational Review Project consisted of eleven task forces, including a Community Policing Policy and Service Review/Survey, Community Support Services, and a Communications Support task force.[23] How this reorganization was structured is significant. Each task force was administered by upper- and middle-level managers (staff sergeants and sergeants), rank-and-file membership was on a volunteer basis, and one strict rule was imposed: "There will be no rank in this room" when issues are discussed. This process allowed for a great deal of real (not cosmetic) participation from all levels of the organization. In addition, an effort was made early in the process to solicit comment (specifically on the pros and cons of community-policing programs) from all members of the service. In general, the eleven groups were assigned the task of determining if the services provided by the organization (currently or proposed for the future) were efficiently provided and "on target" in terms of the organization's goals. They were charged with identifying and analysing obstacles or "tasks or activities [that] are currently impeding the quantity and quality of direct service by our officers."[24]

The combined task forces' report to the HRPS board included fifty-five structural and 115 procedural recommendations. The primary changes that have resulted are the move to a "team policing" approach and a "flattening out" of the entire organization. The structural recommendations involved reducing the number of supervisors in patrol from fourteen to eleven per platoon (all shifts), as well as the elimination of eight other management positions and five civilian (mainly clerical) positions. A few positions were to be shifted around and three more created, for a net decrease of nineteen jobs, almost all of them in management. Also, the existing divisions of "Administration" and "Operations" were to become "Community Policing Administration" and "Community Policing Operations." An additional division of "Community Policing Support" was to be added, in which a new department of "community support" was included. In addition to these changes, some existing strategies remained in place. These include Community Directed Patrol (including the village constables), the "project visibility" officers, bike patrols, and the community-consultation committees.

Although the HRPS has undergone a lengthy, all-encompassing reorganization, it is important to note that neither the stated philosophy nor the specific strategies were significantly altered. The emphasis on a mix of proactive, reactive and preventive police activities is still an official part of the "service-delivery philosophy," as is the reliance on the constable generalist approach and the notion of participatory management.[25] Rather than change, there is a noticeably sharper focus on some of the concepts. For example, the new statement of principles (draft) is "more specific about the community's role as a "partner" in contribut[ing] to creating an environment that examines, anticipates, prevents, or reacts to concerns resulting in positive solutions" and in making the maintenance and improvement of quality of life one of its primary goals.[26] It is also more specific in terms of the role of the front-line officer: "The H.R.P.S. will empower its members with the responsibility and opportunity to provide the community with an interactive and innovative service; being accountable to the community and the organization."[27]

The newly developed "service-delivery philosophy" sharpens the focus on problem-solving as a tactic, continuity of service and communication among various officers servicing a community, and flexibility (ability to "adjust to changing environment"). The dependence on fellow constables and focus on problem-solving that characterize the team-policing approach have always been implicit in the goals of the organization, but they have been made more explicit. In short, the latest change has come more in the process of the implementation, not the substance of what is being implemented. It should also be noted that the new plan is still evolving, and not all of the task force's recommendations have been officially approved by the police-services board.

From "professional" to "community-based" policing: internal obstacles to change

The process of organizational change faced many internal obstacles in the Halton organization throughout the decades of its implementation. A 1987 study found that strategies put into practice prior to that time (such as the proactive/reactive patrols) faced such obstacles as a perceived lack of leadership and commitment in the lower ranks; difficulty in the coordination of tasks and the communication of expectations; and anti-CBP cultural attitudes of some officers.[28] Frustrations came closer to the surface after the 1991 strategic plan was implemented. These included a lack of commitment to the concept of community policing, low morale, a lack of adequate training in community policing, and inadequate assessments of community-policing activities. Although these obstacles overlap to a certain degree, I discuss each separately.

Lack of commitment

One of the most commonly mentioned variables influencing the success of the community-based policing programs is the attitudes of individuals involved in the process. Whoever is making the decisions varies from situation to situation, but the sincerity of decision-makers' motives is always of essential importance to the effectiveness of the resulting program. A genuine desire for change at the top brings legitimacy to the process and makes the possibility of long-term commitment more likely. Insincerity in the part of top decision-makers can lead to debilitating resistance from the rank and file, particularly if the upper-level lack of follow-through is perceived as an ongoing pattern. Table 1 outlines the effect commitment and the attitudes of management often have on CBP programs in general and the effects these variables have had on the HRPS program in particular. The text in the top portion of each box is a practical description of a particular variable, stated first in positive terms (effective programs) and then in negative terms (ineffective programs). Beneath this, in italics and in brackets, is an evaluation of the HRPS program as it relates to the same variable.

Despite its long history of philosophical approval and uninterrupted implementation of community-based programs, lack of commitment was repeatedly identified by administrators and front-line personnel as the single biggest obstacle to the effectiveness of community policing in Halton. There are two sides to this problem. First, from the administrators' point of view, there is the lack of internal cooperation, that is, "getting people to 'buy into' the philosophy" rather than looking at community policing as a grocery list of programs. From the point of view of the front-line officer and middle management, there is the problem of a perceived lack of commitment from above. In traditional hierarchical structures, officers often learn about new initiatives from the distant, upper levels of the administration and may perceive community-based policing efforts as political lip-service or a "selling out" to special-interest group pressure at the expense of the officers.[29]

Line officers in Halton often felt they were "thrown to the wolves" when upper management "imposed a program [on them] from above" without any input from them, without any details about how or why they were supposed to go about implementing it, or without the necessary support, including guidance and support from immediate supervisors and resource support (extra time, etc.). In other words, front-line officers felt they were being asked to "do" community policing, "but no one told us what that was ...

They expected us to carry something out that they [upper management] didn't even understand." (interviews)

An oft-cited example was the community-conference committee. Line officers were informed (without consultation) that it was now their responsibility to organize a community-conference committee in their patrol area. Details were minimal. Constables were told that this was part of a community-oriented policing approach and that their task was to go out and find out what was going on with the public. No specific directions or guidelines were offered, nor was any training required or even offered. It was not made clear to the constables that the purpose of the meetings was to attempt to identify and solve community problems. One front-line officer who received this mandate believes that it represented not only a lack of commitment but a lack of knowledge and understanding of exactly what community policing is supposed to be. He suggests that this led to a disorganized, sporadic ineffective outcome. Some officers were meeting regularly with citizens and seeing positive results, while other meetings were a complete waste of time, because the officers did not have any training in how to go about organizing such a meeting, how to encourage community involvement, or how to facilitate discussion in a meeting once it got going. Managers also agree that there is a problem with lack of consistency, skills training and lack of direction with the community-conference committees.[30]

An internal survey, conducted in the fall of 1994, asked all front-line officers, middle managers and supervisors to name some of the positive and negative points of Halton's community-policing program.[31] Some typical responses were "lack of support from management," "community policing not (really being) practiced, only window dressing for the politicians,"[32] "manpower seems very low all the time," and "[community-conference committee] meetings are not consistent/time wasted/not focused on their functions."[33] One of the officers who participated in the solicitation of comments observed a pattern of complaints related to number of years of service. The views expressed from the police officers with ten years or more of service were directly related to the lack

Table 1. *Comparison of Effective and Ineffective Programs*

	Effective Programs (Evaluation of HRPS programs)	Ineffective Programs (Evaluation of HRPS programs)
Commitment-related variables		
Depth of commitment	Changes must pervade organization and grow from a fundamental change in departmental vision. *(Vision of top leadership appears to have remained consistent; no evidence of efforts to "switch streams" and abandon community policing in twenty years.)*	Changes only "add-ons"; essence (vision) of organization remains unchanged. *(Vision has remained consistent over time, but depth has faltered; vision often lacked depth which led to a lack of credibility (failure to provide support, follow-up, or training in various projects).)*
Length of commitment	Long-term; changes are given a chance to show they are effective *(Halton's strongest asset; commitment to CBP principles has been very consistent over time)*	Short-term; an element of impatience, political expediency; programs are discarded if positive results are not immediately forthcoming. *(In-service training uses the City of Houston's abandonment of CBP as an example of an organization that did not allow projects to prove their viability (gave way to political expediency).)*
Attitude/motives of management	Sincere, genuine concern, desire to make a change *(Actual solicitation of input, resource support, training, as represented in 1994-95 reorganization.)*	Insincere; only a PR "ploy" to quiet community criticism. *(Lack of instruction/guidance in CCC mandate; lack of input in previous decisions (previous team-policing program, proactive/reactive patrol program).)*
Morale-related variables		
Attitude/motives of rank and file	Trust leader's motives, genuinely welcome new responsibilities and autonomy (new decision-making role)	Feel like "scapegoats" for weak management; perception that front-line officers are being used to deflect criticism from political leaders. Adversarial relationship between rank and file and management, as well as community.

Table 1. (Concluded)

	Effective Programs (Evaluation of HRPS programs)	Ineffective Programs (Evaluation of HRPS programs)
	(This is the sort of "increased job satisfaction" organizers hope the constable generalists will feel in the new team-policing project. It appears to have worked well in many of the village-constable positions: they have welcomed new responsibilities, formed creative solutions to problems, and have an increased level of satisfaction.)	*(The resentment of the "grin and wave squad" that was perceived as a ploy "to make the politicians look good": the proactive/reactive patrol perception that reactive officers were being made scapegoats by having to answer more calls, keep the crime rate down, and make the politicians (with their "pet" CBP projects) look good.)*
Level of rank and file involvement in ongoing functioning of CBP program	Constant, continuing *(Use of volunteer task forces in restructuring: town-hall sessions; solicitation of input; and commitment to flexibility and responsiveness to ongoing concerns or needs.)*	Ineffective, fades over time; no real internal power/ influence *(Lack of initial participation was identified as a problem in the past, but initial participation in the reorganization will not be enough to sustain its effectiveness over time (i.e., continuing input is required).)*
Level of training/preparation	Formal training in community-policing skills (problem-solving, teamwork, public relations, interpersonal communication) at all levels of the organization, for existing officers and new recruits. *(Many of the various task forces cited the need for the Service to address the problem of training, indicating at least a recognition of the need for an integrated training program.)*	Inadequate; vague, superficial and/or brief introductions; little or no formal training; mixed messages. *(Only a few hours of CBP technique training is conducted at the Ontario Police College; and only a few in-service training programs on CBP-related topics have been offered.)*
Level of perceived (internal and external) effectiveness	Measurable effects identified, communicated to the public and rank and file *(More "fair" assessment procedures, more descriptive record keeping)*	No effort made to produce measurable effects; community and front-line officers have no conception that program is "working" *(Identified as a problem in the past: officers asked to do community policing, but assessment still based on "catching bad guys.")*

of commitment towards the concept, the poor marketing plan, and the lack of training/education at the initial outset which caused confusion and misdirection within the organization. It appeared that there was no leadership to implement this new idea and everyone was left on their own with no guidelines. This created a lack of confidence within the Service, which is still present today. The police personnel that were under ten years service, were not tainted with the initial implementation problems and confusion.[34]

An example of a lack of commitment was apparent in Halton's early attempts to implement a team-patrol concept. It is interesting to note that the new team project and the failed attempt implemented in the mid-1970's are similar in both structure and objectives.[35] What appears to most distinguish the two is level of commitment. As Police Chief Peter Campbell points out, design of who will do what, where, and when is not enough to make the team concept work. He identifies five issues that relate to the long-term success of team policing, all relating in some way to the idea of commitment:

1. *leadership*, in the form of support from supervisors; a relationship that reflects "guided autonomy" of constables. Front-line officers are "empowered" by being allowed to make their own decisions, work out solutions with fellow constables and members of the community, yet are given technical support, guidance, advice, etc., and broad boundaries are set by the supervisors;
2. *coordination* of the activities of team members (the constable generalists), supervisors, and specialists within single communities, and the coordination of activities of other teams operating at different times and in adjacent areas;
3. *communication*, or the development of effective channels of communication among team members and among teams operating at different times and in adjacent areas;
4. *planning,* or making a concerted effort to identify problems and the development and planning of creative solutions to those problems; and
5. *training,* for constables in skills related to team building, problem solving, etc.[36]

The fact that such issues are recognized, that they are being addressed by upper management, and that there is a concrete plan for following through on them increases the likelihood that a much-needed perception of commitment will result within the ranks. This level of commitment, or "follow through," was not present in earlier efforts or even alluded to at the outset of the program. The 1976 team-policing effort focused on structural changes (zones were redrawn and platoons re-deployed), and only vague references were made to constables being allowed more time "out of their cruisers" and having a "great[er] change of following up" on crimes.[37] The failure of administrators to "follow up" on the program's implementation led to a perception that upper management was not committed, and it also led to a great deal of resentment and frustration, which in turn led to low morale.

Low morale

In the Halton internal survey, there were numerous examples of complaints based on low morale brought about by a lack of participation in decisions, lack of guidance, lack of support, and lack of resources. Some of the most common complaints can be categorized into these areas:

- feelings of isolation: "Confines officer to a single community";
- feelings of being overworked: "More demands on police," "Stacking of calls, impression we are always backlogged";
- resentment towards community-assigned workers: "[There is] still bitterness between [community-directed patrol] and other officers";
- feelings of ineffectiveness: "Ability to respond to emergency situations is being affected," "Not enough hours in the day to do a thorough job"; and
- lack of appreciation from the community: "Public calls and expects police to solve all their problems," "Resentment from the community."[38]

The specific programs that were repeatedly blamed for reducing morale (by line officers and supervisors alike) were the "proactive-reactive" programs (both approaches). At first, when all front-line officers were required to document half of their time as "proactive policing" and half as "reactive policing," there was confusion as to what exactly was expected of them. Not only was there no training provided, but many complained that there was no clear definition provided of what proactive policing was. The result was that most officers just logged whatever time they were not answering calls as "proactive policing," and very few made any special efforts to change what they had been doing all along. In other words, the plan had little positive effect on the quality of police work but had a negative effect on morale because of the frustration caused by the vagueness of the directions and the feeling that they were being given more responsibility without additional resources.

The morale problem worsened when administrators concluded that the original plan needed re-working. Since it proved unworkable to ask each officer to split his or her time in half, it was decided that the platoons would be split up, with some officers doing proactive policing and others doing reactive policing. The problem remained, however, because of the vagueness of the term "proactive policing." The overwhelming impression that was created within the ranks was that "those guys over there (the proactive officers) are sitting around while we (the *real* police) are doing all the work." The proactive officers became known by others as the "grin and wave squad." Officers assigned to the reactive patrol saw their call-load increase, and they perceived the proactive officers were getting most of the credit for solving problems. The program caused a great deal of tension in the ranks and between front-line officers and supervisors. One officer, working in the reactive patrol at the time, saw the peak of this tension when the chief of police was reported to have said, "We don't catch bad guys, we do community policing." Whether this quote is accurate, the fact that it took hold and spread throughout the organization shows how one remark can focus feelings of frustration into an intense distrust and lack of confidence in the upper levels of management.

With little education and direction provided, the commitment cannot be fully implemented if the tools and knowledge are not provided.

In the recent review process, the HRPS appears to have taken some account of these morale problems. It sought to promote morale by reducing feelings of ineffectiveness, confusion, and frustration by empowering the rank and file. More than twenty per cent of the organization (107 out of 540 members) *directly* participated in the task forces, making the reorganization more of a bottom-up process than the "imposed from above" plans of the past. Close to one hundred per cent participated at least indirectly via a solicitation of e-mail comments, anonymous suggestion cards and an internal survey.[39]

In addition, after the task forces came up with concrete proposals, many of which have been approved by the board, a series of meetings was held (July 1995) before implementation actually began. Members of the organization were encouraged to address the chief directly with any concerns, questions, suggestions dealing with the reorganization. The goals were to "dispel any rumours or inaccurate information relating to the [reorganization] as well as the ongoing implementation of it."[40]

According to the chief, these meetings were well attended, and many members of the organization took advantage of the opportunity to vent frustrations and air complaints to the highest-ranking officer in the service. A common question posed came from the "imposed from above" fear: "Is this [policy] cast in stone?" Campbell says he used the opportunity to assure officers that the new plan was flexible and that at any time in the implementation the rank and file felt unhappy or uncomfortable with a part of it, he and other managers would try to be responsive to those concerns and open to suggestions from the field.[41]
Government retrenchment may add to morale problems. The chief points to the reduced promotion prospects and the lack of additional funds as the primary sources of low morale. While the staff is being cut and officers are being required to become more "generalist" (i.e., to do more and to know more than they were previously required), they feel frustrated by a lack of additional resources (manpower, equipment, etc.).[42] This will present a challenge to promote morale in the group, and the organization will have to offer necessary support and incentives to make it worth their while to stay in patrol. The obvious solution is to somehow balance the costs of the new organizational structure with the benefits of improved job satisfaction, fulfillment and so on. Chief Campbell says he recognizes the importance of

promoting job satisfaction and will seek to provide it through more participation in decision-making and managerial flexibility.

The new approach to team policing is expected to enhance job satisfaction at the "front-line" level. Several (four to six) patrol constables (including existing village constables) are assigned to larger "zones" that allow greater freedom of movement and more opportunities to engage in group problem solving. The hope is that team members will provide support to each other in the form of knowledge, experience and expertise about particular problems. The team-policing project will also, in theory, provide more consistency in problem identification and crime prevention. Teams are encouraged to share information and work together with their own team members and teams working the same area on other shifts to solve problems and conduct investigations. In previous team-policing experiments officers have complained that manpower was not being used efficiently because of the arbitrary nature of the "community" boundaries. Officers often felt they were "locked in" to their own communities and became frustrated, because they were restrained from going across the street to answer a call just because it was in someone else's area. Table 1 summarized the effects of the morale-related variables of employee participation in the CBP process, the attitudes of the rank and file, as well as two other related variables: training and assessment procedures.

Inadequate training

As will now be evident, one of the main sources for low morale and perceived lack of commitment to community-based programs in the HRPS was a lack of preparation and training. One veteran officer who participated in the internal survey by conducting interviews with more than fifty of his fellow officers observed that a lack of training created a perceived lack of commitment:

> [I]t is disappointing to learn that there is an inadequate amount of effort and time placed into the education process either at the Ontario Police College or inservice-training within the service when they are recruited. With little education and direction provided, the commitment

cannot be fully implemented if the tools and knowledge are not provided.[43]

In the internal survey, it was concluded that "[o]nly a few members had the actual opportunity or time to read any literature on Community Policing."[44] One task force member concluded there was "[i]nadequate training and education for all members of the H.R.P.S. This lack of knowledge created confusion, misdirection and loss of confidence and trust within the service."[45]

Based on these experiences, the success or failure of the latest team-policing effort will depend largely on support (both actual and perceived) and training. The proposal already put forth addresses the support element, but relatively little has been put in writing addressing the need for training in problem solving, small-group communication, or in the additional policing skills that is required of front-line officers. Since they are required to be "generalists" rather than specialists, the average officer is doing more crime-scene investigation, witness interviewing, etc., that is traditionally done by specialists.

Many of the task forces dealt directly or indirectly with internal communication and training. Some of the specific proposals that have emerged include:

- delivery of management training;
- development of a partnership with Sheridan College (the community college within the region);
- training of all uniform employees for crime analysis and use of criminal investigation databases;
- the assignment of training responsibilities to one person for consistency;
- the establishment of training requirements for all officers; and
- the improvement/increase of in-service training that addresses "questions being repeatedly raised/areas of concern"[46]

Training is now seen by upper management as a primary issue in the success of the new effort, particularly in terms of the philosophy of community policing, problem-solving techniques, how to work with a team, and how to plan, structure and run community-consultation committees.

Because the administration of police services in Ontario is governed by the provincial government, the HRPS is limited to training its members after they are already working the streets (i.e., "in-service training"). New Halton Region constables are trained at the Ontario Police College, where the curriculum has very little subject-matter related to community-policing techniques (eight hours total), and the HRPS has no direct input into the course of study.

Inadequate assessment procedures

The perceived effectiveness of the program depends to a great degree on the measurability and assessment of the activities involved. If the police participants in the program are made to feel that community-based policing is working for them, then its continued success is more likely. Likewise, if decision-makers are led to believe that CBP "works," by objective standards, they are likely granted more funding when necessary or are at least less likely to cut funds. The traditional police approach to quantifying the crime-fighting function is carried out primarily by charting activities in three basic categories: offence/incidents, arrests/citations, and charges filed. These are the basic reports that rank-and-file officers fill out and are the traditional means for assessing their performance (and that of the department). The number of "offences cleared" reflects the number of arrests made in relation to offences reported, and "charges filed" (or "charges laid") figure is a ratio of arrests that actually result in the suspect being charged with a crime.

Neither of these ratios accurately reflects the goals of CBP, however, nor does the traditional measure of response time to calls. Community-based policing seeks to *avoid* crime and avoid the need to call police so often. Thus, the problem of measuring the effects of CBP efforts is one of the most prominent difficulties to be overcome. If not addressed, it obviously invites morale problems and internal division. Although many researchers have lamented the difficulties in measuring results, only a few studies have been produced with tangible measures of CBP "output." One recent study measured levels of fear of crime in areas targeted by foot patrols and community ministations.[47] Others have attempted to quantify problems identified, the strategies employed and the resources used to implement them.[48] Researchers in the Netherlands have developed a system that measures the "countable products" of police activity (arrested suspects, crimes reported, assistances performed; unplanned, assistances performed; planned, licences processed and advice given) and "presence in society" (surveillance, controls, external contacts, and large-scale actions). Countable products are weighted by an "appropriate standard time" and summed, yielding a figure representing the total production of the police force, which in turn yields a production-unit-per-dollar (guilder, in this case) figure. Likewise, "presence in society" figures, measured in hours, provide a figure of presence in society per dollar spent.[49]

As many have noted, "documenting actual practice in the field [is] a difficult and demanding task" that needs to be routinized.[50] But it is also a task that "involves inescapable value and qualitative judgements,"[51] which do not lend themselves to a smoothly calibrated scale of measurement. "At best all that could be reasonably aspired to are allocations of individuals into very rough and crude categories: outstanding achievements and/or potential, broadly satisfactory, totally unacceptable."[52] R. Reiner argues that such broad measures are sufficient "in order to make the crucial and unavoidable management decisions" about who must be sanctioned or who merits promotion.[53]

Some strides have already been made in Halton to address the assessment problem. Community-based police officers file "monthly performance summaries" that tally not only the "traditional" crime-reporting activities, such as arrests, seatbelt tickets, etc., but also provide details of "community work." In addition, non-community-based patrol constables are provided with the opportunity to log "case activity data," which includes problems that an officer has identified in his or her community and what activities can be undertaken to address them.

Despite these efforts, Halton officers still complain of a "lack of recognition for community policing," and "appraisals are still structured around reactive goals, not proactive goals," despite management's claim that proactive policing was a priority.[54] Among the latest proposals, few directly address the assessment issue. However, there are several that focus on reducing paperwork by allowing for direct computer entry of reports, transferring reporting responsibilities for some incidents to non-sworn officers, and reducing the amount of reporting required of front-line officers in general.[55] Although these do not directly address the assessment issue, in theory, they should provide constables with more time to document non-traditional "community-related" activities, which in turn will allow for these activities to be considered more fully in assessment procedures. Development of assessment procedures that more accurately measure the CBP goals of crime identification and prevention, however, is clearly a challenge that Halton Region will have to devote more attention to in future if the service's commitment to community policing is to be sustained.

Summary

Despite these obstacles, it should be noted that the overall internal and external response to Halton's community-policing policies over the years has been positive. Their model has been one that has been the subject of study by similar organizations across North America and around the world.[56] The same internal review that revealed problems with low morale, a perceived lack of commitment and poor assessment procedures also found some significant positive feelings towards the policy. Most of the "pro-community policing" comments fell into one of four categories:

1. *efficiency:* consistency of area coverage; officers develop knowledge of a specific area; chronic problems readily identified; informants developed; better information gathering; manpower more evenly distributed.

2. *personal fulfillment:* officers become experts in their communities; friendships developed; more one-on-one problem solving.

3. *good community relations:* create a positive impression on the public; improve service's image; face-to-face contact with the public; bring police and community closer; police are more accountable; trust built between police and public; communication improved between police and public; better support from community regarding serious incidents; police are

more approachable; bring people more peace of mind in terms of how their tax dollars are spent.

4. *high degree of community involvement:* participation in the Neighbourhood Watch programs; more involvement of the community with problems in their areas; more interaction with community; better community input towards policing; creates teamwork within the community.[57]

Most in the service agree that the philosophy, or idea, of community policing is good; one respondent noted that it provides a focus for "why we are here." While the positive comments are instructive as to what is working well and should be continued, the obstacles that have confronted the Halton Region CBP programs over the years have also provided some valuable lessons not only for Halton but also for other Canadian municipalities.

Lessons learned from the Halton Region experience
1. Community policing is a philosophy
The belief that community policing is a philosophy and not just a set of programs differentiates the Halton program from other less successful community-policing efforts. Organizers there have recognized that there is no "magic pill" in the form of a program that will immediately result in positive police-community relations, contented, fulfilled police officers and lower crime. Real problems must be solved "from the inside out" by the slow, painstaking process of instilling the values of community policing in the hearts and minds of all the participants, one at a time.

New York criminal-justice professor, David H. Bayley, asserts that "[t]he formulation that community policing is a philosophy rather than a program ... allows programmatic development to fit local circumstances and perceptions of need," but falls short in its dependence on too vague a definition of programmatic content. The problem is, he argues, that "everyone can claim to be doing it,"[58] presumably no matter what they are "doing." Halton Region Police Chief Campbell disagrees with that interpretation. He suggests that CBP should be viewed as a comprehensive program, encompassing the philosophy of community-based policing *and* the various programs that come out of it. In other words, the programs themselves do not make community policing; a commitment to community policing produces the programs that all work together to fulfill the goals of the CBP "vision."

2. Don't expect results overnight

This lesson is perhaps the most valuable to be drawn from the Halton Region experience. It is important to recall that this approach to policing (radical at the time) started in Burlington nearly twenty years ago, and there are still some serious bugs being worked out. As one architect of the new program pointed out, they are not expecting it to work "overnight." They expect it to continue to be hard work. As another officer pointed out, "This is not a single program or even a series of programs; community policing is a *process*," and the implementation of that process is an ongoing concern. Acknowledging that one hundred per cent of the organization will never "buy into" the community-policing philosophy, Campbell stresses the need to develop a "critical mass" of support. In other words, with proper instruction and internal responsiveness to concerns, eventually more and more members of the organization will take "ownership" of the philosophy, until a level is reached at which the philosophy can be implemented effectively without total commitment from all members.

Meaningful reform also takes a consistent commitment over a long period of time, an objective that is extremely difficult to achieve, as the failures of so many efforts in other localities demonstrate. Despite its mistakes and failures (and changes in leadership), Halton Region has obviously benefited from the positive momentum provided by a consistent commitment to the philosophy of community policing by some key members of the organization. Whether by chance or by design, the Halton Regional Police Service (in all of its twenty years of existence) has been headed by individuals dedicated to the principles of community policing.

Halton Region has obviously benefited from the momentum provided by consistent leadership. In contrast, an organization that has seen radical shifts in philosophy brought about by changes in leadership will have greater obstacles to overcome in terms of perceived commitment and morale. The Halton experience is most likely explained by a combination of different factors: decision-makers in Halton Region having the foresight to be consistent with their choices of leaders, resisting any temptations to send the organization off in a different direction by choosing a new leader who is radically different from his predecessor; the longevity of leaders in the position (only three have held the post in more than twenty years); and the fact that the reputation of this organization and previous leaders attracts like-minded, qualified applicants to the job.

3. Allow for innovation from within

If there is a universal agreement on one thing the HRPS did right with its community policing program, it was to "allow good people the opportunity to innovate and excel, and make some of the things we were talking about work." Despite its shortcomings, throughout the years of trying different approaches, creative, dedicated, somewhat entrepreneurial individuals were empowered to develop crime-reduction and community-awareness techniques that have proved to be effective in their areas and have started to spread throughout the organization.

One example is a patrol officer who set up a medication-labeling program for the elderly, with the help of a local pharmacist. The constable found that in one apartment building with a concentration of elderly residents in his area there was a problem of identifying possible causes of illness or death in responding to calls. The stickers provide him and other officers, as well as emergency medical personnel, with vital information as to what drugs the resident has been taking and what ailments they may be suffering from. The pharmacist is happy for the advertisement, the residents feel safer, and it makes the police's job a little easier.

4. Learn from and admit your mistakes

The latest effort by the HRPS to restructure its operations proves to some members that decision-makers are sincere, mainly because they are perceived to be admitting that mistakes were made in the past. This perception is important, because, otherwise, line officers may feel that any new programs will be "more of the same." And, if past efforts were perceived as merely "window dressing," then subsequent ones will be viewed as insincere as well, unless there is some admission that mistakes were made in the past. The newest effort represented a willingness to admit that problems existed with the way things were operating and how they had been implemented in the past. A lot of effort was put into trying to convince members of the organization that this was not "more of the same" but a sincere effort to implement the philosophy of CBP by integrating everyone into the decision-making process throughout the life of the program.

5. Start from the bottom up

Some of the harshest lessons learned in Halton have to do with the fact that the line officers perceived that the programs were being implemented from "on high" by people who did not understand what police work was. The problems with team policing, proactive-reactive patrol and community consultation committee programs are all examples of this. The participation of twenty per cent of the organization's members in the reorganization, the solicitation of information from numerous sources of input, and the town-hall meetings with the chief all represent genuine attempts to make this latest effort a "grass-roots" concern.

At the beginning of this case study, it was asserted that Halton learned that community policing had to be done "the hard way," that there were no easy solutions, and no matter how well a police service is managed, there will still be obstacles to be overcome. That is perhaps the most important lesson of all to be learned. The Halton experience shows that it is a combination of patience, commitment, ideas, and creatively constructed programs that will allow for the success of a comprehensive community-based policing approach. With all these lessons in mind, if the Halton Regional Police Service continues to take advantage of its strengths (long-term commitment, a structure that allows for freedom and innovation) and continues to monitor and address problem areas (lack of training, morale) by maintaining flexibility and listening to the members of the organization, it will likely maintain an effective, community-based policing organization that can act as a model for many others in North America.

Endnotes

*Reprinted with permission, Canadian Public Administration, Volume 41, No. 1, (Spring) pp.120-146.
The author acknowledges the help and assistance of Professor William D. Coleman and the members of the Halton Regional Police Service.

1   For case-study analyses of community-based policing in Metro Toronto, Halifax, New York City, Brooklyn, Chicago, Madison, and rural America, see A.M. Pate and P. Shtull, "Community policing grows in Brooklyn: An inside view of the New York City Police Department's model precinct," *Crime & Delinquency* 40, no.3 (July 1994), pp. 384-410; D. Clairmont, "Community-based policing and organizational change," in J. Chacko and S.E. Nancoo eds., *Community policing in Canada* (Toronto: Canadian Scholars' Press 1993), pp. 91-138; R.A. Weisheit, L.E. Wells, and D.N. Falcone, "Community policing in small town and rural America, *"Crime & Delinquency* 40, no. 4 (October 1994), pp. 549-67; n.a., "The experiment that worked," *Liaison* (February 1987), pp. 10-14; A. J. Lurigio and W.G. Skogan, "Winning the hearts and minds of police officers: An assessment of staff perceptions of community policing in Chicago," *Crime & Delinquency* 40, no. 3, (July 1994), pp. 315-30; M.A. Wycoff and W.G. Skogan, "The effect of community policing management style on officers' attitudes," *Crime & Delinquency* 40, no. 3, (July 1994), pp. 371-83; and C.J. Levy, "Walking the beat, the police find many allies on the street," *The New York Times* 4 April 1993, pp. 35, 42.

2   D.Clairmont, "Community-based Policing Implementation and Impact," *Canadian Journal of Criminology* 33, nos. 3-4 (July-October 1991), pp. 469-84, p. 470.

3   Interviews were conducted with the current chief, Peter Campbell, twenty-five years with the Halton Regional Police Service, two staff sergeants (both with the service since the early 1970s), two village constables (ten and five years, respectively, with Halton), and one patrol constable (with service since the early 1970s and a participant in the community-policing task force.)

4   Chacko and Nancoo, *Community Policing in Canada*, pp. 3-11, especially pp. 5-6.

5   Cited in a *Halton Community Policing Programme* open memo: "To: The citizens of Halton Region and members of the Halton Regional Police Service," 1991.

6   B.N. Leighton, "Vision of community policing: Rhetoric and reality in Canada," *Canadian Journal of Criminology* 33, nos. 3-4 (July-October 1991), pp. 485-522, p.512.

7   Ibid.

8   Ibid.

9   Chacko and Nancoo, *Community Policing in Canada*, p.7

10 G.L. Kelling, and M.H. Moore, "The evolving strategy of policing," *Perspectives on policing*, no. 4 (Washington, D.C.: National Institute of Justice and Harvard University); W.G. Skogan et al., *The Reactions to Crime Project: executive summary* (Washington, D.C.: National Institute of Justice); W.G. Skogan, *Disorder and Decline: Crime and the Spiral of Decay in American Neighborhoods* (New York: The Free Press, 1990); J.H. Skolnick and D.H. Bayley, *The New Blue Line* (New York: The Free Press; 1988). These citations were made in Chacko and Nancoo, *Community Policing in Canada*, Introduction [emphasis added].

11 Clairmont, "Community-based Policing," *Canadian Journal of Criminology*, p. 471.

12 Ibid., pp. 476-8.

13 D.H. Bayley, "Strategy," in Chacko and Nancoo, *Community Policing in Canada*, pp. 39-47, at p. 39.

14 n.a., "Experiment Spreads to Cover Entire City", *The Burlington Post* 4 February 1976, pp. 3,5.

15 M. Rapsey, "Skerrett's Aim: Halt a Crime Before it's Committed," *The Burlington Spectator* 12 January 1971.

16 n.a. "First Police Social Worker," *The Burlington Spectator* 19 January 1971, p. 8.

17 n.a., "Community Policing is Coming to Aldershot," *Weekend Post* [Burlington] 20 March 1982, p.10.

18 Presumably since it is the area with the greatest population and the highest crime rate, most new programs that have been implemented in Halton were given a "trial-run" in Burlington. This is true of the major effort that was undertaken between 1975 and the early 1980s, as well as the new effort that is planned for the fall of 1995.

19 n.a., "Proactive Policing Going Full Scale," *Weekend Post* [Burlington] 16 April 1983, p. 4.

20 The "constable generalist" is defined in several HRPS internal documents as a "highly trained professional, capable of delivering a full range of quality services to the community."

21 *Halton Regional Police Force Policing Philosophy* [internal document, 1982].

22 Ibid, p.24

23 Halton Regional Police Service, *Directions* [internal newsletter, Summer 1995].

24 *Halton Regional Police Service Organizational Review Project: General Scope of Activities for all Task Forces* [internal document, 1994].

25 This is based on a comparison of the mission statement from 1982 and strategies dating from then and the 1991 strategic plan to that in *Halton Regional Police Services Community Policing Principles* and *Service Delivery Philosophy.*

26 *Halton Regional Police Services Community Policing Principles* [internal document, 1994].

27 Ibid.

28 D.J. Loree, "Innovation and change in a regional police force," *Canadian Police College Journal* 12, no. 4 (1988), pp. 205-39, 170-7.

29 L.A. Cooke, "Low morale at DPD," *Dallas Observer* 27 October 1988, p.1, 14-17.

30 Problems with the community-conference committees, while they represent a perceived lack of commitment and adequate training in terms of *internal* shortcomings, also represent one of the most striking *external* shortcomings of the Halton CBP program, which is beyond the scope of this analysis. If the HRPS is serious about becoming a legitimate "partner" with the community (as stated in the 1994 *Service Delivery Philosophy*), then it is possible that the issue of how to integrate true public input into the system will need to be further addressed. However, as one referee of this article aptly pointed out, the perceived legitimacy of a CBP program may be defined more by the public's perception of the *effectiveness* of the program in terms of crime control rather than by the actual level of input or participation of the public in its implementation. In defining the problem thus, Halton's problems in dealing effectively with the public would more accurately be considered an internal one of enhancing overall effectiveness rather than the external problem of improving the level of authenticity of the public's input.

31 *Community Policing Committee Status Report (Draft)* [internal document, November 1994].

32 In interviews, front-line officers often use the term "politicians" to refer to upper management, police-services board members, and (of course) politicians.

33 *Status Report.*

34 HRPS Community Policing Task Force, *Informal Survey on Community Policing in Halton* [internal document, November 1994].

35 n.a., "Experiment spreads to cover entire city," *The Burlington Post* 4 February 1976, pp. 3,5.

36 Police Chief Peter Campbell, others [personal interview].

37 "Experiment spreads," *The Burlington Post*, pp. 3,5.

38 *Status Report.*

39 Chief Campbell [personal interview].

40 HRPS, *Directions*

41 Chief Campbell [personal interview (conducted one day after the final town-hall meeting)].

42 Chief Campbell [personal interview].

43 HRPS Community Policing Task Force, *Informal Survey.*

44 *Status Report.*

45 HRPS Community Policing Task Force, *Information Survey*.

46 HRPS, *Directions*.

47 D.P. Rosenbaum and A.J. Lurigio, "An inside look at community policing reform: Definitions, organizational changes, and evaluation findings," *Crime & Delinquency* 40, no. 3 (July 1994), pp. 299-314.

48 J.E. McElroy, "Evaluating service delivery of police agencies: suggestions for focus and strategy," *Workshop on Evaluating Police Service Delivery Report* (Montreal: University of Montreal, International Centre for Comparative Criminology, 1995) pp. 199-217, at p. 210.

49 G. Terlouw and M. Kruissink, "Police performance assessment: perspectives and problems," *Workshop on Evaluating Police Service Delivery Report* (Montreal: University of Montreal, International Centre for Comparative Criminology, 1995) pp. 376-400, at pp. 399-400.

50 McElroy, "Evaluating service delivery," *Workshop*, pp. 211-12.

51 R. Reiner, "Process or product?: problems of assessing individual police performance," *Workshop on Evaluating Police Service Delivery Report* (Montreal: University of Montreal, International Centre for Comparative Criminology, 1995), p. 195.

52 Ibid.

53 Ibid.

54 *Status Report*.

55 HRPS, *Directions*.

56 HRPS *Halton Regional Police Service Annual Report, 1993* [internal document]; and personal interviews.

57 *Status Report*.

58 Bayley, "Strategy," in Chacko and Nancoo, *Community Policing in Canada*, p. 39.

5

Organizational Change and CommunityPolicing: Fredericton Police Force

Leanne J. Fitch*

Introduction

In the early 1980s community policing was heralded as the "new way" to conduct business. This philosophy brought with it a need for significant changes in the long-standing traditions and ideologies of the professional police organization. Consistent with this movement the police have steadily re-evaluated their traditional priorities and service delivery and continue to implement organizational changes that are considered "landmark" events in the evolution of policing. An analysis of such change involves the complex study of informal cultures, managerial practices, and external pressures as organizational theories focus on empirical and conceptual observations of the factors that influence social behavior and working structures. Change may be beneficial or destructive, may bring progress or decline, but whatever the impact of change, it will inevitably lead to some form of organizational and relational transformation (Hall, 1991; Louis, 1992). Undoubtedly, tampering with traditional structures and social systems will cause a rippling effect that is felt throughout the organization and beyond.

In this chapter, some of the complexities of implementing organizational change will be explored in a review of the Fredericton Police Force as we trace its movement from the formative stages of community policing to its present status as a proactive community centered organization. The following pages will focus on the fact that while policing is steeped in tradition, it must now, more than ever, be dynamic and continuously evolving to meet the needs of our rapidly changing and complex communities. The first section will briefly explore change in terms of a *social system tapestry*, which theoretically explains the reciprocal relationships between the external environment, being the community, and the formal and informal cultures within the police organization. Central to the successful implementation of organizational change is the cooperation and involvement of all three groups. Next, a review of the case study organization will provide a framework for understanding the changes envisioned and implemented in Fredericton from 1985 to 1995. Next, a summary of the case study methodology will reveal the processes used to capture qualitative and quantitative feedback from the three primary reciprocating groups. This will be followed by a review of the primary findings, which were derived from the community surveys, management interviews and rank and file interviews. Finally, this chapter will provide a profile of the current state of community policing in Fredericton.

Organizational Change and Community Policing

As illustrated in the *social system tapestry* below (Fig.1), the formal police organization, informal organizational cultures and the external environment exist as separate, yet related, entities. These entities are interwoven to create a paradigm of reciprocal relationships with each piece of the pattern invariably affected when a significant organizational change is introduced. Police *management* for example is a piece of the *social system tapestry*, which possesses the power to direct the function and style of policing services. The ability of management to sell ideas to those affected by change is crucial to the success of new policing strategies. On the other hand, the **rank and file** possess the ability to either carry out the duties to fulfill new functions or sabotage change thereby, stunting organizational growth. In policing, a degree of resistance can be anticipated if administrators implement change without regard for long-standing sub cultural traditions and values within the rank and file (Punch, 1983; Guyot, 1991). Resistance can also be found in the upper echelons of the organization as new organizational strategies such as "bottom-up" versus "top-down", "flattening" and "employee empowerment" are introduced. When police organizations talk of greater autonomy across the superior/subordinate divide, managers and members alike may rebel for fear of shifting the traditional hierarchy, losing promotional opportunities, and tinkering with the status quo (Johnson, 1994; Clairmont, 1990; Forcese, 2002).

Figure 1. The Police Organization as a Social System Tapestry (Fitch, 1995)

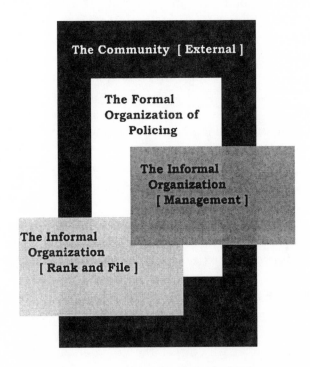

The ***external environment,*** which includes communities, government, independent agencies and various citizen groups etc., may have different interests at stake and cannot be overlooked in our attempt to understand the process and outcome of organizational change in policing. the external environment may be a driving force of change and directly involved, or conversely may be the passive receivers of change that is imposed upon them.

As illustrated in Figure 1 the external environment, (as activists, participants or receivers) combined with the formal and informal arrangements of the police organization must be considered in our attempts to understand the shift to community policing.

It is true that the "police are but one component of the informal and formal network of social control in the community, and must share with the community the responsibility for solving policing problems" (Murphy, as cited in Griffiths et al. 1994:181). This is especially true when we consider the strategic partnerships, which are required to reach the goals of community policing. Nancoo (2000:174) explained that:

> The elements of strategic partnerships find expression through consultative and collaborative patterns of partnership behaviors between the police and the community. Organizations involved in the strategic planning and strategic management process are expected to engage in extensive consultations with their communities through focus groups, town hall meetings, surveys, and advisory committees. Collaborative efforts are intended to forge strategic alliances with members and agencies of the community in pursuit of the goals of crime prevention and control of crime and disorder.

Similarly, Mills et al, (1995:196) noted that it is not possible or "desirable" to separate the study of organization from that of society. They explained that organizations are "part of the history and culture of their respective societies and cannot meaningfully be analyzed in isolation from larger influences". Blau (1962:9) likewise explained that organizations do not exist in vacuums, but rather in communities and societies, and that research should consider the importance of the relationship between organizations and their environment. As illustrated in the *Social System Tapestry* we see that organizational change in the form of community policing is dependent upon the reciprocal relationships between the external environment, internal policing cultures and the formal organization of policing. With a theoretical appreciation of reciprocal relationships, the Fredericton case study sought to examine the transition to community policing on these three fundamental levels. This was accomplished by drawing out qualitative and quantitative information from sample groups involved in, and affected by the shift. The primary sample groups in the study included the community of *Marysville* in Fredericton, *Police Management* and *Rank and File* from across the organization.

The Fredericton Police Force - A Case Study (1985-1995)

The Fredericton Police Force is one example of an organization that experienced change in ideology, structure, function, cultural values and traditions. The primary catalyst for that change was the growing interest in community policing as a method of improving service delivery and problem solving in the mid 1980s. Over a ten-year period from 1985 to 1995 the Fredericton Police Force re-evaluated its traditional methods and embraced a community policing philosophy. Tangibly, during this period the Force's commitment to community policing was demonstrated by the implementation of a series of structural changes, which included: two Storefront Operations, four Mobile Community Police Officers, a Mobile Office, Bicycle Patrol, Foot Patrol, six Neighborhood Constables, six Community Offices and a School Resource Officer. The Force also engaged in a strategic planning process, which established core values and a mission statement that revolved around a community-based philosophy. Internally and culturally, the organization also took some steps to inform the membership of changing ideologies and strategies, albeit this information was not presented until well after the creation of the Mobile Community Police. Externally, police managers introduced politicians to the new concept, and citizen surveys were conducted throughout the city in an attempt to more aptly adjust policing strategies.

Organizational Change and Community Policing

In the fall of 1985, the concept of community policing was introduced in Fredericton as an alternative solution for a socially and criminally troubled area of the city. Doone Street, a subsidized housing project, was an area that had experienced many social problems; high youth crime rates; fear among area residents, negative stereotypes of the police and repeat calls for police service. In an effort to address these issues, the Chief of Police submitted a proposal to City Council, which asked for the employment of one full-time police constable to act as the coordinator for a Storefront Operation. On May 2, 1986 the *Doone Street Storefront* was officially opened, which provided a means for decentralized, personal, community oriented policing services to be delivered in that neighborhood. The Doone Street Storefront experienced such success in terms of reduced crime rates, calls for service and increased police-public interaction, that it received the Solicitor General's Crime Prevention Award in 1987. That same year, a second Storefront Operation was opened in another troubled housing development on Hawkins Street.

In the spring of 1991, yet another innovative plan was introduced in Fredericton in response to budget cuts and demands for police efficiency. This time, senior managers and the Storefront constable devised the concept of *Mobile Community Police* [hereafter MCP]. The team consisted of four police officers that were mandated to respond to "hot spots" throughout the city, in an attempt to resolve specific crime and disorder problems. Their focus was to develop proactive and problem-solving strategies, enhance police-community interaction, and increase police visibility through foot patrol and bicycle patrol. Their goals were to lessen calls for service, reduce fear of crime and improve the quality of life for citizens, one neighborhood at a time. The theory behind this strategy was that a team of four mobile officers, whose focus was to empower the community, would be equivalent to the work of 16 officers. The community of Marysville was the first target area for the MCP officers. This decision was based on a variety of factors including: public pressure stemming from a community meeting where residents expressed their desire for more effective policing to address drug trafficking, fear of crime, loitering and traffic concerns. Over the course of the year, the MCP worked diligently with the community and met with considerable success (further details to be discussed under the caption of External Surveys).

In late 1992 and early 1993 community policing in Fredericton took a somewhat unexpected twist of fate. Upon learning that the MCP finished their work and were preparing to move onto the next electoral ward, the residents of Marysville cried out and refused to accept police withdrawal from their community. As a result of political and public pressure for a permanent police presence in their area, the *Neighborhood Constable* [hereafter NC] was created. The role of the neighborhood constable was essentially to work within the communities of two adjacent electoral wards and nurture a healthy, productive relationship between his/her citizens, ward councilors, and the police force. By the fall of 1992, three of the four original MCP officers were redeployed from Marysville to another trouble area in the city. One team member remained behind as the NC to establish and man the newly founded *Marysville Community Office*. Another officer replenished the team by joining the MCP as they traveled to the next "hot spot" beside the local University campuses. This time however, the team relocated in their new, fully equipped 32-foot *Mobile Office*. As the MCP completed their tasks once again and prepared to move on, one more neighborhood constable remained behind to establish yet another community office. This trend of depositing a neighborhood constable, and replenishing the team, continued until six community offices, serving twelve electoral wards were established throughout the city. While the state of community policing in Fredericton has continued to evolve since the conclusion of the case study in 1995, for the purposes of this chapter, we will now review the methodology and results of the study. An updated profile of community policing in Fredericton will be provided in later pages.

Methodology

The case study method as employed in Fredericton provided the opportunity to investigate and analyze organizational change from the "inside-out" and the "outside-in". Field research in the form of quantitative surveys and qualitative interviews were synthesized with academic literature to analyze organizational change and community policing. The Fredericton case study (Fitch, 1995), sociologically examined organizational change and community policing by exploring the complex internal and external relationships that influence how the police conceptualize, legitimize and respond to changes in their traditional ideologies and practices. As this change was examined the study also sought to reveal whether or not community policing was truly becoming engrained in the values and practices of the rank and file, management and the community. Simply stated, the study was designed to analyze change and the processes of change that had taken place in terms of community policing in Fredericton. And, to develop an understanding of the various roles played by the three primary reciprocating groups. Change was examined from two main sociological perspectives. First, combinations of social system and structuralist approaches were introduced to illustrate the complex social and structural relationships that exist with the organization and within the community in which it functions. Secondly, Weber's formulations on bureaucracy were used to analyze the traditional hierarchical nature of the Police Force and how change in structure and function alters the traditional patterns and relationships within a paramilitary organization.

The findings illustrated that the external environment is in fact a source of influence on the organization, and how the police conceptualize and legitimize policing strategy or attach "subjective meaning" to their own role. The findings also revealed that the shift to community policing resulted in ideological, structural and functional changes that subsequently altered internal relationships and external service delivery. Furthermore, and most importantly, the shift to community policing relied on public feedback and ultimately enhanced a reciprocating relationship between the police and the external environment. This was due in part to the decentralization of police services that increased the division of labor, reduced internal/cultural social cohesion, and increased external interaction and communication. The study illustrated that change, in the form of community policing, revived a sense of "Peeler" in the Fredericton Police Force and increased police-public cooperation and partnerships in the attempt to solve local problems of crime and disorder. The following pages will review the methodology used, and illustrate how these conclusions were drawn out of the survey responses and interviews.

In the first part of this section on methodology we will review why external quantitative surveys are important and discuss the survey results from the community of Marysville. The latter part of this section will focus on the results of the internal quantitative interviews with members and management of the Fredericton Police Force.

External Environment – Community Surveys

Police organizations across North America have conducted community surveys since the 1950s in an attempt to understand public perception of police services and crime. More recently, such surveys have been used for strategic planning of police services and to evaluate innovative police programs. The use of public surveys has gained credibility as a management tool in progressive police organizations as noted by Forcese (2002:43), "a community-based system must be reflexive, responsive and flexible. Community perceptions and demands must be identified and appraised, and performance of police service personnel must be appraised and, as necessary, amended". Similarly, Linguanti and McIntyre (1992: 251) noted if we accept the historic principles of Sir Robert Peel "it follows that the public's approval of its police force is a vitally important aspect of policing. One way of measuring the public's attitude towards the police is through surveying the policed community". In the Fredericton study, community surveys served a number of purposes. In a 1991-92 (Keating) random survey of Marysville, citizen's perception of police service and area concerns were captured. The results were collected and strategically used by the MCP officers that were assigned to address problems in that area during the year. The officers relied on this data along with crime statistics and calls for service in Marysville, and tailored their policing strategies to solve local crime and disorder problems relating to youths, speeding, rowdiness, drugs and a plethora of other issues.

One year later a post-survey (Fitch, 1993), was conducted in an attempt to gauge the impact of community policing in Marysville and capture change in citizen perception regarding public safety issues and the police. The 1993 survey instrument consisted of various categories in a ten-page questionnaire. The questionnaire was modeled closely to the 1992 (Keating) survey for later comparative purposes. Areas covered in the surveys included socio-demographic characteristics of respondents, fear of criminal victimization, citizen perception of crime, police-community communication, and a range of police services. Three hundred surveys were randomly distributed on all streets in the enumeration area of Marysville. The response rate of completed and returned questionnaires was 48%. This post survey was also a means to determine whether or not the police had listened to citizen feedback on the pre-survey and tailored their policing strategy to meet the needs of the community. Hanton (1994) noted that community policing "earned its praise from Fredericton residents" and that there was hard evidence that the program was working in the 1993 survey results from Marysville. The results showed a substantial drop in a variety of problem issues over the one-year period in which community policing was implemented. One of the most significant conclusions reached, was the reported increase in positive communication between the police and the area residents, which is quite remarkable considering "communication between the police and the public" in 1992 received the lowest ratings.

It is interesting to note that although the survey respondents valued police programs and felt that crime prevention should be a joint responsibility, less than ten-percent were actively involved in initiatives such as Bicycle Safety, Operation ID, Block Parent and Neighborhood Watch. In a recent study involving top police executives from across Canada, they reported that a limitation to the effectiveness of community policing is the reluctance of citizens to become actively involved and share responsibility for public safety (Murray and Alvaro, 2001:74). Despite this reality, the police and the public continue to be supportive of community policing initiatives. In Marysville, for example, one year after the implementation of community policing, there was an increase in those who believed that the police were more visible, provided more crime prevention information and were doing a good job of informing the public of police roles and objectives. Virtually all of those polled agreed that the local police were friendly and showed a genuine concern for community problems, and extend this concern beyond routine police matters. A very high percentage either agreed or strongly agreed that the police were doing a good job responding to calls for service, law enforcement, protection, investigations and crime solving.

Both the 1992 and 1993 Marysville surveys were a means of illustrating how feedback from the external environment can shape the direction of police services as they accept or reject new strategies. The surveys, (which have since been conducted throughout the city) are useful in many ways. First, they provide quantitative data on public perceptions and policing needs. Second, the comparative surveys (pre and post community policing) provide a measuring stick to gauge the citizen responses and effectiveness regarding policing initiatives in specific areas. And, based on the belief that community expectations have a considerable influence on the police function and self-conceptualization of role, they complement the notion that the police and the people are on the move toward a new reciprocating relationship. In fact, the surveys illustrated that public perceptions and expectations are having an even greater influence on police function and on the subjective meaning the police attach to their role in society (Fitch, 1995). Indeed, the community of Marysville had a direct influence on policing services by voicing what they wanted and expected from the police through their responses to surveys, and by their participation in community meetings. Police managers and a selected few officers responded to community needs and subsequently implemented a series of policing initiatives to address their concerns. Most notably, when the Mobile Community Police completed their original mandate in Marysville and prepared to move to another troubled area in the city, the residents strongly voiced their objection and demanded a permanent police presence. In response to the outcry from the citizenry and the city councilor for that area, a full-time Community Office and Neighborhood Constable were established.

Knowing the Organization: Internal Interviews

The previous section provided an example of how an enhanced relationship between the external environment and the police can yield positive results and that this relationship must be based on communication and a mutual interest to improve the quality of life in a given area. The community influences not only what police service is needed, but also influences how the police conceptualize and legitimize their own role. In the following sections of this chapter we will discuss how police managers and the rank and file officers fit into the social system tapestry of change. Personal interviews were conducted with 39 of its 96 members of the Fredericton Police Force in an effort to capture their thoughts and feelings regarding the shift to community policing. The sample was broken down to three subgroups, which included 29 rank and file officers, five community officers and five management personnel. The 29 rank and file members were randomly selected and consisted of mostly males with an average age of 14 years service. The sample included male and female officers from various divisions including patrol response, criminal investigations, and street crime unit. The five community officers and five management personnel were randomly selected, with the exception of the Chief who was intentionally chosen based on his lead role in the organization. The interview guides for each group were primarily the same, but slightly adjusted to capture the differing roles and experiences of the subgroups. For example, the rank and file was asked, "what training have you had with respect to community policing". Whereas community officers and managers were additionally asked "and what role did you have in training others in community policing"? All interview guides were designed not to test their knowledge of community policing, but rather to gain information about their feelings and attitudes towards organizational change in the form of community policing. Each rank and file member was interviewed for approximately one hour, and while the interview guide was strictly adhered to, there were allowances for open-ended responses to probe beneath surface answers. Management and community police interviews were two hours in duration each. Typed transcripts were prepared for each interview and a detailed coded category and index system was created to identify patterns and deviations and aid in the analysis of over 900 pages of qualitative data. The interview questions were grouped into nine general categories including: knowledge of community policing, origins of organizational change, response to change, references to community policing projects, professional to community style policing, leadership and authority in hierarchy, informal organization, the community expectations and patterns of social action.

Results garnered from the interviews with rank and file and management will be discussed in further detail according to respondent groups in the following pages. Suffice to say here, that the interview results in Fredericton revealed that the shift towards community policing was significant in five primary areas. First, police managers were required to *re-think* traditional ideologies and operational strategies. Second, the formal organization of policing was required to *re-organize* structure and function. Third, the rank and file police officers needed to *re-conceptualize* their values and practices to fulfill newly defined roles. Fourth, in keeping with the philosophy of community policing, police managers and members alike were required to "let go" of the traditional vestiges of power and authority, and *decentralize* both internally and externally. And finally, the police were required to change their insular crime-fighting image of the professional era and *empower* the citizenry to once again have a voice in how the police serve their community.

Police Management and Organizational Change

In this section we will see how the managers in Fredericton, who advocated new ideologies and implemented community policing strategies, altered the structure and service style of the organization and subsequently influenced the role fulfillment of the rank and file. To understand the dynamics of change in Fredericton we will first review how police managers, in general are sources of influence over the rank and file and approach policing from a different vantage point. This will be followed by a brief overview of how changes in the form of community policing were introduced in Fredericton.

The consensus view of management suggests that managers and members of the organization are "mutually linked together by strong common interest". This view tends to "overemphasize shared interests and commonly held goals...and overlooks the existence of opposed interest groups, as well as conflict, power and inequality within the organization" (Mills et al. 1995:213). Organizational change cannot be understood by presuming that managers and the rank and file exist as a consensual whole, free of differences between them. To accurately gauge the impact of organizational change it is necessary to explore management and the working membership independently. Regardless of the "shared occupational identity" of the police they can have very different perspectives and strategies relating to their work (Skolnick, 1967:42). In a discussion of cultural perspectives in organizational theory, Schein (1992: 94) noted that there are a number of informal cultures within organizations including: "a managerial culture, various occupationally based cultures in functional units, group cultures based on geographical proximity, working cultures based on shared hierarchical experiences and so on". Furthermore, he observed that the focus in organizational analysis should not be on "what culture is", but rather on "what culture does". Police managers for example have the power to influence the organization by instituting rules, regulations, orders and policies that filter through the ranks of authority, and literally "come down" from above. As such, managers, who advocate new ideologies and implement new strategies in line with community policing, have the capability of altering the structure and service style of the organization and subsequently influence the role fulfillment of the rank and file.

The paramilitary hierarchy in policing further serves as a psychological and physical divide between the cultures of police management and membership. Wilson (1968:57) defined the role of police administrator as that of leader, manager, disciplinarian, democrat and politician, who is supposed to set policies, obtain human and monetary resources, harness public support and lead the organization. Managers and leaders have been traditionally expected to control, direct and implement strategies designed to keep the organization moving forward. The introduction of community policing in Fredericton, was a fundamental ideological and functional transformation and one in which police managers were faced with influencing the community, politicians and the rank and file into accepting a new service style of policing. Griffiths et al. (2001:181) noted, "identifying the principles of community policing and paying lip service is easy. It is making the required organizational changes required to actually implement community policing that is the most difficult".

In Fredericton, the Chief of Police was aware that community policing was the "way of the future", and initiated a bold move in response to local area problems in the Doone Street area. In his proposal to City Council in 1985, the Chief revealed a blue print of action by introducing the concept of the Storefront Operation. This action plan, which was spurred by innovative thinking and rooted in research, was an effort to enhance police effectiveness and reduce calls for service. The impetus for change was captured in the following quote from a senior manager in Fredericton:

> After realizing that we were going to have to do something to reduce our calls for service, we looked at what areas were affecting us most. That probably boiled down to the Doone Street area...just the proportion of the amount of calls for service in a small area, and a lot of repetitive calls...we decided to mount the storefront. It really had the results we were looking for. The sense of community, the mobilization of the community...the positive results we got. We planned a five-year window in Doone Street; to try to improve the quality of life in that community and reduce our level of service at the same time and then pull the officer back out. We figured by that time the community would be self-sufficient. We realized all of our objectives except pulling the service back out, we got tremendous resistance from the community...but that was really the genesis of our whole community based policing issue.

All management agreed that the Storefront was the initial phase of community policing in Fredericton and because of its success, a base was created from which future community policing initiatives evolved in the city. The Mobile Community Police for example, were considered an evolution of the Storefront operation. The implementation of the MCP also illustrates the changing management orientation towards decentralized policing as explained by a senior manager:

I think what we have now is not what we first sat around talking about. We first looked at how to expand the role of the storefront coordinator. And we talked about a mobile unit that could be used on Hawkins Street, up in Perry Court, in kind of what is known as our projects. And we looked at renting a construction trailer sort of thing and setting it up in different areas, and hauling it on a flatbed. And then we realized what we were talking about was a whole new philosophy that the department should adopt. And our Chief was becoming very knowledgeable in this area of community-based policing and so I think one of the inspectors, a constable and myself kind of took our ideas that we had thrown back and forth to him, and then encouraged the idea of community policing throughout the city.

More and Unsinger (1992: 49) observed that enlightened management strategies can have a "profound impact on the direction and activities of an organization". In particular, they explained that "knowing how" to introduce change is as important as the actual change being introduced. In fact, the method of implementing organizational change can be a determining factor of whether or not change will be embraced by those affected by it. Initially in Fredericton, only the senior managers and a few front line personnel were informed about community policing and the new strategies surrounding the Doone Street Storefront Operation. The general rank and file was largely uninformed or involved in the process of change. Rather, the primary step in management's plan focused on securing external approval and financial support from City Council. The Chief of police noted that the implementation process was eased by political support and commitment towards community-based initiatives, yet acknowledged that while City Council and citizens had been very receptive, the last to be brought "on-line" were the masses within the police organization. This process is somewhat contrary to the experience in the Edmonton Police Service where a careful plan was invoked to educate the organization through an "internal marketing strategy" which was designed to solicit input from the officers and create an atmosphere conducive to change" (Griffiths, 2001:181).

The implementation of community policing into a traditional paramilitary organization is a tremendous undertaking and getting the rank and file "on board" is a major hurdle to overcome (Clairmont, 1991; Loree, 1993). The initial plan to invoke change in Fredericton only involved the transfer of one constable, and the decentralization to one Storefront Operation. As such, the introduction of community policing at that time was not a threat to the status quo. It was not until much later, with the introduction of the Mobile Community Police that the general rank and file questioned the direction the organization was moving in. Although the initial plans in Fredericton did not focus on informing and educating the rank and file about community policing, management indicated that "one of the keys to the success of the community-based policing initiative in Fredericton was the buy-in of the members" Carlisle (1994:12). Central to the "buy-in" of the members was the taken-for-granted trust in the historically "amicable" labour-management relationship within the organization. In fact, all the managers noted that the Fredericton Police Association was neither radical nor resistant to management direction, which accounts, in part, for management initially neglecting to concentrate on changing the attitudes and beliefs of the membership. The initial emphasis was placed rather, on securing external support and funding, followed by careful selection, and subsequent training of community oriented constables. Key managers responsible for the implementation of community policing in Fredericton explained that, the bulk of the organization had been informed through internal memorandums, standing orders, "scuttlebutt" and "hall-talk". In the Victoria policing experience, administrators similarly failed to educate and integrate all of the sworn members regarding community policing. As a result, the lack of integration throughout their organization had a negative impact on how the rest of that department accepted community-based. It seems that, in Victoria, the training was focused on the senior administrators, who were responsible for most of the planning and development. Walker et al. (1992:79) concluded that total implementation must include an understanding and acceptance throughout the organization if community policing is to be considered more than an "add-on". Clairmont (1990:80) similarly noted in his Halifax study that the implementation of community policing entails much more than a "new structure" or additional programs. It requires a shift in management ideology, strategy, and a new philosophy of policing. If divergence exists between management vision for organizational change and understanding on part of the rank and file, "buy-in" may be stunted.

Another challenging experience for many police agencies during this era, was adjusting the traditional hierarchy of the paramilitary organization to be commensurate with the philosophy of community policing. Many programs and projects under the philosophy of community-based policing require members from across the ranks to participate in innovative strategies, which require increased autonomy and a break in the chain of command (Clairmont, 1991; Trojanowicz et al. 1988; Loree, 1993 and Griffiths et al. 1994). Managers, supervisors and members faced the challenge of letting go of the vestiges of power and control because traditionally subordinate officers have been trained to "follow orders", "not buck the system" and "not to ask questions". In Fredericton, the changing structures of accountability initially caused some concern and confusion within the organization. On one hand it was becoming commonplace for constables to have more direct access to division commanders, effectively jumping ranks at the lower end of the hierarchy. And, to aggravate internal tension, constables were becoming increasingly responsible to the public and City Councilors than they were to patrol supervisors within the organization. As one Fredericton interviewee stated "it is going to be very problematic for the supervisor, because the role of supervisor in community policing is a coach. Nothing more". On the other hand, the physical decentralization created by placing carefully selected officers into storefront offices, a mobile community office and neighborhood office gave those constables unfamiliar latitude in their work by reducing internal mechanisms of accountability. This newborn autonomy was very unfamiliar to constables who were accustomed to "working by the book". According to one Fredericton source, they "became somewhat like fish out of water". Mobile Community Police officers during the early 1990s actually returned to the Force asking to have a supervisor assigned to the unit. Loree (1993) attributed this quandary in community policing to the fact that in most organizations police management is encouraging autonomous actions on one hand, while holding a book of regulations and policy in the other. Hall (1991:69) described the traditional paramilitary model as one inundated with formalized rules, which create a "vicious cycle". Generally, workers will follow institutionally defined rules because this is how they are traditionally evaluated; they know what is expected of them and the rules actually become "security" for the worker. Hall further noted that the drive for autonomy has been stunted because organizations usually have built in "safeguards" that are rigid and reduce the amount of freedom within the organization. This point is supported by the findings in Fredericton that indicated that, despite moves to flatten the hierarchy of policing and increase employee autonomy it was not entirely accepted in the formative years of community policing. In general, the power to introduce and implement organizational change in the form of community policing remained primarily in the hands of senior management. As illustrated thus far, the community and police managers, have an impact on organizational change. The following section will provide an overview of the reactions and involvement of the rank and file regarding community policing in Fredericton. It will address whether or not community pressures and expectations, combined with internal hierarchical influences, have revived a sense of "Peeler" in the rank and file.

The Rank and File and Organizational Change

The rank and file is more than a structural component of the organization; they are, rather, people bound in an informal organizational culture with ingrained values, traditions and practices. This culture is based on strong "social cohesion" and beliefs in their collective action (Goodwine et al. 1994). In policing, the rank and file has a unique informal relationship and sense of *esprit de corp* that separates them from police mangers and the external environment (Skolnick, 1967; Wilson, 1968; Punch, 1983; McConville et al, 1992; Forcese, 2002). The police culture includes "an understanding of how police officers see the social world and their role in it" and this "is crucial to an analysis of what they do, and their broad political function" (Reiner,

1992:107). The culture of policing is a way in which officers discover their working personality and assign legitimacy to their work through the process of socialization. Consequently, cultural "cop" cohesion is instrumental in the consensus building of, or resistance to organizational changes (Punch, 1983; Guyout 1991; Loree, 1992; Mills et. al, 1995; Vincent, 1979; Ericson; 1982). The ability of management and/or the community to change the cultural tradition and ideology of the rank and file is directly linked to the composition of that informal grouping. Successful implementation and future of community policing is therefore very dependent on the informal acceptance to transform ideology and policy into organizational reality.

Research has indicated that "change triggers rational and irrational emotional reaction" because of the uncertainty and lack of understanding involved (Donnelley, et.al, 1987:448). Negative response to change is aggravated when the nature and impetus for change is not made clear to the people who are going to be affected by it and their input is not solicited. Brown (1992:21) stated that the art of communication and keeping people informed is essential in organizations to ward off damaging rumour and speculation that often accompanies change. In Fredericton, the majority of the rank and file explained that the lack of membership input and lack of training were considered to be something of a downfall during the implementation process of community policing. Many indicated that they received little or no formalized training in the new philosophy and that changes were sprung upon them in a less than formal or communicative fashion. The exception to this response was the fact that some community officers attended conferences and in-service training sessions on the philosophy of community policing in Atlantic Canada and/or elsewhere in the country. While the community officers had a higher response than patrol officers and detectives in terms of their training in community policing, half of the community officers stated their knowledge was primarily gained through self-directed reading and media coverage. This is troublesome when we consider the research that has found that the level of training and "real support and opportunity that top management provides" with respect to community policing will affect the resistance to, or success of, new policing strategies (Clairmont, 1991: 477).

Inferences drawn from 34 interviews with rank and file of the Fredericton Police Force revealed several interesting details regarding change and the informal culture of a paramilitary organization. The rank and file generally acknowledged several positive aspects of community policing, however, they were keenly aware of some of the practical limitations such as deployment of human resources, scheduling, training and conflicting job expectations. Interestingly, the Neighborhood Officers acknowledged increased job satisfaction, but explained that conflicting and continuous demands from the community and within the organization could potentially lead to burnout. For some officers, the impact and implications of change were minimal, while to others it was a considerable shift that required a fundamental rethinking of culture, values and tradition. Several officers explained that change of any kind is sometimes met with a degree of resistance, fear and/or indifference by at least a few members in the organization. They recognized that there are some officers who are reluctant to forego their traditional "crime fighter" image as stated by one constable:

> Yeah the only ones I think that would resist it (community policing) to the bitter end are the... type of person who is really afraid of the community and they think, "I'm Mr. Policeman and I'm different from those guys and I want to stay that way".

The majority of frontline officers and community officers noted that contemporary policing requires a balance between proactive and reactive strategies, mobilization, technology, emergency response and enforcement. And, many referred to policing, as an evolutionary process that is continually changing according to social needs, demands, standards and expectations. One officer explained that the ability to succeed is related to the ability to cope with change. This patrol officer also commented that the organization is fortunate to have a receptive and educated membership.

> Change is the hardest thing. I think the ability to be a successful police officer or successful at anything you do

and success with the force depends on the individual...I think one thing this department is very fortunate in, is it has a very high standard of education and I think with that education, the ability to cope with change is probably better.

The findings also indicated that the rank and file in Fredericton is not radically unionized. This is important because it is consistent with management's perception of the flexible nature of the police association. In Fredericton, one officer aptly explained that as a collective unit, the association was not radically resistant to organizational change and the implementation of community policing.

I think that there's a partnership here. You know the association is not against it because, you know, like we negotiated a contract based on realizing, yeah, there are certain needs for some fluidity there, some widening of constraint. ...I don't think we are [passive]. I think we are reasonable.

The overall findings derived from the rank and file interviews of the Fredericton Police Force indicated that they possess a genuine willingness to accept change as a learning and growing experience. The organization was considered by many to be one with a comfortable working atmosphere, which enjoys amicable management-labour relations. Outside of the challenges associated with the shift in hierarchy, this finding is somewhat contrary to literature, which emphasizes police resistance to change due to culturally engrained traditions. In Fredericton it seems that the rank and file observed the external support from citizens and councilors who were excited about the new strategies and who perceived community policing as legitimate. This observation combined with a perceived managerial commitment to the directional shift towards community policing resulted in a sense of legitimacy that "filtered" through from the outside and "filtered" down from the top of the hierarchy. Interestingly, this shift in ideology was noted by almost all of the members. One of the community officers explained further that:

The people who are in management, you know, they
have been in policing for a long time and have done a lot
of changing of their own attitudes, I think in some areas
and this was harder for them, I think because of the old
school of policing. And making change for people like
me, I didn't find that hard.

Despite the fact that the majority of the rank and file did not feel
they were adequately informed about community policing via
formal training, they became keenly aware of the external and
managerial legitimacy that was attached to it. This observation
eventually had a degree of positive influence over the acceptance
of community policing by the rank and file throughout the
organization. The final section of this chapter will profile the
current status of community policing in Fredericton.

Community Policing in Fredericton: A Current Profile

Frederictonians have, without a doubt, had an impact on
community policing in their city. The residents of Marysville first
illustrated this when they expressed their concern about policing
issues and the possibility of losing the Mobile Police from their
area. Their voices combined with political support, innovative
management and dedicated officers, created a ripple effect
throughout the city as the Mobile Community Officers worked
their way through various neighborhoods and established
neighborhood constables and community offices in their wake. A
trend was indeed established and by the year 1999 there were eight
community offices, which included one in each of the two city
high schools and one at Saint Mary's First Nation. The 32-foot
Mobile Community office is now defunct, the unfortunate victim
of arson, but the spirit of community policing remains alive in
Fredericton. The two original Storefront Operations on Doone
Street and Hawkins Streets are now referred to as Community
Centers and remain fully functional. The true success in this
scenario is that area residents now exclusively operate both
Centers. The neighborhood constables have been assigned to their
ward offices and respond to these previously troubled
neighborhoods to provide occasional mediation to help solve local

issues, information on Block Parent, Neighborhood Watch, and other programs. Both of these neighborhoods experienced and sustained a sense of ownership and empowerment that was introduced through community policing in the mid-1980s. The Fredericton Police also have two full-time *Community Resource Officers* who focus on the educational needs of young children from kindergarten to middle school and safety needs of the elderly. These officers provide information sessions and lectures on more than thirty crime prevention topics and work closely with the *Neighborhood Constables* and *School Resource Officers* to provide timely information to the citizens of Fredericton. By the year 2003, Fredericton is boasting a number of new partnerships and programs within the community. A select few have been highlighted below:

Fig. 2

Fredericton Community Crime Prevention Council

Teens Against Drunk Driving

Spray No to Violence – Graffiti Contest and Scrub-Club

Senior Take Extra Precautions Program

Third Age Center for Seniors

Fredericton Multicultural Association

Muriel McQueen Fergusson Foundation for Family Violence Research

Down Town Business Development

Main Street Business Development

Fredericton Trail Patrol and Liaison Officer

Crime Prevention Association of New Brunswick

National Strategy for Crime Prevention

911 Stock Car (high school program)

Bike Patrol

John Howard Society

Partners for Youth

Saint Mary's First Nations

University Communities

Block Parent Program

Neighborhood Watch Program

Emergency Shelter Liaison Officer

Queens Ward Neighborhood Association

Community Action Group On Downtown Vandalism

Over the past several years, there has also been a conscious effort to increase training for the Fredericton rank and file, on community related topics. Officers from across the organization have been exposed to *problem oriented policing, basic community policing, managing community policing* and *crime prevention through social development* and *crime prevention through environmental design.* Several members have also had an opportunity to work in various community postings, and when they have returned to traditional positions such as patrol response, have done so with a new understanding and appreciation for community policing which is applied to their daily practices. New recruits and seasoned veterans alike are also encouraged to abide by the community philosophy as set out by New Brunswick Policing Standards and re-affirmed in the Force's strategic plan, core values and mission statement.

Conclusion: Lessons Learned about Change

The organizational shift towards community policing in Fredericton was initially the result of innovative management and was formalized by public and political support and carried out with the work of a few dedicated and flexible community officers. At the time of the initial case study, the majority of the rank and file indicated that the shift to community policing had not directly affected their traditional role as police officers, however, most believed community policing to be a valuable proactive strategy that would continue to evolve within the community and the organization. It is reasonable to conclude that given the authority and persuasive powers of managers in a paramilitary organization, their attitudes and actions regarding institutional issues will be reflected in their subordinates. The enthusiasm and commitment displayed by management regarding community policing, coupled with legitimate political and public support, most certainly played a role in how the rank and file adjusted to change. Although community policing was establishing a "foothold" in the organization in the early 1990s, it was unrealistic to assume that the philosophy was being unconditionally embraced throughout, as less than 10 percent of the force was re-deployed to community policing, and training was virtually non-existent. Implementing change should be a slow process designed to infiltrate the roots of the organization and the community and can only be accomplished through commitment, patience and understanding on the part of all stakeholders. In lessons learned from the Halton Regional experiences, a service that has been at the forefront of community policing, they recognized and responded to the difficulties of thoroughly integrating community policing. Of the most important lessons gleaned from their experiences is that: Change must be gradual and requires support and commitment; their plans must be carefully communicated throughout the organization; they had to undergo significant organizational change; they must be able to learn from their mistakes and adapt readily to change. And finally, that the organization must be prepared to accept change that is inspired from the bottom up (Griffiths, et al. 2001:189).

In Fredericton it seems that over the past 18 years, a community-oriented philosophy has seeped into their culture of policing. It is interesting to ponder why the members of this police organization were generally willing to forego traditional "trappings", regardless of an implementation process that largely neglected to include them in the initial stages of change. It was revealed in the Fredericton study that this was attributed in part, to the amicable police-labour relations, which existed between managers and the rank and file at that time. While the transition to community policing in Fredericton was relatively smooth in comparison to some organizations, it would have been more widely received and engrained in the organizational values, if emphasis were placed on force-wide participation and education about community policing from the onset. To ensure that organizational reforms continue to develop appropriately, future managers must conduct ongoing evaluations, commit to continuous learning and facilitate communications within the organization and the community. As police organizations continue to evolve in response to the changing expectations and demands, these three-way reciprocal relationships must be nurtured and strengthened. Police mangers, the rank and file and citizenry must be evermore prepared to work with each other to solve problems of crime and disorder. Suggesting that police organizations will have to adjust their own strategies to reflect Canada's changing demographic composition, social and legal expectation, is an oversimplification of a very complex reality. As noted by Nancoo (2000: 180) "quality policing will come from a visionary leadership and the active participation of a trained and empowered workforce in the service of and in partnership with the citizens of a diverse and democratic society." Although police organizations remain quasi militaristic, they must continue to listen to the public and encourage their partnership and must "continually modify and improve the way (they) operate and serve the citizens of Canada" (McCallum as cited in Lockhart, 2002: 42). Equally important, police managers must value the input of their own people and enlist the participation of the rank and file, in the decision-making processes that affect the neighborhoods they police.

Endnote

*The views expressed in this paper are those of the author and based on case study research, but do not necessarily reflect the views of the organization with which she is associated.

References

Blau, P., and R. Scott. (1962). *Formal Organizations: A Comparative Approach*. San Francisco: Chandler Publishing Company.

Brown, M. F. (1992). Leadership and the Front line Supervisor: The Sergeants Role in a modern Law Enforcement Agency. *The Police Chief: The Professional Voice of Law Enforcement. May: 18.*

Carlisle, G.M. (1994). *Address to City Council*. Fredericton, NB.

Clairmont, D. (1990). *To the Forefront; Community-Based Zone Policing in Halifax*. Ottawa: Canadian Police College.

Clairmont, D. (1991). Community-Based Policing: Implementation and Impact. *Canadian Journal of Criminology,*33:469-484.

Donelly, J., J. Gibson, and J. Ivancevich. (1987). *Fundamentals of Management*. Plano, TX: Business Publications Inc.

Ericson, R. (1982). *Reproducing Order: A Study of Police Patrol Work*. Toronto: University of Toronto Press.

Fitch, L. J. (1995). *Reviving the Peeler: A Case Study of*

Organizational Change and Community-Based Policing.
Fredericton: University of New Brunswick.

Fitch, L. (1993). *Survey Results: Community of Marysville.*
Fredericton: Fredericton Police. (Unpublished).

Forcese, D. (2002). *Police: Selected Issues in Canadian Law
Enforcement.* Kemptville, ONT: Golden Dog Press.

Goodwin, J. and M. Emirbayer. (1994). Network Analysis,
Culture, and the Problem of Agency. *American Journal of
Sociology,* 99:1411-1454.

Guyot, D. (1991). *Policing as Though People Matter.* Philadelphia:
Temple University Press.

Griffith, C.T., and S. Verdun-Jones. (1994). *Canadian Criminal
Justice.* Toronto: Harcourt Brace and Company Inc.

Griffiths, C.T., B. Whitelaw, and R. Parent. (2001). *Community
Policing in Canada.* Scarborough: Nelson Thompson
Learning.

Hall, R.. (1991). *Organizations: Structures, Processes and
Outcomes.* Englewood Cliffs, NJ: Prentice-Hall Inc.

Hanton, E. (Sept 27, 1994). Community-based Policing Working.
. Fredericton, NB: *The Daily Gleaner.*

Hornick, J., B. Leighton, and B. Burrows. (1993). Evaluating
Community Policing: The Edmonton Project. In J. Hudson
and J. Roberts (Eds.), *Evaluating Justice: Canadian
Policies and Programs.* Toronto: Thompson Educational
Policy.

Johnson, R.. (1994). Police Organizational Design and Structure.
FBI Law Enforcement Bulletin. June: 5-7.

Keating, E. (1992). *Report of Findings of the Fredericton City
Police Force: Neighborhood Survey.* Fredericton, NB:
Saint Thomas University.

Linguanti, F., and J. McIntyre. (1992). "Public Attitudes Toward
The Police: Methodology and Questionnaire. Ottawa:
Canadian Police College Journal. 16(4).

Lockhart, D. (2002). Cross Border Partnership Builds Community
Policing Ties. *RCMP Quarterly,* Summer Vol. 167.

Loree, D. (1993). Personal Communication. Ottawa: 14 June 1993

Loree, D. (1992). *Policing: A Long Fork in the Road.* Ottawa:
Canadian Police College.

Louis, M.R. (1992) Organizations as Culture-Bearing Milieu. In

Jay M. Shafritz et al., *Classics of Organizational Theory*. Pacific Grove, CA.

McConville, M. and D. Shepherd. (1992). *Watching the Police Watching Communities*. New York: Routledge Inc.

Mills, A., and T. Simmons. (1995). *Reading Organizational Theory:A Critical Approach*. Toronto: Garamond Press.

More, H. W., and P. C. Unsinger. (1992). *Managerial Control of The Police: Internal Affairs and Audits*. Springfield, IL: Charles C. Thomas Publisher.

Murray, T., and S. Alvaro. (2001). *A Profile of the Canadian Police Executive Community*. Ottawa: CACP Police Futures Group.

Murphy, C., and R.G. Muir. (1985). Community-Based Policing: A Review of the Critical Issues. In Griffiths, C.T., and S. Verdun-Jones. 1994. *Canadian Criminal Justice*. Toronto : Harcourt Brace and Company Inc.

Nancoo, S.E. (2000). *21st Century Canadian Diversity*. Mississauga: Canadian Educators Press.

Punch, M. (1983). *Control in the Police Organization*. Cambridge, MA: MIT Press.

Reiner, R. (1992).. *The Politics of the Police*. Toronto, ON: University of Toronto Press.

Skolnick, J. (1967). *Justice Without Trial*. New York: Wiley Inc.

Singer, Zev. May 2, 2002 B-1. Police rethink usefulness of satellite sites. Ottawa: *The Ottawa Citizen*.

Trojanowicz, R.C., and M. Moore. (1988). *The Meaning of Community Policing*. Michigan: The National Foot Patrol Center.

Vincent, C.L. (1979). *Policeman*. Toronto, ON: Gage Publishing.

Walker, S.G., and C. Walker, and J. McDavid. (1992). *The VictoriaPolice Stations: A Three Year Evaluation*. Ottawa: Minister of Supply and Services.

Walker, S. G., and C. Walker. (1991). *The Fernwood Survey Report:The Victoria Police Department*. Victoria: C.O.P.S. Evaluation Project.

Wilson, J.Q. (1968). *Varieties of Police Behavior*. Cambridge: MA:Harvard University Press.

6

Policing and security in four remote Aboriginal communities: A challenge to coercive models of police work*[1]

Tammy Landau

Most of the early literature on police work begins by paying homage to Goldstein's (1960) "discovery" of the use of police discretion not to invoke the criminal law even in cases where the law was apparently clear and there was sufficient legal evidence to prosecute. The role of formal and informal rules, including that of criminal law, has pervaded much of the literature on policing since then (Skolnick 1966; Wilson 1968; Bittner 1967a; 1967b; Manning 1977; Ericson 1981a; 1981b; 1982; Reiner 1992; Moore 1992) and has influenced the way in which the essential police function has been conceptualized in terms of the legitimate use of force (Bittner 1970; Reiss 1971; Shearing 1984; Klockars 1985). As a consequence, much of the research on policing has placed insufficient emphasis on the variety of functions which may be performed by the public police, in which their coercive powers may only play a minor role. Indeed, the particular role played by the public police in a given situation might be more a function of the strength of the network of social services and agencies, many of which themselves possess considerable coercive powers (Lustgarten 1986). The current research moves the literature in this direction by decentring the coercive powers of the police and placing them within the broader context of community security needs and the ability of the existing network of social resources to meet those needs.

The functions of the police in four remote aboriginal communities in northern Ontario form the basis of this study. This context, in which the public police operate in a situation of high risk and service needs but low availability of resources to address them, highlights the security functions performed by the police and the necessity to transcend the coercive framework within which they have been traditionally placed.

The literature on policing

Goldstein's (1960) "discovery" of the use of police discretion led to an early emphasis on police deviance (Cain 1979) and methods of controlling the police through increased professionalism (Bittner 1970; Reiss 1971; Klockars 1985), training (Banton 1964; Bittner 1970) and technological advancements which should professionalize and "scientificate" (cf. Ericson and Shearing 1986) the police. The "second generation of police studies" (Punch 1979) extended the discussion beyond the fact of police deviation from the rule of law to detailed analyses of the nature of rules and the ways in which the police use both formal and informal rules to achieve desired goals and avoid negative outcomes during the course of the work (e.g., McBarnet 1981; 1979; Ericson 1981a: 1981b; 1982; Ericson and Baranek 1982; Ericson and Shearing 1986). Rules, not police, became the unit of analysis, while police work became the vehicle through which they were viewed.

Ultimately, attention turned to what the police actually do. Research routinely revealed the unlimited range of situations in which police became involved, and the variety of actions they took to resolve them (Bittner 1967a; 1967b; Reiss 1971; Punch 1979). Nevertheless, there emerged a virtual consensus in the policing literature: "[t]he policeman's role is defined more through his responsibility at order maintenance than law enforcement" (Wilson 1968: 16; Reiss 1971; Lab 1984). Others described this role as peacekeeping (Bittner 1967a; 1970), or reproducing order (Ericson 1982; Ericson and Baranek 1982). While enforcing the law has a place in policing, it is secondary to the essential police function: "[P]atrol officers sometimes find it appropriate to use the criminal law to reproduce order. Such occasions are relatively rare, and their occurrence certainly does not indicate that the officers' primary task is criminal law enforcement. Rather, the law is occasionally invoked because it comes in handy as an enabling device to assert order" (Ericson 1982: 175)

The police function and the legitimate use of force

The order maintenance function of the public police is itself linked to how many have conceptualized the essential nature of the police, i.e., the legal power to use physical force or coercion to resolve situations and achieve desired outcomes (Bittner 1970; 1974; Reiss 1971; Shearing 1984; Klockars 1985). Indeed, it is this power which permits the police to achieve other ends. Since most of the research centred only on the uninformed public police in isolation from other services, the debate on the nature of the public police as essentially linked to their coercive powers remains largely unchallenged.

The service function of the police

The symbolic importance of the law enforcement function of the police and the functional importance of their order maintenance/order producing role is critical. Most of the literature on public policing, however, has placed serious limitations on the production of knowledge about the nature of police work. Those functions which do not emerge from within a framework of coercion have received only scant attention in the literature.

One consequence of this narrow approach is that the service function of the police has been largely overlooked in the literature. While there have been several studies which have documented the extent to which the police are called to provide a variety of services (such as aiding physically or mentally ill persons, finding lost children) (Cumming, Cumming, and Edell 1965; Bittner 1967b; Webster 1970; Bercal 1970; Punch and

Naylor 1973; Punch 1979; Antunes and Scott 1981; Shearing 1984), this function of the public police has been relegated to something less than a secondary role. Cumming *et al.* (1965) were the first of the police scholars to identify the police officer as "philosopher, guide and friend" who becomes involved in various sorts of "personal problems" which might require police support. Findings on the proportion of service calls to police range from 17% (Webster 1970) to over 50% (Cumming *et al.* 1965; Punch and Naylor 1973). The role of police as "veterinary surgeon, mental welfare office, marriage guidance councilor, home-help to the infirm, welfare worker friend and confidant" (Punch and Naylor 1973: 360) emerges repeatedly. These services are relegated to the "latent" police function, as the police specialize primarily as an agency of control (Cumming *et al.* 1965). Perhaps even more revealing of the insignificance attached to the service function of the police is Wilson's (1968: 4) work. While he found that 37.5% of the calls to the Syracuse Police Department were calls for service, i.e., first aid, rescuing cats, helping older women, those data "are omitted from [this] study because they are intended to please the client and no one else". The most common explanation for why the police are called in to provide various types of services to the community is that they are the only 24-hour service in the community (Cumming *et al.* 1965; Reiss 1971; Klockars 1985; Griffiths and Verdun-Jones 1989). Conceptually, this does not place them apart from all-night gas stations or diners.

The literature nevertheless hints at some interesting aspects to the provision of services, which might lead us to question the simplicity of the "24-hour service" model. For example, Cumming *et al.* (1965), Reiss (1971), Punch (1979), and Shearing (1984) have all pointed to a social class element with respect to calls for service from the community. "Poor, uneducated people appear to use the police in the way that middle people use family doctors and clergymen – that is, as the first port of call in time of trouble" (Cumming *et al.* 1965: 285). Shearing (184: 60) found that people from the lower socioeconomic strata "use police more as troubleshooters in the case of interpersonal conflict" than people from middle and upper strata, as well as for dealing with "accidents." For Bittner (1967b), emergency apprehensions of the mentally ill are related to the absence of other alternatives available to aid in the situation. It may symbolize "the inability of some people to solve their own frictions and problems" (Punch 1979: 137), which have the greatest effect on the group in which other social services are not interested (i.e., "the poor and the ignorant", Cumming *et al.* 1965). But none of these issues have been, or can be, addressed within the policing literature which has been generated for the last three decades by an emphasis on a framework of coercion.

Policing and security in aboriginal communities

It is the theme of the involvement of the public police in the provision of security and its relationship to the service function of the police which is the focus of the present research. Of particular interest are the primary security services provided by the public police to four remote aboriginal communities, and the availability of other service agencies from inside and outside the community to meet the security needs of the communities. "Primary security" services refer to those services which ensure and protect one's physical well-being in the immediate situation.

There are important ways in which the police activity may be deeply involved in the provision of primary security in communities which are socially and economically underdeveloped, and in which the threat to personal security from accident, illness, violence, and death are elevated. Indeed, the Ontario Native Affairs Secretariat (1992) reports that the death rate among Indians(2) is two to four times the rate for non-Indians: accidents, poisoning, and violence account for over 33% of deaths among Indian people (vs. 9% for the non-Indian population), Indian people die from fire at a rate which is seven times that of the rest of Canada, and the overall rate of violent deaths among Indian people is more than three times the national average. Suicides are almost three times as high, infant mortality is 60% higher than the national rate, and life expectancy is ten years less than for non-Indians.

In addition, it is becoming increasingly well documented that the rate of reported crime on Indian reserves far outstrips the rate off-reserve, among aboriginal and non-aboriginal population (Brodeur and Leguerrier 1991; LaPrairie 1993). The role of excessive alcohol use in many communities contributes to, and complicates, risk (Shykilnyk 1985). Alcohol is a predominant feature in criminal occurrences (LaPrairie 1991; Brodeur and Leguerrier 1991; Auger, Doob, Auger, and Driben 1992; Depew 1992); in the incarceration of aboriginal people (Jolly and Seymour 1983; Ontario Native Council on Justice 1990; LaPrairie 1993) in aboriginal homicides (Doob, Grossman, and Auger 1994); and likely contributes to the risk associated with much of reserve life such as poorly constructed frame houses heated with primitive woodstoves, severe winter weather conditions, and reliance on water transportation in summer months.

Placed in the context of a general lack of resources, institutions, and agencies available to service many reserves or to deal with the risks of reserve life, the public police become pivotal in managing risk and providing security. Indeed, this may be one of the most critical roles fulfilled by the police in the earlier literature (Cumming *et al.* 1965) on the provision of services to the socially and economically marginalized in urban communities. Analysis of the range of demands on the public police and the kinds of services they provide, including those related to the provision of security, can highlight the critical functions of the police in this context.

The task, then, is how to place the police in aboriginal communities. As we have seen, the provision of a wide range of services by police to most communities is substantial, although difficult to assess quantitatively, or qualitatively due to the secondary role these services have played with respect to traditional frameworks within which policing has been conceptualized. From the little research that has been done, it appears that socially and economically marginalized groups tend to use the police as service providers more than do other groups (Cumming et al. 1965; Reiss 1971; Bittner 1967b; Shearing 1984). Indeed, LaPrairie (1993) suggest that aboriginal over-representation is more a function of socioeconomic status than race. While it may also be the case that there is a higher degree of offending behaviour in aboriginal communities (Department of Indian and Northern Affairs 1990), we can expect that the role of the police in many aboriginal communities will be related to the existence, adequacy, and accessibility of other central social services and agencies involved in the provision of primary security. Hence, the role of the police cannot be considered independent of functions such as health care, transportation, and various types of crisis intervention mechanisms, such as shelters for assaulted women and children, detoxification centres, fire-fighting equipment, and ambulance services.

The current research

The research reported here analyzes the provision of public policing services as revealed in community-based interviews carried out in four remote Cree communities in northwestern Ontario and an analysis of police occurrence reports for two years for those same communities.

Face-to-face interviews were carried out with community leaders (the Chiefs and other elected members of the First Nations government), service providers (community health representatives, nurses, mental health workers, teachers, family services workers), police, and "regular" members of each community to assess the nature of the most serious social problems in the community, the role and involvement of community leaders and service providers in dealing with those problems, and the role and involvement of the various public policing bodies in dealing with community problems. The strengths, weakness, and limitations to dealing with those problems in the community were assessed. In the final analysis, interviews were carried out with 74 regular members of the communities, 10 community leaders, 23 service providers, and 13 police personnel.

Ontario Provincial Police occurrence reports for the 1990 and 1991 calendar years were analyzed as a way of capturing the range of situations in which the public police become officially involved and some of the official action taken by the police to resolve them. Occurrence reports were coded for information with respect to who contacted the police (community leader, service provider, or "regular" member of the community), the type of incident (family or other violence, suicide, fire or other emergency, request for various types of assistance from community leaders, service providers, or community members), involvement of alcohol or solvents, and the action taken by the police to resolve the incident. This might include such things as carrying out some kind of service, referring the case to other service providers from inside or outside the community, or dealing with the occurrence informally.

Research Sites

The data must be viewed within the context of the particular communities visited. While this is a general comment which would apply to any research, it is of critical importance in the case of Indian reserves or settlements. It is here that the social impact of Canadian policy of paternalism, assimilation, and neglect of the aboriginal population is so starkly evident (Shkilnyk1985; Gibbons and Ponting 1986; Ponting 1986; Siggner 1986; Frideres 1988; York 1990). Community descriptions which have been pieced together after relatively brief stays in each community can give only a vague hint of the impact of these policies on the day-to-day lives of many aboriginal peoples. In addition, relatively brief field work does not clearly reveal the "unofficial" community structure and dynamic with deep historical, social, and political roots. These dynamics may well significantly influence official and unofficial role of police, community workers, and elected leaders. Nevertheless, these descriptions are meant more to provide a context which highlights the uniqueness of the current living conditions of the communities under study, rather than a complete anthropological account of reserve life.

There are many things which the four selected communities have in common. All four communities are Cree communities in relatively close proximity to each other in northwestern Ontario. All are considered by the Department of Indian and Northern affairs to be "remote" (i.e. more than 350 kilometres from a major center), "fly-in" (i.e., only accessible by plane for most of the year) communities. Three of the four communities are Indian Reserves under the *Indian Act*, while the fourth is an Indian Settlement.

All communities are governed by an elected Chief and Council as specified under the *Indian Act*. While a small number of jobs are filled with the First Nations government (e.g. Band Manager, Welfare Worker), it is estimated that close to 90% of the labour force in each community is jobless or receiving some form

132

of social assistance. Medical care is inconsistent and limited. In almost all emergencies, included family, child, or welfare crises, the person must be evacuated from the community to a hospital in the "south", such as Sioux Lookout, Moose Factory, or Kingston. Three of the four communities do not have indoor plumbing or running water, and two do not have safe portable water.

Each community has a small population of service providers from outside the community, such as teachers and nurses. At the time of data collection, two communities were policed only by First Nations Constables (formerly Special Constables) under the Indian Special Constable Programme in the Ontario Provincial Police, one community had a First Nation Constable and a Band Constable appointed under the authority of the Indian Act, and one community had First Nations Constables and had recently appointed "peacekeepers" from the community to search luggage and packages for alcohol entering the community.

One of the most pressing issues facing many northern communities is how to deal effectively with community concerns over alcohol use. Despite the complex jurisdictional problems, and their clearly limited effectiveness (Landau 1995; May and Matthew 1988), a common approach, available only to those communities with reserve status under the Indian Act, is the passing of by-laws prohibiting alcohol and/or other intoxicants on reserve land. The particular wording of the by-laws usually makes it illegal to bring alcohol into the community, to manufacture alcohol on the reserve, or to drink alcohol or be in an intoxicated state while on reserve land. Penalties upon conviction for violating the by-law are usually fines. Jail terms in default or payment are common. All three reserve communities have alcohol by-laws currently in effect. Enforcement has usually meant having most of the formal policing bodies (i.e., First Nations Constables or Band Constables) search passengers and packages at the airport, often at the request of, and in the presence of, the Chief or other member of the First Nation government. Indeed, one community has created a group of "Peacekeepers" with the specific mandate to search for alcohol. "Suspicious" packages arriving at the post office are also singled out for opening in front of the police or Chief. In most cases, any alcohol which is discovered before it enters the community is confiscated and poured out in front of everyone present. In most such cases, charges are generally not laid.

Other points of access to the community, such as the winter road, are much more difficult to monitor. While no official action can be taken until the alcohol reaches reserve land, the prohibition and the limited access to these communities has made it an attractive financial venture for community members. In 1992, a 375 ml bottle of liquor sold in one community for between $150-$300, and a 40 ounce (1.14 litres) bottle sold for between $600-$800. one woman recounted that she made three thousand dollars upon her return to the community one evening by strapping numerous bottles to her body. Less frequently community members make "home-brew", although it may not be necessary since alcohol remains generally available.

Findings from community interviews

In order to give meaning to, and recognition of, the fact of variation across communities, the data are generally presented for each community separately. In fact, one of the theses of this paper is to emphasize the importance of the particular policing environment (here, remote aboriginal communities) on the role and response of the police. Factors such as personal and family history of individual officers, social and political relationships among community members, and the nature of formal and informal mechanisms for controlling social behaviour will influence both community interviews and occurrence data. At the same time, the current research deals largely with the range and variety of police functions performed by the police across communities.

For the interview data which follow, the actual numbers in each cell are often quite small. This has been kept in mind in the discussion of the data. Where denominators are not so small as to make percentages meaningless, the data will be reported as percentages. Otherwise, general statements are made based largely on visual analysis of the data. In order to protect the identity of individual communities, they will not be referred to by their actual names.

View of the most serious social problems in the community

Alcohol use was identified by majority of "regular" community members as the most serious social problem in their community (see Table 1). Respondents across communities often identified alcohol use as closely related to many of the other social problems facing the communities, such as unemployment, marriage problems and child neglect. At times, alcohol is viewed as the root of the problem, while at other times it is seen as the result of the poor social and economic conditions of these particular communities.

Table 1

Community members' responses to "What is the most serious social problem in the community?"

	Community One	Community Two	Community Three	Community Four
Alcohol	13 (68)**	15 (68)	9 (56)	6 (35)
Gas sniffing / Drugs	4 (21)	2 (9)	-	10 (59)
Lack of employment/ Housing /Medical and Social Services	-	4 (18)	3 (19)	-
None/ Hard to say	-	-	6 (38)	-
Other***	3 (16)	4 (18)	1 (6)	3 (18)
Total number of respondents	19	22	16	17

*   More than one response is possible for each respondent. "Don't know" and missing data are omitted from the tables.

**   Number in parentheses is the column percentage.

*** Includes "marriage problems", "parents who don't take care of their kids", "sexual/child abuse", and vandalism".

For example, respondents from Community 1 commented that "alcohol is the root of every problem in this community", and that "solvent abuse is a symptom of something else – a cry for help".

Table 2 presents the range of responses by community members about who should be involved in dealing with the social problems identified in Table 1. the police, and the Chief and Council, were the most frequently identified problem-solvers. When respondents were asked what police should do, only 3 people (all from Community 2) stated that they should lay all charges in dealing with the problem (see Table 3). Instead, putting the (presumably drunk) person in a jail cell is the single most frequent response, followed by a variety of other actions, such as talking to the parents, restoring peace, and checking for alcohol. The use of the jail cell emerges early on as one important way in which the respondents state alcohol use should be handled. And, given the role that alcohol is assigned as both a cause and effect of other serious social problems (child neglect, marriage problems, poverty), there is clearly some perceived value in securing the individual in a cell. As the agency with the only access to jail cells, the police become pivotal in handling the most serious social problem in the community.

Table 2

Community members' responses to "Who should be involved in dealing with the most serious social problem in the community?"*

	Community One	Community Two	Community Three	Community Four
Chief and Council	12 (63)**	13 (59)	2 (13)	4 (24)
Police***	12 (63)	8 (36)	6 (38)	7 (41)
Service providers	10 (53)	9 (41)	3 (19)	2 (12)
Peacekeepers	NA	NA	NA	5 (29)
Other****	7 (37)	11 (50)	2 (13)	7 (41)
Total number of respondents	19	22	16	17

* More than one response is possible for each respondent. "Don't know" and missing data are omitted from the tables.
** Number in parentheses is the column percentage.
*** Includes Band Constable in Community One.
*** Includes parents, elders, and priest.

Table 3

Community members' responses to "In dealing with the most serious social problems in the community, what should police do?"*

	Community One	Community Two	Community Three	Community Four
Talk/Stop them/Tell to stop	2 (12)**	-	-	2
Charge	-	3	-	-
Put in cell	4 (33)	1	3	2
Other***	3 (25)	2	2	3
Total number of respondents	12	8	6	7

* More than one response is possible for each respondent. "Don't know" and missing data are omitted from the tables. Asked only of those who said police should be involved.
** Number in parentheses is the column percentage.
*** Includes "talk to parents", "check for alcohol", "investigate", "pass laws", and "restore peace".

The views of community leaders and service providers closely mirror those of regular community members. In each community, again with the exception of Community 3, alcohol was identified as the most serious social problem facing the community, and which also creates high-risk social situations. One elected community leader in Community 2 stated that "everything is related to alcohol –domestic problems, physical or child abuse, abuse of elders, stealing gasoline". The role of the police in such situations is reinforced by police managers from the Ontario Provincial Police, community leaders, and service providers. For example, while Community 2 does have agencies in place to deal with social problems, such as a child and family services worker, or a mental health worker, the Chief states that "when violence emerges, they leave and we call in the police." Indeed, the child and family services worker stated that "alcohol is involved every time" she is called in to check on a child welfare case. This may involve fires that burn out when parents are out drinking, child abandonment, or sexual and physical abuse of children. She will not go to homes alone unless she is certain that the parents have not been drinking recently. She usually takes one of the First Nations Constables with her: "I never know what to expect".

Clearly, then, alcohol has emerged as a serious social problem for community members, community leaders, and service providers in three out of four communities. It is situated at the core of a multitude of social problems, which communities are trying to confront. Bylaws. Peacekeepers, social services, and specialized programmes are part of the long-term solutions in the communities. Nevertheless, when individual situations of alcohol use emerge, the police are seen, over the Chief and Council and other services providers, as the most central social resource available to deal with the situation. Many of the actions that respondents said police should take are not unique to their uniform. Access to the jail cell, which is the only relatively certain way to ensure security, is.

Views on the effectiveness of community resources

The involvement of the police in the provision of social services may be related to the extent to which the police are perceived to have, or in fact possess, a relatively high degree of material resources or competence in dealing with social problems. Several respondents from each community made unsolicited comments about the ineffectiveness of community service providers specifically, or community resources more generally, in helping to deal with community problems. For example, comments, such as "[t]hey don't have enough education to do what they're doing", or "[w]e need outside resource people to help solve problems. There are hardly any qualified, permanent resource people in the community" are demonstrative. The mental health worker there stated that he must often attempt to have people sent out of the community for alcohol treatment, since "[p]roblems at the reserve level are not being dealt with effectively". He also noted community members' hesitance to talk openly with him, as his office is not soundproofed. Additional concerns over confidentiality in small communities with close family ties also emerge. Even in Community 3, where social problems are less salient in the minds of those who participated in this research, concerns over the lack of training of the child and family services worker to deal with problems (and even then only after they occur) were mentioned.

In interviews with Chiefs and other elected members of the council, the police often emerged in these discussions as more appropriate to deal with various social problems, including alcohol. In Community 1, the view of the Chief and Council is that "[the] police are there to solve problems in the community. They are trained, they know the law, they shouldn't have to be told by us". Indeed, they would like the police in the community to have more powers "to take care of certain things, such as drinking problems". Very similar sentiments were expressed by the Chief in Community 2: "Police know the rules, they don't have to consult me... I don't want to be involved, except over funding at the broad level – it's just another programme." Such views might, in part, suggest that the police have been specifically allocated a central role in solving social problems, including alcohol and solvent abuse, at least in these communities. The extent to which the police have resources, or are perceived to be able to accomplish the desired ends of community members, must be a factor. This is so despite the fact that police in these communities are not well resourced, particularly by standards of off-reserve, public police. There is quite a bit of consensus among police personnel across the communities that "the police are the main people called all the time for every little thing in the community... since [they] are the only people here". One respondent in Community 2 stated that [i]t would have to be the constable who is called in when someone is hurt – there's no ambulance service, even for chronic hospital care". It makes calling the police in cases of attempted suicide understandable if "that's all we have here". To understand their role, however, one must go beyond the coercive model of policing to one which more fully integrates other social and security services. Indeed, such a model may also account for the following examples of calls received by the police officers, as evidenced from the texts of occurrence reports.

Mental Patient (Time: 23:45, December, 1990). M. reports he's hearing things and he thinks there's something up in his attic. Attended M.'s residence with A., M. had made a hole in his bathroom ceiling because he believed something or someone was up there. His residence was very cold and his water pipes were frozen. It looks like the house had been neglected for a long time. Reported incident to L. and T.. We made a fire and fixed bathroom ceiling for him 'cause cold wind was coming from there. M. kept poking at ceiling with broom while we were there and he was getting scared for no reason. After a while M. went to bed. No further action.

Domestic Dispute (Time: 14:50, July, 1990) K. requested police to his residence and did not say why. I attended to K.'s residence. K. informed that he had an argument with his wife and wanted police to talk to her to prevent further problems. I spoke with Mr. and Mrs. K. and also issued warning. Any further incidents charges will be laid.

Finding from police occurrences

This section presents the findings from an analysis of police occurrence data. Occurrence reports give only a partial, albeit carefully constructed picture of police activity. For the most part, they have been used to create official statistics about crime. Occurrence reports are useful to the present research, not because they provide a relatively accurate portrayal of the frequency of certain type of events, such as "criminal" occurrences, but rather because they document the kinds of social situations in which the police become officially involved, and the range of official actions taken to resolve them. Occurrence data can, therefore, complement data about the ways in which community members view the police role, and their involvement in the provision of various social and security services.

All of the Ontario Provincial Police occurrences recorded in each community in 1990 were included in the analyses. For 1991, all of the occurrences for Community 1 and Community 3 were included. Due to the high number of 1991 occurrences in Community 2 and Community 4, a 50% random sample of occurrences only was selected for these two communities. Because only 50% of the occurrences for these two communities were coded, each should, for descriptive purposes, be weighted by 2.0 in order to approximate the full population of occurrence reports for 1990 and 1991. For statistical purposes, this would artificially inflate the total "N" from the 2166 occurrence reports actually coded. In order to compensate for this, and still to maintain the appropriate relative weights of the four communities for each of the four years, a weight of 0.7989 was given to occurrences in Community 1 and Community 3 and to the 1990 occurrences for Community 2 and Community 4. The 1991 occurrences from Community 2 and Community 4 were, then, weighted 1.5978 (2 x 0.7989) which resulted in an overall (weighted N) of 2166 – the number of occurrences coded. To get back to an estimate of actual numbers, the 1991 occurrences from Community 2 and Community 4 should be given a weight of 2.0, using the unweighted data.

All analyses are collapsed across both years. While previous research (Auger *et al.* 1992) has shown considerable variation in the number of occurrences across years in some communities, variation in numbers of occurrences are not of particular interest here. Nor is there necessarily any reason to suspect that any such variation, whatever its cause, would affect the interpretation of the data for this particular study.

The nature of recorded occurrences

Table 4 presents the occurrence type recorded by the police in the four communities. In order to examine more easily the extent to which various occurrence types account for the overall percentage of occurrences in each community, the type of call which initiated the occurrence was collapsed into the following six categories:

1) **"service"** occurrences: some type of service is requested of the police, such as incidents involving child neglect, fires, people overdue back to the community, attending to suicide attempts or other medical emergency, attending at the airport to check for alcohol, or responding to some other request for service by an individual or agency inside or outside the community.

2) **"alcohol"** occurrences: initiated largely by the use of alcohol, or other intoxicants, such as a call that someone in the community was drunk, or reports that someone was bringing alcohol onto the reserve (i.e., bootlegging).

3) **"order"** occurrences: disturbances such as unwanted visitors to someone's home or visitors who refuse to leave, someone shouting in the street, arguing, weapons offences.

4) **"property"** occurrences: stolen, missing or damaged property, mischief or vandalism, arson.

5) **"person"** occurrences: domestic (between immediate members of the same family) and non domestic assaults, serious violence, sexual offences. As it was often difficult to determine from the occurrence report the relationship between the victim and the suspect, any distinction between domestic and non-domestic assault is dubious in any case.

6) **"other"** occurrences: update of previous occurrences, offences against the administration of justice (escape custody, failure to appear, breach of probation).

The data reveal a fair degree of consistency in the occurrence types recorded across communities, particularly with respect to calls for service (18% of all occurrences, order occurrences (23% of all occurrences) and property occurrences (8% of all occurrences). Alcohol occurrences (at 24%) and person occurrences (at 21.2%) were the most frequently recorded overall.

Nevertheless, there is a significant amount of variation across communities. For example, Community 3 had a higher proportion of calls for service (27%) and property occurrences (17.2%) but the fewest alcohol occurrences (12.3%). This makes sense in light of the fact that the police are virtually the only service in the community, and people from that community expressed relatively low levels of concern over alcohol use as a social problem. In addition, there is no possible offence (i.e., no alcohol bylaw) simply for drinking.

Table 4
Occurrence type (collapsed) by community

	Community One	Community Two	Community Three	Community Four	Total
Service	24 (16.4)*	209 (18.6)	26 (27.0)	118 (14.9)	378 (17.5)
Alcohol	50 (34.4)	300 (26.7)	12 (12.3)	157 (19.7)	519 (24.0)
Order	38 (25.7)	253 (22.5)	21 (21.3)	181 (22.8)	492 (22.7)
Property	10 (6.6)	76 (6.7)	17 (17.2)	75 (9.5)	177 (8.2)
Person	20 (13.7)	204 (18.1)	16 (16.4)	218 (27.5)	458 (21.2)
Other**	5 (3.3)	84 (7.4)	6 (5.7)	45 (5.6)	139 (6.4)
Total	146 (100)	1126 (100)	97 (100)	793 (100)	2163 (100)

*   Number in parentheses is the column percentage.
**   Includes update of previous occurrences and offences against the administration of justice chi-square = 75.75, df = 15, $p < .001$.

The "24-hour service" model of the public police has traditionally been conceived in terms of the availability of other social services in the community, to which community members would otherwise turn. One way of evaluating this model is to look at the proportion of calls for service received by the police at various times during the day. As can be seen in Table 5, 58% of all occurrences were received by police between 6 p.m. and 6 a.m. although there is significant variation across communities with respect to the time of the occurrence. For example the number of occurrences involving calls for service between 6 a.m. and 6 p.m. is significantly higher in Community 4 than in the other communities. Indeed, police in that community recorded a higher percentage of calls for service during the day than after 6 p.m.. This is interesting since a broad range of services in the community are more available and accessible than after regular hours. In Community 3, over 40% of calls for service were recorded during the day. In this case, however, there are so few other services available in the community at any time, a more even distribution of calls for service across time would be expected.

Table 5

Time of occurrence by community, for service occurrences

	Community One	Community Two	Community Three	Community Four	Total
Night (6pm-6am)	16 (72.7)*	135 (67.2)	13 (59.1)	44 (39.6)	208 (58.4)
Day (6am-6pm)	6 (27.3)	66 (32.8)	9 (40.9)	67 (60.4)	48 (41.6)
Total	22	201	22	111	356

*   Number in parenthesis is the column percentage.
       chi-square = 24.30, df = 3, $p < .001$.

If we expand the 24-hour service model to include the provision of primary security services, many of which, in these communities at least, will involve alcohol, the case for the security function of the police becomes stronger. Table 6 presents occurrence type by whether intoxicants were mentioned in the report, for all four communities pooled. Almost two-thirds of occurrences overall mentioned the use of intoxicants (virtually always alcohol), although there is a significant degree of variation across occurrence types. In particular, intoxicants were mentioned in 31.3% of recorded service occurrences, 61.2% of recorded order occurrences and 64.7% of recorded person occurrences. Intoxicants were mentioned in only 14.2% of property occurrences.

Table 6
Occurrence type by mention of intoxicants pooled
across all communities

	Service	Alcohol	Order	Property	Person	Total
Not mentioned	260 (68.7)*	2 (0.3)	190 (38.8)	150 (85.8)	161 (35.3)	763 (37.8)
Mentioned	118 (31.3)	518 (99.7)	300 (61.2)	25 (14.2)	296 (64.7)	1257 (62.2)
Total	378 (100)	519 (100)	491 (100)	175 (100)	458 (100)	2020 (100)

* Number in parenthesis is the column percentage.
chi-square = 637.50, df = 4, $p < .001$.

These collapsed data obscure some additional important findings which indicate that alcohol was mentioned as a factor in a high percentage of extremely high risk situations: 70% of child welfare cases, 68.8% of attempted suicides, 28.9 % of medical emergencies, 59.4% of weapons occurrences, and 66.7% of domestic and non-domestic assaults, combined. Indeed, some of these types of occurrences question the value of invoking a simply coercive model of policing here at all. For example, the ability to use coercion would be an important resource in resolving cases involving weapons or physical violence. But the same cannot be necessarily be said for incidents involving attempted suicides or medical emergencies. On the other hand, child welfare cases are examples where coercion may be required at the same time that security is provided.

The nature of police action in resolving occurrences

As stated earlier, analysis of the kinds of actions which are traditionally interpreted as reflecting law enforcement activity, such as laying charges or lodging someone in a jail cell, further demonstrates the problematic nature of invoking a coercive model of the police in these communities. This may be particularly true in the case of calls for service, where the police action, which is typically associated with coercion and law enforcement, is ironically, more of a service in some contexts. In fact, in responding to calls police took law enforcement action alone (i.e., laying charges, contacting other public policing personnel, or lodging in a cell) in only 32% of occurrences, and 55% of occurrences involved no law enforcement action at all. All other occurrences were resolved with some combination of referrals to other services, informal actions (e.g., taking the victim or suspect home, issuing a warning) or providing some type of service, such as taking someone to the hospital or checking for alcohol at the airport. In addition, however, two thirds of all charges laid by the police were for alcohol offences (See Table 7). Twelve percent were for property offences and 11% were for offences against the person: only two of these involved serious violence.

The security role of the public policing bodies in these communities is not limited to the direct provision of primary security services. The role of other agencies involved in the provision of security, such as provincial or federal medical services, the Child and Family Services, the Ministry of Natural Resources, and the Ministry of the Attorney General, also emerges in the context of particular types of occurrences, such as missing or overdue persons, child welfare cases, and sudden deaths. The texts from the following occurrences highlight the extent to which the public police work in conjunction with other workers in providing primary security, and at other times work for those other security institutions in providing information about risk and security.

Overdue Person (Time: 10:30, June, 1990). Mrs. P. 10-21 (called) at the police officer and reported her husband who is 80 years old is long overdue from his hunting camp. Mrs. P. was worried and requested some action be taken to locate her husband.

13:00 – Sgt. A of Patrol Unit notified.

16:15 – Ministry of Natural Resources flew over the campsite of Mr. P. and did not see anyone.

Next day – conducted search at the coast, accompanied by Sgt. B., on an O.P.P. Long Ranger helicopter and located Mr. P. 15 miles south of the river. The ice was close to the shore which kept Mr. P. from traveling. Mr. P. was alright and advised he should be home in about a week. Sgt. A. advised of Mr. P.'s location. Family and Chief informed, satisfied with action taken.

Table 7

Type of charges were laid, by community

	Community One	Community Two	Community Three	Community Four	Total
Provincial liquor	-	24 (6.0)*	2	6 (1.7)	32 (4.0)
Bylaw	44 (84.6)	252 (63.5)	-	239 (69.5)	535 (67.0)
Property	2 (3.8)	32 (8.1)	1	58 (16.9)	93 (11.7)
Person	3 (5.8)	53 (13.4)	2	27 (7.8)	85 (10.7)
Weapons	2 (3.8)	8 (2.0)	-	5 (1.4)	15 (1.9)
Administration of Justice	-	13 (3.3)	-	4 (1.2)	17 (2.1)
Other federal/ provincial statutes	1 (1.9)	15 (3.8)	-	5 (1.4)	21 (2.6)
Total	52	397	5	344	

*   Number in parentheses is the column percentage.

Assist Hospital Staff (Time: 03:50, February, 1991).
Hospital Staff requests that we attend T. residence and check to see what people are drinking there. Two people have been admitted to the hospital who have confusing symptoms. Staff advise if they know what they were drinking they could better help patients. Attended residence but could detect no party and could not find out where patients were drinking.

The provision of security services, either directly to the community or to the network of other security institutions, many of which are off-reserve, provides an important framework for understanding much of police work in the communities in this study. Nevertheless, community interviews and occurrence data suggested a much broader range of social activity in which police become involved. The texts from the following demonstrated the incompleteness of a policing and security model, and highlight the broader social service function of police work.

Medical Assistance (Time: 03:30, January, 1991). M. reports his son has back pains and can't walk on his own. Needs stretcher to transport him to hospital. Attended at residence, stretcher used to transfer victim to the hospital. Admitted in for the night. No further action.

Compassionate Message (Time: 21:00, February, 1990). T. requested assistance in delivering a message to her brother-in-law. T. requests police assistance to deliver a compassionate message to A. regarding the death of his sister. The deceased was a resident of (another village). After the message was delivered, Mrs. M. and T. needed further assistance to A. regarding the death of his sister. T. left residence because she almost fainted and M. left as well. After a couple of hours, T. and another woman came to residence to comfort A.

Domestic (Time: 10:30, July 1990). H. reports she's having problems with live-in boyfriend J.H. reports she wants to leave J. because they're always arguing. However, she states he has not hurt her physically. Her problem is that J. will not give her extra money although she has enough to get herself to Timmins. Attended J. residence and spoke to both and advised them that no one can tell them what to do and that they will have to solve this problem by themselves. Both parties understand. No further action.

Conclusions

The findings in this research are similar to those of Brodeur, LaPrairie, and McDonnell (1991), who found a similar role of alcohol with respect to social problems, a wide range of demands made on the police in each community, the lack of confidence expressed in other social service providers, the limited referrals made to these other services, and the unique use of the jail cell. The real and perceived risks created by the presence of alcohol in these communities sets a general context for reinterpreting conventional views about the essential nature of police work. The particular position of the uniformed, public police in the broader network of social services further raises questions about the extent to which their coercive powers define their social involvement. Instead, this research suggests an important role for the public police in the provision of primary security. Community members turn to the police to solve a wide range of social problems because they are seen as best at dealing with social and not, as Bittner (1970) states directly as a result of their coercive powers. Alcohol is perceived to be the most serious social problem in three of the four communities. It is also perceived to create and increase social and physical risk. As a consequence, it is appropriate that the police should spend so much of their time dealing with alcohol problems, but as a social and security problem, rather than a law enforcement or crime control problem (also see Depew 1992).

Implications for the indigenization of policing services

The trend toward indigenizing the provision of policing services to aboriginal communities originally emerged out of a growing concern over the apparent over-representation of aboriginal peoples in the criminal justice system generally, and in correctional facilities specifically. The data presented here seriously question the extent to which such a policy can have much of an impact on reducing the risk of incarceration of aboriginal peoples in communities similar to those in this study. The social involvement of the public police exceeds the crime control framework from which the policy of indigenization has emerged. At the same time, the few resources available to deal with social risks, particularly those involving alcohol use, are deeply embedded within this framework. As we have seen, lodging people in a jail cell is a frequently relied upon option of the police, and is often specifically requested by the community, to deal with high-risk situations. Due to the nature of the social problems in the community, the use of the cell often goes hand in hand with alcohol use and the laying of liquor-related charges. Both of these measures occur in a context of low availability of alternatives, and have serious implications for official criminalization and incarceration. Changing who wears the uniforms without simultaneously reducing risk or providing alternative resources to deal with it, does nothing to change the ability of any type of policing service to meet the security needs of the community. As has been amply demonstrated by Ericson's (1982) work on patrol officers, the law remains a powerful tool for the police in achieving various desired goals, whether they are reproducing order, keeping the peace, or providing primary security.

Many communities are approaching the indigenization of police services as part of the larger trend toward self-government (Brodeur *et al.* 1991), irrespective of the issues of over-representation. It is not likely that the basic form and structure of urban models of policing (with their emphasis on centralized, hierarchical, armed, and uniformed forces) will be abandoned. This is so despite protests that a largely punitive, individualist model of conflict resolution, characteristic of Euro-Canadian justice, is foreign to most aboriginal cultures. There is very little funding available at the level of individual First Nations to experiment with creative community-based alternatives to the provision of policing services. The development of the peacekeepers in Community 4 is an example: while there have been, from the outset, long-term goals of having the peacekeepers become involved in a broader range of social problems (especially with respect to young people at risk of solvent abuse), funding for the programme is extremely tenuous, particularly when it must compete with desperately needed housing and employment programmes. As a result, the peacekeepers are limited to a high narrow mandate of checking for alcohol at the airport and post office. The bureaucratic constraints placed on aboriginal communities to negotiate policing agreements with federal and provincial governments, who not only hold the purse strings but themselves harbour highly conventional, crime control models of appropriate police services, adds to the problems of innovation and reform of indigenized policing services.

The emphasis on the essentially coercive nature of police work reflects the conceptual framework of social control which has pervaded much of criminology throughout the 1970s and 1980s (See for example, Cohen 1985; also McMahon 1992, for discussion of this trend in the literature on corrections). This view of policing has determined a priori the nature of the interpretations which would be assigned to particular police actions. While this research suggests a shift away from the framework of coercion, a complete shift to a framework of security would be equally misconceived. There is still a wide range of police activity which cannot be adequately accounted for by reference to the provision of primary security or the five types of security which Ericson (1994) has defined. The point is more that there are multiple dimensions to police work the complexity of which is lost when a single explanatory concept is invoked.

Nevertheless, the security work of the public police is clearly critical to their function. At the same time, many other state agencies provide related security services with equal, if not greater, social ramifications. There should, then, be greater research emphasis on the broader network of social institutions involved in the provision of primary security, and the range of similar, or overlapping, services which they provide. The nature of police work involved in providing primary security, referring to other security to other institutions and the provision of information to those institutions, is one approach. While this approach is useful it remains within the vast body of policing research which uses as its starting point the police organization and a relatively constricting view of the essential nature of police work. A fresh approach would be to begin with those other security institutions which are concerned with the assessment and prevention of risk and piece together the functions they assign to the uniformed public police in providing various security services. This would have the advantage of breaking further with the coercive framework of police work, and permit the discovery of a range of police functions whose legitimacy is often lost in narrowly constructed theories of the nature of police work.

Endnotes

*From the Canadian Journal of Criminology, Vol. 38 No.1 (January1996).
Reproduced by permission of the *Canadian Journal of Criminology*. Copyright by the Canadian Criminal Justice Association

1. This research was conducted while the author was at the Centre of Criminology, University of Toronto. The author would like to thank Anthony Doob, Richard Ericson, and Martin Friedland of the University of Toronto, for their comments on an earlier manuscript. Special appreciation is extended to Don Auger and the late Dennis Cromarty for facilitating research access to the communities and police occurrence data. This research received funding through the contributions programme of the Ministry of the Solicitor General of Canada. The views expressed in this article do not necessarily reflect those of the Commission of Inquiry into Certain Events at the Prison of Women.

2. While language is constantly in transition, for the purposes of this paper, certain terms will be used only in certain contexts, to reflect the current legal, political and social considerations. The term "Indian" refers, in only a technical way, to people defined as such under the *Indian Act*: a person who is registered as an Indian or is entitled to be registered as an Indian under the Act (see Frideres 1988, for a broader discussion of the various categories of "Indian" under the *Indian Act*). As Frideres ([1988: 11) notes, the term is strictly a legal one, and "does not reflect social, cultural, or racial attributes". This means that non-registered Indians, Metis, and Inuit people are excluded from this definition, where these very attributes and others (i.e., historical and political) may be shared. The more inclusive term "aboriginal peoples" will be used to reflect this.

References

Antunes, G. and E. Scott. (1991). Calling the cops: Police telephone operators and citizens calls for service. *Journal of Criminal Justice* 9: 165-179.

Auger, D., A. Doob, R. Auger, and P. Driben. (1992) Crime and control in three Nishnawbe-Aski communities: an exploratory investigation. *Canadian Journal of Criminology* 34(3/4): 317-338.

Banton, M.(1964). *The Policeman in the Community*. London:

Tavistock.

Bercal T. (1970). Calls for police assistance: Consumer demand for governmental service. *American Behavioural Scientist* 13: 681-691.

Bittner, E. (1967a). The police on skid row: A study of peacekeeping. *American Sociological Review* 32(5): 699-715.

Bittner, E. (1967b). Police discretion in the apprehension of mentally ill persons. *Social problems* 14: 278-292.

Bittner, E. (1970). *The Function of the Police in Modern Society*. Chevy Chase, Md.: National Institute of Mental Health Centre for Studies in Crime and Delinquency.

Bittner, E. (1970). Florence Nightingale in pursuit of William Sutton: A theory of the police. In H. Jacob (ed.). *The Potential for Reform of Criminal Justice*. Beverly Hills: Sage Publications.

Brodeur, J.P.. C. LaPrairie and R. McDonnell. (1991).*Justice for the Cree: Final Report*. Grand Council of the Crees (Quebec), Cree Regional Authority.

Cain, M. (1979). Trends in the sociology of police work. *International Journal of Sociology of Law* 7: 143-167.

Cohen, S. (1985). *Visions of Social Control: Crime, Punishment and Class*. Cambridge: Policy Press.

Cumming, E., I. Cumming and L. Edell. (1965). Policeman as philosopher, guide and friend. *Social Problems* 12: 278-286.

Department of Indian and Northern Affairs. (1990). *Indian Policing Policy Review*. Ottawa: Indian and Northern Affairs Canada.

Depew, R. (1990). Policing native communities: Some principles and issues in organizational theory. *Canadian Journal of Criminology* 34(3/4): 461-478

Doob, A., M. Grossman and R. Auger. (1992).Aboriginal Homicides in Ontario. *Canadian Journal of Criminology* 36(10): 29-62.

Ericson, R. V. (1981a). Rules for police deviance. In C. D. Shearing (ed.), *Organizational Police Deviance: Its Structure and Control*. Toronto: Butterworths.

Ericson, R.V. (1981b). *Making Crime: A Study of Detective Work*. Toronto: University of Toronto Press.

Ericson, R.V. (1981). *Reproducing Order: A Study of Police*

Patrol Work. Toronto: University of Toronto Press.

Ericson, R.V. (1992).The division of expert knowledge in policing and security. *British Journal of Sociology* 45.

Ericson, R.V. and P. Baranek (1981).The scientification of police work. In G. Bohme and N. Stehr (eds.), *The Knowledge Society*. Norwell, Ma: Reidel Publishing Co.

Frideres, J.S.(1988). *Native Peoples in Canada: Contemporary* Conflicts. 3rd Edition. Scarborough: Prentice Hall.

Gibbons, R. and J.R. Ponting. (1985). Historical overview and background. In J.R. Ponting (ed.), *The Arduous Journey: Canadian Indians and Decolonization*. Toronto: McClelland and Stewart.

Goldstein, J. (1960). Police discretion not to invoke the criminal process: Low visibility decisions in the administration of justice. *Yale Law Journal* 69: 543-594.

Jolly, S. and J. Seymour. (1981). Anicinabe Debtor's Prison. Final Report. Toronto: Ontario Native Council of Justice.

Klockars, C. (1981). The idea of the Police. *Law and Criminal Justice Series*, Vol. 3, Beverley Hills: Sage Publications.

Lab, S. (1984). Police productivity: The other eighty percent. *Journal of Police Science and Administration* 12(3): 297-302.

Landau, T. (1992). The Prospects for a Harm Reduction Approach to Alcohol Abuse in Aboriginal Communities, unpublished.

LaPrairie, C. (1990). Justice for the Cree: Communities, Crime and Disorder. Grand Council of The Crees (Quebec), Cree Regional Authority.

LaPrairie, C. *Dimensions of Aboriginal Over-Representation in Canada: Correctional Institutional and Implications for Crime Prevention*. Ottawa: Department of Justice, unpublished.

Lustgarten, L (1981). *The Governance of the Police*. London: Sweet and Maxwell.

Manning, P. (1977). *Police Work: The Social Organization of Policing*. Cambridge, Mass.: MIT Press.

May, P. and S. Matthew. (1981). Some Navaho Indian openness about alcohol abuse and prohibition: A survey and recommendations. *Journal of Studies on Alcohol* 49(4): 324- 334.

McBarnet, D. (1977). Arrest: The legal context of policing. In S. Holdway (ed.), The British Police. London: Edward Arnold.

McBarnet, D. (1979).Conviction: Law, the State and the

Construction of Justice. London: The MacMillan Press Ltd.

McMahon, M. (1991). *The Persistent Prison?: Rethinking Decarceration and Penal Reform*. Toronto: University of Toronto Press.

Moore, M. (1991). Problem-solving and community policing. In M. Tonry and N. Morris (eds.), *Modern Policing. Crime and Justice: A Review of Research*. Chicago: University of Chicago Press.

Ontario Native Affairs Secretariat. (1992). Social and Economic Indicators Relating to Aborignal Peoples. Toronto: Ontario Native Affairs Secretariat.

Pointing, J.R. (1984). Assessing a generation of change. In J.R Pointing (ed.), The Arduous Journey: Canadian Indians and Decolonization. Toronto: McClelland and Stewart.

Punch, M. (1977). *Policing the Inner City*. London: Macmillan Press.

Punch, M. and T. Naylore. (1973) The police as a social service. *New Society* 24: 358-361.

Reiner, R. (1992). *The Politics of the Police*. Brighton: Wheatsheaf Books.

Reiss, A. (1970).*The Police and the Public*. New Haven: Yale University Press.

Shearing, C.D. (1984). *Dial-A-Cop: A Study of Police Mobilization*. Toronto: Centre of Criminology, University of Toronto.

Shkilnyk, A. *A Poison Stronger Than Love: The Destruction of An Ojibwa Community*. New Haven: Yale University Press.

Siggner, A.J.(1984).The socio-demographic conditions of registered Indians. In J.R. Ponting (ed.), *The Arduous Journey Canadian Indians and Decolonization*. Toronto: McClelland and Stewart.

Skolnick, J. (1964). *Justice Without Trial*. New York: Wiley and Sons, Inc.

Webster, J. Police task and time study. *Journal of Criminal Law, Criminology and Police Science* 61(1): 94-100.

Wilson, J.Q. (1968). *Varieties of Police Behaviour*. Cambridge: Harvard University Press.

York, G. (1988).The Dispossessed: Life and Death in Native Canada. London: Vantage.

PART 111

SUBCULTURE, ETHICS AND TECHNOLOGY

Police Subculture

Police Ethics

Information Technology

7

Canadian Police Subculture

David MacAlister

Introduction

In the early morning of January 14, 2003, three known Vancouver drug addicts were picked up off the Granville Street pedestrian mall by six Vancouver City police officers (Mickleburgh, 2003; Richards, 2003). They were taken to Stanley Park – a massive urban forest in the heart of Vancouver. Once there, the three individuals were beaten (Richards, 2003). After the incident, the six officers filed a misleading report on the events that transpired in the park that night (Fong, 2003). In the months that followed, the six officers apologized to their chief, while they awaited trial on a total of 33 charges arising from the beatings and subsequent filing of false documents (Fong, 2003; Richards, 2003). This event followed less than three months after a scathing report was published by Vancouver's Pivot Legal Society, detailing fifty first-hand accounts of abuse allegedly suffered at the hands of Vancouver police officers (Howard et al., 2002).

Are the Vancouver police unique in their problems of physical abuse? Why do such problems arise? How can we explain why six young police officers, sworn to uphold the law, became embroiled in allegations of police brutality. Police in Canada, as in other countries, exhibit a clear occupational subculture.

Explorations of police subculture lie at the heart of a great deal of the research and theorizing that has been conducted regarding the police in North America. This occupational subculture has numerous readily identifiable characteristics that set it apart from other occupational groups. While one must be careful not to over-generalize, looking at the police as possessing a clearly identifiable culture is useful for better understanding the police role and the behaviour of police officers.[1]

Efforts to understand the police inevitably lead one to look for similarities among police officers, and across police agencies, over time. While many differences can be found among police agencies, and among individual officers within the various agencies, consistencies are apparent and help in attempting to understand police behaviour. The study of police subculture represents a longstanding aspect of "cultural criminology" (Ferrell, 1999) that attempts to infuse meaning into the crime control practices of the police.

Culture, Subculture, and Organizational Culture

As social creatures, we live in a socially constructed world. This social world may be viewed as a culture, a way of structuring our perceptions in common with the way those around us structure their perceptions (Tepperman and Rosenberg, 1995). The notion of a subculture denotes a culture within a culture that shares a world view, including assumptions, norms, beliefs and values, that differ in significant ways from the larger culture around them. Formal organizations, like police agencies tend to develop their own organizational culture, reflecting the group's internal and external interactions. Each organization may be viewed as having its own set of assumptions, norms, and values that manifest themselves in the actions of its members (Schein, 1984). Organizational culture is one type of subculture.

Since police agencies across the country perform similar tasks, and operate under similar circumstances, it should come as no surprise that police organizational cultures display considerable consistency. Accordingly, it is possible to speak in terms of police culture or police subculture as a singular idea, although one should keep in mind that variation will be found within police organizations and among the various police organizations across the nation. Police culture has been defined as:

> The informal, but important relations among police officers and the values they share. Police work is characterized by its own occupational beliefs and values, which traditionally include a perception of the police as sexist and macho (Roberg, Crank and Kuykendall, 2000, p. 544).

The evolving literature currently makes frequent reference to "police culture" as a way of coming to understand the informal factors that affect police behaviour. The unique occupational beliefs and values are the key topics in such research. Academic research referring to the "police subculture", historically occupied much of the academic attention on the police in North America, and tended to look at those aspects of policing that separated the police from the rest of society. More often than not, it seemed to look at the unique aspects of the police subculture for explanations of police wrongdoing. The terms "police culture" and "police subculture" are virtually interchangeable. One must keep in mind however, that while some consistencies clearly exist among police agencies, considerable variation exists between these agencies. It is possible to speak of an RCMP organizational culture, or an Ontario Provincial Police organizational culture, but even within a single organization like these ones, considerable variation exists across the jurisdiction, and even within smaller regions of the country or province, depending upon the function being performed by organization members in a particular unit or detachment.

While some might argue it is overly simplistic to speak of a monolithic organizational culture that remains constant over time (Lippens, 2001), there can be no doubt that half a century of research continues to identify consistent police subcultural characteristics.[2]

Characteristics

Beginning around the 1950s, American policing researchers identified the key characteristics of the police subculture, and began to identify the importance of the subculture in understanding police behaviour. One of the first to identify the feeling of social isolation experienced by police officers was William Westley, who described the police officer as feeling like a "pariah," resulting from a perception that the public views them as "corrupt and inefficient" (Westley, 1953: 54). This creates a sense of alienation, whereby the police view the public as the enemy, resulting in a shared emphasis among police officers on secrecy and a series of dysfunctional consequences.

In the decades after the 1950s many academics, engaged in the study of American policing, have identified a distinct police subculture (see Manning, 1977; Neiderhoffer, 1967; Skolnick, 1966). Common to these analyses has been a tendency to view the police subculture as displaying two common characteristics: (1) Police officers are socially isolated from the rest of society, with the resulting group solidarity among. Police officers, and (2.) Police officers tend to perceive the public as hostile, unsupportive, untrustworthy, and unable to comprehend the true nature of police work. An" unsympathetic, critical, untrustworthy, and uncomprehending" public inclines the police to become suspicious and isolate themselves from the rest of society (Carter & Radalet, 1999: 179).

Not all members of a police department have the same role to play. Of course, there are many similarities in background, training and experience that are shared by all police officers. However, police officers often enter specialized units, or take on management responsibilities. One author has argued that police subculture can be divided into two: "street cops" and "management cops" (Reuss-Ianni, 1983).

Management Subculture

Elizabeth Reuss-Ianni (1983) noted that most policing research has focused on street or "line level" police officer subculture. However, police subculture is best understood, in her view, by taking into account interactions between line level patrol officers and police management, which has its own subculture. Considerable antagonism was found between these two groups in the New York Police Department, which she investigated during her research. Each had their own interests. The difference between the two is perhaps best exemplified by the concern of line level officers with simply obtaining desirable results (ends). In contrast, management are concerned with the process that is used (means) as well as the results (ends).

Image conscious

Management level officers are charged with running the police organization, rather than engaging in routine patrol activities. More direct lines of accountability to the public, civilian oversight, and the media weigh heavily on the minds of police management.

Senior level management is typically held directly accountable to some form of civilian oversight. Depending on the police agency, this may involve accounting to a police board responsible for developing overall policy for the police agency, or a cabinet minister charged with overseeing policing at the provincial or national level. All levels of management are image conscious. They must maintain the police agency in a positive light in order to maintain ongoing support from civil authorities. In contrast, line level officers often make low-visibility decisions in the context of day-to-day survival out on the streets.

Management level police officers are usually politically savvy. It is an essential part of their role to deal with political authorities, particularly with regard to budgetary and resource-based matters, and with regard to accountability. Portraying the department in the best possible light is a constant matter to be kept in mind.

Double bind: management caught in the middle

Line level police officers face a role that they perceive places them in a difficult bind. They experience conflict each day from at least three sources (Griffiths and Verdun-Jones, 1994: 83-4). This conflict includes:
- The discrepancy between their own conception of their role as "crime fighters", and the actual demands and expectations of the public that place mostly service-related demands on them;
- A perceived lack of support from the public; and

- Difficulties associated with performing "crime control" tasks in a "due process" oriented legal 'system.

These conflicts typically lead to an increased cohesion of the police, as against the public at large. Essentially, the conflict is a relatively simple one, and exists between the police and the public. To a large extent, the line level officer may be frustrated by the odd demands made upon them, but the real conflict arises from trying to protect society from devolving into chaos and anarchy, all the while being hamstringed by legal and regulatory restrictions. At the management level, things are considerably more complicated.

Management level police officers have the same conflicts to deal with as line level officers. They too must ensure that formal social control takes place, maintaining law and order in society. However, they also must contend with fiscal realities, accountability of the organization and its members, and respond to unwanted police officer behaviour. In many cases, they must also deal with police union influence. Decisions by oversight agencies control the department's policy and resources. Management has little control over such matters, yet they greatly affect the ability of the management team to deliver police services.

Decisions made by management that back up line level officers are open to critique by the public, civilian oversight, and the media. Assumptions are made that the police are covering for one another, maintaining the blue wall between the organization and the outside world. However, if management decisions fail to support line level officer activity and decision-making, the management will be critiqued by the line level officers and their union or employee association, for failing to be supportive. It will inevitably be alleged that management is leaving the line level officer out to hang.

Decisions must be made with regard to resource allocation. Which ever units get additional funding will result in those which do not obtain additional resource allocations feeling slighted and underappreciated. Being caught between the public and the line level officers, causes police management to be in a double bind. They are in a cross-fire between the public and the street level officers, with decisions rarely appeasing either set of interests.

Management culture: changing the line level culture

In the last fifteen years, police agencies have been heavily influenced by calls for change. Public cries for greater input, judicial and political calls for increased accountability, and educated management interest in organizational reform have all left their mark on Canadian policing. An important role of police managers today is serving as a medium to bring about organizational transformation. In this regard, the line level subculture is often perceived as a villain or obstacle that must be overcome.

The last two decades have witnessed the adoption of community policing and problem-oriented policing strategies by police departments across the country. This has often accompanied new management strategies, such as the adoption of a "learning organization" philosophy.[3] These changes have had considerable support from the public and civilian oversight authorities. In many cases, management has strongly promoted such forms of organizational renewal. However, line level officers have frequently proven to be unreceptive to such reforms (Griffiths, Whitelaw & Parent, 1999: 138-142). Police subculture has frequently proved to be an insurmountable obstacle to organizational renewal.

In police agencies across the country, reform minded chiefs have hit roadblock after roadblock in the form of line level resistance to change. In many cases, frustrated police managers have walked away, taking early retirement opportunities, leaving the organization to return to its status quo, response-driven and enforcement oriented approach to policing. Recent research in the United States has revealed that police departments exhibiting a participatory management style are more likely to have police officers who display positive attitudes towards community-oriented policing (Adams, Rohe & Arcury, 2002). However, penetrating a subculture resistant to change presents an ongoing problem for police reform.

The necessity to engage in street policing under some degree of management control is a source of conflict for many line level officers. Herbert (1996b) identifies this possibility, noting an example of an officer being called off of a high-speed pursuit:

If a patrol officer team pursuing a fleeing felon is ordered to stop by a superior officer, normative orders conflict. The patrol officers value adventurousness, competence, and morality; they want to prove their courage, to defeat those who would challenge their authority, and to rid the area of an evil menace. Conversely these same officers may want to ensure their own safety and to protect their chances for bureaucratic advancement against the potential damage from ignoring a command. Both actions are simultaneously supported and challenged by conflicting normative orders (1996b: 579).

Herbert argues that this conflict explains, in part, the divergent subcultures of police managers and line level personnel, with managers likely to favour "legality, control and safety" while line level patrol officers tend towards "adventure, competence, and morality" (1996b: 579). Divergent motivations will result in conflict between these two groups.

Line level Subculture

The line level police subculture, like many subcultures, has certain clearly definable characteristics. From the 1950s onward, most research has identified the police as clannish, isolated and secretive. Shared activities and work routines lead to shared ways of thinking. Over the years, various researchers in different countries have identified key themes inherent in the police subculture. Studies on this topic have a rich history in the United States,[4] however Canadian researchers have also explored the topic:

Table 1

United States Research:

Researcher	Year	Publication	Major Subculture Themes
William Westley	1953	*Violence and the Police*	Blue curtain
Jerome Skolnick	1966	*Justice Without Trial*	Working Personality
Arthur Neiderhoffer	1967	*Behind the Shield*	Cynicism

Researcher	Year	Publication	Major Subculture Themes
John Van Mannen	1973	"Observations on the Making of a Policeman"	Police Personality develops through learning
George Kirkham	1976	*Signal Zero*	Chronic suspicious-ness: a survival strategy
Herman Goldstein	1977	*Policing a Free Society*	Difficulties of policing in a democracy
Peter K. Manning	1977	*Police Work*	Ambiguous police mandate
Egon Bittner	1980	*Functions of Police in Modern Society*	Police solidarity
Carl Klockars	1980	"The Dirty Harry Problem"	Good ends only attained through bad means
Michael K. Brown	1981	*Working the Street*	Anxiety and stress management
Elizabeth Reuss-Ianni	1983	*Two Cultures of Policing*	Street cops' informal code of conduct
John Crank	1998	*Understanding Police Culture*	Activities & Sentiments tied to work environment
Steve Herbert	1998	Police Subculture Reconsidered"	Formal and informal dynamics interplay

Canadian Research:

Researcher	Year	Publication	Major Subculture Themes
Clifford Shearing	1981	"Subterranean Processes in the Maintenance of Power"	Reproducers of structures of dominance

Richard Ericson	1982	*Reproducing Order*	Recipes for action; maintenance of order
Claude Vincent	1990	*Police Officer*	Police Occupational Identity, older officer more isolated
Jayne Seagrave	1995	*Changing the Organizational Culture*	Policing as a "mission"

Different researchers focus on different aspects of the subculture. Additionally, researchers looking into the subculture in different agencies are naturally going to find variation from what other researchers have identified elsewhere. However, what is so impressive about the literature in this field is not the diversity of what has been found, but rather, the consistency of findings from place-to-place and across time. Among the findings consistently identified are the following:

1. Social isolation
2. Perception of public hostility
3. Informal code of conduct
4. Working personality

Some researchers focus on one aspect of the above factors. Other researchers group factors together differently. Regardless, academic inquiry has consistently turned up a collection of norms values and behaviours that reflects a shared adaptation to the stress and conflict experienced in the policing role.

Social isolation

Police work tends to involve unorthodox shifts of duty. Many departments operate on a twelve hour shift rotation, splitting patrol officers into four platoons or squads. Each squad works together on a particular shift (e.g. 7 a.m. to 7 p.m.) for a period of time, followed by a rotation of the squad to nights (e.g. 7 p.m. to 7 a.m.). A squad will typically work two day shifts, followed by two night shifts, followed by four days off. Since this puts the squad on an eight day cycle, the days off change from one week to the next. As one shift is working its days, another is working its nights. For each two shifts working on a particular day, two other shifts are on days off. This has the effect of isolating police officers from those who work routine Monday to Friday jobs – it also isolates them from their own co-workers assigned to different shifts. The result can be significant pride in one's squad, however socializing with non-police officers requires considerable effort and planning.

This isolation is exacerbated by the nature of police work. After a busy shift, officers often find sharing the experiences of the shift with those who came through it with them to be a form of relaxation. They are often tense, and shared experiences help in coping with recurring anxiety and emotional stress (Brown, 1981: 82). They frequently find non-police officers can not relate to the day's events. Getting together for drinks after a shift is a routine practice carried out in many police agencies.

Police officers find mutual support in one another. Backing each other up on the job protects officers from the dangers of the streets. Emotional backup provided off the job provides protection from the ongoing stress associated with the job. In protecting one another from outside threats, police officers may be said to erect a "blue wall of silence" that ensures the availability of unquestioned support and loyalty" that officers believe is essential in what they perceive to be a dangerous occupation (Bittner, 1980: 63).

In time, police become untrusting of non-police officers. Even senior management within the police organization itself is perceived as being unsympathetic to the role played out on the streets. Peer group support becomes increasingly relied upon. In a cyclical process, the exchange of war stories among peers emphasizes the dangerous aspects of the job, and the importance of peer support or backup intensifies. Chronic suspicion of non-police officers develops, with danger being seen in almost all situations, leading to a mind state bordering upon paranoia (see Kirkham, 1976). Police officers see themselves as the crime fighters in society, who are under appreciated, and misunderstood. Aggressive policing leads to the development of a "siege mentality" where the public at large are viewed as potential offenders, causing further alienation of the police from the rest of society (Christopher, 1991).

Perception of public hostility

A common feeling among police officers is that the public is, at a minimum, unappreciative of police efforts in stemming the crime wave. At worst, they perceive the public as outright hostile towards police efforts. Police officers are frequently cited as being a "cynical" group. According to Neiderhoffer:

> Cynicism is an emotional plank deeply entrenched in the ethos of the police world and it serves equally well for attack or defense. For many reasons police are particularly vulnerable to cynicism. When they succumb, they lose faith in people, society, and eventually in themselves. In their Hobbesian view, the world becomes a jungle in which crime, corruption and brutality are normal features of the terrain (1967: 41-2).

Cynicism and pessimism reinforces social isolation, police officers "know the public generally resents their authority, and is fickle in its support of police policy and individual officers. Older officers teach younger ones that it is best to avoid civilians" (Baker, 1985: 211). Acts of police wrongdoing appear elevated in those parts of the community that are the most socially "disorganized", perhaps due to the higher levels of police-citizen conflict in those areas intensifying the "us versus them" mentality among police officers (Kane, 2002).

The perception of public hostility is undoubtedly exacerbated by the police always dealing with people in conflict with the law. This leads to the adoption of an oppositional "us versus them" mind set. John Van Mannen graphically illustrates how police officers develop "typifications" – a sense of what to expect in various situations. He claims the police analyzed in his study exhaustively divided the citizenry into three categories: (a) suspicious persons, (b) assholes, and (c) know-nothings (1999: 348). Suspicious persons are those who do not fit into their surroundings, thereby arousing police suspicions. Assholes are those who deny, resist, or question police authority. Know-nothings are in the residual category of everyone who does not fit into one of the first two categories. It is very easy to not respect someone whom you believe does not respect you. The perception of public hostility is a key to the rise and maintenance of the police subculture.

Informal code of conduct

Belonging to the police subculture involves commitment to an informal code of conduct. This informal code tends to over-ride more formal rules and procedures, and operates to reinforce the occupational subculture. Some key aspects of the code include:[5] 1.Take care of your partner first, then the other officers. 2. Don't turn in fellow officers – if you protect them, they'll protect you when you need them. Be loyal – don't aid in the investigation of fellow officers. 3. Be tough – take control, never back down, be the one in control. Honour attaches to being tough. 4. Carry your fair share of the workload. 5. Don't do too much work – it makes all the other officers look bad – stick to the quota. 6. If you get caught doing something wrong, take the fall yourself, and don't bring other officers down with you. 7. Don't trust new officers until they've proven themselves. 8. Mind your own business – keep out of other officers' affairs. 9. Cover your ass, don't give supervisors anything to hold against you. 10. Don't trust management, they don't look out for your interests

Secrecy and loyalty to one's colleagues are important aspects of the informal code. Of course, this code is not unique to policing. Experience has shown students in post-secondary academic settings also display a strong code of secrecy and loyalty![6] However, the "Code of Silence" of the police is particularly insidious given the role that it plays in insulating police corruption and brutality (Skolnick, 2002).

Working personality

As the police officer becomes absorbed into the world of policing, the norms, values and beliefs of the police subculture become incorporated into the officer's sense of self. Policing is an identity-defining occupation (Vincent, 1990). The social psychology of identity appears to be going through resurgence in the academic literature.[7] Personality traits or characteristics emerge in the individual officer mirroring the subcultural norms. This process was first clearly articulated by American policing researcher Jerome Skolnick (1966, 1994). According to Skolnick, the police officer's constant exposure to danger and the need to use force and authority shape the police officer's working personality.

Key characteristics of the working personality were identified by Skolnick. Others investigating the phenomenon have added to his analysis. There is at least some research to show the police personality may include the following characteristics:
1. suspiciousness
2. preoccupied with danger – symbolic assailants
3. cynical
4. authoritarian
5. clannish
6. racist
7. hostile
8. conservative
9. dogmatic/moralistic
10. macho

Not all police officers display high levels of all of these variables. Police officers can be quite dissimilar along such dimensions. However, the research points to general trends reflecting significant enough levels of such variables among a large enough number of the population of police officers to assert that a police working personality with these dimensions can be identified.

Police tend to be highly suspicious of people and situations. They are constantly on the look out for unusual conduct that seems to indicate criminal activity is afoot. In 1993, the Ontario Court of Appeal ruled in *R. v. Simpson* that the police have the authority to detain and question an individual, even in the absence of statutory authority, so long as the police officer can justify the detention by a "reasonably based suspicion" giving rise to "articulable cause" in the circumstances.[8] Police may detain the individual to investigate for possible criminal activity without meeting the traditional standard for detention of reasonable grounds to believe the suspect is involved in the commission of an offence. The court decision affirms and supports a key characteristic of the police personality: to remain vigilant and suspicious of unusual conduct that may be a harbinger of criminal activity.

The preoccupation with danger reflects a heightened state of vigilance to possible violence. Even coffee breaks are spent on edge, as police officers typically take a seat in a restaurant with their back to the wall, and a clear view of people entering and leaving the establishment. As a result of always looking out for danger, police develop perceptual shorthand to allow them to identify certain individuals as "symbolic assailants", who are people whose "gestures, language, or attire" are of a sort that the police have come to identify as potentially dangerous (Skolnick, 1994: 44-7). Many police tasks are not as dangerous as police folklore implies (Lichtenberg and Smith, 2001), however, their apprehension and sensitivity is very real, and sets the police apart from those being policed, adding to a sense of isolation.

Many aspects of the police job bring on cynicism. Police view the other components of the criminal justice system as inefficient, and often working at cross-purposes to the police. Judges are viewed as soft on crime. Defence lawyers are despised for vigorous cross examination of police witnesses and complainants. Correctional rehabilitation programs are believed to coddle offenders. Law makers are criticized for liberal approaches to justice issues. Even the police hierarchy is criticized for inefficiency and lack of support for police on the street. Increased cynicism and pessimism results in police becoming hardened to the work they believe they have to do.

Much debate exists in the academic literature regarding the extent of authoritarianism among police officers. An authoritarian personality denotes an individual with minimal ego development, often described as rigid, prone to think in stereotypes, intolerant of deviations and punitive (Skolnick, 1994: 59). Much research conducted in the 1970s focussed on levels of authoritarianism among police officers, identifying higher levels in less educated police officers and lower levels among college educated officers (Roberg, Crank & Kuykendall, 2000: 412).

The social solidarity of the police creates a sense of belonging. Strong feelings of empathy, combined with cooperation in a teamwork atmosphere, produce what many officers describe as clannishness (Skolnick, 1994: 57). This may be connected to the perception of omnipresent danger and the experiences of hostility endured by the police as a collective group.

Research in North America and the United Kingdom has shown that the police frequently display racially prejudiced views (Seagrave, 1997: 118). In the United States, police have been said to identify the African American as the symbolic assailant, or

171

presumed danger on the streets (Skolnick, 1994: 47). In Canada, the police in the prairies have periodically come under fire for alleged racism against aboriginals, and in Toronto the police have recently come under considerable criticism for alleged racial profiling of blacks. Racial profiling involves targeting citizens for police attention on the basis of their race rather than their behaviour. In a series of articles run in the *Toronto Star* from October 19 to October 26, 2002, the newspaper reported on police arrest data showing blacks were much more likely to be arrested in Toronto for drug and other offences, out of all proportion to their representation in the population (Rankin et al., 2002). Canadian police have also come under attack for racial profiling by the academic community (Tanovich, 2002a; 2002b).

Police researcher William Ker Muir (1977) noted that many police officers are caught in a paradox that arises from their belief that the tougher their reputation, the less often they will have to resort to force. By displaying hostility and bravado, an officer believes they are essentially setting up a deterrent against anyone getting involved in an altercation with them. Overt displays of hostility may be used by the police as a defence mechanism.

As a group, police officers tend to be conservative in both their political views, and their personal lives. Collectively, they tend towards conformity (Frewin and Tuffin, 1998). The political right advances political and moral themes consistent with the police crime control perspective, so police allegiance to conservatism is not unexpected. John Lee (1981) found Canadian police hold conservative views. In their daily world view, police officers tend to be pragmatic, preferring down to earth approaches, shying away from innovation, experimentation, or new research (Reiner, 2000).

In a related personality attribute, police tend to be dogmatic. They are reluctant to abandon long-held views. Steve Herbert (1996a) found in Los Angeles that police officers regularly view their role through a lens of morality. They tend to view their world in black and white (sometimes quite literally) terms, perceiving themselves to be involved in the pursuit of good over the forces of evil. Characterizing the targets of their attention as evil-doers has a variety of functions. It reduces the ambiguity inherent in many encounter situations. The perceived omnipresence of evil helps the police come to grips with their inability to prevent crime. They are tasked with the reduction of crime levels in the areas they police, but this is an impossible task. It also permits them to cognitively rationalize how they can run roughshod over inherently ambiguous situations that they encounter. The police are expected to enforce order but are denied the resources and time necessary to fully deal with the complete range of disordering influences. Their moralistic views also allows them to cope with the myriad of situations in which they are required to act contrary to the interests of at least one party in an encounter. The police are required to use coercive force in rapidly evolving situations of conflict. While there are positive benefits to the police, Herbert asserts that the moralistic worldview has negative effects on police-community relations, and it condones overly aggressive police actions.

In policing, masculinism, sometimes referred to as a macho self-image (Reiner, 2000; Young, 1991), has been frequently identified as a key component of the police subculture. This characteristic frequently manifests itself in frequent indulgence in alcohol and sexual escapades (Reiner, 2000). An important negative consequence of masculinism, according to Herbert (2001), is that it has effectively crippled the community-oriented policing reform movement:

> Community policing implies a definition of the police role that runs counter to the masculinist crime fighter image, and thus faces resistance from officers. In community policing, officers are instructed to downplay their derring-do and instead engage in the involved and complicated process of establishing cooperative relations with the citizenry. For many officers, community policing thus amounts to social work. This is so inconsistent with their masculinist self-image that many officers refuse to redefine their role. Masculinism in policing thus works to disable efforts to enable greater citizen involvement in police practice (2001, p. 56).

Accordingly, Herbert claims that this has resulted in a suppression of the move towards greater democracy, in that community-oriented policing reflects an increased level of citizen-participation in society, and masculinism inhibits officer adoption of community-oriented policing norms. Taken to its extreme, it has been found that some police officers engage in sexual violence. In a review of three years of news media accounts and fourteen years of judicial decisions in the United States, 124 cases of police sexual violence were identified by Kraska and Kappeler (1995). These authors placed police sexual violence on a continuum. Of course, not all of these incidents involve a full blown sexual assault, however such incidents were indeed uncovered. In recent months in Canada, several police officers have been investigated for alleged sexual assaults.

In Ontario, investigations of serious allegations of police wrongdoing are carried out by the Special Investigations Unit. On September 24, 2002, Peter Tinsley, the Director of the Special Investigations Unit caused a charge of sexual assault to be laid against a Constable of the Toronto Police Service (Special Investigations Unit, 2002). This charge arises from an incident in which the female complainant alleges she was sexually assaulted in the lobby of a police station. Indeed, even a member of the Ontario Special Investigations Unit has become the subject of a sexual assault complaint (Madigan, 2002). An S.I.U. investigator was arrested in March of 2002, after it was alleged that he committed a sexual assault on a woman who met with him during an investigation. In Nova Scotia, a Halifax Regional Police officer, was charged with sexual assault, however the charge was dropped when he pleaded guilty on October 24, 2002, to lesser offences of common assault and unsafe storage of his service sidearm (Ware, 2002a; Ware 2002b). This constable was given a suspended sentence by the court and remains the subject of an internal investigation. Another incident arising in the maritimes involving an allegation of police sexual assault occurred on Prince Edward Island. A constable of the Charlottetown R.C.M.P. detachment pleaded guilty in June of 2002, to a lesser charge of common assault and was fined for his actions (CBC, 2002a). During his off duty hours, the Constable engaged in acts of kissing and rubbing against a woman who was asleep at a friend's house. Both of the parties to the incident had been drinking.

Of course, not all allegations of sexual assault against police officers are substantiated. In June of 2002, a corporal received $1.3 million in an out of court settlement of a lawsuit in which he claimed he had been the subject of a malicious prosecution (CBC, 2002b). The corporal was accused of being involved in the 1992 Martensville, Saskatchewan day care incidents. The officer and a number of other individuals had been charged after it was alleged that they had engaged in bizarre rituals, and forced the children to engage in sex acts at the day care centre. The corporal was acquitted of the charges against him in 1993. However, masculinist police attitudes may contribute to the surprising number of police sexual violence incidents that are found to be substantiated.

Masculinist attitudes were found by Rigakos (1995) to be prevalent in the Delta (B.C.) Police Department's response to domestic violence incidents. He concluded that the conservative, victim blaming patriarchal views of the police officers being studied failed to treat court order violations pertaining to battered women seriously.

While recent research efforts question the extent to which the police working personality or "identity" is all-consuming (Oberweis and Musheno, 1998), there can be little doubt that policing is an identity defining occupation unlike most others in our society. Why is there such a clearly definable subculture in policing? What brings it about?

Causes

The police subculture appears to be endemic to policing. However, competing views exist regarding how the police subculture arises. Drawing on the literature used to explain the presence of an inmate subculture in prisons,[9] it is possible to posit at least two competing explanations. Police subculture may arise as a result of police departments hiring individuals possessing personality characteristics that, when combined with like-thinking individuals in the work environment manifests itself as a police subculture. That is, police agencies may simply be hiring individuals who are already committed to the norms and values that we have come to associate with police subculture. Alternatively, it is possible that the police subculture is a result of socialization practices. According to this view, new recruits are inculcated into the subculture, they begin their career as basically neutral entities, but the subculture gradually convinces them to accept the norms and values of their fellow officers. These two perspectives may be referred to as the predisposition theory and the socialization theory.

The importation theory suggests that police departments tend to recruit individuals with similar personalities; when working together, they combine to produce the police subculture. Considerable evidence supports this thesis. Police departments tend to hire like-minded individuals. Considerable energy is expended by police recruitment authorities to select those who will best fit into the police role. While new recruits tend to be more idealistic than experienced officers (Catlin & Maupin, 2002), they tend to display consistent personality traits.

Predisposition

Considerable debate prevails over why individuals are drawn to a career in policing. Certainly, there are as many reasons as there are people applying for new recruit positions. However, it is not particularly clear whether a particular personality type is drawn to policing as a vocation. Police recruits have consistently tended to be male. Currently, about 85% of police officers in Canada are male (Statistics Canada, 2002). Policing also runs in families, with the children of police officers frequently choosing policing as a career (Forcese, 1999: 125). Significant numbers of new police recruits are known to engage in the drinking of alcohol (Obst, Davey & Shehan, 2001), an important factor affecting how the recruit will fit into after-shift drinking sessions. Educational requirements remain low in most jurisdictions. Historically, few police recruits have come from the ranks of ethnic minorities. Interviewing and personality testing seeks to screen potential candidates, in order to find those "most suitable" for police work. While the official goal is to find those with desirable characteristics such as "integrity, honesty, and respect",[10] the inexplicit and unofficial hiring agenda of police agencies has been to select individuals who are going to fit well into the police organizational culture. Has this resulted in the selection of a particular personality type? It may be that police organizations hire individuals in whom the foundation of a police personality is already present, with this being what draws them to police work (Bennett and Greenstein, 1975). Some early theories suggested that people with an authoritarian personality type were attracted to policing (Roberg and Kuykendall, 1993: 278). This would suggest that individuals who are deferential to authority, able to see issues in black and white, intolerant of defiance, minimally empathetic, politically conservative, susceptible to peer influence, and self-confident are attracted to policing. Bonifacio argues that a "desire to master dangerous situations" so as to display one's "bravery and power" is the primary motive behind people applying for police work (1991: 146) According to this view, police officers are born, not made. They have certain personality constructs that impel them towards a career in policing. They suffer from "recognition hunger", are unconsciously conflicted by desires for "power and nurturance", and are seeking the "thrill" of mastering danger (Bonifacio, 1991: 142-3). If this is indeed the case, it would lend considerable support to the predisposition theory of police subculture. However, it is not a widely supported position today.

John Van Mannen observes police recruits as non-authoritarian (1997: 90). They enter the job environment with a normative commitment to the police organization and its goals (Van Mannen, 1997: 91), but there is no identifiable pre-existing personality. It seems to be readily accepted in the current policing literature that the traits common to police officers do exist, however, they arise through the process of socialization rather than from pre-existing personality characteristics (Seagrave, 1997: 72).

Socialization

From the moment a police officer begins the recruitment process, forces of socialization are brought to bear indoctrinating the new recruit into an occupation-based identity that exists in a subculture with its own norms, values and beliefs that are unique from those in the dominant culture in the wider society (Vincent, 1990). Major forces that come to play in socializing the new officer extend from the recruitment practices, through the realities of life in the police academy, and extend even further. Early days on the street are devoted to field training, arguably the most powerful force in teaching and reinforcing the norms of the police subculture. Additional factors that will have some impact are the individual department's style of delivering policing, and the task environment within which policing must occur.

At the point of initial screening, police officers quickly realize the competitiveness for the position they seek. Potential recruits frequently hear about the large number of applications who are screened down to a smaller number that are eventually invited to write an exam. Often, there will be hundreds of potential recruits writing an exam for a department with relatively few openings. The applicant comes to believe that they will be part of a select group if they make it through the process. At each stage in the recruitment process, the pool of candidates shrinks, enhancing the feeling that one is very special to have made it all the way through to the final stages. Successfully passing tests of physical ability reinforce or foster a self-perception of strength and stamina. Psychological evaluations that are passed reinforce a sense of mental strength and stability. Passing stressful interviews, and other evaluation procedures combine to create a sense that the new recruit is going through rites of passage into a select and special subgroup of society.

Recruit training often takes place in a cloistered atmosphere in a police academy or other similar venue shared with other justice system recruits. At the academy, the learning of the rules and procedures governing police work are only the beginning of the socialization process. A much more important dynamic is the development of a sense of camaraderie or esprit de corps that is shared among the recruit class (Van Mannen, 1997: 92-3). The recruits come to admire the adventures of veteran officers who typically serve as academy instructors. The department's tradition is "absorbed" as the student comes to identify more and more with their police agency (Van Mannen, 1997: 93).

In the words of symbolic interactionism, the recruit is mortified, going through a process of status change that is symbolized by the new haircut, the uniform, the long hours of work carried out in a more or less cloistered atmosphere. New friends are made among classmates, new titles are adopted (cadet or constable), daily routines are regimented by the academy. In a sense, the recruit goes through a process of becoming reborn, with a new status and identity as a probationary police officer. The recruit comes to absorb the subcultural "ethos" and begins to think like a police officer (Van Mannen, 1997: 95). Firearms and self-defence training enhance and expand the feelings of power and the ability to master unforeseen and dangerous situations.

In all departments, classroom training is followed up by a period of field training. The new recruit will be assigned to a senior officer who formally carries forward the task of overseeing the implementation in the real world of the skills and abilities mastered by the recruit at the academy. Informally, the field trainer plays a powerful role in bringing the recruit into the occupational subculture. Some trainers have been known to express sentiments such as "forget everything they told you at the academy, everything...they do police work one way at the academy and we do it another way on the street..." (Cordner and Sheehan, 1999: 467). The recruit takes in the myths, folklore, and stereotypes from their field trainer and other officers encountered in the field. The sentiments and behaviours of senior officers are readily adopted, and in doing so, the new officer avoids ostracism and critical evaluations by the field supervisor (Van Mannen, 1997: 97-8).

Among the important things absorbed by the new officer are the following identified in Van Mannen's experience and research:

- Skills and attitudes are learned from fellow patrol officers, not supervisors
- Fellow officers are open and welcoming
- All dilemmas faced on the street can be handled – start by watching, listening and mimicking the field trainer
- Avoid the mistakes made by others who came before
- Handling the "heavy call" shows you have what it takes
- Backing up your field trainer is an important test of loyalty
- The "first arrest" experience cements the passage to a new status (1997: 95-100).

Since formal training in a police academy can never teach a new recruit everything they need to know to be an effective police officer, it is natural that a lot of learning will occur during the field training period. The stories and actions of senior officers inevitably tend to stress the dangers of police work, and the problems associated with relying on the community for support during dangerous encounters. This helps to reinforce the police subculture and leads towards the development of a working personality.

Idealism does not last long once a recruit has entered field training (Catlin and Maupin, 2002).

Each department has its own organizational style or ethos. In a pioneering work on the subject, James Q. Wilson (1968) identified three different organizational styles in different American police departments: the watchman, the legalistic, and the service style.[11] It is debateable whether such a typology is accurate in the Canadian context (Seagrave, 1995), however the point to be made is that organizational style can have a significant impact on the specific form police subculture takes in a particular agency. To some extent organizations exert control over their organizational culture. Management can mould the style of an agency they oversee through overt and covert manipulation (Gibson, Ivancevich & Donnelly, 1985; Ivancevich & Matteson, 1990). For example, recent efforts in many police agencies have concentrated on developing a "learning organization"[12] stressing systems thinking, personal mastery, mental models, shared vision, and team learning. In the policing context, this involves officers putting aside their old ways of thinking (or mental models) and learning to be open with co-workers. In this way, they will come to understand how their agency really works (developing systems thinking), and together form a plan that everyone can agree upon (a shared vision). The members of the police agency then work together, in order to achieve their shared vision. If management is successful in implementing this, or some other current management reform, they will develop a working environment in which elements of the police subculture are modified. Police departments employing a participatory management style appear to have greater success in getting the rank and file to accept community policing reforms than traditional organizational structures (Adams, Rohe & Arcury, 2002). However, the police subculture is notoriously difficult to bend.

Finally, it should be noted that the task environment within which a particular police agency operates will impact on the police subculture. Very small departments with a few strong personalities often develop a subculture moulded around the views of these few strong personalities. Larger departments are more likely to exhibit the full panoply of subcultural elements found in the classical literature. Little research has been conducted on the effects of the task environment on police attitudes and behaviour in Canada.

Positive aspects of police subculture

Most of the literature on police subculture has focused on the negative aspects of it. However, there has recently been a view advanced indicating that the subculture may provide some benefits to the officers (Griffiths, Whitelaw & Parent, 1999: 109). Under this view, the subculture, and its accompanying working personality have arisen for very good reason. They are important aspects of a survival strategy.

The police occupation often requires police officers to adapt to frequently changing shift rotations. This naturally leads to difficulties in maintaining consistent contacts with friends and family who work regular week-day shifts. As a result, fellow officers fill a void, providing a support network for similarly situated work mates. Additionally, the specific encounters and situational dynamics encountered in policing are often not as well appreciated by those who do not engage in police work. Fellow officers provide a useful outlet for thoughts and experiences generated during a shift together. Officers on the same shift play a particularly important role in an officer's life. They are exposed to the same situations, and have the same days off, often leading to the development of close personal friendships.

Since the role of the street police officer exposes the individual to the potential for violence, the close bonds developed in the occupational subculture of policing provide a means to cope with the stress arising from the constant threat of danger. Research has indicated that stress in policing is a major concern (Loo, 1984; Loo, 1985). Negative aspects of stress in policing include resultant job burnout, cynical and negative attitudes in general, conservative and authoritarian belief systems, and poor health (Stearns and Moore, 1993). Stress in policing is typically viewed in a negative light. Accordingly, efforts to minimize or control stress levels are generally viewed as positive goals. It may be that the sense of belonging and social cohesion provided by the occupational subculture of the police helps to minimize stress levels that would otherwise be very difficult to accommodate.

Not all individuals who enter policing experience the same levels of stress. The highest levels of stress and career burnout have been found among those entering the profession with a "social activist" orientation (Burke and Kirchmeyer, 1990a). Such individuals hope to bring about social and institutional change through their efforts. Such individuals seek to "rock the boat" and disturb the status quo. The lowest levels of stress and burnout were found by Burke and Kirchmeyer to be amongst "artisans", individuals who enter policing seeking intrinsic rewards in their career, such as personal growth, professional development and the mastery of new skills. Socialization into the police subculture is likely welcomed, integrating the new recruit with this orientation being a natural course of conduct. The relatively few social activists who remain in policing over a lengthy period of time eventually report lower levels of stress and burnout (Burke and Kirchmeyer, 1990b). However, relatively few officers holding such attitudes remain in policing over the long haul, and their eventual satisfaction may rise despite, rather than because of any positive impact of police subculture.

Homicide investigators typically deal with the stress resulting from attending homicide scenes through a number of coping mechanisms, including the adoption of dark humour, emotional distancing from the victim, and adopting a professional focus to the tasks at hand (Sewell, 1993). However, the child murder investigator appears to be particularly stressed by exposure to a victim from whom it is difficult to emotionally distance oneself. Van Patten and Burke (2001) argue that the police homicide investigator experiences critical incident stress when exposed to the murder of a child. The police subculture may aid the investigator in coping with the stress associated with such cases.

The social isolation associated with police subculture that insulates police from the rest of society may allow child homicide investigators to maintain "psychological and emotional distance from civilians" (Van Patten and Burke, 2001: 144). Indeed, exposure to death, and the display of a non-emotional, aloof, and even casual reaction may be a rite of passage into the police occupational subculture (Henry, 1995). Van Patten and Burke found that relatively few homicide investigators seek out critical incident stress management programs. Only one third of those homicide investigators studied had reported participating in such a program (2001: 146). For the majority of homicide investigators, the support and solidarity provided by the peer group within the occupational subculture may provide the primary coping strategy for dealing with the psychological consequences of traumatic incidents.

Police Deviance

The police, like all groups in society, engage in acts of deviance. Such acts are of particular concern if they reflect acts of corruption or brutality. The police role carries both power and authority, making their exercise of discretion a matter of public concern. The public expects the police to act fairly and with restraint, given the privileged position they hold with regard to the exercise of discretion in their use of power and authority.

Corruption

Police corruption has been defined as the use of police power and authority for personal gain (Goldstein, 1977). Thomas Barker (1994) asserts that occupational socialization into the norms of the police subculture plays an instrumental role in leading to corrupt behaviour. Peer group support for corrupt practices combines with the widespread opportunities for corrupt acts that policing entails to create a situation in which corruption can easily flourish: "The peer group indoctrinates and socializes the rookie into patterns of acceptable corrupt activities, sanctions deviations outside these boundaries, and sanctions officers, who do not engage in any corrupt acts" (Barker, 1994: 53).

Corruption is most likely to occur where the risk of getting caught is minimal, and where the consequences of getting caught are not sufficient to deter such activity. In 1996, a staff sergeant head of the RCMP's anti-drug profiteering unit pleaded guilty to stealing $138,454 from a sum of money taken into evidence by him in a major heroin arrest (Ogilvie, 1996a; 1996b). In 1989, constable of the Toronto Police Service was charged with a number of offences pertaining to a "pay-for-sex escort agency" he had established with a prostitute he knew at the time (Stansfield, 1996). His charges were withdrawn after he agreed to resign from the police service. In cases such as these, the officers must believe there is very little chance of being caught, and if the risk of being caught arises, they surely believe the police subculture will operate to shield them from an effective investigation.

Subculture provides support for police corruption in a variety of ways. It may help corrupt police officers to live with the apparent contradiction of being paid to uphold the law, while violating the law themselves. Kappeller, Sluder and Alpert (1998) argue that this can arise through the adoption of techniques of neutralization. This concept is adapted from Sykes and Matza's (1957) view that most offenders do not conceive of themselves as criminal. Their own criminal behaviour contradicts their self-image, and accordingly they justify their behaviour by arguing to themselves that their conduct is not really criminal. Five techniques of neutralization are noted: denial of responsibility ("They made me do it, it was not my fault"), denial of injury ("No one got hurt, they can afford it"), denial of victim ("They deserved it"), condemning the condemners ("They do not know anything, everyone is crooked"), and appeal to higher loyalties ("Protect your own, no one hurts the platoon")(Kappeller et al., 1998: 114).

The police subculture provides police officers with the necessary ideology or mindset for corruption to arise and remain justified. It also helps to understand how those who enforce the law can occasionally break the law without experiencing any significant conflict.

Brutality and abuse of authority

Barker and Carter define abuse of authority as "any action by a police officer without regard to motive, intent, or malice that tends to injure, insult, trespass upon human dignity, manifest feelings of inferiority, and/or violate an inherent legal right of a member of the police constituency in the course of performing 'police work'" (1994: 7). While abuse of authority includes psychological abuse, and legal abuse, it is physical abuse or police brutality that is of most concern to the public and police management. Estimating the extent of police brutality in Canada is very difficult (Ross, 1996; 2000), in large part due to the efforts of the police subculture to cover it up.

A major contributing factor towards police brutality appears to be the "us versus them" mentality that is so prominent in the police subculture. As noted earlier, Steve Herbert's analysis of morality in police work, claims that the police viewing themselves and others in terms of good and evil, can lead to excessive use of force. A situation in which the police use more force than is necessary in the circumstances can be condoned from a police stand point if it is "understood as ultimately motivated by a desire to expunge evil from otherwise peaceable streets" (Herbert, 1996a:815). Instances of excessive force are the price to be paid for the ongoing effort to keep the city safe. Police morality "crudely characterizes" people and actions, with a result that needlessly aggressive and insensitive treatment of individuals encountered by the police are condoned.

Skolnick and Fyfe (1993) argue that the police subculture may be responsible for some of the increase in the frequency of police brutality complaints found in many jurisdictions. Like Herbert, they attribute the "us versus them" mentality to the problem. Too often, police view themselves as "soldiers" waging a "war on crime". It is a war they cannot win, and the realization of this produces frustration, demoralization and anger: "police brutality is inevitable when, as has happened in some places, officers describe themselves as ghetto gunslingers or as troopers assigned to isolated outposts of civilization" (Skolnick & Fyfe, 1993: 133).

Built into the occupational subculture of the police are attitudes, prejudices and language that make police brutality too easy for the police to rationalize to themselves. They are not beating on ordinary citizens, but "scumbags and pukes" (Jackson, 1992) or others who have been depersonalized and categorized as the "other" in a battle between us and them. It takes special efforts for agencies to overcome the "powerful prescriptions of silence and loyalty" manifested by the subculture of policing (Skolnick & Fyfe, 1993: 112).

Conclusion

Recent concerns regarding police subculture have centred on two areas. First, the role police subculture plays in hiding police deviance, shielding it from accountability mechanisms is a cause of considerable concern. Second, the subculture has been identified as a stumbling block for police management pursuing reform efforts, whether in the guise of community policing or some allied reorganization (Marks, 2000; Haarr, 2001).

The first concern is an ongoing live issue that concerns the public, the media, politicians, oversight officials, and police managers. The vignette described at the opening to this chapter poignantly displays the concern over police subculture's role in shielding the police from accountability. If the officers are found responsible for the harm that befell the three individuals who found themselves at the wrong end of a police baton in the wee hours of the morning, it shows that the subculture of the police is alive and well in that jurisdiction, operating to allow a mindset to prevail that considers brutality an acceptable practice. There is no other way to adequately describe why several police officers would collectively engage in acts of brutality and then engage in acts of deceit in the aftermath.

Meanwhile, it appears that the second matter may not be as great a problem in the years ahead as was envisioned during the last decade. However, it is not because the police subculture has come to embrace organizational reform. In recent years, policing has witnessed the birth of a "performance culture" incorporating pressures on all levels to achieve performance levels in key tasks associated with the police role, particularly in the area of reactive enforcement (Scott, 1998). In the post-September 11th environment, the public and politicians appear to be content with police agencies reasserting a crime control mandate that, despite the inevitable adverse effect on civil liberties (Heymann, 2002; Toope, 2002), plays into the hands of the police subculture. This appears to signal a return to reactive, law and order based policing in many communities. There will be little subcultural interference in organizational changes of this nature.

It is unlikely that we will witness significant change to the police subculture in the years ahead. It has remained substantially intact for at least half a century, and has shown to be robust across jurisdictions. The police subculture is not yet showing cracks in its old age. As education levels of new police recruits have increased, and the gender (Linden and Fillmore, 1993) and ethnic (Jain, 1994; Jaccoud & Felices, 1999) make up of police agencies has diversified, it was natural to expect a softening of the police subculture over time. However, the research does not lend much support to support this contention.[13] However, very little research on policing is carried out in Canada.

While American and British policing academics have an active research agenda in place that continues to investigate police subculture, Canada has been lacking in this regard as of late. How do police handle internal conflicts and contradictions in the subcultural normative order?[14] Sporadic research efforts have only scratched the surface of the topic in this country. Does the subculture differ in the RCMP compared to municipal departments? Is there variation within the RCMP, or within various units in different police agencies? American research has found rural policing reflects the same subcultural themes found in urban policing (Christensen and Crank, 2001), however only fieldwork will determine if this holds true for the police in Canada's remote regions. How has transnationalization affected police subculture? James Sheptycki, (1997) argues this is having a significant impact on police subculture. Despite the difficulties in carrying out sound, ethical observational research on the police, this still appears to be the best avenue for uncovering the mysteries of police subculture (Phillips and Brown, 1997; Westmarland, 2001).

Endnotes

1   Shearing and Ericson (1991) advance the idea that the police (sub)culture provides a "tool kit" which will be used differently by different police officers, recognizing that human agency is not stripped away by a very powerful subcultural influence on the behaviour of police officers. Problems with overly simplistic "(sub) culture causes behaviour" approaches have also been recently identified by Shover and Hochstetler (2002).

2　Eugine Paoline (2003 in press) has presented a particularly strong call for the continued analysis of police subculture. The concept remains a powerful analytical tool in understanding police decision-making and police deviance

3　See discussion with note 10 below.

4　A fair amount of police subculture research has also been carried out in Australia (e.g. Chan, 1996; 1997) and Britain (e.g. Banton, 1964; Holdaway, 1984; Reiner, 2000), however work in this area has been most prolific in the United States.

5　A code of secrecy or a code of silence has been noted throughout the police subculture literature. However, some authors have identified a more complex code with specific behavioural requirements. In the American context, see Niederhoffer (1967) and Reuss-Ianni (1983) in this regard.

6　I am not alone in noting this code of silence among post secondary students. It has also been noted by policing researchers Albert J. Reiss, James Fyfe and Jerome Skolnick (see Skolnick & Fyfe, 1993: 110-111).

7　Howard (2000) has recently explored the various developments in sociology and psychology pertaining to identities, illustrating a variety of approaches to the phenomenon. Most police subculture research appears to adopt, implicitly or explicitly, a symbolic interactionist approach.

8　Other provinces have since adopted the Simpson approach to suspicion-based detentions: See, for example R. v. Cooke (2002)(B.C.C.A.), R. v. Ladouceur (2002)(Sask.C.A.)

9　See Griffiths and Verdun-Jones (1994: 504) for a discussion of the deprivation and importation theories on the rise of the inmate subculture. Deprivation theory posits that the inmate subculture naturally arises as a means to mitigate the pains of imprisonment. Importation theory hypothesizes that criminal attitudes and behaviours characteristic of the inmate subculture are brought in to the prison by inmates who followed criminal careers on the outside.

10　These are key values looked for and ingrained in the RCMP's training program: see RCMP Cadet Training (2003).

11　An examination of Wilson's typology, and those of other police management analysts, is beyond the scope of this chapter.

12 Much of the work on learning organizations is derived from the seminal work of Peter M. Senge (1991) The Fifth Discipline: The Art and Practice of the Learning Organization New York: Doubleday Books, and Peter M. Senge (1990) "The Leader's New Work: Building Learning Organizations" in Sloan Management Review 32(1): 7-23. The idea behind a learning organization is based on five elements:

1. Team learning – A working group suspends their assumptions and thinks freely together. This involves an exchange of dialogue, getting past personal defensiveness to present ideas openly.

2. Building shared vision – By sharing visions of the future, the group becomes excited about what they are doing together. Since their motivation to change comes from themselves, it is an inner motivation which will result in them going out of their way to implement it.

3. Mental models – The group identifies previously hidden assumptions or mental models, bringing them into the open and working on them.

4. Personal mastery – Each worker personally develops their vision, developing an inner drive that results in performing to their very best.

5. Systems thinking – By consistently re-examining the whole process or system, the group works together to accomplish the organization's goals, rather than addressing localized or individual problems. This is the "fifth discipline".

13 For example, Alley, Waugh and Ede (1996) failed to find that increases in the proportion of women in policing had a significant impact on police subculture. In particular, they found little difference between female and male officer attitudes towards matters such as police misconduct. In any case, women (Suriya, 1993) and minorities may be held on the periphery of the police subculture, negating any positive influence they could have on its strength.

14 An issue raised by Steve Herbert (1996b) as prevailing in his look at policing in Los Angeles.

References

Adams, Richard E., William M. Rohe, & Thomas A. Arcury. (2002). Implementing Community-Oriented Policing: Organizational Change and Street Officer Attitudes. *Crime Delinquency* 48(3) 399-430.

Alley, Avril, Linda Waugh, & Andrew Ede (1996). *Police Culture, Women Police and Attitudes Towards Misconduct.* Paper presented at the Australian Institute of Criminology Conference, First Australasian Women Police Conference, Sydney, July 29-31, 1996.

Baker, Mark. (1985). *Cops: Their Lives in Their Own Words.* New York: Fawcett.

Banton, Michael. (1964). *The Police and the Community.* London: Tavistock.

Barker, Thomas. (1994). Peer Group Support for Police Occupational Deviance, Chapter 4. In Thomas Barker and David L. Carter (Eds.), *Police Deviance* (3rd ed.). Cincinnati, OH: Anderson Publishing.

Bennett, Richard & Theodore Greenstein. (1975). The Police Personality: A Test of the Predispositional Model. *Journal of Police Science and Administration* 3: 439-445.

Bittner, Egon. (1980). *The Functions of Police in Modern Society.* Cambridge, MA: Oelgeschlager.

Bonifacio, Philip. (1991). *The Psychological Effects of Police Work: A Psychodynamic Approach.* New York: Plenum Press.

Burke, R.J. & C. Kirchmeyer. (1990). Initial Career Orientations, Stress and Burnout in Policeworkers. *Canadian Police College Journal* 14(1):28-36.

Burke, R.J. & C. Kirchmeyer.(1990). Present Career Orientations, Stress and Burnout in Policeworkers. *Canadian Police College Journal* 14(1):50-57.

Carter, David & Louis Radalet. (1999). *The Police and the Community* (6th ed.). Upper Saddle River, NJ: Prentice Hall.

Catlin, Dennis W. & James R. Maupin. (2002). Ethical

Orientations of State Police Recruits and One-Year Experienced Officers. *Journal of Criminal Justice* 30: 491-498.

CBC (2002a). Mountie Sentenced for Sexual Assault. CBC Prince Edward Island – online. Web posted June 27, 2002. Retrieved October 28, 2002 at: http://pei.cbc.ca/template/serv;et/View?filename=dawson 260602

CBC (2002b). Policeman gets $1.3 million in Martensville Settlement. CBC News – online. Web posted June 19, 2002. Retrieved October 27, 2002 at: http://cbc.ca/storyview/CBC/2002/06/18/popowich 020618

Chan, Janet (1996). Changing Police Culture. *British Journal of Criminology* 36(1):109-134.

Chan, Janet. (1997). *Changing Police Culture: Policing in a Multicultural Society*. Cambridge, UK: Cambridge University Press.

Christensen, Wendy & John P. Crank. (2001). Police Work and Culture in a Nonurban Setting: An Ethnographic Analysis. *Police Quarterly* 4(1):69-98.

Christopher, Warren. (1991). *Report of the Independent Commission on the Los Angeles Police Department*. Los Angeles: City of Los Angeles.

Cordner, Gary & Robert Sheehan. (1999). *Police Administration* (4th ed.), Cincinnati, OH: Anderson Publishing.

Ericson, Richard (1982). *Reproducing Order: A Study of Patrol Work*. Toronto: University of Toronto Press.

Ferrell, Jeff (1999). Cultural Criminology. *Annual Review of Sociology*. 25: 395-418.

Fong, Petti (2003, March 25). Officers Filed Misleading Report: Court. Vancouver Sun online at Canada.com News. Retrieved April 3, 2003 at: http://www.canada.com/search/story.aspx?id=11a46038-cb64-401e-ae47-b9423e5a125a

Forcese, Dennis. (1999). *Policing Canadian Society* (2nd ed.). Scarborough: Prentice Hall.

Frewin, Karen, & Keith Tuffin. (1998). Police Status, Conformity and Internal Pressure: A Discursive Analysis of Police Culture. *Discourse and Society* 9(2):173-185.

Goldstein, Herman. (1977). *Policing a Free Society*. Cambridge, MA: Ballinger

Griffiths, Curt T. & Simon N. Verdun-Jones (1994). *Canadian Criminal Justice* (2nd ed.). Toronto: Harcourt Brace.

Griffiths, Curt, Brian Whitelaw & Richard Parent. (1999). *Canadian Police Work*. Toronto: ITP Nelson.

Haarr, Robin N. (2001). The Making of a Community Police Officer: The Impact of basic Training and Occupational Socialization on Police Recruits. *Police Quarterly* 4(4): 402-433.

Henry, V.E. (1995). The Police Officer as Survivor: Death Confrontations and the Police Subculture. *Behavioral Science and the Law* 13: 93-112.

Herbert, Steve, (2001). Hard Charger or 'Station Queen'? Policing and the Masculinist State. *Gender, Place and Culture* 8(1) 55-71.

Herbert, Steve. (1998). Police Subculture Reconsidered. *Criminology* 36(2): 343-369.

Herbert, Steve. (1996a). Morality in Law Enforcement: Chasing 'Bad Guys' with the Los Angeles Police Department. *Law & Society Review* 30(4) 799-818.

Herbert, Steve. (1996b). The Normative Ordering of Police Territoriality: Making and Marking Space with the Los Angeles Police Department. *Annals of the Association of American Geographers*, 86(3) 567-582.

Heymann, Philip B. (2002). Civil Liberties and Human Rights in the Aftermath of September 11. *Harvard Journal of Law & Public Policy* 25(2): 441-456.

Holdaway, Simon. (1984). *Inside the British Police: A Force at Work*. Oxford: Basil Blackwell.

Howard, Judith A. (2000). Social Psychology of Identities. *Annual Review of Sociology* 26: 367-393.

Howard, Tim, Michael Jackson, Thomas Kerr, Katrina Pacey, John Richardson & MarkTyndall. (2002). *To Serve and Protect:* A Report on Policing in Vancouver's Downtown Eastside Vancouver: Pivot Legal Society.

Jackson, Eric. (1992). Police Brutality and the Prejudice Reduction Model. *Law and Order Magazine* 40(11) Reproduced online at: http://www.ncbi.org/accomplishments/mediacoverage/polic e_brutality.pdf

Jaccoud, M., & M. Felices. (1999). Ethnicization of the Police in Canada. *Canadian Journal of Law and Society* 14(1):83-100.

Jain, H.C. (1994). An Assessment of Strategies of Recruiting Visible Minority police Officers in Canada, 1985-1990. In R.C. Macleod and David Schneiderman (Eds.), *Police Powers in Canada: The Evolution and Practice of Authority.* Toronto: University of Toronto Press.

Kane, Robert. (2002). The Social Ecology of Police Misconduct. *Criminology.* 40(4): 867-896.

Kappeller, Victor E., Richard D. Sluder & Geoffrey P. Alpert. (1998). *Forces of Deviance: Understanding the Dark Side of Policing* (2nd ed.). Prospect Heights, IL: Waveland Press.

Ker Muir, William. (1977). *Police: Streetcorner Politicians.* Chicago: University of Chicago Press.

Kirkham, George L. (1976). *Signal Zero: The True Story of a Professor who Became a Cop.* New York: J.B. Lippincott.

Kraska, Peter B. & Victor E. Kappeler. (1995). To Serve and Pursue: Exploring Police Sexual Violence Against Women. *Justice Quarterly* 12(1), 85-111.

Lee, John Alan. (1981). Some Structural Aspects of Police Deviance in Relations with Minority Groups. Chapter 3 in Clifford D. Shearing (ed.). *Organizational Police Deviance.* Toronto: Butterworths.

Lichtenberg, Illya D. & Alisa Smith. (2001). How Dangerous are Routine Police-Citizen Traffic Stops? A Research Note. *Journal of Criminal Justice* 29: 419-428.

Linden, Rick, & Cathy Fillmore. (1993). An Evaluation Study of Women in Policing. In Joe Hudson and Julian Roberts (Eds.), *Evaluating Justice: Canadian Policies and Programs* Toronto: Thompson Educational Publishing.

Lippens, Ronnie. (2001). Rethinking Organizational Crime and Organizational Criminology. *Crime, Law & Social Change* 35: 319-331.

Loo, Robert. (1984). Occupational Stress in the Law Enforcement Profession. *Canada's Mental Health* 32, 10-13.

Loo, Robert. (1985). Policy Development for Psychological Services in the Royal Canadian Mounted Police. *Journal of Police Science and Administration* 13, 132-137.

Madigan, Tracey. (2002). Police Investigator Arrested for Sexual Assault. CBC Montreal – online. Retrieved October 27, 2002 at:
http://cbc.ca/storyview/CBC/2002/06/18/popowich020618

Marks, Monique. (2000). Transforming Police Organizations from Within: Police Dissident Groupings in South Africa. *British Journal of Criminology* 40: 557-573.

Mickleburgh, Rod. (2003, January 25). Vancouver Police Accused of Brutality. *The Globe and Mail* online. Retrieved April 3, 2003
http://www.globeandmail.com/servlet/ArticleNews/front/R TGAM/20030125/wxbeat0125/Front/homeBN/breakingne ws

Niederhoffer, A. (1967). *Behind the Shield: The Police in Urban Society*. New York: Doubleday.

Oberweis, Trish & Michael Musheno. (1999). Policing Identities: Cop Decision Making and the Constitution of Citizens. *Law and Social Inquiry* 24(4): 897-923.

Obst, Patricia L., Jeremy D. Davey & Mary C. Sheehan. (2001). Does Joining the Police Service Drive You to Drink? A Longitudinal Study of the Drinking Habits of Police Recruits. *Drugs: Education, Prevention and Policy* 8(4): 347-357.

Ogilvie, Clare. (1996a). Senior Cop Stole Cash. *The Province*. Tuesday, March 5, 1996, A4.

Ogilvie, Clare. (1996b). Never Meant to Keep Drug Money: Narc. *The Province*. Friday, May 17, 1996, A13.

Paoline, Eugene A. (2003). Taking Stock: Toward a Richer Understanding of Police Culture. *Journal of Criminal Justice* 31(3): 199-214.

Phillips, Coretta & David Brown. (1997). Observational Studies in Police Custody Areas: Some Methodological and Ethical Issues Considered. *Policing and Society* 7: 191-205.

Punch, Maurice. (1983). *Control in the Police Organization*.

Cambridge, Mass.: MIT Press.

Rankin, Jim, Jennifer Quinn, Michelle Shephard, John Duncanson, & Scott Simmie (2002). Singled Out. *The Star* – online, retrieved October 19, 2002 at http://www.thestar.com

RCMP Cadet Training Handbook-online (2003). Retrieved April 6, 2003 at http://www.rcmp-grc.gc.ca/ctp/ctp/resr/hnbk/index_e.htm

Reiner, Robert. (2000). *The Politics of the Police* (3rd ed.). Oxford: Oxford University Press.

Reuss-Ianni, Elizabeth. (1983). *Two Cultures of Policing: Street Cops and Management Cops*. New Brunswick, NJ: Transaction Books.

Richards, Gwendolyn. (2003, March 31) Accused Officers Apologize to Chief. *Vancouver Sun* online at Canada.com News, retrieved April 3, 2003 at: http://www.canada.com/search/story.aspx?id=6f1b77bf-b2be-4b4b-af4a-8534bab41a61

Rigakos, George S. (1995). Constructing the Symbolic Complainant: Police Subculture and the Nonenforcement of Protection Orders for Battered Women. *Violence and Victims*.10(3): 227-247.

Roberg, Roy & Jack Kuykendall. (1993). *Police and Society*. Belmont,CA: Wadsworth Publishing.

Roberg, Roy, John Crank, & Jack Kuykendall. (2000). *Police and Society* (2nd ed.). Los Angeles: Roxbury Publishing.

Ross, Jeffrey Ian. (2000). *Making News of Police Violence: A Comparative Study of Toronto and New York City* Westport, CT: Praeger Publishers.

Ross, Jeffrey Ian. (1996). Violence by Municipal Police in Canada: 1977-1992, Chapter 8. in Jeffrey Ian Ross (ed.) *Violence in Canada: Sociopolitical Perspectives.* Oxford: Oxford University Press.

Schein, E.H. (1984). Coming to a New Awareness of Organizational Culture. *Sloan Management Review* 25(2), Winter, 3-16.

Scott, Jan (1997). Performance Culture, The Return of Reactive Policing. *Policing and Society* 8: 269-288.

Seagrave, Jayne. (1995). *Changing the Organizational Culture:*

Community Policing in British Columbia. Unpublished
Doctoral Dissertation. Burnaby, B.C.: Simon Fraser
University.

Seagrave, Jayne. (1997). *Introduction to Policing in Canada.*
Scarborough: Prentice Hall.

Sewell, J.D. (1993). Traumatic Stress of Multiple Murder
Investigations. *Journal of Traumatic Stress* 6, 103-118.

Shearing, Clifford (Ed.). (1981). *Organizational Police Deviance:
Its Structure and Control.* Toronto: Butterworths.

Shearing, Clifford & Richard Ericson. (1991). Culture as
Figurative Action. *British Journal of Sociology* 42:481-
506.

Sheptycki, James W.E. (1998). The Global Cops Cometh
: Reflections on Transnationalization, Knowledge Work
and Policing Subculture. *British Journal of Sociology*
49(1): 57-74.

Shover, Neal & Andy Hochstetler. (2002). Cultural Explanation
and Organizational Crime. *Crime. Law & Social Change*
37: 1-18.

Skolnick, Jerome H. (2002). Corruption and the Blue Code of
Silence. *Police Practice and Research* 3(1): 7-19.

Skolnick, Jerome H. (1994). *Justice Without Trial: Law
Enforcement in a Democratic Society.* (3rd ed.). New York:
Macmillan.

Skolnick, Jerome H. (1966). *Justice Without Trial: Law
Enforcement in a Democratic Society.* New York: Wiley.

Skolnick, Jerome H. & James J. Fyfe. (1993). *Above the Law:
Police and the Excessive Use of Force.* New York: The
Free Press.

Special Investigations Unit (2002) "Toronto Police Officer
Charged, September 24, 2002" News Release online at:
http://www.siu.on.ca/siu_publications_documentation_deta
il.asp?id=156

Stansfield, Ronald T. (1996). *Issues in Policing: A Canadian
Perspective.* Toronto: Thompson Educational Publishing.

Statistics Canada (2002, December 20). Police Personnel and
Expenditures in Canada, 2002. The Daily online at:
http://www.statcan.ca/Daily/English/021220/d021220c.htm

Stearns, G.M. & R.J. Moore (1993). The Physical and

Psychological Correlates of Job Burnout in the Royal Canadian Mounted Police. *Canadian Journal of Criminology* 35:115-136.

Suriya, S.K. (1993). The Representation of Visible Minorities in Canadian Police: Employment Equity Beyond Rhetoric. *Police Studies* 16:44-62.

Sykes, Gresham M. & David Matza. (1957). Techniques of Neutralization: A Theory of Delinquency. *American Sociological Review* 22: 664-670.

Tanovich, David M. (2002a). Operation Pipeline and Racial Profiling. *Criminal Reports* (6th) 1:52-55.

Tanovich, David M. (2002b). Using the Charter to Stop Racial Profiling: The Development of an Equality Based Conception of Arbitrary Detention. *Osgoode Hall Law Journal* 40(2): 145-187.

Tepperman, Lorne & Michael Rosenberg. (1995). *Macro/Micro: A Brief Introduction to Sociology* (2nd ed.). Scarborough: Prentice Hall.

Toope, Stephen J. Fallout from '9-11': Will a Security Culture Undermine Human Rights? *Saskatchewan Law Review* 65: 281-298.

Van Mannen, John. (1999). The Asshole, Chapter 20. In Victor E. Kappeler, *The Police and Society.* Touchstone Readings (2nd ed.). Prospect Heights, IL: Waveland Press.

Van Mannen, John. (1997). Observations on the Making of Policemen, Chapter 5. In Robert G. Culbertson and Ralph A. Weisheit (Eds.), *Order Under Law: Readings in Criminal Justice.* Prospect Heights, Ill: Waveland Press.

Van Patten, Isaac T., & Tod W. Burke. (2001). Critical incident Stress and the Child Homicide Investigator. *Homicide Studies* 5(2):

Vincent, Claude. (1990). *Police Officer*. Ottawa: Carleton University Press.

Ware, Beverley. (2002a). Conditional Discharge for Officer: Cop faced assault on Woman, Firearm Charges. *The Daily News*, Canada.com News Thursday, October 24, 2002.

Ware, Beverley. (2002b). Trainor May Keep Police Job. *The Daily News*, Canada.com News, October 27, 2002.

Westley, William. (1953). Violence and the Police. *American*

Journal of Sociology 59: 34-41.

Wetmarland, Louise. (2001). Blowing the Whistle on Police Violence. *British Journal of Criminology* 41: 523-535.

Wilson, James Q. (1968). *Varieties of Police Behavior: The Management of Law and Order in Eight Communities* Cambridge, MA: Harvard University Press.

Cases Cited

R. v. Cooke (2002), 2 C.R. (6th) 35 (B.C.C.A.)

R. v. Ladouceur (2002), 165 C.C.C.(3d) 321 (Sask.C.A.)

R. v. Simpson (1993), 79 C.C.C. (3d) 482 (Ont.C.A.).

8

A Social-Psychological Model of Unethical and Unprofessional Police Behaviour*

*D.F. Sunahara***

Introduction

The following proposes a model of unethical and unprofessional police behaviour. This model differs from much of the existing literature on police ethics in several important ways. Most importantly, it is not prescriptive, i.e., it does not talk about the values that police officers should have. Rather, the emphasis is upon the processes that translate external conditions into attitudes, emotions, beliefs and values which in turn cause some officers to act unethically or unprofessionally.

The current model of unethical and unprofessional behaviour also differs in scope from much of the existing literature. Any discussion of ethics is a discussion of relationships. Understandably, given their public role, most discussions of police ethics focus on the relationship between the police and the public. These discussions have addressed such issues as the use of force, discretion, gratuities, conflict of interest, abuse of authority, wrongful convictions etc.. The current discussion takes a broader approach. It adopts the perspective that unethical actions, whether directed against the public or against colleagues and the organization can be understood best by treating them as instances of the same phenomenon. For example, the current discussion treats exploiting the public for private gain and exploiting the organization for private gain as the same. By expanding our understanding of whom, or what, may be the victim of unethical behaviour we are able to develop a more comprehensive and yet more parsimonious model of unethical and unprofessional police behaviour.

The current discussion differs from much of the literature on police ethics in a third way. The current discussion takes as given the wrongness of certain actions. It makes no attempt to provide a nuanced discussion of the moral philosophy that lies at the heart of most discussions of ethics. The goal here is to propose an explanatory model of unethical and unprofessional police behaviour that can be subjected to empirical verification. That is, the goal is to propose a causal, rather than a philosophical model.

Before proceeding, one additional clarification is in order. While much of the following will address behaviours that conventionally are described as ethical failings, it will also address behaviours that fall outside the realm of moral wrongdoing. Behaviours that are unprofessional, rather than strictly moral failings will also be addressed. Professionalism, or rather its absence, which Kleinig (1996:45) describes as a dedication to doing what one does out of a commitment to it, with a determination to do it to the best of one's ability . . also forms part of the subject matter of this report.

Unethical and Unprofessional Behaviour

This report argues that unethical and unprofessional behaviour is not a homogeneous set of acts sharing a common etiology. Rather, it begins with the premise that there are six different classes of unethical behaviour. And the report further argues that officers move along different paths to reach these undesirable end points. Unless we recognize the possibility of different development processes we are in danger of obscuring the possible policy levers that can be applied to prevent problems. The following section provides a brief description of the six classes of unethical and unprofessional behaviour under examination here.

Affective Acts

Affective acts are expressions of emotion. Not all such acts are unethical or unprofessional. Both acts of great villainy and acts of heroism and sacrifice can be driven by emotion. Those that cause unjustifiable injury form the content for the class behaviour under discussion here.

Perhaps one of the most frequently cited examples of this kind of behaviour is the overly aggressive behaviour exhibited during and following high speed pursuits. The adrenalin induced emotion brought on by such pursuits has caused officers to drive recklessly and physically and verbally assault the pursued driver. Affective acts need not, however, be directed against members of the public. They can include emotionally driven actions directed against the organization and colleagues. Many of the wrongful actions triggered by anger, fear and frustration fall into this category of behaviour.

Discriminatory Acts

Typically we think of discrimination in terms of ascribed characteristics such as race, ethnic origin, sex and religion. That is, we link the idea of discrimination to section 15 of the Canadian Charter of Rights and Freedoms. In the present context, however, discrimination captures a broader range of actions.

Discrimination is conceived of here as actions that flow from a negative assessment of a person's group characteristics. Both racism and the disrespectful treatment accorded by some officers to society's marginalized members are based on assessments of a person's group membership. For example, the flippant attitude displayed by some police officers to a poor or homeless person flows from their assessment of their victim's group membership. Like racism, it does not flow from any knowledge of that person as an individual. Examples of discriminatory behaviour include the presumption of guilt based on race, sexual harassment, biased human resource practices and the disrespectful treatment of the poor.

Noble Cause Corruption - The Problem of Dirty Hands

Noble cause corruption refers to police using unacceptable, but what they feel to be necessary methods, to achieve ends deemed beneficial to society[1]. Examples of this behaviour can include coercing confessions, using witnesses of dubious quality and incomplete or perjured testimony to ensure the conviction of a dangerous person. The release of information to publicize and thereby halt internal waste or wrongdoing, i.e., whistle blowing, also falls under the heading of noble cause corruption.

The current discussion departs from Klockars (1985) examination in that it makes no attempt to specify the conditions under which noble cause corruption can be justified. Rather, it takes as a given, the wrongness of the action. As was noted at the outset, the goal here is to present an explanatory model of unethical and unprofessional behaviour that can be subjected to empirical examination rather than a model that addresses the defensibility of a given act.

Self-interested Corruption

Much of the literature on police ethics conceptualizes self-interested corruption in more limited terms than the approach adopted here. Typically, the literature describes this form of corruption as (1) police officer using their positions to (2) realize personal gains, that are (3) material in nature and (4) entail a loss to a member of the public (Cohen 1986). For example, both the Mollen and Fitzgerald[2] inquiries into corruption in New York City and Queensland examined cases of police officers using their positions to extract bribes from members of the public. The current discussion adopts a more expansive definition. There are several crucial differences.

Much of the literature conceives of self-interested corruption as actions which deprive a member of the general public or the public as a whole of some material good. Thus there is an extensive literature that discusses such issues as conflict of interest, bribery, aggressive shopping, accepting gratuities and in some of the more egregious cases, stealing from the public. The current approach does not limit itself to this perspective. The essential quality of the action is not who is being exploited but the exploitation itself. Thus exploiting one's colleagues or the police organization itself is treated the same as exploiting a member of the public.

When a police officer demands a gratuity from a member of the public, there is the implied threat that the officer will misuse his or her peace officer authority to the detriment of that person should he or she refuse to comply. By expanding our understanding of self-interested corruption to cover the exploitation of colleagues or the organization, we adopt the perspective that there is no necessity that peace officer status be an enabling condition for the self-interested action.

In the present discussion, self-interested acts are not limited to acts that benefit the police officer who performs the action. The benefit may be realized by a group in which the police officer holds membership and the officer may be only an indirect beneficiary. This approach is more consistent with our understanding of conflict of interest. Public officials act improperly when they direct benefits to family, colleagues or friends.

The final difference between the current approach and the existing literature concerns the nature of the benefit being realized. The present discussion goes beyond the receipt of material benefits. That is, the benefits need not be reducible to money. Rather, the benefits may be nonmaterial. This expansion allows such practices as sexual exploitation and the code of silence to be considered equivalent to accepting a gratuity.

Failure to be Diligent

The behaviours that fall in this category do not entail actions that contravene broadly held moral values. An action may be unprofessional because the police officer fails to apply his or her skills with energy and care. Swope (1998:37) argues that mediocrity. . . (the) lack of commitment, laziness and excessive tolerance is a looming problem. A wide range of behaviours can fall under this heading, e.g., careless record keeping, tardiness, poor deportment, neglect of duty etc... A failure to be diligent presupposes the ability to perform the action. Police codes of conduct in Canada commonly include neglect of duty as a disciplinary issue.

One must be cautious when reproaching or assigning a moral weight to those who exhibit a lack of diligence for a failure to be diligent may simply reflect burnout. Pines makes the following observation in this regard:

> While the definitions of burnout vary, they all describe the end result of a process to which highly motivated and committed individuals lose their spirit. Individuals who enter a profession (e.g., nursing or counselling) with a cynical attitude are unlikely to burn out; but those with a strong desire to give of themselves and who feel helpful, excited, and idealistic are susceptible to the most severe burnout (1993: 386)

While the quote makes reference to nursing and counselling, a reference to policing would have been equally appropriate. While a failure to be diligent may be injurious to the public or organization, placing it in the realm of a moral failure may be problematic.

Lacking Technical Skills

An action may be unprofessional because the police officer lacks the technical skills to perform the task properly.

Exogenous Conditions

Exogenous conditions represent the givens in a model. That is, they are the parts of the model that are deemed causal and left unexplained. This does not imply that they cannot be explained but rather that the current exercise makes no attempt to do so. For example, in studies of educational achievement, the socioeconomic status of a student's parents is often treated as an exogenous variable. It is used to explain the child's school performance but the researcher does nothing to explain how socioeconomic status was achieved in the first place. Exogenous variables are the causes of the behaviour being examined by the model.

The following discussion presents five exogenous variables

for the proposed model of unethical and unprofessional behaviour. Each of them has received substantial attention in the literature so only a brief discussion is included for each of them.

Corrosive Street Experiences

Operational police work is characterized by the conflict inherent in attempting to control the behaviour of others. Oral and physical confrontations can be a staple of everyday life for a police officer. But negative street experiences are not limited to the direct dealings with members of the public. Policing, far more than most state activities, is subject to a degree of scrutiny and comment that most other government agencies would find unimaginable. Critical media and political scrutiny and hostile private observations are also part of everyday life for police.

It should also be emphasized here that the corrosive nature of police work goes beyond the actions of the public. Clearly, police officers are placed in positions where they must act in ways that they find, if not distasteful, at least not entirely to their liking. A regular diet of performing such acts can be as wearing as being the target of the public's hostility and disrespect.

Corrosive Experiences Inside the Organization

Living within any formal organization is never an unalloyed joy. The effects of complex rules, personalities, labour-management conflict and at times intrusive organizational practices range from the simply fatiguing to the stressful and offensive. Liberman et al. (2002), for example, observed that stressors coming from within police services correlated more strongly with post traumatic stress symptoms than did exposure to operational risks. Amongst the stressors originating inside the organization were problems such as relationships with colleagues and management and shift work. Amongst the operational stressors were exposure to serious violence, death and making decisions that harm innocent bystanders. Lee and Stoneham (1993) observed that, while operational events such as the use of lethal force were seen as the most stressful by RCMP officers, internal events such as excessive paper work, shift work and employee relations were far more common. Indeed, in their study they observed that none of the most stressful operational events registered amongst the 20 most frequently reported stressors. Whether policing is more prone to these forces is not the issue under discussion here. Rather, this model takes these forces as a given. Their presence in police organizations has been well documented.

Motivated Workforce

Perhaps one of policing's greatest strengths and ironically one of its greatest vulnerabilities is the motivation of those who become police officers. Those who choose policing as a career, more than most, value public service. They are motivated by the desire to do good, to contribute. Policing, from this perspective, can accurately be called a vocation. Crank argues that

> In the heart of every cop is a sense of morality, strong
> in some and weak in others, but always present. In
> spite of all the statistical chaff used as hiring criteria
> in the contemporary era, morality is the bottom line -
> if they lack it they will not be hired, they will resign,
> or they will be weeded out (1997:43).

While perhaps giving too much credence to the effectiveness of police discipline to weed out the undesirable, Crank does capture the generally strong moral underpinnings that bring new recruits into policing and that motivate them once employed.

Occupational Sub-culture

The occupational sub-culture of police is treated as an exogenous variable. But as will be discussed in a later section, it is not truly exogenous in that it is a function of one of the other variables discussed by the model. It is, however, treated in this way because our focus is on explaining its consequences rather than its origins.

The term sub-culture is used here in its formal sense. That is, it refers to a variation in the overarching culture of a society. There is no implication that sub-cultural differences are degenerate. Typically, members of a sub-cultural group have the same values as the larger society. How they differ is in the emphasis placed on one or more of the values shared by the larger society.

While not synonymous with the police sub-culture, loyalty represents one of its dominant features. Numerous inquiries and academics have examined the issue of loyalty in policing. Given the often value-laden debate that surrounds this issue, a brief digression is probably in order here.

Loyalty, as discussed here, is neither a virtue nor a vice. The value we assign it is essentially situational (Ewin 1993: 39). When the object to which loyalty is shown is valuable, then acting loyally is a virtue. But where loyalty is attached to an unvirtuous object, loyalty is a vice. The loyalty that causes a police officer to risk his or her life to save another police officer is virtuous because the life of that officer, like all human life, is valuable. The loyalty that underpins a cover-up is corrupt.

The previous paragraph argued that whether loyalty was a vice or virtue depends on the object of the loyalty. Loyalty in policing has two such objects. There is a closing of ranks when a police service or the institution of policing is under assault from external sources. That is, there is loyalty to the police community as a whole. There is also the loyalty that causes the rank and file to close ranks when one of their colleagues is under pressure from management. In this instance, the object of loyalty is more narrowly defined in terms of the rank structure.

Poor Human Resources Development

Much of the police ethics literature talks about police officers who knowingly engage in actions that are injurious to the public or the police organization. Malice or wilfulness does not lie at the heart of all the injuries done by police officers to the public or to their organizations. How an organization develops its staff also contributes to whether the public and the organization are well or ill-served.

Until recently, the generalist model held sway. That is, police focussed on a set of skills common to a broad range of operational roles and limited their human resource development to ensuring these core skills were developed. Given this focus, it is not surprising that the outcome too often has been skills that represent the lowest common denominator. Little attention was paid in either formal training or the development of career paths to nurture specialized skills. This holds true with respect to the development of operational and managerial skills.

The Model

To this point, the discussion has presented six classes of unethical or unprofessional behaviour and four exogenous or causal conditions. What remains to be done is to identify those processes that link the two sets of variables together. In the following section of this report, we examine how the causal variables lead to unethical and unprofessional behaviour.

The reasoning adopted in the development of this model is the one that has dominated most of the social psychological literature for the past century. It is also the reasoning that underpins most of our common sense notions of human behaviour. In this model, behaviour finds its roots in the environment. The environment's control over our behaviour, however, is mediated by psychological process internal to the person. An event in the environment stirs emotions, raises memories and beliefs and elicits attitudes and values. These internal psychological changes, in turn, shape our behaviour.

The Effects of Corrosive Street Experiences

The Police Subculture

Street experiences affect both individual police officers and police officers as a group. Its effect on the group is to shape an occupational subculture that values loyalty (Hunt and Magenau 1993:74-75). And this should not be surprising nor should it be automatically condemned. A culture of loyalty is an inevitable consequence of working in any environment such as policing, nursing, team sports or the military that depends upon solidarity for success and security. Because of the environment and role of police, loyalty emerges both as an instrumental cultural trait and a trait that can undermine ethical standards.

Emotion

At the level of the individual, perhaps one of the most obvious consequences of operational police work is emotion. The dangers, cruelties and stupidities routinely encountered by police officers naturally give rise to heightened emotions. While situationally specific, anger, fear and frustration are the natural outcomes of police work. And these emotions, if not managed, can lead to affective behaviours that breach the normative standards of democratic policing.

Stereotyping

Corrosive street experience is almost synonymous with frequent and often unpleasant contact with society's marginalized members. Bouza provides a colourful description of some members of the American underclass.

> City streets became dotted with bag ladies, bearded wanderers with backpacks, disoriented spirits mumbling to themselves, and newly impoverished women and their children. Many stood lone vigils, with cups extended, begging coins. At night they emerged, zombie like, to wander the dark streets (Bouza 1990:223)

The picture differs only by degree from the urban core of many Canadian cities. Membership in the groups described by Bouza, and indeed membership in most social groups, comes with visible markers. Markers, such as the shopping cart loaded with the detritus of the streets and an unkempt appearance are sufficient to identify a bag lady's group membership. Markers of race, i.e., facial features, skin and hair colour, markers of economic status such as residence or neighbourhood, clothes and vehicle, lifestyle markers, language etc. identify group membership.

Operational police work generates a disproportionate number

of calls for service involving society's marginalized members. From this differential exposure, police officers can begin to develop stereotypes where the outward markers of group membership, such as the dishevelled condition of the homeless, begin to control the behaviour of officers. That is, police begin to respond to the outward signs of group membership rather than to the actual behaviour of the person in question. Mastrofski et al. (2002:540), for example, observed that police were more likely to be disrespectful to people they encounter in impoverished neighbourhoods than in wealthier settings.   In such situations, the citizen need not do anything untoward to become the object of the police officer's attention. And should this attention turn into more intrusive behaviours, we would describe the officer's behaviour as discriminatory. The issue with respect to stereotyping is that the control these visible markers exert over the behaviour of police is independent of the actual conduct of the person.

Returning again to Bouza.

> Cops make shorthand judgements, based on myths and realities. They stereotype because it speeds up their processes. They react on the basis of their expectations and, although no one is going to say this publicly, their expectations are that blacks are more likely to be wrong than whites. This accounts for why so many blacks get pulled over. The odds are better for getting someone who has an outstanding warrant or obtaining evidence of a crime (1990:252)

This differential treatment is not limited to the United States. The United Kingdom's Police Complaints Authority reports that

> Black people are five times more likely than white people to be checked under these powers. Just under 2 per cent of the population is black and yet they comprise 11 per cent of those stopped and searched. Asians represent 3 per cent of the population but made up 5 per cent of those stopped last year. (Police Complaints Authority 2002)

The inclination to view and treat the marginalized members of society differently from others is also evident when we examine cases of wrongful conviction in Canada. In the most widely publicized cases: Donald Marshall Jr., Guy Paul Morin, David Milgaard and Thomas Sophonow,[3] all the accused were marginal members of society. And in each case, police pursued their investigations with the *a priori* belief that these men were guilty. Various inquiries into the relationship between police in Canada and the aboriginal community have come to similar conclusions. The current controversy over racial profiling that has recently moved to Canada is an expression of concern over the control that visible markers can exert over police behaviour.

What is important to emphasize here is that the development of stereotypes, while neither inevitable nor desirable, is natural. It is a psychological process that helps us all to make sense of and to deal with a complex environment. That being said, when actual behaviour falls under the control of these stereotypes, then discrimination replaces the equitable treatment that is every society member's right.

A Sense of Entitlement

By a sense of entitlement we mean the feeling that we have a rightful claim to something. Like loyalty, a sense of entitlement is neither inherently good nor bad. Whether it is a vice or virtue depends on what the person feels entitled to. It is legitimate for everyone to feel they have a rightful claim to equal treatment before and under the law. Entitlement in this context is good because equal treatment is a widely held moral value. A sense of entitlement becomes degenerate when the object of one's sense does not have this moral standing. For example, the right to own a luxury car and live in a lavish home is not a widely held moral value. Similarly, being able to break traffic laws with impunity is not a widely held moral value. Consequently, feeling entitled to these objects is unvirtuous.

When a person is victimized, it is natural for that person to feel entitled to some form of compensation. An eye-for-an-eye, our notions of equity and justice, the norm of reciprocity all speak to this issue. In the words of Pynoos et al.

> A victim is sanctioned to assume a social role that warrants restitution and/or special treatment and to expect society to bring the perpetrator to judicial accountability (1993: 573).

This connection between victimization and a sense of entitlement was explored by Gilmartin and Harris (1998). These authors observe that police officers routinely are on the receiving end of verbal abuse and physical assault and this can translate into a sense of entitlement. Gilmartin (2002) characterizes this sense of entitlement in the following way you owe us cops for all we have to put up with on the street to serve and protect you. That is, police officer can begin to feel they are entitled to something more because they must work in a corrosive street environment.

This sense of victimization finds concrete expression in the Canadian Police Association website. It opens with the following quote from Victor Hugo's novel, *Les Miserable*.

> A . . . society closes its doors, without pity, on two classes of men, those who attack it and those who guard it.

The use of this quote from Victor Hugo by the Canadian Police Association aptly captures the sense of victimization felt by many police officers.

The question that Gilmartin's characterization raises is what do police officers feel entitled to? The literature reveals many answers. Some officers feel entitled to material benefits while other officers have extracted sexual favours and yet other officers manifest their sense of entitlement by demanding deference. What is common to all of these is that a sense of entitlement is a precursor to the pursuit of self-interest.

It's important, when trying to understand the concept of entitlement, to recognize that, from the claimant's perspective, the rightfulness of the claim is not in question. This belief in the non-negotiability of the claim has important implications when a claim is thwarted.

Of particular relevance to this issue are two areas of research.

The first is the literature that examines the relationship between demeanour and police behaviour. This research suggests that the expectation of a deferential demeanour plays an important role in shaping police behaviour.[4] Worden and Shepard (1996) observed that a person who was disrespectful to police, i.e., who violated an officer's expectation of deference, was more likely to be arrested than a person who was respectful. This relationship held true regardless of the legal quality of the person's actions. The related and clearly parallel line of investigation is the research that has examined the relationship between frustration and aggression. This literature is the more general and provides an explanation for the observed relationship between demeanour and police behaviour.

Part of a literature that extends back over 70 years, the research on the frustration-aggression hypothesis has observed that the frustration of a goal can lead to an increase in aggressive behaviour. Tying together these two bodies of research, if we assume that deference is an important goal for police then it follows that police officers will experience the lack of deference or a disrespectful demeanour as frustrating and that this frustration can lead to more aggressive behaviour. In such situations, aggression can be instrumental for it enforces a deferential demeanour.

Alienation

Alienation is a multidimensional phenomenon. The dimensions of greatest relevance to the current discussion are mistrust and hopelessness. The mistrustful person constantly searches for ulterior motives, conspiracies and ambushes and their absence is merely proof that the enemy is clever. This mistrust is not the same as the prudent wariness that every police officer must possess. It is a debilitating and bleak world view that causes the police officer to engage the world with extreme and unfounded pessimism.

The second relevant dimension of alienation is hopelessness. Hopelessness, as the term suggests, is the sense that there is no light at the end of the tunnel and, indeed if there is such a light, that it will soon be extinguished. The future is bleak and any effort to improve the situation is pointless. The world is in a downward spiral.

The connection between alienation and the police experience

is made clear by the following quote from Graves (1996) when he describes police cynicism.

> (Police) Cynicism is an attitude of contemptuous distrust of human nature and motives. A cynic expects nothing but the worst in human behaviour. (Graves 1996)

The roots of police alienation are clear. Repeated exposure to the corrosive world of the street with its attendant cruelties and stupidities and a social world of like minded police officers destroys the positive motives that bring recruits into policing and leaves him or her debilitated. Reinforcing this sense is the insider knowledge and rumour that often circulates amongst police officers. Where the average person sees only surface reputations, the police officer is often privy to information about others that paints a more sinister picture. Rather than the respected business man, the police officer sees an alleged arsonist or wife beater and rather than the upright politician, they see a man known to the police. This private knowledge shapes a belief that nothing is as it seems to be and that respectability may only be a mask for deceit. The world comes to be seen as a hostile and degenerate place populated by the unworthy.

Little of value can come from this alienated world view. Alienation brings with it its own justification. If the world is corrupt, then why should the police officer be the only one not benefiting from the material, sexual and self-serving opportunities the world has to offer? If the world is corrupt, then the police officer has little reason to believe in the efficacy of the criminal justice system and therefore must obey rules of his or her own making to ensure justice is done. The pursuit of noble causes divorced from adherence to procedural justice becomes the rule. And if the world is hopeless why should the police officer waste his or her energies and talents trying to do good? Mediocrity and outright neglect become the officer's guiding principles. In short, the alienated officer is ripe for self-interested corruption, noble cause corruption and the failure to be diligent.

Corrosive Experiences inside the Organization

While the world of the street may appear degenerate and corrupting, life inside the police organization can also be a world of insults and injuries. Prunckun describes the problem this way:

> I identified eighteen separate stress theme. . . . I'll quote you the five most frequently cited cases by the police officers I interviewed. The first and most common was, Anger and a sense of betrayal with management practices and administrative policies that cause unnecessary distress . . . (1991:13)

Prunckun is not the only author to identify problems within the police service as an important cause of distress. Liberman et al. (2002) discussed briefly earlier drew similar conclusions. Some have interpreted these internal conflicts as amounting to a class struggle that pits the rank and file against management. The theme of this body of research is clear. There is substantial conflict within police organizations and rank and file police officers often feel they have been betrayed by management.

Emotion

The consequences of corrosive experiences internal to the organization run parallel to the consequence of corrosive operational police work. They are emotion, a sense of entitlement and alienation. There are, however, some differences.
Shernock argues

> . . . police officers who are frustrated and resentful over the lack of respect shown to them by police supervisors and administrators and over the inflexible hierarchical structure of the police department may compensate by acting overly authoritarian in the community where it is safer to express themselves without the consequences of being insubordinate to higher-ranking officers (1990:28).

So in addition to their anger and frustration manifesting themselves in affective acts directed against the organization and colleagues, some is displaced outward to victimize the public.

The affective acts caused by conditions internal to a police service can take various forms. The filing of frivolous grievances and complaints, the undermining of management controls and the ongoing criticism and conjecture over management's motives and virtue typify the affective acts routinely seen and heard in police services.

Entitlement

The feeling of being victimized, whether on the street or by the organization, can lead officers to feel they deserve something better; that they should be compensated for the insults done to them. This sense that they deserve compensation can translate into various forms of self-interested corruption. Officers may manipulate expense or overtime claims, close ranks to prevent management from disciplining a colleague or use public resources for private benefit.

Alienation

Caution must be taken when identifying the object of an officer's sense of alienation. It is probably common for officers to remain loyal and attached to others of their own rank or immediate work group while becoming estranged from the management and rules of their police service. Under these circumstances, any sense of moral obligation to obey management or the rules it makes disappears. This breakdown in respect and credibility has the potential to be very disruptive. Like the alienation that flows from negative street experiences, the alienation caused by negative internal experiences can lead to the same kinds of the unethical and unprofessional behaviour, i.e., self-interested corruption, noble cause corruption and a failure to be diligent.

But the alienation from management brings with it special problems. Various enquiries and academic research into police wrongdoing have pointed out the inability or unwillingness of police to correct the unethical behaviour of another officer. In such situations, the bonds of loyalty both prevent officers from reporting bad behaviour and taking action to stop the behaviour personally.

Given this general reluctance, management's responsibility to create policy and programs to prevent or correct ethical problems is particularly critical. Unfortunately, the problem that management must correct contains its own obstacles to a solution. When a gulf exists between management and labour, management's ability to cause change to happen is badly diminished. In studying the effectiveness of communications to cause changes in beliefs and attitudes, psychologists have consistently pointed out that the effectiveness of communications is, in part, a function of the communicator's credibility. To the alienated officer, management is not credible and any new ethics initiative is likely to be greeted with cynicism. The alienated officer is prone to look behind such initiatives in search of hidden and nefarious management motives or mentally discard them as another instance of hypocritical political correctness.

Motivated Workforce

Police officers carry with them the desire and intention to do good. And day to day, these good intentions become concrete in the officer's performance. Typically, people expect their good deeds to be rewarded. That is, when we do good, we feel entitled to some recognition. But this is often not the experience of police officers. The very nature of police work virtually guarantees that an officer will be rebuffed, castigated or orally or physically assaulted for doing his or her duty. To compensate for these rebuffs, some officers may take it upon themselves to generate their own rewards. That is, they may engage in self-interested corruption.

A criminal justice environment that many officers deem to be overly protective of individual rights, where the penal system is derisively described as "Club Fed" and where many members of the public are contemptuous of the police's efforts can leave officers frustrated with the system of which they are a part. This frustration in combination with the desire to do good can turn high ideals into a degenerate form of justice. Officers may step outside the criminal justice system from which they have become alienated and mete out justice according to their own standards. They may begin to turn their noble motivations into ignoble deeds. The presumed nobility of their cause becomes sufficient justification for their disregarding the tenets of procedural justice. From the police officer's view point, justice becomes whatever the officer choses to do.

Occupational Sub-culture

Given the nature of police work, it is not surprising that the police occupational sub-culture causes police officers to become estranged from the larger society and to seek security within the narrow confines of the police community. This small world is one of the few refuges available. Unfortunately, how this security manifests itself can be corrupt for the self-interested protection of other officers can begin to take precedence over obligations to the general public and police organization. Numerous inquiries and studies have clearly demonstrated the degenerate effect of misplaced loyalty; how it transforms into an alienated world view and how it causes officers to subordinate their duties to their self-interest.

Poor Human Resources Development

Police work amounts to little more than the labour of police officers. Therefore the quality of police work is virtually synonymous with the quality of the labour force, its knowledge, skills, motivation, diligence etc.. Where the labour force has been well developed, the public and police organization are well-served. To the extent that this is not the case, the public and organization can suffer injury. The organization plays a critical role in ensuring that the labour force is skilful, motivated, well supervised, etc.. Should the organization fail in its responsibility to develop its labour force, it can expect that its services will periodically fall below professional standards and the public will be ill-served.

Summary and Discussion

If we are to understand the causes of unethical and unprofessional police behaviour, we cannot limit our inquiry to questions of character. For in Canada, we have probably been as fortunate as any nation in attracting those who value public service. We must look to the day to day experiences of police officers to understand why some diverge from the ethical and professional. Clearly, the two most dominant influences on the behaviour of police officers are the treatment accorded them as police officers and as employees. And research suggests that both sides of an officer's life may be corrosive.

Operational police work brings negative emotions to the fore. Frustration, anger and fear are part of every officer's street experience. For some officers, these emotions are left unchecked and drive behaviours that are overly aggressive, disrespectful or abusive. And the police organization, rather than being a refuge from the injuries of the street, can contribute its own indignities.

It is also every officer's fate to come into routine contact with those who are criminal, injured or who simply cannot control their own behaviour. And given the social hierarchies that exist in Canada, inevitably certain socially identifiable groups will figure more prominently in an officer's experience. The danger of this differential exposure is the creation of stereotypes that can cause officers to respond to the image rather than the substance of a person's behaviour.

The notion of fairness and equity pervades our thinking. When a person injures another, the Judeo-Christian rule of an eye for eye demands retribution. In the same way, when one is injured, we expect compensation. We feel entitled to sympathy, support and even material recompense for the damage done us. The roots of this sense of entitlement, however, extend beyond the experience of being victimized. They also can be traced to misplaced pride. The elitism that comes with being a member of a special group that has been set apart to perform onerous duties also contributes. The critical problem with this sense of entitlement is that its frustration will cause some to ensure personally that the debts owed them are paid in full. This pursuit of narrow self-interest, while problematic in all walks of life is particularly problematic for public office holders such as police.

Much has been written about the alienation of police officers. And alienation, whether treated as a rationale, political comment or as a psychological defence mechanism to protect the police officer from further injury, remains a pivotal issue. It is central in that it links the environment to much of unethical or unprofessional police behaviour. It is part of a world view that both helps to trigger and rationalize unethical and unprofessional behaviour.

Endnotes

*Reprinted, with D.F.Sunahara's permission, from
http://www.cpc.gc.ca/research/pbehav_e.htm
**The views expressed in this paper are those of the author and do not necessarily represent those of the Canadian Police College, the Royal Canadian Mounted Police or any government department or agency.

1   Those who engage in noble cause corruption can be seen as falling into the philosophical tradition of consequentialism. That is, they view the Rightness of their actions to be a function of whether their outcomes are good or bad. Those who diligently pursue due process fall into the nonconsequentialist camp for they are concerned with the propriety of the process and not the outcome. For a discussion of this issue, see Catlin and Maupin (2002).

2   New York Commission to Investigate Allegations of Police Corruption and the Anti-Corruption Procedures of the Police Department, Queensland Criminal Justice Commission.

3   Donald Marshall Jr. was a poor Mi'kmaq youth from Cape Breton Island. Guy Paul Morin was a working class neighbour of the victim whose peculiar behaviour, possibly the result of his being a schizophrenic, caused police to target him. Both David Milgaard and Thomas Sophonow were transients.

4   Formal police training and the folk lessons taught by one generation of police officers to the next emphasize the importance of officers taking control. Obedience, or a respectful demeanour marks how successful a police officer has been at doing so. A disrespectful manner challenges the officer's authority and is clear evidence that he has not achieved his objective.

References

Bouza, Anthony V.1990. *The Police Mystique*. New York: Plenum Press.

Canadian Police Association. 2002. *Canadian Police Association* [Online]. [cited September 11, 2002] Available from Internet: <URL:HTTP//www.cpa-acp.ca/>

Catlin, Dennis W. and James R. Maupin. 2002 Ethical orientations of state police recruits and one-year experienced officers. *Journal of Criminal Justice*. Vol. 30 (2002): p.491-498.

Cohen, Howard. 1986. Exploiting police authority. *Criminal Justice Ethics*, Vol. 5, 2 (Summer/Fall 1986): p. 23-31.

Crank, John P. 1998. *Understanding Police Culture*. Cincinnati, Ohio: Anderson Publishing Company.

Graves, Wallace. 1996. *Police Cynicism: Causes and Cures* [Online] [cited June 2, 2002]. Available from Internet: <URL:HTTP//www.fbi.gov/publications/leb/1996/june964.txt

Gilmartin, Kevin M.2002. *Ethics-Based Policing. Undoing Entitlement* [Online]. [cited August 20, 2002] Available from the Internet: <URL:HTTP://www.gilmartinharris.com/ entitlement.htm. >

Gilmartin Kevin M. and John J. Harris.1998. The law enforcement Ethics...the continuum of compromise. *The Police Chief Magazine*, January 1998: p. 25-28.

Hunt, Raymond G. and John M. Magenau.1993.*Power and the Police Chief*. Newbury Park, CA:Sage Publications Inc.

Lee, Daniel, C. and Brenda G. Stoneham. 1993. *Survey of Work Stress*. Ottawa: Health Services Directorate, Royal Canadian Mounted Police.

Kleinig, John. 1996. *The Ethics of Policing*. Cambridge: Cambridge University Press.

Klockars, Carl B. 1985. The dirty harry problem. In *Moral Issues in Police Work*. Edited by Elliston, Frederick A. and Michael Feldberg. Totowa, New Jersey: Rowan & Allanheld Publishers: p. 55-75.

Liberman, Akiva M.et al.2002. Routine occupational stress and psychological distress in police. *Policing: An International*

Journal of Police Strategies & Management, Vol. 25, 2: p. 421-439.

Mastrofski, Stephen D. et al. 2002. Police disrespect toward the public: an encounter-based analysis. *Criminology*, Vol. 40, 3 (August 2002): p.519-551.

New York Commission to Investigate Allegations of Police Corruption and the Anti-Corruption Procedures of the Police Department. 1994. *Commission Report: Anatomy of a Failure: A Path for Success.* New York: City of New York.

Pines, Ayala M. 1993. Burnout. In *Handbook of Stress Second Edition.* Edited by Leo Goldberger and Shlomo Breznitz. New York: The Free Press: p. 386-402.

Police Complaints Authority. 2002. *Race Relations and Racism.* [online] [cited October 16, 2002]. Available from Internet: <URL:HTTP://www.pca.gov.uk/investig/racerel.htm >

Pynoos, Robert S. et al. 1993. Interpersonal violence and traumatic stress reaction. In *Handbook of Stress Second Edition.* Edited by Leo Goldberger and Shlomo Breznitz. New York: The Free Press: p. 573-590.

Queensland Criminal Justice Commission.1997.*Integrity in the Queensland Police Service.* Brisbane: Criminal Justice Commission.

Shernock, Stan K. 1990. The effects of patrol officers' defensiveness towards the outside world on their ethical orientation. *Criminal Justice Ethics*, Vol. 9, 2 (Summer/Fall 1990): p.24-42.

Swope, Ross E.1998. The core-virtue bell curve. *The Police Chief Magazine,* January 1998: p. 37-38.

Worden, Robert E. and Robin L. Shepard. 1996. Demeanor, Crime, and Police Behaviour: A Re-examination of the Police Services Study Data. *Criminology*, Vol. 34, 1: p. 83-105.

9

Policing and Information Technology in Canada

Marcel-Eugène LeBeuf*

Introduction

Information technology (IT) has entered the field of policing and law enforcement as it has for many other sectors in society. But only recently has IT started to become integrated in law enforcement. As a result, Canadian police today are facing a number of major changes resulting not only from the integration of IT tools but also from the incredible drive toward globalization and from the constraints stemming from the standardization of work tools, procedures, and methods in general. These changes reflect an inescapable and irreversible trend toward a new model for public law enforcement. The police have seen the gradual end of one period where, for many years, they had full control over their field of action, to a period, which is not transitory, where three new factors are to be observed simultaneously: technology-based criminal activity that has none of the characteristics of traditional crime; new high-performance working tools that require very specialized training for their use; and a stronger articulation by the public at large as to the role they wish the police to play within their environment.

At the same time profound changes have happened since the tragic events of September 2001 in the field of security. They highlight among other things, the complexities of the globalization process, and the role of risk in security (national security, national infrastructure, organized crime). IT tools are currently used in offices or in the field.

The very expression "information technology[1]" is ambiguous, general and yet restrictive. The term is used to designate a variety of more or less complex gadgets, machines and software which, as Nogala (1993) put it, have each their own specific development, use and impact. The term "information technology" leads us to ask the following question: How does the integration of such technology change the role and task of the police?

This paper provides a summary of the various issues and problems related to the introduction, integration and use of information technology within public security. It also evaluates the issues related to the cost, impact and accountability process. It takes into account the upsurge in a new type of criminal activity that makes use of technology and that has abandoned traditional means of the past.

Information Technology and Society

The evolution and penetration of information technology in society[2] and within organizations, including governments, is proceeding at a fast pace. Information technology also gives rise to a new work culture[3] characterized by a wider and more open flow of ideas, by the use of innovative work methods, such as e-mail[4] and by temporary one-time alliances for specific tasks. Similar networks are being created by criminal organizations.

In Canada, a two-pronged initiative by the federal government warrants special attention. The first prong, called the Government On-Line initiative is aimed at increasing electronic transactions[5] between the government and the community and developing the legislative tools required for large-scale electronic commerce. The second prong focuses on reinforcing user confidence, improving the electronic commerce information infrastructure, and optimizing its benefits. The goal was to capture a 5% share of the world electronic commerce by 2003 (Canada, 2000). To this end, the Government passed the *Privacy Act* (C-6) as of January 2001, which legally recognizes electronic signatures. In this, Canada is following the example of the United States, the European Union, and several European countries (Murray, Vick, Wortley, 1999).

The emergence of information technology gives rise to new threats relating to security and human activities. The destruction of technological infrastructures is still a real threat and is taken very seriously. To that effect, the Office of Critical Information Protection and Emergency Preparedness (OCIPEP[6]) was created by the Prime Minister in February of 2001. It constitutes the federal lead department responsible for co-coordinating a federal response to cyber and physical threats or incidents. There is also the Communications Security Establishment (CSE) which ensures the protection of Government of Canada electronic information and information infrastructures[7].

The criminal environment is also changing. After a major investigation on telemarketing involving 951 individuals, the FBI confiscated 92 computers but only three firearms (Robertson, 1999). As noted by Boni and Kovacich in 1999, crimes are facilitated by the criminals' familiarity with the new technology and the information superhighway. The tools required to commit crimes are readily available. Microchips, nanotechnology (Drolet, Moen, 2000; Rees, 2000), and wireless are all used by the public. What was considered futuristic a few years back is now commonplace.

Information warfare is a real threat and includes money laundering, gaming, all forms of extortion including credit cards or the use of computers to falsify data, economic crimes, MIS sabotage, computer hacking, spying and other activities by groups linked to organized crime (Coutorie, 1995; Dobeck, 1997; Carter, Katz, 1998). Committing such crimes does not depend on geographical proximity. Real crime and real issues are to be found in a new virtual universe which is now well established (Rosé,

1996). The new connections are horizontal and invisible (Marx, 1997). The winner of this universe will be the one holding the joystick.

The growth in Internet has been rapid, jumping from 19% in January 1996 to 60% in January 2000 in Canada. Among the G7, Canada is the number one of Internet use (RCMP, 2002). This is a dramatic increase (Ekos Research Associates, 2000). The Internet gives Canadians great potential for legal use and for illegal use. Electronic transfers of funds are fast and unsupervised (Alexander, Munro, 1996), and because of the large number of them, they provide an easy avenue for money laundering. The Internet provides users with a certain level of anonymity through, among other things, encryption (FBI, 1999) and other software (Scientific American, 2000). It is a kind of buffer that reduces and delays the likelihood of getting intercepted because the evidence is non-physical and can be easily eliminated (Robertson, 1999; Sullivan, 1999). Furthermore, time and space are irrelevant. Today, it is still relatively difficult to highlight criminal activity on the Internet. Crimes may not be reported. Brenner (2003) asserts that law enforcement agencies still do not know how to receive and compile complaints about crimes involving information technology.

Cybercrime[8] or e-crime (as Etter would say, 2001) affects law enforcement, business communities and society in general (Livanos Cattaui, 1999). Currently, cybercrime is viewed in two ways by the law enforcement community. A computer is involved in a crime (for example could be the target of a crime), or is associated with the crime (for example a crime could be committed with the assistance of computers). These two approaches are somewhat contradictory. On the one hand, some feel that computer crime as a concept is nothing new. The only novelty is the use of the new and sophisticated tool. On the other hand, others believe that cybercrime represents a new form of criminal activity because it is perpetrated in a new environment. Hacking, for example is essentially due to a huge increase in the number of computer users. Stealing hardware is also a crime. According to estimates, losses from hardware theft reached US$34.7 million between October 1997 and June 1998 (Dertouzos et al., 1999). As police see the rising concern about IT crime, they are faced with the immediate demands from IT crime victims and demands from citizens for order and security in their living environments.

Information Technology and the Police

The interaction between the police and technology is complex. It concerns both power and information. With respect to power, information technology promotes actions and secures results that were previously impossible to achieve; although police operations are improved, performance is not necessarily improved (Manning, 1992). In fact, as police work is ecologically scattered (to use Manning's (1992) expression), its sought-after effectiveness depends on a number of factors including the organizational culture of the various groups of workers, the type of information that is stored and the methods of doing so. It depends also on the capacity to plan IT integration in police organization and to control IT usage. Without such planning and integration, police use of IT tools may fall short of the potential.

Moreover, the public image of the police and their impact on society are significantly enhanced. For example, the Web pages published by police departments constitute an innovative exercise in public relations which allows them to inform the public of crime prevention activities in their locality, supply statistics on the level of criminality and provide information about missing persons (Eisenberg, Porter, 2001; Strandberg, 1998; Haley, Taylor, 1998; Goodman, 1997; Wilsker, 1997; Corsentino, Pettinari, 1996).

With respect to information that police have gathered, Ericson and Haggerty (1997) assert that technology allows the police to remain a symbol of authority within communities. This is because access to data banks and other computerized data provides them with more information than ever in the past, allowing them to develop more effective strategies for combating both traditional and high-tech crime (McLean-Lipinski, 1999).

If law enforcement agencies hope to outsmart criminals, they will need to adopt the best technological tools available on the market (Campbell, 1997). Moreover, the challenge is not so much to adopt information technology as to adapt information technology that can systematically be helpful to the police in dealing with these new problems and issues.

Integration of the Technologies into the Police Environment

Technology has been part of the police environment for more than 150 years (Soullière, 1999). It has changed police mobility (from the horses to the patrol car laboratories), the processing of information (data gathering, fingerprints, etc), the focus on training capacity and the analytical components (data base, networks, etc.). However, to date it would seem that, as a whole, this technology has been used in a transient and sporadic manner in a number of police departments across Canada because of lack of strategic planning exercise and lack of national coordination. In that sense one can argue that policing remain largely unchanged (Manning, 2000).

At one time, the premise for equipping the police with new technologies was that new technologies put a fresh face on the services offered in order to meet the needs of the taxpayer (Audet et al., 1996). It was hoped that IT could contribute to transforming police departments into organizations that would truly serve their citizens, a community police force, as it were. To meet client needs, policing organizations have set up intelligence structures allowing them to intervene rapidly, effectively and autonomously in their local neighbourhoods. Currently, a number of police departments are equipped with technology such as the AFIS (Automated Fingerprint Identification System) for fingerprinting, or the GPS[9] (global positioning system) for communications, or even mobile data computers. But, as of today we still need to construct a more detailed chart of the situation of the police forces on a country-wide basis.

It is relatively difficult to chart the current use of technologies by the police. A survey done in 2000 in Canada with police departments (328 questionnaires) was an attempt to determine which technological tools were used most frequently by Canadian police services (LeBeuf et. al., 2000a). Excluded from the survey were management software and the new biometric technology. Police departments indicated whether they had a list of IT tools, what use they made of the tools, what plans they had over the next two years for the tools and what type of training was provided to use the tools. The survey showed that police use of technology is advancing quickly. In general, knowledge is fragmented and related to the field it is designed to improve (such as, for example, fingerprints). We concluded that police have become dependent on IT, just like criminals and businesses. The costs inherent in the purchase and use of technology are not yet well known for public services. More or less all police services use some IT for operations. There was also general request to get more information about the available tools, standards and best practices[10].

The proliferation of IT tools occurs far more quickly than decision-making in public-sector police departments. In order to deal effectively with the IT market, the police must determine both their own needs and those of the community they serve in order to make an informed choice of the most appropriate technological tool. Decision makers do not always have the skills required to make the necessary decisions since, in many cases, they deal with a number of overlapping elements: the technology as such, the link between technology and traditional work, and the ability to fully exploit this technology. During one research project, we visited a certain number of police departments. On one occasion, a police officer demonstrated the crime-mapping system. At some point, the police officer admitted that he had taken more than eight months to learn how to handle the software. With good training, his learning curve could have been much shorter.

This example shows that technological tools can be very effective if they have been developed specifically for the police or in cooperation with the police. The performance of these tools would appear to be a relative matter since the amount of extra information obtained through the use of the software will depend on whether or not the user is capable of fully exploiting its potential. The performance of any apparatus will vary according to the way in which the user exploits it. However, one should not forget that all software has built-in restrictions which come into play when it is integrated into a larger technological whole.

The private security market, which is innovative and

primarily concerned with the protection of property, has developed and uses tools that are often well ahead of any system that public security organizations can afford. It won't be long now, certainly not a question of decades, before the major areas of protection, whether of places, property or persons, will be ensured not by human beings, but by robots, satellites, nanotechnology and micro-engineering (Moore, 1995; Akrich, Méadel, 1993). Moore (1995:2) describes security zones that can now be protected by invisible movement-sensitive light rays or by laser or pulsars. Robotics has also an exceptional role to play in laboratories, thanks to the delicate handling operations which it allows when, for example, extracting chemical compounds (Johnson, 1997). Biometrics, a technology which brings together finger prints, palm prints, specific features of the face, and readings of the retina or the iris, will constitute the future identification system. In the same way, DNA (deoxyribonucleic acid) identification will become commonplace. Indeed, the Canadian Parliament has adopted the *DNA Identification Act* which authorizes the setting up of a DNA data bank for genetic identification of persons convicted of serious crimes. Closer to us are the CCTV (closer circuit television) systems used in private and public spaces. They allow electronic surveillance at distance from the object or contact observed. It is said that CCTV is most effective in reducing property crime. The development and introduction of video surveillance is no longer exclusive to private security firms, but has become a working tool for public security services as well (Ocqueteau, Pottier, 1993; Deisman, 2003).

According to recent estimates, one million CCTV systems are installed in Great Britain (Crawford, Lister, 2003). CCTV systems have become a control tool as well as a property security tool, giving police a permanent watch on citizens (Foucault, 1977). Public police departments are not the only ones exerting a permanent watch on the citizens. They collaborate with other experts, vendors or manufacturers, who may assure the quality of the system's usage[11].

Technology Users within a Police Department

There are as many technology users in a police department as there are tasks to be accomplished. It is not the same person who uses a crime-mapping system or a mobile data computer. In the first case, analysts with access to crime-mapping software obtain as much information as possible for the benefit of investigators and of patrol officers. But investigators and patrol officers themselves do not have either direct or even limited access to this tool. In the second case, however, the patrol officers deal with the information directly in their patrol car. They access the material that allows them to work better and more simply, often by getting rid of all the paper work.

Without losing too much of the actual complexity, we can classify users into four main types: executives, investigators, patrol officers and partners.

Police executives are facing declining financial and human resources. They seek technology gains to gain efficiency in operations (Morrison, 1996). But executives trained in a pre-technological environment (Rodriguez, 1995) have to articulate their needs using their own understanding of technological tools, by taking a technological standpoint that corresponds to the strategic and corporate vision of their organization. They need to create flexible organizational structures to manage both the work and the individuals, to encourage horizontal cooperation between the units and, most of all, to understand and control a decision-making process based on skills and not on rank (Martin, 1996).

The officer investigating organized crime or computer crime is now required to understand and use new tools. Search warrants in hand, they are more likely to confiscate PCs and hard drives than ledgers or paper documents and they intercept encrypted cell phone communications rather than taping telephone calls. The crime scene is no longer only a physical setting. In other words, they deal with the world of communication technology as it affects society as a whole and as it is used for criminal activity.

Analysts, for their part, can now access an enormous number of data banks that offer material for their work. How can they set priorities with all the available information? One of the first consequences of having such vast amounts of information is that analysts must learn to think differently. Rather than concentrating on a single problem, they need to develop the ability to address several problems and several possible solutions at the same time, and sometimes collaborate with colleagues scattered across the world, whose experience and language are different from theirs (Dorn, 1998). Like everyone else, analysts find themselves faced with too much information. Data has no significance unless it is transformed into meaningful ideas for operations and / or management. New IT tools necessarily change the way of looking at crime and analyzing it. The ViCLAS (Violent Crime Linkage Analysis System), for example, which is used in the case of serial murders, totally changes the investigators' use of their accumulated data (Sheptycki, 1998). Could unlimited technology become a hindrance for the police because of the difficulty in processing it all?

Depending on their department, patrol officers are now using patrol cars that have been transformed into mobile technological laboratories. On the one hand, a number of repetitive tasks have been simplified thanks to data banks and software. Nevertheless, patrol officers still manage and coordinate the technology on board, whether it is the camera that photographs them when they leave their car, the mobile data computer, e-mail and so many other tools. These items improve police safety and police performance (Parsons, 1993). Whether tomorrow's patrol officers are community based or not (LeBeuf, 1999), undoubtedly they will be technology-based.

Moreover, the introduction of management information systems (MIS) also requires the ability to take in experts to look after the running of the system for the short or medium term. It is quite fascinating to note that police departments have taken in experts from computer companies or have created positions for civilians, computer engineers, computer technicians, etc. to ensure the proper management, planning and replacement strategies related to the new systems. The new creative spirit within the police department (Pitcher, 1995) is the computer technician or technology manager. Police departments are welcoming highly qualified specialists, not so much as managers of scientific areas such as laboratories, but rather in order to plan and develop IT for their whole staff[12] (for example, mobile data computers) (Breton, 1996).

The product offered by a company does not always correspond adequately to the needs of the police. The need of the users within the police must be met as they gradually move from being a traditional reactive force and become a more pro-active service. This could happen when the police look at developing, in collaboration with a company, a product that does meet their needs. Researchers aware of the complexity of police work are designing new IT policing tools[13]. The role of the police is to adapt the appropriate technology to its own needs.

Within the confine of this new strategy, police are encouraged to cooperate with experts rather than to play the role of experts themselves, as they do traditionally. One could imagine that there will be a sense of collegiality and cooperation between colleagues and IT specialists. These specialists must get out of their offices and be encouraged to cooperate with police officers in order to adapt technology to their needs.

This means that the police will adapt their normal work methods on the basis of their own ability to handle the high-performance tools available to them. It should be noted that, although their tasks will be refined and simplified by technology, the final result may not be greatly enhanced. New technologies do not create competence or experience.

However, contrary to what is generally thought, technology confines individuals even more closely within the perimeters of their tasks, demanding a high level of competency and the development of a cutting-edge skill. Once analysts have learned to handle crime-mapping software, for example, they will begin to discover the full potential of the tool. In other words, individuals achieve a high level of performance not so much as police officers, but as experts in the management of a piece of software. This restructuring of their working approach leads them to understand and define the reality of crime in its full complexity, thus eliminating simplistic explanations (Catalyst, 1996). Once these individuals are transferred, the loss of the expertise leads to an indecisive period where the analysis of criminality will not be carried out at the same level of competency as previously.

Finally, there is another category of users, who have a very specific relationship with technology. We are talking here of industry and government which themselves may be involved in partnerships with the police. Reports of various experiments in US partnerships of this kind indicate the advantages for the police of cooperating with major private industries or para-governmental organizations (Fulton, 1995, BJA, 2000), or with government services such as the army (Smietan, Ferris, 1996; Preimsberger, 1996). Research into non-lethal weapons has had major impact on police work, giving rise to technologies such as the smart gun or the taser gun (to immobilize a dangerous suspect), the road patriot (which stops a vehicle by disconnecting its electrical system), imagery process mirrors (developed by space researchers to significantly enhance blurred or inaccurate images).

Another form of partnership is based on the possibility of exchanging information between the police and community groups through the use of a more effective information system (Catalyst, 1996). The premise is that constructive exchanges can easily be envisaged through the use of various technologies. A recent study on Canadian investigators and technologies shows that even when information sharing technologies are introduced, sharing of information may fail because of lack of access or limited access, incompatibility of technological systems, lack of coordination between local and national systems or lack of training and interest from the individuals (LeBeuf, 2002a).

We should avoid making hasty generalizations at a time when the police forces are often still learning by trial and error how to handle instruments that are new to them and that were not included in their original job-training process.

Incentives and Disincentives to the Integration and Use of IT

How does one make it easier for a police organization to adopt a technological approach? Nogala (1993) identifies the internal and external incentives and disincentives. Let us take a look at them. Internal incentives result from factors at different levels. One, for example, is the improvement of performance in the application of the law and in cooperation between police departments. The incentive may be to combat major banditry, day-to-day criminality and the fast developing area of technological crime. It is in this last area that we find the new types of crime linked to the use of technology, an area that is still difficult for the police departments to handle. Consequently, the orientations or strategies favoured by the police will promote and accelerate the use of technology and integrate it more and more into the system as a whole. There are essential conditions to be met in order to do this, including the ability to pay for the technology and the ability to integrate it into the working environment. It will also be necessary to strengthen cooperation between various police forces, cooperation which may, for example, involve the use of special squads, like Joint Task Force operations under the sponsorship of a large police department that come together to fight organized crime. Cooperation of this kind facilitates rapid exchanges, adequate communication and information sharing (LeBeuf, 2002b). We still need to assess how, in fact, the information exchange process works, particularly where information technology systems are not compatible.

There is a second, rather different factor involved. The police are involved in a definitive professionalization and specialization process. Investigators dealing with organized crime have had to add to their working tools the use of the ACIIS II (Automated Criminal Intelligence Information System) which allows them to identify the position and role of criminals within organized crime (Kerr, 1999). The introduction and full use of cutting-edge technology requires that the users have highly specialized technical qualifications. Should the personnel, therefore, be trained on-site so that they can fully exploit the potential of these technologies or should experts be brought in who not only can handle the technology, but can also monitor the rapid process of changes? More generally, the issue is the strategic vision to be developed by police departments, in order to meet the needs of their communities and of the members of their departments. They must also be able to make informed decisions as to the technologies they select, so that such technologies do not become obsolete too rapidly.

A third factor worth bringing out is that these new technologies appear to be effective weapons of incredible potential. For example, *compstat*, following its initial testing by the New York police department (Bratton, Nobler, 1998) has developed into a strategic tool for neighbourhood crime management and has also helped project an image of the police force as being active both in prevention and repression (Green Mazerolle, Haas, 1998). Today, advanced seminars are held on this subject alone. This means that the police are perceived as able to solve more problems and to maintain their power of social control through the use of technologies placed at the service of the community (National Institute of Justice, 1997).

External incentives are linked to technological progress and rapid social development. One of the new and irresistible driving forces is the incredible speed with which both current and developing technologies are changing (Castells, 1996). The innovative cycle has become very short, equipment has become more powerful and cheaper, as complex processes are transformed into day-to-day tools. After two or three years, a management information system is often out of date or no longer compatible with other computerized systems that have been acquired since the initial installation. This means that police departments are likely to find themselves faced with one or more of four problems: they may be overtaken by the technological market; they may lag behind the most recent developments; they may be hindered in their development by the fact that their systems are no longer compatible, or they may be unable to expand because they lack the financial resources to upgrade the systems they do have. The technological market is knocking on the public security door, having first saturated the private security market which is less and less people-dependent (Moore, 1995). Moreover, the security needs of individuals and private commercial interests had led to a search for technological solutions to security problems (Boullier, 1993; Clarke, 1993).

Disincentives to progress are numerous and relate to several factors concurrently. At the beginning of the 1990s, a major police department decided to adopt a new forensic identification technology. The process which lasted five years allowed the implementation of the AFIS and eliminated a great number of forms and documents from the files. This was the beginning of the paperless era. However, these five years of major change had their ups and downs. The operation had been only partially planned out on paper, and a certain number of major problems developed during the process of change: suppliers went bankrupt; certain data bases could not be activated because of incompatible platforms; the systems sometimes went down while manual data contained in files was being transferred to computerized data banks, arousing a great deal of critical comment. Finally, the destruction of old handwritten files led to concern expressed by employees whose notes were destroyed. Once the process was completed, the system required only two work stations compared with twenty-eight stations previously.

Consequently, one of the major difficulties faced by the manager is to develop a business plan to meet the daily needs of the process. However well change is planned out, it will not give good results if it does not take into account simultaneously the development of tools, of professional mentalities and of the factor of resistance to change[14]. Technology is handled by men and women exposed to diverse levels of stress because of their police work, and because of the professional framework in which they operate. The degree to which the hoped-for results of technological innovation are achieved will depend as much on one as on the other factor.

As of now, the police will be using more and more sophisticated and costly equipment. However, there is a clear gap between what we hear from engineers and specialists and the daily experience of police users. Technology does not always carry out its promises and sometimes makes only a slight difference. In fact, if we can make a simple analogy, having a word processor isn't enough to make you a writer. Technology becomes effective when a certain number of ideal conditions are met, such as proper training, backing by experts, in-depth knowledge of the use of the apparatus. Sometimes technology only becomes really useful after expensive adaptations.

Another important and determining factor is the limits of police financial resources. It is not possible to finance all the desirable technical options and all the products available on the market. Direct and indirect costs are high and recurrent. The purchase of a system now means that soon it will be necessary to change or to upgrade the system. Likewise, the development, research and maintenance of technological skills are relatively costly for the police, which mean that even today these technologies are often not seen or perceived as a priority. Moreover, since it is necessary to develop and adapt training for each change in the technologies used by the police, immediate and direct costs ensue. The police have moved into the era of permanent and ongoing change.

Another important aspect of the changes created by technology, which is proving to be a major and complex obstacle, is the situation of the police forces around the country. According to the Canadian Constitution, police forces, with the exception of the RCMP, come under the jurisdiction of the provinces. This means that there is a fragmentation of the overall police entity which is difficult to deal with when trying to create harmonized national standards. Moreover, the various police departments tend to go their own ways and don't have a natural impulse to get together in order to create a critical mass, for the purchase of material, for example. This means that it is very difficult to ensure compatibility of the technologies that have been developed by different companies. Finally, small and medium-sized police departments do not have regular on-staff experts who can assess the technologies, the appropriateness of purchasing and ensure strategic planning of the technology to be acquired (Brady, 1996).

The Cost of Technologies

It is difficult to determine the direct cost of technologies. Do these costs only cover the systems or the software, or should they also include costs linked to personnel training, to the restructuring of human resources and system security? There are recurrent costs related to the purchase and upgrading of apparatus and technological tools of all sorts. And budgets should take these into consideration. Then there are hidden costs linked to the introduction of the technology. They include the expense of recurrent or prolonged sick leave taken by individuals who resist change or wish to sabotage it. Another problem is that of demotivation and apathy, factors that are more difficult to evaluate, but are nevertheless significant and which can contribute to the costly failure of a technological venture.

Another cost factor is the training[15] of both personnel and senior executives. Though the issues and training costs may be complementary, they are nevertheless different. It is indeed astonishing that there is so little literature regarding the training of top-level executives within the field of information technology or on the type of information required for the development of a strategic vision and an informed decision. However, training is a constant priority and subject to continuous upgrading. Tomorrow's training programs must be developed bearing in mind the concerns and needs of tomorrow. Again, a wider vision is needed to compass the new issues raised by technology.

Finally, technology security itself raises significant and costly problems – problems to be resolved and problems to be eliminated. If there is a general consensus that information technology substantially enhances the effectiveness and performance of police users, what is perhaps less well known is that the same technology increases public vulnerability (Grabosky, et al., 1996). Examples of this vulnerability are the development of new crimes such as telemarketing fraud, embezzlement of electronic transfers, illegal tapping of cell phones and electronic vandalism. In the latter case, we refer to a virus attacking a hard drive in the same way that viruses attack human beings. It costs an enormous amount of money, not only to protect oneself against illegal attacks and invasions, but also to reboot the weakened or destroyed system.

The Impact of Technology on Police

The impact is various and varies according to the sectors concerned. The opening hypothesis is that technology is integrated into police work on the basis of the benefits that they will engender for police operations. This hypothesis remains to be proved. The hypothesis is in line with Metcalfe's law that says that until the number of people using a network reaches critical mass changes in technology only affect the technology. But once critical mass is attained, social, political and economic systems change. The telephone is a good example (as reported by Boyd, 1999). For Metcalfe in order to change his strategic thinking one must see advantages. What remains to be seen is how the police will change when its critical mass is attained, and what will be the incentives for changes?

Within the information technology sector in particular, one can identify three major forms of impact. Recourse to technology increases the effectiveness of one's work by eliminating or reducing the number of repetitive tasks, in particular for patrol officers. This leads to an improvement in performance, more rapid response time and a higher solution rate (Seaskate, 1998, Lingerfelt, 1996). By transferring some part of the administrative tasks of the police officer to civilian personnel, patrol officers have more time to devote to their community. Again, in the field of forensic identification, the fact that one can access computerized files that already contain basic information, significantly reduces the time needed to complete electronic forms. There are less repetitive actions required. Moreover, the information obtained is of higher quality, since police officers can immediately check out the data banks and, where necessary, fill in missing information.

Technology opens the door to the installation of an extended communication network which has a high performance level and interconnects departments that otherwise would not be in touch. However, one still has to assess the quality of these contacts and the results obtained by the new network. An analyst working in a major police department reports that she was able to contact a large number of analysts and investigators in her department thanks to e-mail and the Internet. However, she also noticed that if she used the telephone, she was able to develop stronger and more personal relationships, which worked in her favour when it came to long-term information exchanges and cooperation. Direct person-to-person contact meets the need to set up a real network of more humane contacts and thus to obtain more accurate and specific information. A more superficial contact created by e-mail comes in handy when you need only general factual information.

The setting up of high performance (or significant) communication networks has an immediate ripple effect which modifies decision-making practices. It means that a police department that wishes to tie in with a powerful high-performance system needs to have equipment that is compatible with that used in other departments or in the major regional departments. The transfer of information and knowledge collated in data banks is more and more dependent on the transfer of technology. From this point of view, information technology generates improvements in working techniques, but it does not replace them.

When police officers work with information technology, there is less emphasis on the evaluation of the task in terms of performance or quantitative results than on the ability to work through different sites with multiple connections. New work divisions are based on the capacities and skills of the worker rather than on the task. For example, forensic identification teams are now much smaller, but their work is completed more rapidly and more accurately, with less personnel. Police officers in the forensic identification program do not inevitably work faster than formerly. This is not necessarily what is asked of them, but the Identification Section offers more effective overall results since a large number of repetitive tasks no longer need to be effected thanks to the inception of computerized data banks.

Ethics, Liability and Accountability

There can be no area where it is more necessary to scrutinize the ethical side of police activities than when it comes to using technology. Indeed, it is true that for a considerable time now we have accepted that a computerized system such as the Canadian Police Information Centre (CPIC) must be protected because it contains a great deal of information on individuals. This also means, given the ease of interconnection and the speed of existing software, that it is essential to ensure that police accessing this type of data bank, to input and extract information, should use it exclusively within the framework of their mandate (Marx, 1998). A commission of inquiry revealed that police officers had used data obtained from a data bank for personal ends (Public Inquiry

Commission, 1998). Something that is unacceptable but exceptional may turn into an everyday habit if an ethical reflection on technology and its use is not begun and pursued. Technology must not be used for purposes for which it was not designed. We should remind those concerned that ethics should be part of the daily life of all police officers, whatever their rank, function or the extent of their personal ambitions within the police force. The ethical approach which is first presented in the classroom should be maintained and encouraged in the police officer's daily activities. It would also be salutary if unethical behaviour were reported, but this seems still a lot to hope for in the light of contemporary police culture.

Conversely the accountability[16] process needs to be evaluated in light of the ever changing technological policing environment. The real issue is to which action or process the accountability refers. Accountability can refer to the performance of the IT tools and conversely to individual practices. It can also be in terms of support to the tools, for example how they are used by individuals. Results can be in term of statistical number of arrest, or broadly speaking it can be in terms of how officers work together in an inter-dependent relationship. Take the example of sensors at the border. Once a sensor sends a message to the police station, it puts into motion a collaboration mechanism between partners on a national and international basis. Here it is less numbers that count (how many arrest) than how the partnership created by the use of new technology opens the door to a number of related questions[17] such as how to cooperate, how to work together, or how to harmonize workings procedures.

Another issue is that of the liability of police departments when they use technology and the legal proceedings that may ensue. The use of non-lethal weapons such as cayenne pepper (oleoresin capsicum), which is permitted because it constitutes an alternative to regular weaponry, has led to court proceedings in the United States which resulted in the conviction of police officers who used pepper sprays against an offender (Cansler, 1998). Intercepting private communications when access is prohibited by the use of keys raises the question of the right to privacy and the right to the protection of the public at large (Cansler, 1996).

However, one thing is certain: technology should not be improperly used or used for purposes for which it was not intended.

One may also suppose that the new work methods based on high-tech apparatus will allow police officers to take suspects' statements at the scene of the crime or in the patrol car, a practice that is current in the London (Ontario) police department. The suspect confirms the accuracy of the statement, not by signing it, but by clicking the "send" button, which immediately transmits the statement to a data bank. Another problem is that mug-shot files, which offer an extended choice of suspects for crime, could be a source of difficulty for crime control. Digital photos can be modified by computer without a trace of the change. In other words, a photograph could be modified to suit the characteristics of a suspect so that they look alike. This rather silly example allows us to stress the fact that police work is being simplified and refined thanks to the technology, but we still have to see how the law will deal with the introduction of these new techniques.

Finally, there is the major question of encryption, which raises a number of basic questions. Encryption is the ability to hide the content of the message by making it incomprehensible except to authorize recipients who possess the key. It is an example of how standard police techniques become non viable (Zaccardelli, 2000). We know that development of the Internet was financed by the US Army during the Cold War in order to increase the number of communication sources in the event of a major nuclear attack. The Internet is a huge worldwide computer network, and in 1997 it was estimated that it included some 80,000 independent computer networks (Dobeck, 1997). This means that it is fairly difficult for law enforcement services to penetrate the system especially when commercial encryption programs make unlawful access largely irrelevant. One of the solutions proposed by the United States is that government should have control over servers, a suggestion which has not been unanimously welcomed and which runs counter to the very principles of the Internet and of the right to privacy (Pilant, 1999).

Concluding Remarks on an Evolving Situation

IT in policing is first and foremost a set of tools to improve the performance of the police. These tools, which transform the police both in its management and its operations, have yet to be examined fully by the accountability process. Yet the use of IT is in part responsible for law enforcement errors (Frost, 2003), and infringement of privacy rights. Moreover, it is because the Internet allows each and every one of us to connect to the Web, to have our own personal Web page, to post any kind of information (such as how to make a bomb), that there have been attempts to control it.

From simple technological tools we have moved to the situation where the content and the container are one. Originally introducing IT to police department was to provide better services for citizens. However today concerns are more focussed on the acquisition of strategic IT tools with greater focus, adaptability and planning integration. This mirrors changes in all sectors of business and public life.

Long before the events of September 2001, a system at the Canada/US border known as CANPASS[18] allowed regular users (such as truck drivers) to pre-register so that they could quickly pass through border customs offices[19]. Strategies for managing these flows are based on segmenting populations on the basis of pre-programmed factors and empowered by biometric scanners to confirm identities. This entails information sharing to secure the border (Sheptycki, 2002). Even though the assumption is that sharing of information is possible, it is not simple, as case study research on investigators working on organized crime in Canada has shown; crime investigation practices, investigation methods, individual professional interest, trust relationships between individuals and access to IT systems have all had an impact on the process of sharing - or not sharing- information (LeBeuf, 2001).

With the availability and dissemination of IT tools, what is relatively new is the expertise that individuals have with the tool even more than the tools by themselves. In other words, database information is useless if not analyzed properly, if access to the information is restricted, or if related systems are incompatible.

Technology means that systems and data banks are more

powerful, that the ability to share information has increased logarithmically and that interconnections between the systems, police departments and data banks are easier to make than ever. The inevitable question is: is this technology creating a new police profession? If so, one would need new material such as that now being integrated into police departments, the recruiting of personnel able to handle tomorrow's police tasks and a training that will ensure the optimal use of the instruments to be used by the police officers. Training, necessarily, will become specialized and high level in order that trainees may understand the operational side of the technology and meet community needs. This is something that the French government noted during a national training conference which took place in Paris (France, 1999).

A great number of the factors affecting the role of technology in the police depend to a large extent on social forces whose interaction and development are not easy to predict. The future of technology is based on strictly human considerations: a police chief who is motivated by technology, specialists who work to get a file accepted, budgets that are developed under pressure from enlightened champions in the field. Technology is available, but it is up to the decision makers to understand the use for it. However, the expansion of technology could also be related to external factors such as a major crises or terrorism attack.

After September 2001, combating terrorism became a policing priority. Meeting this priority has required new tools and controls to meet the new focus on integrated teams of law enforcement at the border. What seems to be relatively simple for integrated teams at first sight is complex and ambiguous on further examination. There is no uniformity in the practice of the partner countries, there is no relevant training to use new tools; there is not always good comprehension of the subtle technical software language; there is no access or limited access to each other's data banks, at the outset the partner members on the team have not yet earned enough trust to work together. Sometimes there is a lack of interest among member teams. As yet. there doesn't seem to be globalization of control through IT. The federal government is urging the law enforcement community to join together to improve national security and reduce organized crime. However the federation of organizations, mainly federal entities at the beginning, is encouraged by federal funding and by the possibility of redefining and broadening their professional mandate.

If the introduction of technological tools requires planning in terms of costs and modification of functions, it is still true that the development of these tools is being pursued at an extraordinary rate, as is their marketing. On one hand, police officers ask their superiors to provide the apparatus to facilitate and improve the carrying out of their tasks; on the other hand, management is under pressure from suppliers touting the benefits of highly developed tools, benefits that sometimes go well beyond the real needs of the departments, or that create new setting-up costs because of incompatible systems.

There are already studies on the way in which police departments collate and analyze data (types, objectives, etc.) and also how the police access such data (O'Shea, 1998). There are others in which the emphasis is on the extent to which technology diminishes the number of reports and forms that have to be drafted or filled in (Amoroso, 2000; Moriarty, Dover, 1998). There are yet again others based on surveys of target groups that indicate that computer crimes (copying or illegally selling software, illegal intrusion by hackers) are not necessarily seen as crimes, and particularly not by students in engineering or technology (Mercier, 1998).

There is, indeed, no rational approach, or harmonized standards for the integration or use of technology in Canada[20]. We suspect that the decision-making in this area is based on a transient rationalization supported by knowledge and skills that are external to and uncontrollable by the police itself. The lack of familiarity with the tools means that they are integrated only partially or superficially, in an attempt to make them compatible with traditional work methods. In the end, technology necessarily goes through a transitional phase during which police have to first learn to come to terms with tools that promise effective problem solving before they can integrate them and use them properly. It is essential not to become too dependent on suppliers and those who control the market (Naulleau, 1998). Once the transitional phase has been completed, a phase that can be quite long, given the human and financial factors involved, it is still necessary to learn how to integrate these new tools with the classic working methods with which the police are familiar and which were developed much earlier. Since it is necessary that users be trained to adapt to the tools, and that experts be on-site or reasonably available to help or to handle the apparatus, which means reorganizing human resources, integration is like a game of leap-frog – up and over, down and across.

Not only must police departments prepare themselves to understand the major changes that will be caused by the introduction of high-performance technological tools, they must also prepare themselves to integrate these tools, to handle them properly, so that they do not lag behind when it comes to dealing either with new forms of crime that derive from such technology, or with more traditional criminal behaviour. The industry brings together a number of technologies that used to be separated. Called convergence, it provides the opportunity to combine for example palm-top computing Internet access and voice communication (Rees, 2002). But in order to be efficient in using this technology the police must first and foremost understand the issues at stake. If it may be fairly easy to understand that combating e-crime requires up-to-date skills and specialized knowledge one must also realize that crime control is also dependent on new connected tools and that these tools have to be available to duty police officers and understood by coherent executives.

Endnotes

*The views expressed are those of the author and are not necessarily those of the Royal Canadian Mounted Police or the Government of Canada.

1   Information technology refers to communication systems (Internet, mobile data terminal, mobile data computer, GPS), experts systems (ViCLAS- Violent Crime Linkage Analysis System, PDQ- Paint Data Query) biometric (to recognize individuals based on unique physical characteristics such as DNA,), robotic, informatics systems (MIS), etc.

2 The technology sector has a major impact on the economy as much in terms of research and development as major losses (human and economic resources).

3 Technology creates conditions that are conducive to innovation such as distance learning, artificial intelligence, virtual reality, and telepresence (see Denning, 1998).

4 Email has been adopted to the extent that an individual may be called an "e-mail person," a phrase used by Field (2000).

5 Electronic commerce is not new, as funds have been transferred electronically for several years now, although the current development, impetus, and interest by corporations and consumers alike rise to another level (Dryden, 1998).

6 See www.ocipep.gc.ca .

7 Initially established in 1946, its mandate as been most recently modified by the Anti-Terrorism Act in December 2001. For details see www.cse-cst.gc.ca

8 Cybercrime refers to such crimes as fraud, computer misuse, hacking, terrorist propaganda and retaliation. (Smith, 1999). It may lead to adjustments to existing procedures. For example, Lloyds of London, an insurance company, is said to be poised to offer its customers a hacking policy insurance (White, 2000).

9 The GPS that provides patrol car latitude and longitude and allows them to be located rapidly.

10 In 2000, the Canadian Police College sponsored a national conference on IT and policing For more details see LeBeuf, 2000b.

11 To that effect, an international company assigned one of its employees to a major police department to help permanently manage their identification software.

12 This cause unexpected consequences such as a high turn over of experts who go from unending attractive work setting to another

13 Actually, improvements results from customers demand not from concern for law enforcement or public safety (Kaye, 2000).

14 If one day the introduction of e-mail within police departments meant direct access to the executive team, it did not take long

before the e-mails were directed to secretaries or the e-mail addresses were removed. Direct access has been redirected through to the traditional formal hierarchical structure.

15 Police training has been transformed with the introduction of technology. Not only is there a prime need to train people in the use of this technology, but technology itself is used to provide training such as distance training (Wells, Minor, 1998), teleconferencing or training programs assisted by computers or CD-ROM (Hutchison et al. 1998). The most recent Canadian initiative is PoliceLearn.com which deliver e-learning over the Internet to the public safety community (www.policelearn.com).

16 Clearly the notion of accountability deserves more space than available here. For an excellent reference book see Stenning, 1995.

17 The same questions are under scrutiny within the new borderless European Union- for more details, Bigo, 2002.

18 CANPASS is one of new and innovative programs and services of The Canada-United States Accord on our Shared Border originally signed in 1995.

19 In September 2001, the border was close down with a major economical impact in the economy that is more than 1., 9 billion daily bilateral trade in goods and services (Manley, 2001).

20 It does not mean that on a regional basis there are no tentative to amalgamate systems or to try to connect systems already in place. The situation is evolving at a fast pace. For example there is now what is called Cross Band Repeater that permits to radio systems using different bandwidth to connect and to talk to each other. Here it is the technology which is adapted to a current situation.

References

Akrich, M., Méadel, C. (1993). Technologies de sécurité et organisation. *Les Cahiers de la sécurité intérieure*,21:53-59.

Alexander, K., Munro, R. (1996). Cyber payments: Internet and

Electronic Money Laundering: Countdown to the Year 2000. *Journal of Financial Crime*, 4, 2:156-160.

Amoroso, E. (2000). Supporting Police Work with Information Technology at the London Police Service. In M.E. LeBeuf (Ed.) *Conference Proceedings. Police and Information Technology: Understanding, Sharing and Succeeding.* Cornwall, May 28-30, 2000. Ottawa: CPC (CD-ROM).

Audet, M., Jacob, R., Lauzon, N., Rondeau, A. (1996). Renouvellement des services publics et autoroute de l'information: vers un modèle stratégique de transformation et de critères d'aide à la décision. Version finale. *Présenté au Centre francophone de recherche en informatisation des organisations (CEFRIO).* Septembre.

Bigo, D. (2000b). Liaison officers in Europe. New officers in the European security field. In J.W.E. Sheptycki (ed.) *Issues in transnational policing.* London: Routledge.

Boni, W., Kovacich, G. (1999). *I-Way Robbery. Crime on the Internet.* . Boston: Butterworth Heinemann.

Boullier, D. (1993). La vidéosurveillance à la RATP: un maillon controversé de la chaîne de production de sécurité. *Les Cahiers de la sécurité intérieure*, 21:88-100.

Boyd, C. (1999). Metcalfe's law www.mgt.smsu.edu/mgt487/mgtissues/newtrat/metcalfe.htm isited March 2003.

Brady, T. (1996). The Evolution of Police Technology. In National Institute of Justice, Office of Community Oriented Policing Services (ed) *Technology for Community* Policing. *Conference Report.* National Institute of Justice.

Bratton, W., Nobler, P. (1998). *Turn Around. How America's Top Cop Reversed the Crime Epidemic.* New York: Random House.

Brenner, S. (2003). Toward A Criminal Law for Cyberspace: A New Model of Law Enforcement. *In Proceedings*, (2003). Law Commission of Canada. In Search of Security. An International Conference on Policing and Security. Montréal, February. CD-ROM.

Breton, P. (1966). L'informaticien et la sécurité: enquête sur un antagonisme. *Les Cahiers de la sécurité intérieure, Entreprise et sécurité*, 24:36-47.

Bureau of Justice Assistance (2000). Operation Cooperation. Visited, 2002-11-14, www.ojp.usdoj.gov/bja

Campbell, F. (1997). High-Tech Advances Bring New Tools. *Police*, 21, 10:60-63.

Canada, Department of Justice. (2000). Electronic Commerce. Http://Canada.justice.gc.ca. Visited 00/09/15.

Cansler, R.E. (1998). Technology Liability Considerations. *The Police Chief*, May:53-55.

Cansler, R. (1996). Technology Liability Considerations. In National Institute of Justice, Office of Community Oriented Policing Services (ed) *Technology for Community Policing*. Conference Report. National Institute of Justice.

Carter, D., Katz, A. (1998). Computer Applications by International Organized Crime Groups. In L. Moriarty; D. Carter (Eds.), *Criminal Justice Technology in the 21st Century*. Springfield: Charles C. Thomas.

Castells, M. (1996). The Rise of the Network Society. *The Information Age: Economy, Society and Culture*. Volume I. Great Britain; Blackwell.

Catalyst (1996). *Denver Partnerships Produce Unexpected Evidence*, 16, 2:1-2.

Clarke, R. (1993). Les technologies de la prévention situationnelle. *Les Cahiers de la sécurité intérieure*, 21:101-112.

Corsentino, D., Pettinari, D. (1996). *A Fork in the Road. Sheriff,* March-April:1012, 35.

Coutorie, L. E. (1995). The Future of High-Technology Crime: A Parallel Delphi Study. *Journal of Criminal Justice*, 233, 1:13-27.

Crawford, A; Lister, S. (2003). Integrated Local Security Quilts or Frayed, Fragmented and Fragile Tangled Webs?: the Patchwork Shape of Reassurance Policing in England & Wales. In Conference Proceedings. Law Commission of Canada. *In Search of Security An International Conference on Policing and Security*. Montréal, February. CD-ROM

Deisman, W. (2003). *CCTV: Literature Review and Bibliography*. Research & Evaluation Branch. Community, Contract &

Aboriginal Policing Services Directorate. RCMP. Available at : www.rcmp-grc.gc.ca

. Dobeck, M. (1997). Taking Advantage of the Internet. *The Police Chief,* January: 35-38.

Denning, P.J. (1998). The Internet after Thirty Years. In Denning D., Denning, P. (Eds.). *Internet Besieged. Countering Cyberspace Scofflaws.* New York: ACM Press.

Dertouzos, J., Larson, E., Ebener, P. (1999). *The Economic Costs and Implications of High-Technology Hardware Theft.* USA. CA, Santa Monica: Rand. Science and Technology Program.

Dorn, N. (1998). Du renseignement au partage des informations: l'intelligence protéiforme. *Les Cahiers de la sécurité intérieure*, 34:91-108.

Drolet, J.F.; I. Moen (2000). Enabling the Next Generation of Defence Capability. Nanotechnology. *Vanguard,* 6:22.

Dryden, J. (1998). La montée en puissance du commerce électronique. L'Observateur, n° 214, octobre-novembre, www.oecd.org//publications/observer Visited 1999/02/10.

Eisenberg, C., Porter, B. (2001). Law Enforcement Web Sites: New Utility for a New Era. *FBI Law Enforcement Bulletin,* 70,8:6-9.

Ekos Research Associates Inc. (2000). *The Public Opinion Environment and Emerging Trends in Public Security.* Presentation to SEC/Co /Directors Planning POWPM. March 28.

Ericson, R., Haggerty, K. (1997). *Policing the Risk Society.* Toronto: University of Toronto Press.

Etter, B. (2001). The Forensic Challenges of e-Crime. Current Commentary. No 3- 10/2001. Australasian Centre for Policing Research. www.acpr.gov.au Visited, January 2003.

Federal Bureau of Investigation (1999). Encryption: Impact on Law Enforcement. www.fbi.gov/library/encrypt/encryppt.htm. Visited 00/04/12.

Field, M. (2000). Organizational Dynamics in a Technology-Driven World; The Impact of Email on Law Enforcement. *The Police Chief*, February, 45-49.

Foucault, M. (1977). *Discipline and Punish: The Birth of the Prison*. London: Penguin Books.

France, Ministère de l'Intérieur (1999). Assises de la formation et de la recherche dans la police nationale (1999). Table ronde no 2: former à l'utilisation des technologies nouvelles. Paris: La Villette.

Frost, (2003). Managing Errors in the New Era of Policing. In Conference Proceedings. Law Commission of Canada. *In Search of Security An International Conference on Policing and Security*. Montréal, February. CD-ROM.

Fulton, R. (1995). When Law Enforcement Met Industry, Transferring Military Technology. *Law Enforcement Technology*, September: 56-60.

Goodman, M.D. (1997). Working the Net. Exploiting Technology to Increase Community Involvement and Enhance Service Delivery. *The Police Chief*, August: 45-53.

Grabosky, P., Smith, R., Wright, P. (1996). Crime and Telecommunications. *Trends and Issues in Crime and Criminal Justice* 59: 1-6.

Green Mazerolle, L., Haas, R. (1998). The problem Solver. The Development of Information Technology to Support Problem-Oriented Policing. In L. Moriarty,and D. Carter (Eds.), *Criminal Justice Technology in the 21st Century*. Springfield: Charles C. Thomas.

Haley, K., Taylor, R. (1998). Police Stations in Cyberspace: A Content Analysis of Law Enforcement Agency Home Pages. In L. Moriarty; D. Carter (eds.) *Criminal Justice Technology in the 21st Century*. Springfield: Charles C. Thomas.

Hutchison, J., Mays, J., Moriarty, L. (1998). Teaching Statistics in the 21st Century: Technology in the Classroom. In L. Moriarty; D. Carter (eds.) *Criminal Justice Technology in the 21st Century*. Springfield: Charles C. Thomas.

Johnson, R. (1997). High-Tech Help. Robots Lend a Hand in the Labs. *Pony Express*, December: 18-19.

Kaye, J. (2000). Information Technology Demystified: A Report of the Informaiton Technology Study Group. *Prosecutor*, 34, 6:26-30.

Kerr, J. (1999). Making Connections, Computer Database Helps Investigators Piece Organized Crime Networks Together. *Pony Express*, January-February: 16.

LeBeuf, M.E. (2002a). Police partnership and organized crime. What works? Four Canadian case studies. Empirical and applied Criminal Justice Review. An Online Journal of the Research on Crime and Justice Network. March 8, 2002 http://qsilver.queensu.ca/rcjnet/journal/cov2.html

LeBeuf, M.E. (2002b). Le renseignement criminel à l'ère de l'Internet. Pourquoi les enquêteurs ne le partagent-ils pas davantage? *Les Cahiers de la Sécurité Intérieure*, 47, 209-229.

LeBeuf, M.E., Paré, S., Belzile, M. (2000a). *Canadian Police Information Technologies: Current Overview*. Ottawa: CPC. Available at: www.cpc.gc.ca

LeBeuf, M.E. (Ed.), (2000b).*Conference Proceedings. Police and Information Technology: Understanding, Sharing and Succeeding*. Cornwall, May 28-30, 2000. Ottawa: CPC (CD-ROM).

LeBeuf, M.E. (2001). *Organized Crime and Cybercrime. Criminal Investigations and Intelligence on Cutting Edge*. Technical Report. Information Technology Series. Ottawa. CPC. Available
at: www.cpc.gc.ca

LeBeuf, M. E. (1999). Police de proximité et contrats locaux de sécurité- Que retenir du modèle canadien de police communautaire? *Rapport présenté à l'Institut des Hautes Etudes de la Securité Intérieure- IHESI*. Paris. Janvier

Lingerfelt, J. (1996). Technology as a Force Multiplier. In National Institute of Justice, Office of Community Oriented Policing Services (ed) *Technology for Community Policing*. Conference Report. National Institute of Justice.

Livanos Cattaui, M. (1999). Alliance Against Commercial Cybercrime. Conference Report. International Chamber of Commerce. London, 7 December. Http://www.iccwbo.org/home/conferences/reports

Manley, J. (2001). Notes For An Address. Canada's Policy Choices. Managing Our Border with The United States.

November 28-29, 2001. Toronto, Ontario. *Public Policy Forum*. Available at http://www.ppforum.com

Manning, P. (2000). Technology Revealed. In Conference Proceedings. *Police and Information Technology: Understanding, Sharing and Succeeding*. M.E. LeBeuf (Ed.), (2000). Ottawa. CPC. CD-Rom.

Manning, P. (1992). Technological and Material Resource Issues. In L. T. Hoover (Ed.), *Police Management Issues & Perspectives*.

Martin, S. (1996). The Impact of Information Technology Upon the Traditional Hierarchical Structures in Highly Bureaucratic Organizations. *Command College Class XXI. Peace Officer Standards and Training*. Sacramento, California.

Marx, G. (1997). The Declining Significance of Traditional Borders (and the Appearance of New Borders) in an Age of High Technology. In P. Drogue (Ed.), *Intelligent Environments*. Elsevier Science.

Marx, G (1998). An Ethics For The New Surveillance. *Visited* 1998-10-2.

McLean-Lipinski, J.R. (1999). Enhancing the Use of Technology in Law Enforcement. *Visited* 1999-05-06.

Mercier, P. (1998). On-Line Crime: In Pursuit of Cyber Thieves. In L. Moriarty; D. Carter (Eds.), *Criminal Justice Technology in the 21st Century*. Springfield: Charles C. Thomas.

Moore, R.H. (1995). Technology and Private Security; What Does the Future Hold? *Journal of Security Administration*. 18,2:1-9.

Moriarty, L., Dover, T. (1998). The Centralized Data Entry (CDE) System: One County's Attempt at Managing Burdensome Paperwork with Innovative Technology. In L. Moriarty; D. Carter (eds.) *Criminal Justice Technology in the 21st Century*. Springfield: Charles C. Thomas.

Morrison, R. (1996). Information Technology 2000. What's Ahead in the 21st Century. *Law Enforcement Technology*, June:40-43.

Murray, A.D., Vick, D.W., Wortley, S. (1999). Regulating E-commerce: Formal Transactions in the Digital Age. *International Review of Law Computers & Technology*,

13,2:127-145.

National Institute of Justice (1997). *Technology for Community Policing. Conference Report.* Sponsored by National Institute of Justice, Office of Community Oriented Policing Services, National Institute of Justice. June.

Naulleau, D. (1998). Le bogue de l'an 2000: un révélateur de la vulnérabilité de nos libertés. *Les Cahiers de la sécurité intérieure*, 34:69-90.

Nogala, D. (1993). Le rôle de la technologie dans la police de demain. *Les cahiers de la sécurité intérieure*, 14, août-octobre:137-158.

O'Shea, T. (1998). Analyzing Police Department Data: How and How Well Police Officers and Police Departments Manage the Data They Collect. In L. Moriarty; D. Carter (Eds.), *Criminal Justice Technology in the 21st Century.* Springfield: Charles C. Thomas.

Ocqueteau, F., Pottier, M.L. (1993). Vidéosurveillance et gestion de l'insécurité dans un centre commercial: les leçons de l'observation. *Les Cahiers de la sécurité intérieure*, 21:60-74.

Parsons, S. L. (1993). Technology Can Boost Safety in the Field . Police and Security. *News,* 9,4:19-22,27.

Pilant, L. (1999). The Debate Over Encryption. *The Police Chief,* LXVI, 1:31-35.

Pitcher, P. (1995). *Artist, Crafstmen and Technocrats: the Dreams, Realities and Illusions of Leadership.* Toronto: Stoddart.

Preimsberger, D. (1996). Cops and Space Scientist: New Crime-Fighting Partners. *The Police Chief,* October:108-114.

Public Inquiry Commission Appointed to Inquire into the Surete du Quebec (1999). *Report of the Public Inquiry Commission Appointed to Inquire into the Surete du Quebec.* Vol. 1, 2. Summary and Recommendations. Québec: Les Publications du Québec.

Rees, A. (2000). Technology Environment Scan. *Report.* Series no 133.1. Australasian Centre for Policing Research. Available at : www.acpr.gov.au

Royal Canadian Mounted Police (2002). *RCMP's Environmental Scan.* Ottawa. RCMP. Strategic Direction.

Robertson, J. (1999). The Changing Face of White-Collar Crime, *Police Chief*, www.theiacp.org. Visited 00/04/12.

Rodriguez, M. (1995). An Overview of Law Enforcement Technology. *The Police Chief*, April: 15-29.

Rosé, P. (1996). L'informaticien et la sécurité de l'entreprise. *Les cahiers de la sécurité intérieure*, 24: 25-35.

Scientific American (2000). Internet Anonymity. Speech without Accountability. October:34.

White, C. (2000). Egg Bank Robbery: Cyber-bandits on a Roll? The R*eport on Crime & Profiteering*, 4,3:17.

Seaskaste, Inc. (1998). The Evolution and Development of Police Technology. *A technical Report prepared for The National Committee on Criminal Justice Technology*. National Institute of Justice.

Sheptycki, J. (2002). Accountability across the Policing Field: Towards a General Cartography of Accountability for Post-Modern Policing. *Policing & Society*, 12, 4:323-338.

Sheptycki, J. (1998). Reflections on the Transnationalization of Policing; the Case of the RCMP and Serial Killers. *International Journal of the Sociology of Law*, 26:17-34.

Smietan, I., Ferris, D. (1996). Detecting Concealed Weapons. In National Institute of Justice, Office of Community Oriented Policing Services (ed) *Technology for Community Policing*. Conference Report. National Institute of Justice.

Smith, R. (1999). Defrauding Governments in the Twenty-first Century. *Trends & Issues in Crime and Criminal Justice*, no.111. Australian Institute of Criminology.

Soullière, Nicole (1999). *Police and Technology: Historical Review and Current Status*. Ottawa: Police Sciences School, Canadian Police College. Available at : www.cpc.gc.ca

Stenning, P.C. (1995). *Accountability for Criminal Justice. Selected essays*. Toronto: University of Toronto Press.

Strandbrg, K. (1998). Websites for Law Enforcement. *Law Enforcement Technology*, January:59-60.

Sullivan, S. (1999). Policing the Internet, *FBI Law Enforcement Bulletin*, www.fbi.gov. Visited 00/04/12.

Wells, J.; Minor, K. (1998). Criminal Justice Students' Attitudes

Toward Distance Learning as a Function of Demographics. In L. Moriarty, D. Carter (Eds.), *Criminal* Justice *Technology in the 21st Century*. Springfield: Charles C. Thomas.

White, C. (2000). Egg Bank Robbery: Cyber-bandits on a Roll? *The Report on Crime & Profiteering*, 4,3:17.

Wilsker, I. (1997). Cops on the Web. In National Institute of Justice, Office of Community Oriented Policing Services (Ed.), *Technology for Community Policing*. Conference Report. National Institute of Justice

Zaccardelli, G. (2000). Crime as a Reflection of Our Society. In *Conference Proceedings. Police and Information Technology: Understanding, Sharing and Succeeding*. M.E. LeBeuf (Eds.), (2000). Ottawa. CPC. CD-Rom.

PART 1V

HUMAN RESOURCES ISSUES

Managing Diversity

Recruitment, Selection and Promotion of Visible Minorities and Aboriginal Police Officers

Women in Policing

10

Managing Diversity
in Police Organizations

Stephen E. Nancoo

The face and fabric of the Canadian workforce are changing. Fundamental demographic changes fueled by changing immigration patterns, an aging population and the influx of women in the workplace are creating a more diverse workforce and workplace. Already a fact of organizational life, a portrait of the new workforce reveals significant dimensions of diversity in terms of age, education, gender, culture, ethnicity and race, religion, values and the physically challenged. Trends indicate that this diversity will become more pervasive, providing organizations, their leaders and managers with enormous challenges and opportunities well into the twenty-first century.

Historically, a defining difference between the Canadian and United States experience is the comparison between the mosaic (Canada) versus melting pot (United States) description of these two countries. In the United States, however, the melting pot theory that was very popular in the first third of the twentieth century is now less popular. Indeed, the social psychologist Triandis (1994) makes a compelling case for "additive multiculturalism" that allows for a policy that elicits increased appreciation of U.S. minorities and their ethnic identities. It is interesting, therefore, that although the case for additive multiculturalism is of relatively recent origin in the United States, most of the published research and writing on diversity reflect the U.S. experience. In terms of the Canadian experience, there is a paucity of research and writing in the area of managing the diverse Canadian workforce, a fact cogently documented by a number of scholars, in an issue of the *Canadian Journal of Administrative Sciences* (Burke, 1991; Kirchmeyer and McLellan, 1991; Joy Mighty, 1991).

In terms of police organizations, there were pressures advancing the cause of making the police more representative of the communities they serve (Chacko and Nancoo, 1993). The increasing diversity in our population has created special strains in our major cities as evidenced by clashes between various ethnic and cultural groups. In 2003, the media has been inundated with discussion of allegations of racial profiling. The Ontario Race Relations and Policing Task Force (1989:25) advised that if the police are seen to eliminate organizational factors which perpetuate prejudice and to punish discriminatory behaviour they will be assured of public confidence. The Report of the Royal Commission on Equality in Employment (1984) asked employers to identify and correct disadvantages to four designated groups – Aboriginal peoples, women, visible minorities and disabled. The Canadian Human Rights Act gave further support to this trend by approving special programs or arrangements designed to eliminate disadvantages suffered by these groups. Samuel and Suriya (1993: 285) observed that the Royal Canadian Mounted Police has made efforts to eliminate all forms of barriers and are diversifying their workforce to correspond more closely to the demographic realities of the communities they serve. The same could be said of some municipal and provincial police services.

Jain, Singh and Agocs study (See Chapter 11, in this Volume) analyze data on the recruitment, selection and promotion of visible minorities and aboriginal people in thirteen police services across Canada. They note that "in general there has been progress in the representation of visible minorities and aboriginal people in some police services, as well as improvements in recruitment, selection and promotion policies and practices in some of the selected police services. Nevertheless, there is still a significant need for improvement since the representation rates generally do not reflect relevant labour markets."

The debate on the representatives of different groups, especially the hiring of more aboriginals, visible minorities and women in police services is broadening to include new variables and dimensions. In addition to a continuous effort to tackle the challenge of increasing the representation of diverse groups within police services, the new frontier to be tackled is how are police organizations managing diversity. In other words, how are police organizations using these individuals, how are they treating these individuals and what opportunities are being created for minority groups to advance in the police organizations. Within the next decade there will be a high attrition rate of senior officers in police organizations and thus there is a strategic opportunity to promote minority groups to higher levels within police organizations. Currently, a number of police organizations are experiencing difficulty in the recruitment and retention of police officers. This is also an opportunity for policing organizations to make their workforce more demographically reflective of the communities they serve. In pursuit of this goal, it is important to remember that the category visible minority does not signify a homogeneous group. Consequently in the recruitment process, it is imperative that in building an equitable organization for the future that members from the various visible minority groups are included.

In light of the profound challenges and opportunities police organizations across Canada are currently experiencing in the areas of recruitment, retention and promotion of members of diverse communities, this chapter (1) examines the impact of diversity, offering some theoretical and empirical arguments in favour of diversity, (2) suggests some approaches to managing diversity through organizational change and cultivating a culture of diversity in organizations. Finally, (3) linkages between diversity and other leadership and managerial techniques will be made and their meaning for the future of organizations and organizational learning will be explored.

Impact of Diversity

Given that diversity is increasingly an organizational fact of life, the question as to how leaders and managers are harnessing the capacities and talents of this diverse workforce suggests a need for empirical answers. Based on her research, Russell (2000) identifies the formidable barriers women encounter in their efforts to build careers in contemporary work organizations. Some of the common approaches used to manage minority and other cultural groups are also faulted by researchers (Kirchmeyer, McLellan, 1991, Joy Mighty, 1991).

One of the approaches employed by organizations in managing diversity is through a homogenization of their workforces. This approach advances a monocultural view of organizational life that ignores potentially valuable new perspectives and interests, deprives the organization of value added human capital, suppresses constructive conflict and places enormous pressure to conform to established practices thereby stifling creativity and innovation (Brown, 1983; Fernandez, 1981).

There are some telling findings based on the limited research in the Canadian milieu. Reitz (1988) found that among minorities there were patterns of wage inequality, a slower achievement of upward mobility and an underutilization of their knowledge and skills. Burke (1991) noted that minority managers experienced more discriminatory treatment and greater resistance to equality He also found that organizations that provided a more favourable climate for minority managers and professionals may experience benefits among white males as well. Zureik (1983) concluded that while Canadian managers view race and ethnicity to be irrelevant to promotional opportunity, minority group members have to be better performers in order to succeed in organizations.

In a review of the research literature, Kirchmeyer and McLellan (1991) listed the following organizational barriers encountered by members of minority groups: isolation from key information and informal networks in organizations, withholding of challenging assignments from minorities, less autonomy and less discretion for minority workers as compared to non-minority workers, low supervisory expectations of the abilities of minorities and a lack of mentoring or sponsoring of members of minority groups.

Advantages and Disadvantages of Diversity

Diversity shows mixed results in organizations. On the disadvantageous end of the spectrum, evidence suggests that intercultural conflict and diverse subjective cultures may lead to reduced cohesion (Jackson et. al 1991). Other diversity effects include conflict and stress (Fernandez (1991), ineffective group interaction (Fenelon and Megatree, 1971); the potential for lower productivity and morale (Solomon, 1989). What, therefore, can an organization gain from diversity? In making the case for treating diversity as a necessary part of business strategy, Morrison (1992:18-28) identified a number of tangible benefits accruing from diversity. These include:

1. A diverse workforce will be valuable in providing better customer service, increasing the organizational competitiveness and facilitate the penetration of an increasingly global marketplace.

2. Cost savings. Morrison's survey revealed that "many executives believe that an effective approach to fostering diversity will save money over the long term and often even in the short run."

3. Increased productivity. Although it is difficult to assess the impact of diversity on productivity, Morrison found that many organizational executives expect greater productivity from employees who enjoy coming to work, who are relaxed instead of defensive or stressed in their work setting, and who are happy to be working where they feel valued and competent. Another group of researchers concluded that there is a positive relationship between employees' perception of being valued and cared about by their organization and their attendance, dedication and job performance (Eisenberger, Fasolo and Davis-LaMastro, 1990). Donna Thomson and Nancy diTomaso (1988) argue that a multicultural approach has a positive effect on employees' perception of equity, which in

turn affects their morale, goal setting effort and performance. Organizational productivity is consequently improved. Cox and Blake (1991) present evidence linking diversity to enhanced creativity and innovation. The Eisenberger group also found that employees who felt valued and cared about by their organization were more innovative without any direct reward of personal recognition. Birnbaum (1981) and Ziller (1972) showed that heterogeneous groups (in terms of race, age, values, background, training and so on) are more productive than homogeneous groups. A number of executives interviewed by Morrison were convinced that diversity would enhance their organization's ability to find innovative solutions to business problems and to create a wide range of goods and services.

4. Better Quality Management. By enlarging the pool of talent from which to choose there is a greater likelihood that the quality of management will be improved.

Other researchers have found that heterogeneous groups tend to be more creative than homogeneous groups, consequently leading to higher quality decisions (McGrath, 1984; Triandis et. al, 1965; Willems and Clark, 1971). On the other hand, homogeneity leads to group think and poor decision making (Janis, 1982).

Jain (1992) makes a significant statement in regards to the postive impact of diversity on economic relations. He postulates "Since commerce and trading with other nations are becoming the mainstay of Canada, and international competition is on the rise, managers of Canadian organizations will increasingly work with their counterparts from different countries, cultures and ethnic and racial groups. Canadian organizations and management must of necessity utilize talent regardless of gender and colour to remain competitive, to survive and to grow. Managing a diverse workforce therefore, has become a critical issue if Canadian organizations are to gain and retain a competitive edge."

This idea is reflected in Canada's strategic direction in terms of its trade policy as exemplifed by the increasing number of governmental trade trips to India, China and Latin America.

Most importantly, organizations, both public and private, should in the final analysis internalize the diversity agenda because of, what I would describe as, the ethical imperative: that is doing it because it is the most appropriate and the right, fair and just thing to do.

Inspite of the obvious advantages that could be derived from a diverse workforce, Morrison concludes that there are important barriers manifesting mindsets that are out of tune with today's workforce and the organizational demands for successful, well-performing organizations. What is needed therefore is for organizational managers and leaders to engage in strategic and determined efforts at changing the culture of their organizations to reflect the values of diversity.

Organizational change

To initiate, sustain and effectively manage and value diversity requires fundamental organizational change, that is, a change in the culture of the organization. This observation is based on this author's involvement in training managers and leaders from different levels of organizations (from supervisory to executive) in every Canadian province over the last decade. Leaders initiating organizational change must undertake three related processes: 1. Leaders must have a clear vision of an ideal or desirable future state. Leaders must ensure that through a process of dialogue with stakeholders, their vision must become a shared vision. 2. Leaders must make a realistic assessment of their organization's current situation. 3. Leaders and organizational members must deliberately plan to close the gap between the present state and the ideal future state. In the transitional period, visionary leaders should develop goals and formulate strategies for moving the organization from the present to the future state. Understanding the state of the present organizational culture is a necessary first stage. Changing the culture is what is required in managing and leading the diversity advantage into the future (See Leadership and Organizational Change Model, p. 274, in this volume.)

Creating a Culture of Diversity

Loden and Rosener (1991), and Gardenswartz and Rowe (1993) and Nancoo (2000) are among the advocates emphasizing the importance of creating a culture of diversity within organizations. "When valuing diversity becomes the norm, not the exception; when others are part of the mainstream and no longer on the periphery; when the organization automatically utilizes the talents of all employees -- then the ultimate goal will finally be achieved, and full lasting benefits of the culture of diversity will be apparent to everyone"(Loden and Rosener, 1991:215).

Three phases of creating a culture of diversity, as proposed by Loden and Rosener, are:

1. Setting the stage by endorsing the value of diversity and communicating this value throughout the organization.

2. Education and change implementation practices through a systematic process of awareness and culture change. This would include awareness education, diversifying decision making groups, creating structures to support organizational change and developing coaching and tutoring mechanisms.

3. Ongoing maintenance of the culture change by the development of on-going activators that ensure that valuing diversity remains a high priority.

Creating a corporate culture that embraces diversity is also proposed by Lee Gardenswartz and Anita Rowe (1993:385-412). They emphasize the importance of nurturing an inclusive organizational culture and introduce assessment tools for measuring the degree of openness in an organization's climate. Recognizing that the resistance to change is a factor in an organization's cultural rigidity, they argued for planned steps to be taken in the transition from a monocultural to a multicultural organization.

Their prescription for a successful diversity effort is for a battle that must be waged on the individual as well as the organizational fronts. In terms of organizational action, they identify the need for (a) creating involvement and commitment at every level of the organization, (b) teaching cross cultural management, (c) building valuing diversity into the bone marrow of the organization, (d) accepting the demographic reality (e) making rapid change the constant and, (f) being willing to pierce the power structure.

Jamieson and O'Mara (1993:34-41) advanced a case for changing the management mindset and introducing a "flex management" model that prescribes new directions for managing the diverse workforce. They identified four strategies: matching people and jobs, managing and rewarding performance, informing and involving people, and supporting lifestyle needs.

In a flex management approach, they explained, by changing an organization's polices and systems, one can also change organizational values. These values are a new corporate mindset based on individualizing, providing choices, seeing people as assets, valuing differences, encouraging greater self management, and creating flexibility.

Morrison (1992:160) recommends a five step action process for developing diversity in organizations:

* Discover and rediscover diversity problems in your organizations.
* Strengthen top management commitment.
* Choose solutions that fit a balanced strategy.
* Demand results and revisit the goals.
* Use building blocks to maintain momentum.

Linkages between Diversity and Approaches to Leadership and Management

For diversity initiatives to survive and flourish, they must be integrated with other leadership and management processes. There are complementary linkages, as outlined below, between valuing diversity and contemporary leadership and management practices as strategic planning/leadership, total quality management, team building, empowerment and creating a learning organization.

Strategic Planning and Organizational Change

Strategic planning is the process whereby organizational leaders in partnership with stakeholders determine the vision, mission, values and goals of the organization and how to achieve them. The Strategic Planning and Organizational Change Model

(See Figure 1) is an empirically tested model that I developed and used in the organizational transformational process in a number of Ontario police services.

Figure 1

Strategic Planning and Organizational Change Model

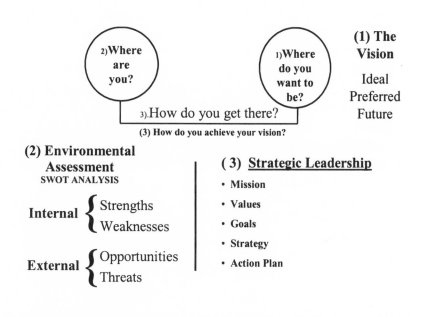

Step 1 of the model is creating **The Vision**, an ideal preferred scenario of the future, a clear sense of where you want to be. Leaders transform their organizations by formulating a compelling, shared *vision* of what the organization is capable of becoming. Vision is a statement of what you want the organization to be; it is a picture of where you want to go and how you want to get there. Vision statements focus on lofty aims with which everyone can identify. The vision statement should become a deep abiding belief and a rallying point that touches everyone. The vision must be shared and supported, positive and inspiring, comprehensive and detailed. For Nanus (1992) the vision attracts commitment and energizes people, creates meaning in workers lives, establishes a standard of excellence, bridges the present and the future and transcends the status quo. The vision is planted in ideality, it is future oriented, it is unique and it can be expressed through imagery.

Step 2 of the Model involves an **Environmental Assessment** of where, as an organization, you are currently. Leaders need to do an *environmental assessment* to form an understanding of an organization's current status in terms of its internal strengths (S) and weaknesses(W), and the external opportunities (O) and threats (T); a (SWOT Analysis).

The Internal environmental scan or assessment is an examination of the status of the key areas of the organization. When conducting an assessment, we want to identify the strengths and weaknesses of each of the key internal areas. We do this so that we can capitalize on our strengths while attempting to overcome the weaknesses. In the External environment it is important for organizations to understand the opportunities that exist and potential future threats. An environmental opportunity is a possible change in the world outside an organization which improves its capacity to meet the needs of employees, constituents and customers. An environmental threat involves a possible change in the world outside an organization which threatens to challenge its ability to meet the needs of employees, constituents and customers.

Irene Sanders (1998) postulates that strategic thinking in the new paradigm is to help an organization identify, respond to and influence changes in the environment. It is a search for information and options, which will ensure an ongoing advantage for the organization given its core skills, strengths and experience. It involves identifying opportunities for innovation and ways to influence what is emerging, as well as ways to achieve other desired results.

Knowing where you want to be and assessing where you are currently allow the leaders to do a gap analysis. **Step 3** of the Model, therefore, involves the **Strategic Leadership** factor which answers the important question how to achieve the organizational vision. Having established the gap between where the organization is and where it ought to be, leaders must strategically lead and manage the process in order to effect the necessary organizational transformations. Strategic Leadership, the core of Step 3 of the Model, involves setting the organization's mission, values, goals, strategy and action plans that are necessary to eliminate the gap between the organization's vision and its current status.

Mission provides the reasons for an organization's existence, the purpose or functions it fulfills, its primary stakeholders base, and the primary methods through which it intends to realize its purpose. The mission clarifies what is really important for the organization, or why it should be doing what it does; and it maintains a clarity and consistency of organizational purpose.

Values are the enduring beliefs, a belief system, that a specific mode of conduct is preferable to an opposite mode of conduct or end state of existence. Values are an expression of what the organization stands for; they tell us how the organization will conduct itself. Values define what is acceptable, they are the rules of the game and the standards of how the vision will be attained; they are the guides in the actualizing of the vision. If vision provides the direction, values are the signposts that guide leaders' decisions and actions on their journey towards excellence. High performing, excellent organizations tend to be values-driven. Values driven leadership is a necessary pre-requisite in the pursuit of organizational excellence. Values-driven organizations spell out their values and what they mean in terms of expected actions. Values are the rules that inform leader's choices and determine their behaviours in an organizational setting.

Goals are the end results that the organization will like to achieve; they are the outcomes against which the organizational performance would be measured. Goals should be specific, measurable, attainable, relevant and trackable.

Strategy spells out the organization's commitment in implementing its goals. Strategy (Bryson, 1995: 12-13) is defined as a pattern of purposes, policies, programs, actions, decisions, or resource allocation that defines what the organization is, what it does and why it does it. Each strategy should generate and be supported by action plans.

For strategic planning and organizational change to be a success there must be action plans: the need to focus on very specific, measurable, person-responsible, time bound actions that serve as the critical success factors. To move from concept to reality, effective Action Plans (Beam, 1993:225) must identify the following actions steps: define specific activities; establish measurement criteria to test that the activity is completed; the activity must be time bond, that is, there is a deadline for the activity; identify who has the authority and responsibility for completing the specific activity; monitor implementation on an ongoing basis and evaluate results to ensure the timely and successful completion of the action plan.

Total quality management (TQM) is a process of continuous improvement, evaluation and adjustment to ensure that the customer/client receives the highest quality service and the product at the lowest cost. Thomas (1991) identified several commonalities between TQM and managing diversity. For example: both TQM and managing diversity are rooted in the possibility of organizational competitiveness. TQM places a high emphasis on employee involvement. Similarly, managing diversity is premised upon the empowerment of the diverse community of employees so that their full potential will be tapped. Furthermore, like managing diversity, total quality management is for the long term. Total quality management and managing diversity programs both call for fundamental organizational culture change to successfully implement these programs. Thomas writes that "when managing diversity is integrated with total quality, the most significant implementation challenges that remain with total quality are more successfully addressed"(p. 165).

Team building. Fostering teamwork is all about getting people to work together toward common goals. Effective teamwork is built on the foundation of cooperative - a sharing of the work - and collaborative - a sharing of the power or authority - relationships.

There is a belief that fostering teamwork and self managing teams enable an organization to achieve its goals in an effective manner. "When properly designed and appropriately nurtured, these teams provide a substantial competitive advantage in the marketplace, as well as a human or social advantage in the workplace" (Jamieson and O'Mara, 1991:130).

Self managing teams have the potential of providing the organization with a competitive advantage in the marketplace through enlightened customer/client practices. Equally important, they also have the capacity of providing for human and social advantage through employee satisfaction.

There is a school of thought which suggests that developing quality teams is becoming more difficult. Fernandez (1991) believes that this difficulty stems from the fact that "customer and employees are becoming more diverse. Quality teams are likely to consist of people who differ in race, ethnic background, gender, age, sexual orientation and other dimensions. They maintain that the difficulties are surmountable if organizations train their people to understand and respect their diversity, as well as to understand teamwork and other tools for innovation" (Canervale and Stone, 1994.)

Empowerment: Empowerment is a central tenet, a core value in the managing/leading diversity paradigm. Managing diversity is a critical determinant of the success of efforts to empower employees.

Rosabeth Moss Kanter (1984) advanced four principles that empower others:

1. Give people important work to do on critical issues.
2. Give people direction and autonomy over their tasks and resources.
3. Give visibility to others and provide recognition for their efforts.
4. Build relationships for others, connecting them with powerful people and finding them sponsors and mentors.

Building a Learning Organization

Developing and nurturing a learning organization is an important factor in integrating the total quality management, teamwork, empowerment and managing diversity processes.

Peter Senge et. al. (1994:6) describes the core elements of the learning organization as:

Personal mastery - learning to expand our personal capacity to create the results we most desire, and creating an organizational environment which encourages all its members to develop themselves toward the goals and purposes they choose.

Mental models - reflecting upon, continually clarifying, and improving our internal pictures of the world, and seeing how they shape our actions and decisions.

Shared Vision - building a sense of commitment in a group, by developing shared images of the future we seek to create, and the principles and guiding practices by which we hope to get there.

Team Learning - transforming conversational and collective thinking skills, so that groups of people can reliably develop intelligence and ability greater than the sum of individual members' talents.

Systems thinking - a way of thinking about, and a language for describing and understanding, the forces and interrelationship that shape the behaviour of systems. This discipline helps us see how to change systems more effectively, and to act more in tune with the larger processes of the natural and economic world.

The relationship between organizational learning and managing diversity is evident. For client/customer centered organizations, where it is imperative to identify the processes that are fundamental for the continuous improvement of the product and service necessary for client/customer satisfaction, it is more likely that the multi-cultural workforce will lead to the realization of the shared vision of safe, secure and peaceful communities in the global villages. We are indeed witnessing a significant internationalization of the workforce and internationalization of cultures within organizations. Organizations and their members have to learn to adapt to this internationalization of culture. They will be able to effectively do so if there is a commitment to the valuing of the diverse workforce, which will be at the heart of the organization of the future. Those who embark on the journey of developing learning organizations which lead, manage and value diversity and capitalize on harnessing "the whole gamut of human potentialities" in their diverse workforce will be better able to adapt productively and creatively to the changes and challenges of the new millennium. Some progress is being made in this area as police organizations have as one of their core values the promotion of continuous learning among organizational members.

Diversity and Good Governance

At the United Nations Expert Group Meeting on Managing Diversity, the Canadian representative O.P Dwivedi (2001) articulated a coherent set of arguments linking diversity with good governance. These include:

- Representative bureaucracy creates an atmosphere for strengthening diversity in the public service.
- Accountability does not get weakened with diversity. On the other hand it gets strengthened with an appropriate administrative culture prevailing.
- Recognition in law for cultural diversity is the foremost prerequisite for good governance because a multicultural society can foster a strong sense of unity and common belonging to its citizens; furthermore, it is a valuable collective national asset. Sustenance of diversity, biophysical or human, is a prerequisite of a just society and good governance.
- Cultural diversity protection is an essential element of good governance. For good governance to be sustained, cultural diversity needs protection because in this context, the administrative culture of a national obligation to foster the convergence of such democratic ideals as respect for individuals, individual freedoms, equality, justice, rule of law and constitutionalism. The world of the 21st Century is the world of cultural diversity. The time has come to learn to live with, accept, celebrate and operationalize its own diversity.

The relationship between diversity and good governance is especially relevant to public policing in a multicultural Canada. It is relevant in terms of the global representation of the number of members of diverse communities represented in police services as well as police training institutions. But it is especially important in terms of having representation of the diverse groups at various levels of police organizations and in ensuring that a nurturing culture of diversity allows for all organizational members to contribute effectively to their fullest potential.

Conclusion

In this Chapter, I have attempted to capture the essence of managing/leading diversity. We have observed that the wider Canadian and police workforces are changing, with significant new dimensions in terms of age, education, gender, sexual orientation, culture, ethnicity, race, religion, values and the physically challenged. The organization of the future is also changing in terms of our understanding, the structure and culture of organizations. Inspite of this, we have noted the limited amount of research in the Canadian literature on diversity within our police, public and business organizations. Even so we recognize the advantages of diversity and the need to create and nourish a culture of diversity within organizations of the future so that the full potential of the diverse workforce can be harnessed to the benefit of the organization as well as Canadian society. We also made linkages between diversity and such contemporary leadership and management practices as strategic planning and organizational change, total quality management, teamwork and empowerment. We have emphasized the need to establish learning communities within organizations. Finally the values of a democratic society and good governance require Canadian police organizations to be more representative, at both the front line and managerial levels, of the communities they serve. This development would enable us to adapt and benefit from the changes and challenges that are an inherent part of the internationalization of the organization's culture and the realities of a diverse workplace which will become increasingly more pronounced in Canadian society in the 21st Century.

References

Beam, William C. (1993). *Strategic Planning That Make Things Happen*. Amherst: Human Resources Development Press.

Birnbaum, P. H. (1981). Integration and Specialization in Academic Research. *Academy of Management Journal,* 24.

Brown, L.D. (1983). *Managing conflict at organizational interfaces.* Reading: MA: Addison-Wesley.

Bryson, John M. (1995). *Strategic Planning for Public and Nonprofit Organizations* San Francisco: Josey Bass

Burke, R. (1991). Managing an Increasingly Diverse Workforce:Experiences of Minority Managers and Professionals in Canada. *Canadian Journal of Administrative Sciences,* 8 (2), 108-120.

Chacko, J. and Nancoo, S.E. (1993). *Community Policing in Canada.* Toronto: Canadian Scholars' Press.

Cox, T. H., and Blake, S. (1991). Managing Cultural Diversity: Implications for Organizational Competitiveness. *Academic of Management Executive* 1991. 5, 45-54.

Cox, T. and Finley Nickeson, J. (1991). Models of Acculturation for Intra-Organizational Diversity, Canadian *Journal of Administrative Sciences*, 8 (2), 90-100.

Dwivedi, O.P. (2001). *The Challenge of Cultural Diversity for Good Governance.* New York: United Nations Experts Group Meeting on Managing Diversity in the Civil Service.

Eisenberger, R., Fasolo, P. and Davis-LaMastro, V. (1990). Perceived Organizational Support and Employee Diligence, Commitment and Innovation. *Journal of Applied Psychology,* 75, 51-59.

Fenelon, J. R. and Megatree, E. I. Influence of Race on the manifestation of Leadership. *Journal of Applied Psychology*, 55, 353-358.

Fernandez, J.P. 1991. *Managing a Diverse Work Force: Regaining the Competitive Edge.* New York: Lexington Books.

Gardenswartz, L. and Rowe, A. 1993. *Managing Diversity*.
Illinois: Business One Irwin.

Jain, H C. (1992). Employment Equity and Visible Minorities:
Have the Federal Policies Worked? *Canadian Labour
Law Journal,* Vol. 1, p. 388.

Jamieson, D. and O'Mara, J. 1991. *Managing Workforce 2000*.
San Francisco: Josey-Bass Publishers.

Janis, I.L. 1982. Groupthink. In J. L. Gibson, J. M. Ivancevich, &
J. H. Donnelly (Eds.), *Readings in organizations*. Plano,
TX: Business Publications.

Joy Mighty, E. 1991. Valuing Workforce Diversity: A Model
of Organizational Change. *Canadian Journal of Administrative Sciences,* 8(2), 64-70.

Kirchmeyer, C. and McLellan, J. 1991. Capitalizing on Ethnic
Diversity: An Approach to Managing the Diverse
Workgroups of the 1990s. *Canadian Journal of
Administrative Sciences,* (8), 72-79.

Loden, M. and Rosener J. B. 1991. *Workforce America!
Managing Employee Diversity as a Vital Resource.*
Illinois: Business One Irwin.

McGrath, J. 1984. *Groups: Interaction and performance.*
Englewood Cliffs, NJ: Prentice Hall.

Morrison, A. M. 1992. *The New Leaders*, San Francisco: Josey-
Bass Publishers.

Nancoo, Stephen E. and Nancoo, Robert S. (Eds.), 1996. *The
Mass Media and Canadian Diversity*. Mississauga:
Canadian Educators' Press.

Nancoo, Stephen E. 2000. (Ed.), *21st Century Canadian
Diversity.* Mississauga: Canadian Educators' Press.

Russell, R. 2000. Women Building Careers in a Diverse Society.
In S.E.Nancoo (Ed.), *21st Century Canadian Diversity.*
Mississauga: Canadian Educators' Press.

Samuel, J.T and Suriya, S.K. 1993. A Demographically
Reflective Workforce for Canadian Policing. In J. Chacko
and S.E. Nancoo (Eds.), *Community Policing in Canada*.
Toronto: Canadian Scholars' Press.

Senge, P., Kleiner, A., Roberts, C., Ross, R.B., Smith, B.J. 1994.
The Fifth Discipline Fieldbook. New York: Doubleday.

Thomas, R. 1991. *Beyond Race and Gender*. New York: AMACOM.

Thompson, B. L. and DiTomaso, N. (Eds.). 1988. *Ensuring Minority Success in Corporate Management*. New   York: Plenum, 1988.

Triandis, H.C. 1994. *Culture and Social Behavior*. New York: McGraw Hill Inc.

Walker, S.Gail (1993). *The Status of Women in Canadian Policing*. Ottawa: Solicitor General of Canada.

Willems, E.P. and Clark, R. D. 1971.   Shift towards risk and heterogeneity of groups. *Journal of Experimental Psychology*, 7, 304-312.

Ziller, R. Homogeneity and Heterogeneity of Group Membership. In C. McClintoch (Ed.), *Experimental Social Psychology*. New York: Holt, Rinehart & Winston.

11

Recruitment, selection and promotion of visible-minority and aboriginal police officers in selected Canadian police services*

Harish C. Jain
Parbudyal Singh
Carol Agocs

Abstract: The demographic composition of the Canadian police services in major cities generally does not reflect the diversity of the communities they serve, especially with respect to the representation of visible minorities and aboriginal peoples. As many commissions and inquiries on race relations issues in policing have reported, this lack of representation may be a factor that is hindering the effectiveness of police work in major urban centres across Canada. Hence, many commentators have called for increased representation of visible minorities and aboriginal people in the police services through effective recruitment, selection and promotion strategies. In this article, through the use of both quantitative and qualitative research methodologies, the authors identify and assess the various staffing and promotional policies and practices of thirteen police services across Canada. Results suggest that there has been some progress in the representation of visible minorities and aboriginal people in policing over the fifteen-year period of this study. However there is still room for considerable improvement in the policies, practices and culture of police services if they are to become more representative of the diversity of the communities they serve.

In recent years, public-sector organizations have been required to respond to the often contradictory expectations of various segments of an increasingly diverse public. The 1996 Census of Canada demonstrated that visible minorities and aboriginal people constitute large and growing proportions of the populations of Canada and its principal cities. Visible minorities made up 11.2 per cent of the Canadian population, 32 per cent of the population of Toronto, and 31 per cent in Vancouver, as well as 16 per cent in Calgary, 14 per cent in Edmonton, 12 per cent in Ottawa/Hull, and 11 per cent in Winnipeg.[1] Aboriginal people comprised 2.8 per cent of the Canadian population, with the following representations in the metropolitan areas: 7.5 per cent of the population of Saskatoon, 7.1 per cent in Regina, 6.9 per cent of Winnipeg's population, 3.8 per cent in Edmonton, 1.9 per cent in Calgary, and 1.7 per cent in Vancouver.[2]

As the institutional embodiment of state power, police services have been challenged to demonstrate fair and responsive treatment of each of Canada's diverse minority communities as a condition of maintaining public trust. Investigations were ordered into the way in which police services in Saskatoon and Winnipeg have dealt with aboriginal citizens.[3] These are only the more recent in a series of numerous investigations, public inquiries and commissions over the past dozen years, which have been appointed in response to conflict between police organizations and aboriginal or visible minority communities in nearly every province and in many of Canada's largest cities.[4]

These studies of police-community tension have invariably pointed to the deep and tangled social and institutional roots of such conflict. In a society where inequalities in the distribution of wealth and power are visibly linked to racial and ethnic differences, police organizations become the most obvious local embodiment of the power of dominant groups in the eyes of minoirites,[5] particularly as the nature of police work changes in ways that integrate police work into daily life. A 1992 Metropolitan Toronto survey of 417 Blacks, 405 Canadians of Chinese descent, and 435 Caucasian citizens, commissioned by the Commission on Systemic Racism in the Ontario Criminal Justice System, illustrates the divergence of perception of police performance among these three groups.[6] The percentages of respondents saying that police treat black people worse than they do white people were 79 per cent of black people, 60 per cent of Canadians of Chinese descent, and 50 per cent of Caucasians. A belief that police treat poor people worse than they treat wealthy people was held by 72 per cent of black people, 46 per cent of Canadians of Chinese descent, and 60 per cent of Caucasians. When asked whether police treat non-English speakers worse than they do English-speakers, 57 per cent of black people, 64 percent of Canadians of Chinese descent, and 47 per cent of Caucasians agreed that this is true. When a regression analysis was conducted to determine the influence of education, age, income, sex, race and other variables on respondents' assessment of police treatment of minority groups, race emerged as the single-best predictor, even when variation in the other factors was considered.

In Canada and other liberal democracies, police services have become integrally associated with roles and values important for the functioning of society. Apart from the traditional function of maintaining law and order necessary in a civilized community, police services have become more diverse to suit the needs of evolving democracies, and now also provide "social services" and services that may be unrelated to crime such as those that deal with domestic disputes and counselling. While peace-maintenance services, as opposed to law-enforcement services, are on the increase, they are not totally new. In fact, Sir Robert Peel's "Bill for Improving Police in and Near the Metropolis," presented to the British Parliament in 1829, emphasized the need to maintain public order and peace.[7] In contemporary society, providing services comprises a large proportion of a police officer's time. In fact D. Hill estimates that approximately eighty per cent of calls for police services are for non-crime related activities such as family upheaval, racial discord and problems associated with youth unemployment. D. Dutton reports that order maintenance and service functions comprise over eighty per cent of a police officer's time, while law enforcement duties take up only about ten to fifteen per cent. Similar figures have also been reported by M. Wycoff, C. Susmilch and P. Eisenbart.[8] Thus, the police service represents a major governmental institution with which a broad cross-section of the public interacts on a regular basis. Given the changing nature of the Canadian "public," it is important that the composition of the police service be reflective of, or at least be sensitive to, the wider community it serves.

A strategy of community policing has been adopted by many police services, at least in theory, as one means of defusing tensions by re-defining the relationship between police and minority communities. While there may be no generally accepted definition of community policing, it encompasses structural and cultural changes in police organizations and the development of a more open, responsive and cooperative relationship between police and communities they serve.[9] Because police officers are recruited from the community, and depend on the cooperation and acceptance of the community for the legitimacy and effectiveness of their work, the relationship between the community and the police service is at the heart of the policing function in society.[10] Community policing, whose goal is the integration of police and communities, depends in part on the presence of members of the diverse communities within police organizations – a visible demonstration of integration.

Hence, it is possible to draw a clear connection between a strategy of community policing and a police service that represents within it the diversity of the community. If minority communities are able to become part of police organizations and then to influence their decision-making processes, police organizations, in time, may become less likely to perpetrate behaviour that is oppressive to minority communities. In turn, visible minority and aboriginal communities are more likely to perceive that they have something to gain from cooperation with police organizations. As the gulf between police organizations and their communities narrows with the provision of more responsive policing, and as a result, the image of the police as an instrument of oppression weakens its hold, minority and aboriginal youth are more likely to consider policing as a career.

According to some commentators, then, tensions and distrust between police organizations and aboriginal and visible-minority communities are related to the continuing pattern of low representation of members of these communities in policing.[11] The reports on investigations and public inquiries into police-community conflict, previously cited, invariably point to the pressing need for police services to become more representative of their communities as one means of improving race relations. Yet, H. Jain, and S. Suriya, among others, have reported that the representation of visible-minority officers in selected major urban police organizations across Canada is lower than their representation in their respective communities.[12]

From a police administration perspective, A. Normandeau suggests that a low representation of visible minorities in police organizations helps to perpetuate Caucasian officers' prejudices against visible minorities; that it creates a climate of harassment for the few "ethnic" police officers and hinders their professional mobility; and that it fails to provide young people from minority groups with role models.[13]

The report of the Race Relations and Policing Task Force (Ontario) indicated that success rates in recruitment and selection into policing are heavily skewed in favour of Caucasian men,[14] creating the perception within minority communities that police organizations do not welcome them as applicants. In addition, many new immigrants from dictatorial or repressive regimes distrust the police[15] and may not consider law enforcement a respectable profession or may view a police job as having few advancement opportunities.[16] Given the obstacles to improving the representativeness of police services, even if there were an organizational commitment to this goal, considerable emphasis needs to be placed on finding more effective ways of increasing visible-minority and aboriginal recruitment and retention as members of police services.

A wide variety of public- and private-sector organizations have taken measures to improve their representation of visible minorities and aboriginal people, as well as of women from all visible-minority groups, in addition to the maintenance of a relationship of trust with their communities. The accommodation of diversity is not just a public-relations exercise, but, as research suggests, it may lead to increased productivity and economic performance.[17] The potential benefits to the effectiveness and efficiency of police services that may be realized through human resource management policies and practices designed to improve representativeness and create a culture accepting of diversity deserve further inquiry.

Although there is some published research on the representation of visible minorities in police services in Canada, to the best of our knowledge there has been no systematic research on the recruitment, selection and promotion of visible-minority *and* of aboriginal police officers, both men and women, in Canada. Nor is there attention in the literature to the need to address the marked underrepresentation of women of visible-minority groups or of aboriginal ancestry. Thus, the main objectives of this article are to examine the following questions:

1. What changes have occurred in the representation of visible-minority and aboriginal women and men in thirteen police services across Canada since 1985? How representative are police services of the diversity of their communities?

2. What policies and practices are used by these police services to govern recruitment and selection of officers? Do these policies and practices contain barriers that may hinder the recruitment and selection of visible-minority or aboriginal applicants?

3. What is the representation of visible-minority and aboriginal people at ranks above the entry level in the thirteen police services? What policies and practices govern promotion decisions? Might these policies and practices present barriers that restrict the promotion opportunities of visible-minority and aboriginal officers?

Literature review and study background

In a series of studies of recruitment and selection of visible-minority officers in fourteen Canadian police agencies, H. Jain reports that while minority representation on police services is gradually increasing, it is still far below the proportion of these groups within the relevant labour markets. For instance, in 1987, visible minorities in Metropolitan Toronto comprised 16.5 per cent of the city's workforce but only 3.4 per cent of the police officers; this latter figure rose to 4.7 per cent in 1990. Using census data, S. Suriya also found that visible minorities and aboriginal people were underrepresented in Canadian police services when compared to their presence in the labour market. There appears to be no published research that provides specific analysis of the under-representation of women who are members of visible minorities or of aboriginal ancestry.[18]

With respect to the inquiries and commissions, the 1989 and 1992 Ontario Race Relations and Policing Task Force reports, the 1988 Quebec Human Rights Commission Report, and the 1993 Task Force (Corbo) Report all dealt with problems in relations between visible minorities and the police.[19] Testimony from provincial justice inquiries in Nova Scotia, Manitoba, and Alberta highlighted the strained relations between First Nations and the police.[20] The Commission of Inquiry Into Policing in British Columbia dealt with problems in the relationship between the police and both visible minorities and aboriginals.[21] In general, a number of these inquires have reported that recruitment, selection and promotional policies and practices are skewed in favour of Caucasian men.[22] Further, as noted by the report of the Commission of Inquiry Into Policing in British Columbia,

> the potential conflicts and inequities that can result from a system of policing that draws recruits from only one segment of the population have been highlighted in many jurisdictions and reports. ...Unless some meaningful steps are taken to make our police agencies more representative, a sense of alienation and antagonism will almost certainly develop between police and minorities. This has already occurred in the United States and, to a lesser extent, in some Canadian cities (most notably Toronto and Montreal). A police chief from a major American city warned the inquiry not to "make the same

mistakes we made." He went on to say that in the inner cities, which are largely populated by African-and Hispanic-Americans, "we are the enemy. Nobody gives us any information."[23]

Despite the differing initial reasons for these inquiries, a remarkable similarity is observed with regard to their findings and recommendations relating to the recruitment and selection of visible minorities and aboriginal people in police services. That is, as a result of the various testimonies before the commissions, *all* the reports stress the importance of some sort of "equity" in staffing and promotional policies in alleviating the troubled relationship between the police and the diverse communities they serve. In fact, U.S. research suggests that the presence of affirmative action programs and court-imposed quotas is the most important factor explaining the increases in the representation of minorities in police organizations and local governments.[24]

Human rights legislation in most jurisdictions across Canada allows for the development of special programs to reduce the labour-market disadvantages experienced by women, aboriginal persons, persons from visible-minority groups, and persons with disabilities. Therefore, employers are free to mount voluntary employment equity programs, in some cases with the express permission of human rights commissions in their respective jurisdictions, such as in Ontario and at the federal level. Canadian employers are largely protected from the charge of reverse discrimination.[25] In turn, the provisions regarding employment equity programs in the human rights statutes are protected by the Canadian Charter of Rights and Freedoms, Section 15(2). The Charter, which forms a part of the Constitution Act of 1982, explicitly states that the equality rights guaranteed in Section 15(1) "do not preclude any law, program or activity that has its object the amelioration of conditions of disadvantaged individuals or groups."[26]

Specifically, employment equity policy has been adopted by law in the federal (that is, Employment Equity Act of 1986 and 1995 and in the Federal Contract Compliance Program, begun in 1986) and some provincial (for instance, the contract compliance program in Quebec) and some local jurisdictions (e.g., Toronto,

Vancouver) as a broad strategy for change aimed at removing discriminatory barriers and assisting organizations to become more representative of the communities for whom they work and from whom they recruit. When they implement employment equity, organizations identify and change policies and practices that impede the access and retention of members of underrepresented groups and work to create an organizational culture that is free of harassment and responsive to diversity. Employment equity also includes attempts to improve the representation of underrepresented groups, including visible-minority and aboriginal men and women.[27] All three components of employment equity implementation are relevant to our analysis of police organizations, although police services vary as to whether they fall under the requirements of an employment equity policy.

The purpose of an employment equity or affirmative action policy is to effectively counter organizational, institutionalized or systemic discrimination, which W. Taylor has defined as follows:

> [A] set of behaviours or institutional acts that create or perpetuate sets of advantages or privileges for whites and exclusions or deprivations for minority groups. It requires, in addition to a set of social mechanisms (institutional practices) and an ideology (policies/norms) or explicit or implicit superiority, the power to implement and maintain systems of privilege or deprivation. Institutional practices, and their support in organizational cultures/norms and power loci, are critical to this definition; they are also vital targets or components of any change effort. [28]

Our research focuses, for the most part, on the employment equity policies of several police organizations in the study and institutional practices that may be linked to improving the underrepresentation of visible-minority and aboriginal women and men in policing.

In a study of institutional practices it is particularly important to consider social scientific and legal analyses of ways in which recruitment, selection and promotion policies and practices may create barriers to the entry and integration of these groups into police employment. Employers may create barriers, either unconsciously or by design, by means of decision-making that involves differential treatment, or adverse impact, or failure to accommodate group-based differences.[29] Adverse impact discrimination is of particular interest in our survey and analysis, since an extensive literature demonstrates ways in which some criteria, such as tests or height standards, that have been used as a basis for decisions about selection or promotion of police officers, may create adverse impacts on women or on visible-minority or aboriginal groups. In other words, the use of criteria that create adverse impact result in a tendency to discriminate against members of these groups in selection and promotion decisions. Courts and human rights tribunals have found that if such discriminatory criteria cannot be demonstrated to be job-related, or cannot be shown to be valid tests that predict job performance, their use cannot be justified.

For example, in a review of court cases related to physical ability tests, J. Hogan and A. Quigley; L. Hoover: and R. Arvey, S. Nutting and T. Landon found that job analysis often fails to adequately tap the relevant duties and performance requirements for a job and that the relationship between test events and the job is questionable.[30] C. Winters reviewed some of the American court cases related to psychological tests used in selection, especially for minority applicants. He argues that the only way police agencies can use such tests is to make them job-related or have corroborating data and use these tests in conjunction with other selection procedures. In fact, in the *Grizzell* v. *Jackson Police Department* case, the court ruled that the Jackson police should no longer rely exclusively on the MMPI (one of the psychological tests used by police) for psychological evaluation and "that no one will be denied employment as a sworn police officer or refused promotion based solely and exclusively on their MMPI score without a psychological interview and other corroborating data."[31]

In Canada, legal cases have also resulted from similar challenges. In a recent case, *British Columbia Public Service Employee Relations Commission* v. *British Columbia Government Services Employees Union, September 1999*, relating to a female firefighter in British Columbia, the Supreme Court of Canada accepted the evidence that owing to physiological differences between men and women, most women have lower aerobic capacity than most men. For instance, most women could not increase their aerobic capacity enough to run 2.5 kilometres in eleven minutes, while most men (65 to 70 per cent) passed the test on the first try relative to few women (35 per cent) applicants. The Government of British Columbia could not provide evidence that the test was related to success on the job. In *ATF* v. *CN* (1984), a Canadian human rights tribunal struck down the use of the Bennet Mechanical Comprehension Test for selection into several entry-level positions because the test had a discriminatory impact on women and could not be shown to be job-related. The Supreme Court upheld the tribunal's decision in 1987. In 1978, an Ontario board of inquiry ruled in favour of the complainant in *Mr. Ishar Singh* v. *Security Investigation Services Ltd.* Mr. Singh was refused a job as a security guard because he wore the turban and beard required in the Sikh faith. The board of inquiry found that while the employer had no intention to insult or act with malice, the effect of the employer's policy, which required that their security guards be clean shaven and wear caps, was to deny employment to Sikhs. It ruled that intention was not necessary to establish contravention of human rights legislation. In *O'Malley* v. *Simpson Sears* (1985), the Supreme Court of Canada found that job requirements that have adverse impact on minorities and women are illegal in the absence of demonstrated "business necessity," or a valid relationship between job requirements and job performance. Over time, then, a relatively large body of jurisprudence on the need for "fair and equitable" criteria in the recruitment, selection and promotion of visible minorities, aboriginal people, and women has developed, which puts the onus on the employer to maintain a workplace free from all forms of illegal discrimination (see, for example, *Ann Colfer* v. *Ottawa Police Commission*, 1979; *Kickham* v. *City of Charlottetown*, 1986; 7 C.H.R.R. D/3339 (P.E.I. Bd. Inq.); *Ahluwalia* v. *Metropolitan Board of Commissioners of Police and Inspector William Dickson*, 1983; 4 C.H.R.R. D/1757 (Ont. Bd. Inq.).

Methodology

This study is part of a larger research project in which

fourteen of Canada's larger police organizations have been studied over a thirteen-year period (1985-98). In the present study, thirteen of these police services were surveyed to identify current and ongoing recruitment, selection and promotion strategies and assess their effectiveness in increasing visible-minority and aboriginal representation. These police organizations included the municipal services of Calgary, Edmonton, Vancouver, Regina, Winnipeg, Toronto, Ottawa-Carleton, Montreal, Halifax, and St. Hubert, as well as the Ontario Provincial Police (OPP), Quebec Provincial Police (QPP), and the Royal Canadian Mounted Police (RCMP). These services are not directly identified in our discussion of some of the results so as to protect anonymity of respondents. The Moncton Police Service was dropped from this study because of its recent amalgamation with the RCMP. Aboriginal officers are included for the first time in the present study; previous surveys in the series focused on visible minorities only. Moreover, this is the first study in the series that includes attention to promotion, in addition to recruitment and selection.

The questionnaire was pre-tested using a selected sample of respondents, and appropriate adjustments were made before questionnaires were mailed to the respective organizations (a copy of the questionnaire can be obtained from the authors). Contacts, usually with the chiefs of police or administrators responsible for human resources, were established in each of the police organizations. These contacts helped in completing the questionnaires and provided supplemental information during follow-up telephone interviews and/or site visits.

In addition, focus group interviews were conducted in two waves (a copy of the protocol for the focus groups can be obtained from the authors). The first set of focus groups was with a convenience sample of potential members of applicant pools and involved women and men who are young adults considering their career options. Ten separate group interviews took place in London (Ontario), Toronto and Montreal and included fifty-eight students and members of community organizations who identified themselves as members of visible minorities or aboriginal people, as well as Caucasian women. The ten focus groups of members of the potential applicant pool for police services provided insights into the perspectives of minority youth regarding policing as a career. *There is no claim that the potential applicant pool members who participated in the study are a representative sample of Canadian minority and aboriginal youth:* assembling a representative sample was impractical for reasons of cost and difficulty of recruiting volunteer participants. *The purpose of these focus group interviews was not to generalize* about the perceptions of all Canadian urban minority and aboriginal youth but to identify some of the considerations that may make policing an attractive career or that may present barriers to the recruitment of members of these underrepresented groups.

The second wave of focus groups included visible-minority and aboriginal men and women who were police officers in the RCMP, OPP, two municipal police services, and a First Nations service in Ontario. The focus groups with serving officers dealt with recruitment and selection, mentoring, career development and promotion, the culture of police organizations, and strategies and prospects for change in police organizations. Several individual interviews were also conducted with officers who hold senior ranks and/or who have done extensive work in an effort to improve the representation of visible minorities and aboriginal people in policing. Altogether, twenty-nine serving officers participated in the second wave. All focus groups were tape-recorded, with the consent of all participants, and the tapes were transcribed for analysis.

In addition, one of the researchers went on a ride-along with an officer during her night shift in order to obtain a first-hand experience of police work. This proved to be very valuable as a source of insight into the demands and challenges of police work, thus facilitating a better understanding of the information provided in this study.

Results and discussion

Overall representation of visible-minority officers
As Table 1 shows, representation of visible-minority and aboriginal officers has increased over the past decade, especially over the last five years. However, the representation rates are still below the percentage of visible minorities in the labour market. This situation is especially noticeable in Vancouver and Toronto,

two of Canada's cities with the highest proportions of visible-minority residents. In contrast, Halifax, Regina and Ottawa-Carleton are approaching representation rates that reflect the visible minorities in the labour market, with the latter two services recording relatively dramatic increases over the last five years.

Visible-minority women's representation rates remain at less than one per cent in all participating police services; two have no visible-minority women as officers. In the case of aboriginal officers, Winnipeg, Regina and the RCMP exceeded the 1991 labour force representation rates, while Edmonton approximates the aboriginal workforce representation rate in the city. Again, the representation of aboriginal women is markedly less than that of their male counterparts in all police services.

Recruitment and selection procedures and strategies

The questionnaire survey

The Canadian police services surveyed in this study utilize an extensive array of recruitment strategies, both traditional and innovative approaches. The traditional strategies, such as recruiting through the standard media (used by 85 per cent of the police services in the current study, versus 71 per cent in 1987), walk-ins and personal contact (77 per cent versus 79 per cent), and employee referrals (69 per cent versus 63 per cent) are still very popular. Over the last five years, police recruitment visits to community colleges and minority organizations have also been fairly widely used (by 69 per cent of the services).

With respect specifically to the recruitment of visible-minority and aboriginal officers, the data reveal that there are important changes in some recruitment strategies. That is, while the use of police officers' contacts with high school teachers and administrators has decreased considerably since 1990 (from 93 to 69 per cent and from 86 to 38 per cent, respectively), the use of visible minority role models is on the increase (from 71 to 92 per cent). With respect to aboriginal recruitment, the use of qualified and trained recruiters, the use of aboriginal community presentations, consultations with aboriginal organizations, and the use of advertisements in the minority media continue to be widely used by the police services (over 85 per cent). Police services

Table 1. Visible-minority (VM) representation in police organizations (1985, 1987, 1990, 1996/97) and availability of visible minorities in labour market (aged 15 years and over)

Minority group / Police organization	1985 Visible Minority % Men	% Women	% Total	1987 Visible Minority % Men	% Women	% Total	1990 Visible Minority % Men	% Women	% Total	1996/97 Visible Minority % Men	% Women	% Total	1996/97 Aboriginals (AB) % Men	% Women	% Total	Area	VM % in Labour market (1991 Census)	AB % in Labour market (1991 Census)
RCMP	n/a	n/a	n/a	n/a	n/a	n/a	n/a	n/a	0.8	2.5	0.4	2.9	3	0.5	3.5	Canada	9.1	3
Vancouver	1.9	0.3	2.2	2.3	0.3	2.6	3.1	0.7	3.8	4.7	0.8	5.5	0.5	0.2	0.7	Vancouver	22.4	2.4
Edmonton	n/a	n/a	n/a	0.7	n/a	0.7	1.6	0.4	2	4.8	0.5	5.3	2.9	0.9	3.8	Edmonton	11.5	3.9
Calgary	0.7	0.1	0.8	0.4	0.2	0.6	Men & Women		1.5	3.5	0.3	3.8	1.2	0.3	1.5	Calgary	12.5	2.7
Regina	n/a	n/a	n/a	0.6	n/a	n/a	0.6	0	0.6	3.6	0	3.6	5.2	2	7.2	Regina	4.8	4.2
Winnipeg	1.3	Men & Women	1.3	1.8	0.1	1.9	3	0.2	3.2	3.1	0.3	3.4	6.8	1.3	8.1	Winnipeg	10.3	5
Toronto	3	0	2.7	3	0.4	3.4	4.3	0.4	4.7	6.7	0.7	7.4	0.05	0.01	0.06	Toronto	24.6	1
Ottawa	0.3	0	0.3	0.3	0	0.3	2.3	0	2.3	n/a	n/a	8.3	n/a	n/a	2.4	Ottawa/Hull	9.4	3.3
OPP	n/a	n/a	n/a	n/a	n/a	n/a	1.4	0.02	1.4	n/a	n/a	n/a	n/a	n/a	n/a	Ontario	12.7	2.1
Montreal	0.1	0	0.1	0.3	n/a	0.3	0.5	0.02	0.5	n/a	n/a	n/a	n/a	n/a	n/a	Montreal	9.9	1.5
QPP	n/a	n/a	n/a	n/a	n/a	n/a	0	0.02	0	1.3	0.3	1.6	0.8	0.08	0.8	Quebec	5.1	1.9
Halifax	1.9	0	1.9	1.9	0	1.9	Men & Women		4.5	4.6	0.2	4.8	0.7	0.5	1.2	Halifax	5.6	2
St. Hubert	0	0	0	0	0	0	0	0	0	0	0	0	0	0	0	St. Hubert	n/a	n/a

The terms "visible minorities" (VMs) and "racial minorities" are used interchangeably. Census data is reported as VMs and hence the term VMs used in this table.

continue to be widely used by the police services as well (over 85 per cent).

The main index used to capture the effectiveness of the various recruiting strategies was derived from a survey question that directly asked what methods generate the most applicants. Respondents ranked newspapers as the most effective, followed by the use of visible minorities and aboriginal people as role models, community outreach programs/presentations, and job fairs. None of the police organizations surveyed collected systematic data on actual figures for each recruitment method, broken down by the relevant groups (visible minorities, Caucasians, etc.). Thus, no direct comparisons across the various methods could be attempted.

Barriers to recruitment of visible minorities, as reported by the police services, remained generally the same over the past five years: home-country perceptions of police, policing not being an acceptable profession for visible-minority women, better opportunities elsewhere, distrust of police, policing not an "honourable" profession, and high physical requirements. There were, however, some significant decreases with respect to significance of barriers due to distrust of police, policing not being an "honourable profession," minorities not being welcomed in police services, and policing as being dangerous. For aboriginals, distrust of police and better opportunities elsewhere were reported by police services as the major barriers.

As in other organizations, Canadian police services, at least in this study, use a variety of *selection* instruments and criteria in screening candidates for positions within the services. In essence, with the exception of one police service, where only a police academy diploma is used, all the other police services in this study use a multiple-hurdle process in screening applicants. Some services require applicants to re-do failed or invalid tests (six services), and others require applicants to do all the tests over again (six services). Table 2 below reveals the failure rates, by group, for the major hurdles (figures are only for the four police services that reported this data). It is evident that the failure rates for applicants from visible minorities are higher than those for Caucasian applicants for most of these hurdles.

The most popular selection instruments used by the thirteen police services include physical fitness exams (100-per-cent usage), background investigations (100 per cent), fingerprint checks (100 per cent), interviews (92 per cent), medical examinations (92 per cent), reference checks (92 per cent), application forms (85 per cent), English tests (69 per cent), and psychological tests (69 per cent). As is evident, two of the most popular selection instruments are the interview and psychological tests (including general aptitude tests). Since many applicants from visible-minority groups fail these tests, it is pertinent that the validity of the tests be assessed. An examination of the data reported suggests that, with respect to the interview, while all the police services have structured formats, only six score the responses. For the psychological test, only four police services have implemented (or are implementing) validation strategies.

As mentioned earlier, in developing a shortlist of candidates for selection, most of the police services utilize a system whereby candidates only proceed to the next stage if they meet the minimum requirements of the hurdles. However, one service uses a top-down procedure to achieve equity priorities: another service adjusts the bio-medical tests for women. Further, in order to encourage minorities to apply (as well as to satisfy some legal requirements), most of the police services have formal and/or informal accommodation policies. For instance, all the respondents stated that they allow Sikhs to wear turbans at work and three have special accommodation policies for visible-minority women.

The choice and development of selection standards varies across police services. However, in general, the human resources division in each service, the police chief, and police services boards feature prominently in the development of these standards, in line with provincial legislation. Ten police services had visible-minority and aboriginal liaison officers, and a similar number had advisory committees with visible-minority and aboriginal members.

Most Canadian police services in this study also administer employment equity programs, with three exceptions. For those services with employment equity programs, five have recruiting goals and timetables specifically for visible minorities and aboriginals, and three have established future hiring goals to the year 2001 and beyond.

Table 2. Failure Rates of Selected Groups in the Multiple Hurdle Process (most recent recruit class)

Type of hurdle	racial minorities		Aboriginals		Non-minorities	
	No. processed	% failed	No. processed	% failed	No. processed	% failed
Case 1						
Police applicant test	86	60	39	46	896	32
Physical abilities test	14	36	33%	33	505	24
Interview (2 on 1)	9	0	50%	50	343	29
Interview (3 on 1)	6	33	n/a	n/a	222	34
Case 2						
Police applicant test	56	71	46	46	348	41
Physical abilities test	17	12	28	7	240	13
Case 3						
Aptitude test	-	-			-	-
PARE test	6	0			142	21
1.5-mile run	6	33			82	33
Essay	4	0			85	14
Case 4						
General Aptitude Test Battery (GATP)	410	62	28	50	860	45
Written Communication Assessment (WCA)	410	26	22	23	860	3
Physical Readiness Evaluation						
For Police (PREP)	410	22	22	14	860	9
Behaviour exit interviews	59	30	6	0	64	17
Background investigation	29	34	4	0	24	13
Psychological interview	17	18	3	33	20	10

Focus group interviews

The first wave of focus groups, in which potential members of applicant pools were interviewed, provided rich data, including powerful images and cogent analyses, related to perceptions of policing as a career. Visible-minority and aboriginal youth reported many negative experiences with police that have created significant barriers to their recruitment into policing.[32] While there were some common themes, there were some differences between respondents of visible-minority and aboriginal ancestry.

When asked what phrases came to mind in relation to "policing as a career," visible-minority participants included the following: authority, interesting job, responsibility, power, racism, harassment, secure career, unwanted, white male, and command respect. Aboriginal respondents mentioned bureaucracy, red tape, racism, discrimination, corruption, tear gas, riot shields, brutality, stereotyping, and judgemental.

> In addition to the barriers identified by the focus groups of serving officers, the survey data suggest that there are significant problems of adverse impact, lack of validation, issues related to the job interview, and prima facie case of adverse impact/illegal discrimination that arise from the selection systems used by some of the services.

Generally, the police were seen as racist and not very knowledgeable of the cultures of First Nations and visible minorities. As one aboriginal participant stated,

> The police [are seen as] a bunch of white guys trying to beat up Indian people. My mother was struck when she was pregnant because she was trying to defend my father who was getting beat up by two officers. My experiences as a young child are negative. ... I know the officers that come on the reserve treat them [aboriginals] like children and talk to them like they are children. We don't have the right services. We do not have the money to build nice

buildings. We do not have the money to set up and draw up our own resources like the way the municipality can.

A visible-minority respondent commented,

> As soon as I came to this country, five months ago, I was walking with my younger brother and some police officers came up to me and said, "Excuse me, sir, where are you going tonight? We just got a criminal call about two black men fitting your description in this neighbourhood who committed a crime." I looked at him, and it was like, "Well, you've got the wrong people – maybe they are further ahead." When he found out I go to [University of] Western [Ontario] and what my dad does – because my dad is a doctor – and because I am well-spoken, he calmed down a little bit. So, it's that kind of experience that had an effect on me.

Yet, participants also conveyed a strong belief in the importance of visible-minority and aboriginal communities of having a representative police force. As one participant stated, "[P]olicing is a form of power. If we are not involved as a people, then we give up the power to govern ourselves."

With respect to ways in which police services can attract and retain visible minorities and members of First Nations, potential applicant pool participants felt in general, that these organizations must change their discriminatory and exclusionary practices. More specifically, participants suggested that the following practices would be helpful:

- having more representatives from their communities on the police services may serve as role models in attracting others;
- applicants should be screened on "moral fibre" and attitudes to minorities" before hiring, in order to ensure that police services do not recruit applicants who have prejudices against minorities;

- mentoring and internship programs for minority and aboriginal youth should be intensified; and
- more informal as well as formal contact should be established with minority communities.

The serving officers of aboriginal or visible-minority ancestry who participated in the second wave of focus groups generally indicated that their career choice had been strongly influenced by relatives or friends who were police officers or by other positive personal experiences with police in their communities. Among the attractive features of a career in policing are job security, the pay, and, most important, the opportunity to be of service to one's community. Many of the visible-minority and aboriginal officers described how their presence in the police service made contributions to their communities, including serving as role models. As one aboriginal officer remarked,

I saw policing as a way to solve problems in our community. I saw that we did a good job. It was safer to walk on the road. Me, my older brother and older cousin (also an officer) began to paint a picture for the aboriginal community. We can do something good, project a model for other young aboriginal people. Now there are thirteen or fourteen other young officers at [community name]. I think we had something to do with that.

Similarly, a visible-minority officer stated the following:

My experience has been that whenever I've been in the community and I've talked with other Black people, they are cognizant of how many other Blacks are on the department. They might not necessarily deal with the police every day, but they are still aware that, "Oh, aren't there two or three other Black guys," ... it seems that, by virtue of our skin colour or structure or whatever, that people know how many of "us" there are within the department. So I've sort of felt that I was ... carrying the torch, or just standing out as a representative of pretty well any and every minority culture or community, just by

300

virtue of my skin colour. I guess that's a good thing in a way, because it gives some people encouragement to say, "Yeah, when I grow up I can be like him. He's Black as well ..." So it's kind of nice to know that by just your presence – you haven't even opened your mouth – that you're giving a positive impression in your community ... It seems that people are not necessarily more receptive to me, but they are just happy to see that there is a little difference, a little mix.

Visible-minority and aboriginal officers identified several barriers that should be removed so as to improve representation of their communities in police services. There is a perception that some unnecessary physical requirements still exist that present a barrier to women, including in particular, minority women. Other barriers to recruitment include a lack of minority and aboriginal representation on interview panels and a lack of minority role models.

In addition to the barriers identified by the focus groups of serving officers, the survey data suggest that there are significant problems of adverse impact, lack of validation, issues related to the job interview, and prima facie case of adverse impact/illegal discrimination that arise from the selection systems used by some of the services.

As data in Table 2, supplied by the police services, indicate, some of the selection methods used by the police services seem to have a prima facie case for adverse impact on either visible minorities or aboriginal people, or both. For instance, for Case 4, applying the 4/5th rule (or the labour market representativeness of an employer's workforce that has been applied in numerous legal cases in the United States and Canada,[33] there is a prima facie case for adverse impact on visible minorities in the General Aptitude Test Battery test, the Written Communication Assessment, and background checks; the number of aboriginals is too small to assess such an impact. Further, the police applicant test appears to have a prima facie case of adverse impact on visible minorities in Case 2 and on both visible minorities and aboriginals relative to others in Case 1.

Lack of validation of selection instruments is also a serious concern. Only four police services validate psychological tests, while two others reported that a validation study was in progress. Three police services have validated the RRST, the cadet examinations, and police constable examination. Another police service indicated that they have performed content validation for the job interview and scoring key, physical, medical and driving examinations, while another service has conducted differential validation of the selection instruments (i.e., a selection method having a differential effect in the selection of minorities). The balance of the police services have not assessed differential validity for their tests for aboriginals and visible minorities.

All police services have structured job-interview formats. However, only seven of the thirteen police departments score job-interview responses. Moreover even though six police departments had aboriginal and visible-minority interviewers, no police service included visible minorities and aboriginal people in the team that does the scoring of job interviews. This is a serious problem, since interviews count for 30 to 100 per cent weight in selection (as reported by the police services). Research indicates that interviews tend to be subjective and to have poor validity unless they are properly structured and validated.[34]

Promotional strategies and criteria

The questionnaire survey

Of the thirteen police organizations in this study, ten provided data on the ranks attained by visible-minority and aboriginal police officers. The typical hierarchy in the police services is chief, deputy chief, chief superintendent, superintendent, staff inspector/inspector, staff sergeant, sergeant, corporal, and constable. With the exception of one police chief, the highest rank attained by aboriginal and visible-minority officers is that of an inspector and/or staff inspector. Only three of the ten reporting police services had a visible minority or aboriginal officer at this rank; these officers represent less than one per cent of each of the police services that reported having them.

Only six police services provided data on the actual number of visible-minority and First Nations officers promoted. Of the

1,506 promotions made by these police services in the 1996-97 period, 77 (5.1 per cent) were among aboriginals, and 129 (8.6 per cent) were among visible minorities. However, over 98 per cent of these promotions were at the most junior level (constable).

Eleven of the thirteen police organizations in this survey provided information on the strategies and criteria for promoting officers. As Table 3 indicates, promotional examinations, seniority, promotional board reviews, and performance appraisals were most often used as criteria for promotion to the sergeant and/or staff inspector position. For inspector and/or staff inspector positions, promotional board reviews, promotional exams, and performance appraisals were most often used as the promotional criteria.

In several police organizations, officers to the rank of inspector (as in Vancouver) and superintendent (as in Edmonton) are covered by collective agreements with police associations. Hence, the criteria for promotion up to and including these ranks are jointly negotiated. This may have an adverse impact on the promotional chances of visible-minority and aboriginal officers, since seniority is one of the major promotional criteria negotiated in these agreements. Police forces hire only at the constable level and at no other rank, except in rare cases when a police chief's position is filled from outside the force. In industry and other organizations, a person can join at any rank or managerial position depending on that person's qualifications and experience. This is not the case in police organizations. No matter how much experience a person has in his or her home country as police chief/ high-level officer, he or she has to start at the constable level in any Canadian police organization. It is for this reason that the Race Relations and Policing Task Force and other inquiries recommended not only lateral or direct entry for qualified visible minorities and aboriginals but also faster promotions for qualified visible-minority and aboriginal men and women.[35]

Using seniority as a criteria for promotion blocks the advancement of underrepresented minority groups, since their members were recruited more recently than their Caucasian colleagues. They are less likely than Caucasian male officers, as a group, to possess the seniority that is necessary to achieve the promotion. For example, in one service, the average seniority of aboriginal members was 6.1 years, but the eligibility to apply for promotion was eight years. The overall results suggest that the average number of years until promotion can occur was approximately eight years for all police organizations reporting. The use of this arguably arbitrary seniority criterion effectively limits the promotion opportunities of aboriginal officers. Visible-minority and aboriginal officers are more likely to remain as constables or be promoted (depending on their length of service) as junior police officers and not achieve higher ranks relative to their Caucasian colleagues hired by police services.

None of the police services in this study have any mechanism in place for lateral or direct entry for visible-minority and aboriginal persons, other than at the entry level. The only exception is at very senior levels such as chief of police. In addition, there were no career development initiatives directed towards these groups. One police service had lateral entry at the second-class constable level from regional police services, while another reported that they had a First Nations direct appointments policy and have hired one aboriginal officer at the inspector level but could not provide any figures for any other lateral appointments.

Almost all police services stated that they have no special measures directed at visible-minority and aboriginal officers for accelerated promotions, as has been recommended by a number of commissions and task forces. The reason cited, in most cases, was that the collective agreement with the respective police associations does not permit any of these measures.

A number of promotional barriers for visible-minority and aboriginal officers are evident in the information provided by the police organizations. They include, but are not limited to, seniority as specified under collective agreements, use of tests, fixed number of applicants per available position, composition of interview panels and other types of decision-making boards, and absence of special measures to promote underrepresented minority groups. Further, there appears to be a lack of proactive communication programs that present diversity at all levels of the organization as a desirable goal for police organizations.

Six of the survey reports indicated that officers could not advance further in the promotion process unless they achieved a "pass/fail" mark (also referred to as a cut-off score). The lower

Table 3. Top Promotional Criteria in Selected (N = 11) Canadian Police Organizations, 1996/97

| Promotional Criteria | Rank | | | | | | | | | | | | | | | |
| | Corporal | | Sergeant/ staff insp. | | Inspector/ Staff insp. | | Chief Inspector | | supt. | | staff supt. | | Deputy chief | | Chief | |
	No.	%	No.	%	No.	%	No.	%	No.	%	No.	%	No.	%	No.	%
Promotional exam	4	36	10	91	6	55	2	18	1	9	n/a	n/a	1	9	1	9
Seniority	3	27	9	82	3	27	n/a	n/a	n/a	n/a	n/a	n/a	n/a	n/a	n/a	n/a
Performance appraisal	1	9	6	55	5	45	2	10	1	9	1	9	3	27	3	27
Psychological tests	0	0	1	9	1	9	1	9	1	9	n/a	9	2	18	2	18
Promotional board review	2	18	7	64	7	64	4	36	3	27	1	9	4	36	4	36
Promotional individual review	0	0	0	0	1	9	1	9	n/a		n/a		2	18	2	18
Assessment centre	0	0	2	18	3	27	2	18	n/a		n/a		3	27	2	18
Other*	0	0	1	9	1	9	1	9	n/a		n/a					

N-13 (OPP – not available; QPP – not completed)

* Other criteria included: knowledge exam, management exam, in-basket exercises, self development and reference checks

pass/fail grade was sixty-five per cent. This may eliminate a number of candidates from the promotion process, with a distinct possibility of adverse impact on the basis of race and gender as a result of these promotional tests.

Several of the police organizations made reference to ratios of number of applicants to available positions. This further reduces the opportunities for many officers. For example, in one police service, for one of every five positions available, the service will review seven candidates per opening. Limiting the number of applicants who can apply for an open position eliminates a number of candidates from going further in the promotion process. This may be especially true of visible-minority and aboriginal officers who have lower seniority to begin with.

Boards or panels are extensively used in the final decision-making process in all cases. Most of these boards use three ranking officers to conduct interviews and make assessments on final candidates. Therefore, the decision to form the board is based on rank. A considerable amount of research has looked at the composition of boards and the effects of race in interviewing situations. It has been found that when a person of one race interviews another person of the same race (a Caucasian person interviews another Caucasian person, or a black person interviews another black person, for example) they tend to assign higher ratings to those candidates who are from the same racial group.[36] Therefore, the police services should consider a mix of participants to reflect differences of both gender and race, when selecting the board, so that visible-minority and aboriginal officers, and women, are not faced with only Caucasian men in the interview process. Considering that only a few visible-minority and aboriginal members, and women, are in higher ranks, the composition of interview boards is another serious barrier to promotion for these officers. Finally, there was an obvious absence of special measures to promote underrepresented minority officers in most police organizations.

Three of the police services reported attempts to remove barriers for minorities from their promotional systems. Some of the positive initiatives undertaken by the three police organizations to eliminate biases and barriers towards minorities in the promotion systems may be emulated in the other police services.

First, recognizing that seniority was creating a barrier to advancement for minority officers, these police services have incorporated the concept of merit into their promotional system. Thus, an individual's accomplishments and abilities are considered, rather than having seniority as the only deciding factor. The necessary competencies required to perform the job duties for each given level are determined. Each officer is then assessed against the competencies that are required to perform the job, and a composite score of tests, abilities, and, in some cases, seniority is determined (one police service used seniority as the deciding factor when candidates have the same score). Junior members of the force thus have an opportunity to be considered alongside more senior members.

Second, each of these police forces has been proactive in reporting their new programs to their members. These programs were developed in consultation with their employees. Each of the groups conducted surveys and town-hall meetings or focus-group interviews to elicit information. In many cases, the changes that occurred were as a result of having listened to their employees.

Focus-group interviews

A dominant theme in the interviews with visible-minority and aboriginal officers was the existence of barriers to promotion within the police services. The perceived lack of promotion opportunities cast a negative light on their experience with policing as a career. Such barriers included the existence of an "Old Boys" network, a fear of backlash if promoted (that is, allegations that promotions were undeserved when achieved by minority or aboriginal candidates), problems with "fitting in" socially, and the "Caucasian male culture" of police organizations. The following quotes from visible-minority and aboriginal officers illustrate the situation and point out how severe the barriers are to the promotion of women who are aboriginal or members of visible minorities:

> I think you're either one of the old boys or you're not. You gotta be one of the boys. The older guys, the guys with more experience. And that's how it works. I'm sure that's a fact to do with promotion and stuff like that. You

want to be liked, you want to be part of the boy's club, before you're even considered for promotion. ... Most guys play hockey, and I feel kind of left out because I don't play hockey. Does that mean that I can't be a sergeant someday? It shouldn't be a factor, but you never know.

I know one thing. Once a minority, whether it's a woman or a Black or a Chinese or whatever, when it comes to promotion, if I get promoted compared to a few other guys, the first thing they are going to say is, "Oh, it must be because you are Black."

I think I had written on my assessment once about not socializing enough. ... I had my friends within the Black community who I also have to go and socialize with.

The police force is very political, basically to go along with the name of the game that is being played to get ahead. Your intelligence and your knowledge, at times, means nothing. It's who your friends are, and how well you accept the criticisms that are thrown at you. You do it with a smile and keep on drinking. You go to all their parties and you're the butt of the jokes, but you take it with a grin and you might succeed, but if you have a mind of your own and are prepared to stand on your own two feet, you will not succeed.

Results from the focus-group interviews suggest that barriers to promotion and lack of career development opportunities were major sources of dissatisfaction to serving officers of minority and aboriginal background. Several officers noted that progress was evident during the brief period when mandatory employment equity was in force in Ontario, but with the Harris government's repeal of Ontario's Employment Equity Act in 1995, the power of the "old boys' network" has been reasserted.

In general, there has been progress in the representation of visible minorities and aboriginal people in some police services, as well as improvements in recruitment, selection and promotion policies and practices in some of the selected police services. Nevertheless, there is still a significant need for improvement, since the representation rates generally do not reflect relevant labour markets.

Several officers expressed a sense of optimism that change is happening and that progressive change will occur as new leadership emerges and younger, better-educated officers replace older officers in the police services. However, the participants were under no illusions about the difficulty of bringing about change. As one officer remarked:

I think that nothing is going to be fixed overnight. ... It's going to take time, and people are just going to have to understand that they should recognize the cultural diversities and intellectual diversities within their own departments. Sure, we all wear the same uniform ... but even though we are all officers, we are all individuals too, with different backgrounds and understandings of things. And if there is any way that a department or organization can tap into those things, the whole organization will be much richer for being able to tap the energies that lie within a person.

Conclusions

We have presented an analysis of data on the recruitment, selection and promotion of visible minorities and aboriginal people in thirteen police services across Canada, using both quantitative and qualitative research methodologies. These findings contribute to the literature in several ways. First, this is the first study that has examined promotion as well as recruitment and selection of visible-minority and aboriginal men and women in Canadian police services. Second, this is the first major study of these issues for aboriginal police officers. Third, this study situates current findings within the context of a wider fifteen-year study:

longitudinal studies are critical in examining change in organizations. Finally, in using both quantitative and qualitative research methodologies, this study provides a richer analysis than previous studies.

Future research should continue to explore these issues over time and with a larger number of police organizations. Further, future studies should address the specific issues of recruitment, selection and promotion with respect to women and persons with disabilities – particularly those of visible-minority or aboriginal ancestry – in police organizations. The lack of data and of initiatives directed towards improving the representation of visible-minority and aboriginal women is noteworthy and needs to be addressed.

In general, there has been progress in the representation of visible minorities and aboriginal people in some police services, as well as improvements in recruitment, selection and promotion policies and practices in some of the selected police services. Nevertheless, there is still a significant need for improvement, since the representation rates generally do not reflect relevant labour markets. The experience of those few police services that have developed progressive approaches, and the experience-based suggestions of members of visible minorities and aboriginal people who have or who are interested in careers in policing, are valuable resources that may be drawn upon to guide future change.

While these findings are of assistance in formulating a current diagnosis of the problem of under-representation of visible minorities and aboriginal people in policing, they are neither essentially new nor surprising. As suggested in our introduction, numerous commissions, task forces, investigations and public inquiries have been struck in provinces and cities across Canada to identify the root causes of the recurring crises in relationships between police services and minority communities. Without exception, their reports have recommended that police organizations become more representative of the diversity of the communities they serve, as a first step towards the renewal of police-community relations. Yet, our data demonstrate that police services are still far from representative and that few have taken effective steps towards this fundamental objective. As a society, we know the distance we have to travel, we understand the social importance of trust between police and the diverse communities of Canada, and we have identified many of the barriers that impede progress towards more representative police services.

Why do we not get on with the task of removing the barriers, improving the diversity of police organizations, and healing the animosity between them and minority and aboriginal communities? The answer to this perplexing question lies beyond the scope of our inquiry, in the realm of social values, political priorities, and power relations between privileged and disadvantaged groups within Canada society.

Endnotes

*Reprinted with permission, Canadian Public Administration, Volume 42, No. 3 (Fall), PP.46-74.
This study was funded by the Canadian Centre for Police Race Relations. The authors would like to thank Ms. Deborah Zinni, a doctoral student, and Ms. Meryl Hodnett, a graduate of the MBA program, both at McMaster University, Mr. Allan Pelletier, Mr. C. Lloyd Stanford, president, Le Groupe Stanford Inc. in Ottawa, for assisting with this research project; Professor Donald Clairmont, Dalhousie University, for lhis comments on an earlier draft; Mr. Michael Foster, for assisting with the focus groups; and the journal's anonymous reviewers for their helpful comments. The authors are solely responsible for the contents and views expressed in this article.

1 In this article, the terms "aboriginal," "aboriginals" and "First Nations are used interchangeably, as are "racial minorities" and "visible minorities." C. Agocs, C. Burr and F. Somerset, *Employment Equity: Cooperative Strategies for Organizational Change* (Toronto: Prentice-Hall of Canada, 1992).

2 Statistics Canada, *The Daily* 13 January 1998, p. 6.

3 David Koperis, "The Saskatoon Police and the frozen bodies," *The Globe and Mail* 17 February 2000, pp. A1, A3.

4   A. Andrews, *Review of Race Relations Practices of the Metropolitan Toronto Police Force* (Toronto: Municipality of Metropolitan Toronto, 1992); Quebec, Human Rights Commission, *Investigation into Relations Between Police Forces, Visible and Other Ethnic Minorities.* Chaired by J. Bellemare (Montreal: Commission, 1988); Alberta, Task Force on the Criminal Justice System and its Impact on the Indian and Métis People of Alberta, *Justice on Trial.* Chaired by R. Cawsey (Edmonton: Queen's Printer, 1991); Toronto, Commission on Systemic Racism in the Ontario Criminal Justice System, *Final Report* (Toronto: Queen's Printer, 1995); Manitoba, Aboriginal Inquiry of Manitoba: The Justice System and Aboriginal People, *Report.* Chaired by A. Hamilton and C. Sinclair (Winnipeg: Queens Printer, 1991); Nova Scotia, Royal Commission on the Donald Marshall Jr. Prosecution, *Report.* Chaired by T. Hickman (Halifax: Queen's Printer, 1989); Law Reform Commission of Canada, *Report on Aboriginal Peoples and Criminal Justice* (Ottawa: Commission, 1991); Toronto, Race Relations and Policing Task Force, *Report.* Chaired by C. Lewis (Toronto: Office of the Solicitor General, 1989 and 1992); British Columbia, Commission of Inquiry Into Policing in British Columbia, *Report.* Chaired by W. Oppal (Victoria: Queen's Printer, 1994); Alberta, Public Inquiry into Policing in Relation to the Blood Tribe, *Report. Findings and Recommendations.* Chaired by C. Rolf (Edmonton: Queen's Printer, 1991).

5   F. Henry, C. Tator, W. Mantis and T. Rees, The Colour of Democracy: *Racism in Canadian Society* (Toronto: Harcourt Brace, 1995).

6   D. Northrup, "Public perceptions of police treatment of minority groups and disadvantaged in Metropolitan Toronto," *Institute for Social Research [York University] Newsletter* 11, no. 1 (Winter 1996), pp. 4-5.

7   D. Dutton, "The Public and the Police: Training Implications of the Demand for a New Model Police Officer," in J. Yuille, ed., *Police Selection and Training* (Boston: Martinus Nijhoff Publishers, 1986).

8 Ibid.; M. Wycoff, C. Susmilch and P. Eisenbart, *Reconceptualizing the Police Role: An Examination of Theoretical Issue, Information Needs, Empirical Realities, and the Potential for Revision* (Washington, D.C.: The Police Foundation, 1980).

9 A. Fleras and J.L. Elliott, *Multiculturalism in Canada: The Challenge of Diversity* (Scarborough, Ont.: Nelson Canada, 1992).

10 Ibid.

11 H.C. Jain, "An Assessment of Strategies of Recruiting Visible Minority Police Officers in Canada: 1985-1990," in R. C. Mcleod and David Schneiderman, eds., *Police Powers in Canada: the Evolution and Practice of Authority* (Toronto: University of Toronto Press, 1994); H.C. Jain, "The recruitment and selection of visible minorities in Canadian police organizations," CANADIAN PUBLIC ADMINISTRATION 31, no.3 (Fall 1988), pp. 463-82; Toronto, Race Relations and Policing Task Force, *Report*. Chaired by C. Lewis.

12 Jain, "An Assessment of Strategies of Recruiting Visible Minority Police Officers in Canada," in Macleod and Schneiderman, *Police Powers in Canada*; Senaka K. Suriya, "The representation of visible minorities in Canadian police: employment equity beyond rhetoric," *Police Studies* 16, no. 2 (Summer 1993), pp. 44-62.

13 André Normandeau, "La police et les minoritiés ethniques," *Journal du Collège canadien de police / Canadian Police College Journal* 14, no. 3 (1990), pp. 231-46.

14 C. Lewis, "The Report of the Race Relations and Policing Task Force," Ibid.

15 Fleras and Elliott, *Multiculturalism in Canada*.

16 C. Jayewardene and C. Talbot, *Police Recruitment of Ethnic Minorities* (Ottawa: Supply and Services Canada, 1990).

17 F. Milliken and L. Martins, "Searching for common threads: understanding the multiple effects of diversity in organizational groups," *Academy of Management Review* 21, no. 3 (July 1996), pp. 402-33; B. Walker, "An approach

to diversity: valuing differences," *Organizational Dynamics* 22, no. 1 (Summer 1993), p. 12; W. Watson, K. Kumar and L. Michaelsen, "Cultural diversity's impact on interaction process and performance: comparing homogenous and diverse task groups," *Academy of Management Journal* 36, no. 4 (October 1993), pp. 590-602.

18 H.C. Jain, "Recruitment of racial minorities in Canadian police forces," *Relations Industrielles* 42, no. 4 (December 1987), pp. 790-803; Jain, "An Assessment of Strategies of Recruiting Visible Minority Police Officers in Canada," in McLeod and Schneiderman, Police Powers in Canada; Jain, "The recruitment and selection of visible minorities in Canadian police organizations," CANADIAN PUBLIC ADMINISTRATION; Suriya, "The representation of visible minorities in Canadian policy: employment equity beyond rhetoric," *Police Studies*.

19 Quebec, Human Rights Commission, *Investigation Into Relations Between Police Forces, Visible and Other Ethnic Minorities*. Chaired by J. Bellemare; Toronto, Race Relations and Policing Task Force, *Report*. Chaired by C. Lewis; Lewis, "The Report of the Race Relations and Policing Task Force," *Canadian Police College Journal*; E. Oziewicz, "Better training on racism urged for Montreal policy: Prejudiced attitude must change, Ryan says," *The Globe and Mail* (Toronto) 19 January 1993, p. A4.

20 Toronto, Commission on Systemic Racism in the Ontario Criminal Justice System, *Final Report*; Manitoba, Aboriginal Inquiry of Manitoba: The Justice System and Aboriginal People, *Report*. Chaired by A. Hamilton and C. Sinclair, Nova Scotia, Royal Commission on the Donald Marshall Jr. Prosecution, *Report*. Chaired by T. Hickman; Alberta, Public Inquiry into Policing in Relation to the Blood Tribe, *Report. Findings and Recommendations*. Chaired by C. Rolf.

21 British Columbia, Commission of Inquiry Into Policing in British Columbia, *Report*. Chaired by W. Oppal.

22 Ibid.; Toronto, Race Relations and Policing Task Force, *Report*. Chaired by C. Lewis.

23 British Columbia, Commission of Inquiry Into Policing in British Columbia, *Report*, p. E-14. Chaired by W. Oppal.

24 Ellen Hochstedler, "Impediments to hiring minorities in public agencies," *Journal of Police Science and Administration* 12, no. 2 (June 1984), pp. 227-40; W. Lewis, "Toward representative bureaucracy: Blacks in city police organizations," *Public Administration Review* 49, no. 3 (May/June 1989), pp. 257-68; Susan E. Martin, "'Outsider within' the station house: The impact of race and gender on Black women police," *Social Problems* 41, no. 3 (August 1994), pp. 383-400; Norma Riccucci, "Female and minority employment in city government: the role of unions," *Policy Studies Journal* 15, no. 1 (September 1986), pp. 3-16; Brent Steel and Nicholas P. Lovrich Jr., "Equality and efficiency trade-offs in affirmative action – real or imagined? The case of women in policing," *Social Science Journal* 24, no. 1 (January 1987), pp. 53-70; Lana Stein, "Representative local government: minorities in the municipal work force," *Journal of Politics* 48, no. 3 (August 1986), pp. 694-716; Samual Walker, "Racial minority and female employment in policing: the implications of 'glacial' change," *Crime and Delinquency* 31, no. 4 (October 1985), pp. 555-72.

25 W. S. Tarnopolsky, "Discrimination and Affirmative Action," in Harish C. Jain and D. Carroll, eds., *Race and Sex Equality in the Workplace: A Challenge and an Opportunity* (Ottawa: Supply and Services Canada, 1980).

26 See also H.S. Jain, "Employment Equity in Canada," *Human Resource Management in Canada* [newsletter] (November 1997), pp. 50,043-50,058.

27 Ibid.; Agocs, C. Burr and F. Somerset, *Employment Equity*.

28 W. Taylor, "Race Relations Interventions Within a Probation Service," in John W. Shaw, Peter Nordlie and Richard Shapiro, eds., *Strategies for Improving Race Relations: The Anglo-American Experience* (Manchester: Manchester University Press, 1987), pp. 149-64.

29 M. Bendick Jr., "Adding Testing to the Nation's Portfolio of Information on Employment Discrimination," in Michael Fix and Margery Austin Turner, eds., *A National*

Report Card on Discrimination in America: The Role of Testing (Washington, D.C.: The Urban Institute, 1999). Chapter 3; Agocs, Burr and Somerset, *Employment Equity*: H.C. Jain, "Race and sex discrimination in employment in Canada: Theories, evidence and policies," *Relations Industrielles* 37, no. 2 (June 1982), pp. 344-66; H.C. Jain and P.J. Sloane, *Equal Employment Issues: Race and Sex Discrimination in the United States, Canada and Britain* (New York: Praeger, 1981).

30 Joyce Hogan and Ann Quigley, "Physical standards for employment and the courts," *American Psychologist* 41, no. 11 (November 1986), pp. 1193-1217; Larry T. Hoover, "Trends in police physical ability selection testing," *Public Personnel Management* 21, no. 1 (Spring 1992), pp. 29-40; Clyde a. Winters, "Socio-economic status, test bias and the selection of police," *The Police Journal* 65, no. 2 (April/June 1992), pp. 125-35; C. Winters, "Psychology tests, suits and minority applicants," *The Police Journal* 62, no. 1 (January 1989), pp. 22-30.

31 Reference for court case; Winters, "Psychology tests, suits and minority applicants," *The Police Journal*.

32 For similar findings from focus groups with about fifty black youth in six Ontario cities, see C.E. James, "'Up to No Good': Black on the Streets and Encountering Police," in Vic Satzewich, eds., *Racism and Social Inequality in Canada* (Toronto: Thompson Educational Publishing, 1998), pp. 157-76.

33 For the United States, see R. D. Gatewood and H.S. Feild, *Human Resources Selection* (Fort Worth, Tx.: Dryden Press, 1998). For Canada, see National Capital Alliance on Race Relations v. Health Canada [1997].

34 Gatewood and Feild, *Human Resources Selection*; Willi H. Wiesner and S. Cronshaw, "A meta-analysis investigation of the impact of interview format and degree of structure on the validity of the employment interview," *Journal of Occupational Psychology* 61, no. 4 (December 1988), pp. 275-90.

35 Ibid.; Toronto, Race Relations and Policing Task Force, *Report*.Chaired by C. Lewis; British Columbia,

Commission of Inquiry Into Policing in British Columbia, *Report*. Chaired by W. Oppal.

36 Thung-Run Lin, Gregory H. Dobbins an Jiing-Lih Farh, "A field study of race and age similarity effects on interview ratings in conventional and situational interviews," *Journal of Applied Psychology* 77, no. 3 (June 1992), pp. 363-71; Amelia J. Prewett, Hubert S. Feild, John G. Veres III and Ph'lip M. Lewis, "Effects of race on interview ratings in a situational panel interview," *Journal of Applied Psychology* 81, no. 2 (April 1996), pp. 178-86.

12

Women in Policing in Canada*

Marcel-Eugène LeBeuf and Julia McLean

Women are in the police to stay. In Canada, they still account for a relatively small percentage that is close to 10%, based on the 1994 figures and including the entire police universe (Statistics Canada, 1996).

Women have been a part of police forces since the turn of the century in America (LeBeuf, 1996; Shores, 1997). In Canada, the first female police officers were admitted into the police between 1912 and 1915. They were very few, that is five, according to Moore's figures (1997). It was not long before they left or were dismissed. They began to invade the ranks of police forces in large numbers in the late '60s and in the early '70s, as a result of the enactment of legislation against all forms of discrimination based on race, gender, religion etc.

The arrival of women in a world in which male-centred (macho) culture, bias and attitudes prevailed, inevitably gave rise to a slow and insidious controversy immersed in the common values of the decade. Unsuited, unadjusted and certainly incapable of carrying out a line of work advocated by and for men, women were initially considered to be unavoidable usurpers. Depending on their standing in the police structure, they were forced to bear the brunt of sarcasm, to deal with the burden of mistakes allegedly the brunt of sarcasm, to deal with the burden of mistakes allegedly attributed to their gender and the forces' inability to adjust to the new social order. They have also had to take on duties, sometimes against their will, in prevention sections and/or child support sections that were not considered to be "real" police work.

In the new century, has the situation of women improved? In other words, as women legally have constituted full-fledged members for at least thirty years, are they assuming their rightful place? Are there any adapted policies in place to help them become integrated in a traditionally male culture and, also, to climb the ladder of a paternalistic structure?

In the next section, we will touch on the women's place in the police organizations, on the actual or presumably granted or expected role and, finally, on the future of policewomen and the organization.

In our compilation of the works on policewomen, we noted that most of the research works compared policewomen with policemen (LeBeuf 1996, 1997). There was never any questioning of police philosophy or even the changes required to integrate them fully. In fact, and particularly during the '70s, several research papers compared the two in terms of performance-related issues, such as the effective performance of duties, the ability to take on similar duties and the opportunities to do real police work. These comparison exercises, which were undoubtedly necessary in view of the very context, did little to discredit women even though it was subtly hinted that women were not of much use in this line of work. They clearly indicated to what extent men were concerned with protecting a male bastion.

Up until recently, not only the selection criteria, but also the admission requirements, the examination requirements and the boards were established by men for men. As the years passed, with the support of men, women began clamouring for policies that took into account their specificity. Large forces such as the Royal Canadian Mounted Police (RCMP) and the Montreal Urban Community Police Department, to name only two, set up a consultancy on women's issues or on diversity programs. The purpose of such a function is to support the institution and to corroborate the policies in place. The question that remains to be asked is the following: what can be done to ensure that the gender issue impacts on police management policy and on related attitudes? It seems to us that the research on policewomen in the years to come should seriously examine this aspect.

Finally, we should point out that the rank and file policewomen, the municipal and RCMP policewomen have made giant strides over the past thirty years, mainly due to the fact that they have begun to join police forces in large numbers, that through their presence they have made waves and clamoured for action that meets their needs. They still have a long way to go. However, the status of senior-ranking policewomen, policewomen in positions of authority, remains relatively undocumented and little known. Based on the statistical data available, 6% of Canadian policewomen have attained the rank of NCO and less than 1%, the rank of officer. If we wish to draw a parallel here, we could say that this category of women, who are pioneers in policing since they slowly went up the rank leading them to such duties, continues to remain cut off from the rest of police officers at a level where men still account for the majority. Some of them continue to experience a state of subservience where it is claimed that the only reason for their success has to do with their benefiting from favouritism because of their woman status, and consequently, has nothing to do with their ability and their leadership. To gain recognition for their work, they have to do better than their male counterparts. Of course, there are always exceptions to this last comment, but we have no intention of making a rule out of it.

Women's Place in the Police Organization

Before dealing directly with the place of women in the police and the inherent problems they encounter, we have to define the place of women in society in general. McTeer (1997) identified at least two key events that enabled women to begin assuming legal and social standing in Canadian society. The first event was the women's right to vote at the federal and provincial levels. The second was the entrenchment of the equality principle under the law in the Canadian Constitution. These events certainly opened doors for women in several activity areas, even though they remained absent in comparison with men. Although they began their ascent; they remained relatively absent from places where power was exercised. For example, in 1997, 18% of judges appointed by the federal government were women. Two of the nine Supreme Court of Canada judges were women. Furthermore, in the Province of Ontario, 7% of the judges were women but women presently account for a little more than 50% of the students in the faculties of law (Eng, 1997). According to Baines (1997), women are generally underrepresented in the legal field, particularly in the courts.

Wondering about the notion of *person* that applied as a privilege for women and not for men as a result of a British court decision that reversed a decision of the Supreme Court of Canada in 1928, Baines asked the representativeness question and its implications for women. Based on Pitkin's definition of representativeness which can be defined in terms of "the fact of making present something that is absent", Baines and others wondered how the representativeness, which can be defined in terms of "the fact of making present something that is absent", of women comes about and what is the rationale behind it? Who is in the best position to carry it out? Representativeness can go against those who are seeking justice when it is not established and/or accepted. Baines illustrated how representativeness can produce a different effect than the one anticipated. In a trial involving a dispute between a black adolescent who claimed to have been physically abused by a white police officer, the judge who happened to be a black woman, commented on the fact that coloured people were being stereotyped by whites. She dismissed the policeman's allegations. The judge was in turn confronted by the judicial council of her province for her comments that were deemed unjustified and biased. Could this mean that there is a connection between representativeness and power?

To quote Maillé (1997), is power gender-related? One of the forms of formal power is electoral representation. The members of the 1993 federal election campaign shows that 18% of those elected to the House of Commons were women representing a population where women were the majority. In such a context, how can power then be defined? Landry, who was quoted by Maillé, felt that "power is"…in other word, helped establish ties beyond the gender of the people exercising it. Such a simplistic view precludes the fact that power is structured mostly by men and, in some cases by women, and the way it is structured it is being challenged. At that point, you can go one step further and ask whether power is exercised differently by women and whether they exercise it the way they would like to. Power can be defined in a binary form. Under a first format, power can be described in terms of domination. It can be further expressed over individuals that is in terms of "power over". Under a second form, it can be expressed in terms of "power of". In this case the persons' skills are of paramount importance. Power is exercised in the form of domination based on an ability to act in relation to the roles of interacting individuals. A teacher who imposes discipline in a classroom could hardly exercise the same influence on adolescents outside the school. He has the power to impose the sort of discipline stemming from his skills as an educator and a figure of authority.

Feminist authors agree in saying that power can be defined in several ways. However, on the basis of this line of questioning, we see that minimum access to the power process on the part of women has yet to be clearly appraised. Just as it is claimed that policewomen slowly go up the police ranks and will, therefore eventually attain the senior management positions in larger numbers, women are also said to have first had access to the right to vote during the 20th century, which gave them the right to representation and, consequently, they obtained the opportunity to become electoral candidates. Now, in such a formal process and with respect to the two examples quoted, there is still too little material on the attitudes of men and women, the obstacles to be overcome, the subtle and difficult to identify forms of opposition to shed enough light on the debate on policewomen. Even though power can be identified differently, that is over individuals or by individuals, it remains a tool that must be mastered, in a struggle where fighting is fierce.

One of the questions to be asked from now on is the following: must emphasis be placed on promoting policies to recruit larger numbers of women in the field of justice and policing in particular? Women have not only made inroads in the police world, they have also made a significant contribution. Eng (1977) noted that women had spearheaded changes to legislation pertaining to tax measures affecting alimony, prosecution in cases of domestic violence, acknowledgement of the battered woman syndrome, to name only a few. In the specific case of the police, the situation is complicated. The Province of Ontario enacted a law in 1991 on employment equity for all public services, including policing. The law was repealed in 1995. If we compare two police forces of different provinces, it seems that the Toronto Police Service is not showing better results in the hiring of policewomen than the Vancouver Police Force, even though the latter was not subjected to the law. To the contrary, it seems that the law has stirred up a wave of backlash and criticism. The recruiting standards have been lowered. The target groups have not shown support for the initiative because they did not want to be accused of not deserving, as the others, the positions. These comments should not stop us from realizing that specific initiatives must be put in place to meet policewomen's requests. The initiatives have to do with parental leave, the policies against all forms of harassment, the policies of job-sharing in a context such as protective re-assignment, daycare, health problems and also educational leave. These initiatives are still incomplete and are far from being implemented in all Canadian police forces. Some of these measures have to be submitted to the members and to the authorities before being incorporated in the collective agreements. Others such as the anti-harassment policies fall within the purview of police commissions (Josiah, 1997). It appears not only, that there is a need to document the types of initiatives but also the goals and objectives sought to establish them. The implementation strategies also have yet to be made known. We think that the initiatives mentioned and others will appear to be modern management tools for all members of forces faced with new family and social realities.

From another standpoint, the review of the literature (LeBeuf 1977) describes how, repeatedly, over the last three decades, the relevance of women, their performance and their leadership have been questioned, appraised and commented on. In the same vein, some authors like to point out that policewomen would be that much more willing to follow the philosophy of community policing seeing that they are more sociable, that they are able to show more empathy and that they have greater introspective capabilities than their male counterparts. They are also endowed with more skills with which to serve the community and tend to be less aggressive in confrontational situations. Such an appraisal has to do with the community policing philosophy and not with a comparison between women and men in a community policing context. Fortunately so. Indeed, if at first glance, such qualities strongly militate in favour of policewomen, the fact remains that the promotion of these skills will work against policewomen over the long haul. Under such circumstances, the skills in question mean, not so much that policewomen approach and carry out policing differently: (they use a rather gentler approach when dealing with the people, a softer language, modified procedures as opposed to their male counterparts (Angers, 1997), which is a given fact that must be acknowledged, but instead that they are effective as police officers only to the extent that they can show these skills. Now, we know that the community policing philosophy has, for the most part, yet to be fully entrenched in day-to-day policing. We also know that the crime prevention aspects and general law enforcement continue to fall within the purview of the police. It would appear that it is mainly by taking into account the complexity of the reality of the police's mission and the questioning of matters related to a police community initiative that the issue of policewomen must be judged on its full merits. In any case, the major changes to which police forces are confronted will come about, whether or not policewomen are involved. Consequently, gender equality analysis becomes a reference tool.

As Frost (1997) says, gender equality analysis takes into account social reality as it is experienced by women and men in a world of equity and relevance. The concerns have less to do with "how to do" (and issues related to the relevance of women in policing) than with "how to make effective use of the potential of women in policing in the light of their personal and occupational concerns. For example, it is known that a majority of women have the greater responsibilities with respect to family and child rearing. Policies could be established to take into account these responsibilities in assigning duties (working hours, job sharing etc.) In the final analysis and more generally, Frost claims that gender equality analysis can contribute to fairer personnel management policies that are better adapted to the various

324

employee needs. For example, such analyses would make it possible to view the career in a positive light in some other way than though a frantic vertical evolution, but instead through the self-realization that comes with it, reconciliation with family values and a sustained and human work place (Desbiens, 1997).

As found in a Statistics Canada study, the number of women in the police in Canada has constantly gone up since 1970. Their number was 5631 in 1994 from an approximate total police population of 56,000 (Statistics Canada, 1996). There are women in 92% of police forces; however, the breakdown varies throughout the country. Most of them are municipal police force or RCMP constables. In fact, the actual number of policewomen is still relatively low.

These summary data show that women are still under-represented in police organizations. Just as their male counterparts, they are required to go through the police culture acceptance phases and also to move up the organizational ranks, which remains a prerogative for a member. Furthermore, they are required to make their own needs and claims known to and approved by their bosses and union leaders or member representatives in the RCMP because the latter do not have the right to unionize. At this stage, we are interested in understanding the process for doing so where policewomen are concerned and access to the facts concerning the use of the process. These are the points that we shall discuss.

The Role Attributed to Policewomen

The present status of policewomen as shown by their numbers and their ranks is a significant factor in understanding the roles that they play. The policemen's expectations of policewomen, the differences in the law enforcement styles of men and women and the problem that the police culture had in accepting women in its work world raise several questions.

Within the police forces, the policemen's expectations of policewomen differ in that the latter are ready to provide or are capable of providing. Previously, policewomen looked after duties related to education and children's aid as well as other duties linked with women's issues because, among other things, policemen have long believed that: women were morally superior to them and could perform certain duties much better than they could. Certain police officers are known to have said that "only policewomen should look after cases involving children because women basically know better than men how to comfort, counsel and question a woman or child who has been mistreated" (Appier, 1992:5). Now, those who joined the police ranks were ready to provide and reach the same levels of acquired skills as their male counterparts. Women consequently felt that what was expected of them was not quite in keeping with the police training that they had received and/or their own perception of police work. In other words, most of the time, women performed, through actions that were more of a verbal than a physical nature, police duties that were perceived to be less demanding from a physical standpoint. This situation clearly led to a different perception of the working styles and characteristics of policemen and women.

While the working style of women differed from the men, the fact of being worthy of police work remained an important criterion for policewomen, coupled with the fact that they could carry out all the police duties. Women wanted to be seen as competent, refused to be discriminated against when promotion opportunities came up, wanted to be recognized for a job well done and be considered able to assist their male counterparts whenever the need arose. As Busson (1997) stated: "the main objectives of policewomen consisted in carrying out all their daily duties the best possible way and in being recognized by their male counterparts as being competent and qualified."

Women flip-flopped between the burden of representing what was considered to be feminine characteristics in a traditionally male world and the challenge of projecting an image of being proficient persons as their male counterparts were. Certain authors have said that the existing police organizations paradoxically force women to fulfill the feminine roles that men instinctively bestow upon them and expect at the same time to show a certain measure of masculinity in their conduct and in the way they approach the public. As Simard (19977) states, organizations have, for a long time, rejected what are commonly known as feminine values.

Consequently, certain policewomen have had to incorporate in their daily lives the language, attitudes and various forms of behaviour of their male counterparts and have set aside a certain portion of their femininity.

In actual fact, the duties carried out these days by policewomen do not conceal the fact that they are still too few of them as indicated earlier and that very few of them have reached officer status. Still this has not prevented them from forging ahead for promotions in spite of the obstacles in their paths. The number of women occupying positions in the line structures of police forces is increasing slowly. The more women in the senior ranks of police forces, the more valuable this will be since (1) they will have proven that they are capable of representing organizations as decision-makers, (2) they will justify the recruiting of a large number of policewomen (3) and they will put emphasis on the differences between the working styles of men and women. These are three factors that can only be of benefit to the profession. It is obvious that women can be found at various organizational levels and that some of them had succeeded in becoming members of elite response teams, such as investigation units and drug squads. However, and this must be emphasized, they still constitute a minority in the police.

Many of the obstacles encountered by policewomen have disappeared; however, others linger mainly because of the police culture which, while questioned by policewomen, still remains a male preserve. According to Simard (1997), identification with paternal authority is practically inconceivable for women, let alone claiming such authority. Within the police organizations, women are assigned to the same duties as their male counterparts; however, they are not always viewed as being fully integrated in the police culture. There has been reluctance in considering the viewpoints of women regarding the adjustment of equipment to the needs of women. Ostiguy (1997), for example, points out that, in the earlier days, policewomen wore a uniform that did not suit them and used weapons that were not designed for people of their build. They had to fight to get people to listen to them. They now have at their disposal the required equipment and facilities. Police stereotypes also had a major impact on the roles conferred onto men and women. In society in general, men are seen as being physically stronger, more rational and logical. The stereotypes are intensified by the police officers because of, among other things, the reputation that they have are peacekeepers under all circumstances. However, the stereotypes can be detrimental to the way organizations and members operate (Dubois, 1997) because they create a rigid standard of behaviour and expectations with respect to the skills of fellow police officers. Yet, it is as a result of these stereotypes that policewomen have had the chance to show their true skills on the job and to question the views of their male counterparts. As stated by Dubois (1997), women have to prove themselves whenever they are reassigned to new work groups or placed in new situations. When they do not have to deal with such stereotypes and the expectations of others, policewomen hope that the stereotypes will simply disappear. It is when a policewoman gets a promotion or when changes are made to the work groups and the regular duties; that problems resurface. According to many members, the police culture remains an environment in which belittling women is still too often the norm.

According to Busson (1997), the only behavioural model that women could follow to succeed in providing effective and professional law enforcement services was that of men. Compared with the women of the '70s, the women of today have a very clear advantage in that they can use, instead of concealing, the attributes that are part of the female stereotypes, such as for example in issues related to the victimization of women and children. In this regard, Lunney (1997) pointed out that "the most widely recognized and accepted role of women is the ability to show empathy and to take care of others in an organizational environment and to positively impact on the socialization and civility aspects". Women complement the traditional police culture by contributing knowledge, points of view and empathy approaches and procedures. Police officers have long believed that these attributes were simply pointless; however, today, they see that they are becoming an indispensable asset to organizations that can now provide their clientele with a more thorough, and in some cases, a more personalized service. Men have come to recognize the importance of their presence within organizations and to stop criticizing them.

The way society has evolved with regard to the roles of women shows that progress is inevitable, but slow. Progress has taken its toll on policewomen, particularly when one considers other male-dominated lines of work in which changes have occurred at a much quicker pace. In the field of education, there is a relatively higher percentage of women at all levels of the administrative structures and women-oriented policies are being designed and implemented. We can see that changes aimed at women in the police field are much more gradual than those occurring in society in general, because this is a male preserve that advocates traditional values. It is obvious that it is not an easy thing for a woman to continue working in the law enforcement field. In actual fact, the positive attributes of women have for much too long been viewed in a negative light and in, some cases, as being a threat to policemen, because they were liable to put in question and improve on the existing law enforcement styles and to bring about a very different method of law enforcement in our societies. Fortunately, as women became permanent members of police organizations, police officers quickly came to realize that each and everyone of them had undeniable qualities and that the differences in working attitudes could be of benefit to the organizations.

Policewomen have succeeded in convincing the police organizations that the procedures and style of law enforcement could be altered. They quickly realized that the obstacles facing them differed from the ones encountered or viewed by their male counterparts (with a few rare exceptions). Sexual harassment, gender discrimination and maternity leave requirements are problems that are restricted to women. Such a situation is hardly conducive to smooth staff relations between men and women within police forces. Bradburn (1997) believes that, in many cases, the role of policewomen is to overcome obstacles that men have never had to deal with. Women have to prove that they are up to the task of policing. Ostinguy (1997), who backs this comment, believes that the strength of today's police forces lies not only in the complementarity of their employees, but also in the reality surrounding the latter, regardless of the level they have reached in the structure or organization for which they work. Whenever men and women successfully carry out the specific duties that are assigned to them, the police organizations realize that their members each have their strong points and their weak points and can then use these skills to their advantage.

Beyond the shadow of a doubt, the women police officers have skills that are equivalent to those of their male counterparts. There remains to ensure a fair working environment, the pooling of information and fair access to the promotion process. Both men and women have had the responsibility of tackling together the broad range of issues related to police women's problems. On the day that the work styles of men and women will be considered assets to the police organizations, a better law enforcement service will be provided and the clientele will be that much more satisfied. In the meantime, the future of policewomen still has to be dealt with.

The Future of Police Women and Police Organizations

During the '60s, the Royal Commission on the Status of Women set up by the Government of Canada described in detail the extent to which women were being discriminated against in Canadian society. This is when the fight for equality for all individuals really started. Since then, women have played a limited social role in society. The social, economic and political status was precisely being recriminated against (McTeer, 1997). Policewomen were necessarily included in the debate for the recognition of equality, which could not be disputed under the Canadian Charter of Rights and Freedoms, but also for the informal recognition of their standing in policing.

One aspect of the issue of women in the police that is relatively difficult to address is precisely the informal aspect of the debate. We see it in literature, at lectures given at seminars and during the discussions that the whole issue of women contains two complementary aspects to wit the aspect of the principles and policies and the informal aspect of networking as illustrated by the adage of Old Boys' Network.

In the first case, the general principles and policies cover, as we have seen, the laws against sexual harassment or administrative policies for managing work-sharing time among members, or terms and conditions related to parental leave included in the collective agreements of each police force. The principles and policies must be considered tools aimed at promoting, not only the integration of women, but their retention until the end of a satisfactory and successful career. The principles and policies are far from being standardized and also far from being integrated in all Canadian police forces (approximately 370), including municipal, provincial and national police forces. These principles and policies are still spearheading the movement promoting the condition of policewomen. They continue to give rise to inquiries and required adjustments in a world in which the critical mass of those in minority has yet to be fully reached. The consensus is that those in minority, who account for approximately 18% of the overall group, are beginning to make some headway regarding the right to criticize and are starting to be heard. It remains to be seen how the police organizations, as a result of the implementation of the general policies and principles will cope in the future with a stronger presence of women that will reflect the new demographic and modern complexities of societies. This is one of the main challenges looming ahead.

In the second case, the situation is more complex and remains to be documented. So far, few researchers and individuals have taken stock of the informal aspect of networking. The notion of networking is relatively unknown. It is in fact a question of maintaining pertinent contacts at conferences, work sessions, extramural meetings and volunteer gatherings. Put more simply, it is a question of ensuring, at meetings with other individuals, to be able to integrate with their networks. By definition, networking is not burdened with a formal structure, it draws little criticism from people who do not support the activity. On the other hand, it very much has to do with personalized invitations and attitudes by means of which the inviters hope to create links, gather details, share confidential information, etc. (Glass 1997). In fact, the motives are probably as numerous and varied as the people bringing them to the forefront. As we have seen, women are still few in numbers and have little contact with the power centres. They are relatively strangers to the existing networks and continue to remain marginalized from an informal standpoint. Incentives, laws and policies can do little to change this. Only a change in attitudes and values on the part of people in positions of authority

If, as we have seen, there is definitely a men's culture in the police, we asked ourselves whether there was a parallel among the elements constituting a women's culture in the police. First of all, the critical mass of the number of women has not been reached. Furthermore, as we have said, the number of women is not distributed equally throughout the various forces. Some have more than others. Finally, it is extremely difficult to see whether there is any solidarity with respect to the women's issue, as compared with the solidarity in relation to the police issue. The interviews that we have carried out show that women are still seeking their own distinction through their policewoman status, their minority standing in the police and as women in society. Some are concerned that calling for incentives to attract more women into the police and measures to retain them in the police ranks are liable to provoke a backlash among their male counterparts. Others, with several years of police service, are backing appraisal efforts and the measures intended to consolidate their status, which is different in any case. Finally, some others fear that, by dwelling on their condition, role and status, they might provoke the type of controversy that cropped up when they first arrived in the '70s. It would appear that a third major challenge is aimed at formally consolidating the women's contribution to policing.

In this regard, police women's groups have the important task of influencing the leaders in the police community to implement polices and practices that will tap the full women's potential in policing and police organizations.

Endnote

*We acknowledge permission to reprint this article, a version of which was originally published in the *Revue International de criminology et de police technique et scientifique* 3/1998, pp. 354-367

References

Appier, J. (1992). Preventive Justice: The Campaign for Women Police, 1910-1940. *Women in Criminal Justice*, 4, 1:3-36.

Baines, B. (1997). The Under Representation of women in the Justice Field. In. M.E. LeBeuf and J. McLean (Eds.), *Women in policing in Canada: The year 2000 and beyond – its challenges*. Workshop Proceedings. Canadian Police College, May 20-23, 1997. Ottawa: Canadian Police College.

Bradburn, L. (1997). Moving beyond obstacles and constraints. In M.E. LeBeuf and J.McLean (Eds.), *Women in policing in Canada: The year 2000 and beyond – its challenges*. Workshop Proceedings. Canadian Police College, May, 20-23, 1997. Ottawa: Canadian Police College.

Busson, B.A. (1997). Women and Policing. In M.E. LeBeuf and J. Mclean (Eds.), *Women in Policing in Canada: The year 2000 and beyond – its challenges*. Workshop Proceedings. Canadian Police College, May 20-23, 1997. Ottawa: Canadian Police College.

Desbiens, M.E. (1997). Course of Action Women Apply to Confront Challenges in the Engineering Field. In M.E. LeBeuf and J. McLean (Eds.), *Women in Policing in Canada: The year 2000 and beyond – its challenges*. Workshop Proceedings. Canadian Police College, May 20-23, 1997. Ottawa: Canadian Police College.

Dubois, G. (1997). Combatting the Stereotypes. In M.E.LeBeuf and J.McLean (Eds.), *Women in Policing in Canada: the year 2000 and beyond – its challenges*. Workshop Proceedings. Cxanadian Police College, May 20-23, 1997. Ottawa: Canadian Police College.

Eng, S. (1997). Policies for women in the justice field – need or necessity? In M.E. LeBeuf and J. McLean (Eds.), *Women in Policing in Canada: The year 2000 and beyond – its challenges*. Workshop Proceedings. Canadian Police College – May 2-23, 1997. Ottawa: Canadian Police College.

Frost, S. (1997). Gender Equality Analysis. In M. E. LeBeuf and

J.McLean (Eds.), *Women in Policing in Canada: The year 2000 and beyond – its challenges*. Workshop Proceedings. Canadian Police College – May 20-23, 1997. Ottawa: Ontario Police College.

Glass, B. (1997). The value of networking. In M.E. LeBeuf and J.Mclean(Eds.), *Women in Policing in Canada: The year 2000 and beyond – its challenges*. Workshop Proceedings. Canadian Police College – May 20-23, 1997. Ottawa: Ontario Police College.

Josiah, H. (1997). Innovative policy development approaches. In M.E. LeBeuf and J. McLean (Eds.), *Women in Policing in Canada: The year 2000 and beyond – its challenges*. Workshop Proceedings, Canadian Police College – May 20-23, 1997. Ottawa: Canadian Police College.

LeBeuf, M.E and McLean, J. (Eds.), *Women in Policing in Canada :The year 2000 and beyond – its challenges*. Workshop Proceedings. Canadian Police College, May 20-23, 1997. Ottawa: Canadian Police College.

LeBeuf, M. E (1997). les femmes dans la police. In *Compte rendu. Journée de formation à' l'intention de policières*. Montreal: Sûreté du Québec. Programme d'acces a l'égalité.

LeBeuf. M.E (1996). Trois décenennies de femmes dans la police. *Une bibliographie commentée*. Ottawa: Canadian Police College.

Lunney, R. (1997). Women's influence in police members responsibilities. In M.E. LeBeuf and J. McLean (Eds.), *Women in Policing in Canada: The year 2000 and beyond – its challenges*. Workshop Proceedings. Canadian Police College, May 20-23, 1997. Ottawa: Canadian Police College.

Maillé, C. The use of power in a traditionally paternalistic system. In M.E. LeBeuf and J. Mc. Lean (Eds.), *Women in Policing in Canada: The year 2000 and beyond – its challenges*. Workshop Proceedings. Canadian Police College, May 20-23, 1997. Ottawa: Canadian Police College.

McTeer, M. (1997). The evolution of women in the justice field. In

M.E. LeBeuf and J. McLean (Eds.), *Women in Policing in Canada: The year 2000 and beyond – its challenges.* Workshop Proceedings. Canadian Police College, May 20-23, 1997. Ottawa: Canadian Police College.

Moore, H. (1997). An historical account of women in policing in Canada.In M.E. LeBeuf and J.McLean (Eds.), *Women in Policing in Canada: 2000 and beyond –its challenges.* Workshop Proceedings. Canadian Police College, May 20-23, 1997. Ottawa: Canadian Police College.

Ostiguy, L. (1997). Encountering barriers in the police field. What femalepolice members must confront. In M.E. LeBeuf and J. McLean (Eds.), *Women in Policing in Canada: 2000 and beyond – its challenges.* Workshop Proceedings. Canadian Police College, May 20-23, 1997. Ottawa: Canadian Police College.

Shores, L. (1997). The Thin Blue and Pink Line. Subject to Debate. *A newsletter of the Police Executive Research Forum*, 11, 11:1-34.

Simard, C. (1997). Social identity, women and police culture. In M.E.LeBeuf and J. McLean (Eds.). *Women in Policing in Canada: 2000 and beyond – its challenges.* Workshop Proceedings. Canadian Police College, May 20-23, 2003. Ottawa: Canadian Police College.

Statistics Canada, *Juristat* (1996). Effectif policier et depenses au chapitre des services de police au Canada -1994. January. 16, 1. Ottawa: Statistics Canada

PART V

OPERATIONAL ISSUES

Making the Pickets Responsible

Police Interrogation

When Police Kill

Transnationalization of Policing

Police Discretion with Young Offenders

13

Making the Pickets Responsible: Policing Labour at a Distance in Windsor, Ontario*

Willem de Lint
Alan Hall

This paper examines the 1987 introduction of a policy for policing labour disputes in Windsor, Ontario. The policy emphasizes the explicit use of consensus-building tactics over coercion in strike situations. Events leading to this policy are traced to the local politics of policing and to changing economic and industrial conditions representing the general decline in Fordist industrial relations. Changes within the police, such as the adoption of community policing, are also considered as important explanations. Both the labour-dispute policy and the broader police changes are understood as reflecting the decline of the Keynesian state and the movement toward neo-liberalism.

The Canadian industrial relations literature on labour-strike violence has tended to cast the police either as a coercive force acting on behalf of business and government interests to suppress strikers or as a neutral force trying to keep the peace (Bercuson, 1974; Grant and Wallace, 1991; Jamieson, 1971; Latornell, 1993; Palmer, 1992). From either perspective, the police are seen as performing a dependent role governed and determined in a relatively straightforward way by the demands of the state or the law. Yet, very little research in Canada has been directed toward looking specifically at police *strategies* and tactics in dealing with labour, whether they have changed over time, and if so, why.

In the wake of major labour/police confrontations during the 1980s, considerable attention has been directed specifically at these questions in Britain. A number of analysts in the U.K. have suggested that, until the 1980s, the British police had a history of accommodation and limited use of force in dealing with labour (Geary, 1985; Morgan, 1987; Uglow, 1988). Since then, the police are seen as becoming systematically more paramilitaristic and confrontational (Fielding, 1991; Uglow, 1988; D. Waddington, 1992; Reiner, 1998; Vogler, 1991). Explanations for this change have often emphasized the role of the anti-labour and home security policies of the neoconservative government of Margaret Thatcher, although some have suggested that the movement began early in the 1970s when the police "lost" a series of industrial disputes leading ultimately to the fall of the Heath government (Reiner, 1998: 45). The increased picket-line violence and arrests are frequently seen as a consequence of the confrontational tactics of the police (Scraton, 1985). Much of the debate has revolved around the authoritarian state thesis initially developed by Hall et al. (1978) that these developments represented a more generalized crisis of hegemony within Britain as Fordism and the class compromise began to unravel, creating a more authoritarian state which relied increasingly on the coercive powers of the police to maintain control (see Uglow, 1988; P. Waddington, 1993; 1994a; 1994b; 1998). P. Waddington (1998) in particular has challenged the authoritarian state thesis, as well as questioning the whole idea that recent confrontations between the British police and labour were a function of a change in policing strategy or tactics. He argues that, on the whole, the police have continued to seek ways of accommodating labour and protesters, often in defiance of government wishes, but he also recognizes that the police have certain "lines in the sand" which they are committed to protect and beyond which they will not move. In those situations, often not of their choosing, the police are well prepared to deploy force (P. Waddington, 1998: 378).

Contrary to much of the British research, a broader international literature on public-order policing has now begun to suggest that the 1970s signalled the beginning of a *consensual* orientation in a number of other countries in Western Europe and North America, with an emphasis on communication, negotiation and flexibility. Interestingly, these were countries such as Spain, France and the United States, where police confrontation and strike violence has historically been more common than in Britain (della Porta and Reiter, 1998; Fillieule and Jobard, 1998; Jaime-Jimenez and Reinares, 1998; King, 1997; McPhail, Schweingruber and McCarthy, 1998). In describing this historical trend, della Porta and Reiter (1998: 7) suggest that three major tactical tendencies that have become more dominant in current protest and strike policing may be contributory to violence reduction: underenforcement of the law, an emphasis on negotiation and mediation, and large-scale collection of information. This is also consistent with the policing literature in general, which indicates a movement within police from a doctrinaire rigidity in law enforcement to a more nuanced, proactive and preventative approach (Brake and Hale, 1992; Ericson and Haggerty, 1997; Murphy, 1998). Specific research on strike and public-order policing points to the importance of centralizing and professionalizing tendencies in police structures and cultures, of shifting orientations and levels of government control over the police, and of the influence of media and public opinion as key factors in this shift (Geary 1985; Morgan, 1987; D. Waddington, 1992). International work has also analysed the influence of police interaction with protest cycles and linked police response to characteristics of the political opportunity structure (della Porta and Reiter, 1998; Lipsky, 1968; Snyder and Tilly, 1974). Evidence on the privatization of policing and public security suggests further that many of the roles formerly carried out by the police are being returned to private security firms, suggesting another line of argument regarding the changes in labour policing (Murphy, 1998).

In one of the few studies on public-order policing in Canada, King (1997) argues that there are actually two distinct, opposing trends emerging at this time. Along with the more conciliatory and consultative approach, he suggests that there is an increasingly militarized potential for confrontation which the police stand ready to use. A similar observation has been made more broadly about the contradictions of community-policing models and the parallel emphasis on heavily armed tactical squads in criminal investigations (Kraska and Kappeler, 1997). While King's study was focussed largely on the policing of natives by the RCMP, the implication was that these trends represented a more general development in public-order policing in Canada. Certainly, recent events in Vancouver, Windsor, Quebec City and Ottawa indicate that the police are willing and able to deploy considerable paramilitary force in protest situations.[1]

What is less clear is whether these two trends are competing, "diametrically opposed" developments, as King (1997) suggests or, as P.Waddington (1998) contends, part of a continuing strategy in which the police prefer to use carrots while reserving their capacity to use an impressive arsenal of nonlethal and lethal sticks when the circumstances call for them to "die in the ditch." As has been suggested in the case of community policing more generally (Green and Mastrofski, 1988), it is also possible that this claim of a conciliatory trend to public-order policing is more rhetoric than substantive development in police practice (Winter, 1998).

While various arguments have been made regarding the origins of these strategic developments, both in Britain and elsewhere (della Porta and Reiter, 1998; Marx, 1998; Reiner, 1998), very little historical research has been conducted on the policing of labour that looks specifically at the emergence of new police policy and differences in practices on the ground. This paper reports on an exploratory case study of Windsor, Ontario that traces the development of a new labour policing policy introduced in 1987. The study involved archival research, interviews with Windsor labour, municipal and police represent-ative involved in drafting or applying the new industrial relations policy (N = 16), and observations of four strike situations and two major protests in Windsor from 1997-2000.[2] All interviews included a series of open-ended questions on the municipal history of labour-policing practices and policies.

The literature suggests that there are two lines of argument that need to be pursued in trying to explain changes in the policing of labour. Among police scholars, considerable emphasis has been placed on the recognition of broader cultural and organizational changes *within* the police, such as professionalization and community policing, along with arguments concerning the connections between police and government, whether at the municipal or state level (della Porta and Reiter, 1998). This focus on the police goes some way toward developing an understanding of the history of strike policing, but the literature also suggests that the police role in strikes has to be tied to an analysis of shifts in industrial relations and the relevant state policies and laws. For us, this requires more than a broad reference to cultural, economic, or political changes. There must be an explicit effort to link shifts in the *practices* of accumulation (i.e., Fordism to Post-Fordism) to changes in *strategies* of social regulation, both within and outside the workplace (i.e. repression or legitimation). Accordingly, this paper ties reductions in police-labour confrontations not only to changes in police structures, policies and practices, but also to the interconnections between police and industrial relations developments over time.

To extend the analysis further, the transformations in labour processes may also be relevant to understanding cultural and structural changes within police organizations (cf. O'Malley, 1997; O'Malley and Palmer, 1996). Liberal theorists have tended to see police as accommodating protest within a frame work of due process and consent (Geary, 1985), while critical criminologists and labour historians have emphasised the coercive deployment of the public police in the interests of capital accumulation and/or political repression (Brogden, 1982; Harring and McMullin, 1975; Silver, 1966). A post-critical account recognizes a more complex relationship between capital and labour and public and private regulation, taking into account how neoliberalism reconfigures the regulatory tableau to privilege private interests and responsibilities over social rights and public obligations. That reconfiguration has been uneven both within and between states but has had profound influences on key aspects of police operations and orientations, including the general thrust to redefine the boundaries and conditions of public order and the role of the public police in regulating this order (Murphy, 1998). As such, it may be that Canada's experience of these developments is different from Britain, New Zealand and Australia, and more similar to Europe.

In this paper, we explore the connections between changes in industrial relations and changes in police tactics in the city of Windsor. After locating this policy within local politics and police and industrial relations cultures, we situate it in macro-level developments, specifically, the crisis in Fordism and the emergence of the neoliberal state. We argue that what has developed in Windsor is a strategy of enhanced responsibilization in which unions and management are encouraged to manage their own labour conflicts in a manner that minimizes the need for public-order policing. Under this policy, police management redefines labour conflict as a field of intervention best managed "at a distance."

The Policing of Industrial Conflict in Postwar Windsor

Windsor, Ontario is a heavily unionized industrial city of 200,000 which is located directly across the river from Detroit, Michigan. As in Detroit, the auto industry is the dominant source of industrial jobs with large numbers of workers employed by the Big Three auto makers and various feeder plants. Most of these workers are represented by the Canadian Auto Workers Union (CAW), by far the dominant union in the community (Windsor and District Labour Council, 1999). In what follows, a short and long view of the development of Windsor's industrial-conflict policing policy is offered, both in explanation for Windsor's introduction of this policy and in an initial effort to situate it in the broader shifts that have occurred across Canada.[3] To suggest a hypothesis, it might be said that police action was predictably routinized until a watershed event occurred, after which the parties were compelled to restate their allegiances. Wisler and Kriesi (1998) call this politicization, or political re-involvement. What at first glance appears to be a dramatic change in approach is, upon further examination, less abrupt and reformative.

Reactive Strategy 1950-1980: Pickets as Law Violators?

Our police respondents agreed that the first training in public-disorder policing was in the use of wedges,[4] that this training began in the early 1950s, and that it was first used in the

342

field in the early 1960s at a labour dispute known as the "Dominion Forge strike." Instruction on the use of public-order equipment (shields, nightsticks, protective gear) and in using formations was further developed in the late 1960s and continued intermittently into the 1970s. While it appears that the use of a platoon formation only occurred once around 1970 and not again afterwards, public-order dress and the use of wedges for snatching agitators and for moving people or equipment through pickets into or out of plants, was used frequently in the 1960s and 1970s. Our police *and* labour respondents generally concurred that decisions and tactics on police intervention appeared to be tied to the defence of property rights and were characterized by reactiveness, inconsistency and inflexibility. The police also used visibility and uniformed surveillance as a deterrent to violence.

For example, in a Kmart strike in which 50 women were on strike for a long period and during which some property damage occurred, one respondent said: "half the cops who were there didn't know what they should be doing, management didn't know what they could do. And that was terrible" (P3).[5] Similarly, a strike at Dominion Forge was also characterized by long stints of passive vigilance interrupted by violent action: "… that was a rough one. We had helmets and sticks. We had to assign a car crew around the clock … that was the way we handled them then, we took the cost of watching them and there had to be a better way … today you just can't afford to tie up officers on stuff like that" (P5). At the Kasle Steel strike in early 1987, just before the new policy[6] was introduced, pickets said that the police had assured them that the company would not try to bring anything out of the plant, but then were on hand when a truck came to pick up a load of material produced before the strike began. On the other hand, in the Bendix strike of 1980 one of our police respondents attended a meeting with the union president and a company representative in which he was able to help broker a peaceable conclusion to the standoff. Strike incidents were sometimes handled proactively by individual officers acting on their own, without written or formal guidelines.

Both labour and police stated that police would always respond in force when management made efforts to bring in replacement workers to continue production. However, in many situations where there was no threat of replacement workers, police often kept both their knowledge of and presence at strike events to a minimum. As a picket captain from a 1960s GM strike recalled: "The police I'd see come around once in a while but they never asked any questions because everything was peaceful" (L3).

However, both police and labour understood that the police were on hand to defend the property rights of employers. Even the police did not define themselves as neutral. As one police respondent stated:

> Until that time [of the new policy] the police took a very adversarial role, definitely falling on the side of management every time and ... we would be there to keep the peace but if management called upon us to do anything we were johnny-on-the-spot. If labour called upon us to do anything they'd have a hard time in getting us to respond because we didn't see our roles as that ... When management called, we went running. We did whatever was necessary to appease management (P3).

This suggests that policy on police intervention from the 1950s through the early 1980s were poorly articulated and inconsistent, reactive rather than preventive, and oriented to the defence of property rights (King, 1997).[7] In practice, there was some evidence of piecemeal adaptations throughout the 1970s and 1980s towards a more proactive policy, but up until a strike and plant occupation at Sheller-Globe in 1987, the handling of labour-management disputes did not undergo any official change.

An archival search of public-order policing procedures and regulations in Ontario reveals that, from the 1960s through the 1970s, police policy viewed pickets through the twin lenses of law and order. Public demonstrations, including strike actions, were seen according to martial metaphors as a tactical problem in which a minimization of the relative disadvantage in police numbers required a maximization in the ethos of coercive decisiveness (see also King, 1997). Police were thus trained in the use of wedges and platoon formations and adopted special public-order gear to enhance their appearance and capacity to withstand thrown objects and hand-to-hand combat. Instruction on the use of the baton also figures prominently in these training manuals. Additionally, they cited relevant sections of the criminal code on unlawful assembly and riot (Ontario Provincial Police, 1972; Canadian Police College, 1981).

As a consequence of the subsumption in this training literature of labour strikes under public-order policing, low rank decision-making was as underdeveloped as the question of the use of abstention from force. Training "policy", such as it was, narrowed the field of labour-police-management relations to a question of the tactical neutralization of public disorder (in which the role of management, the public and police-union negotiation are excised from view). It assumed police were on site to enforce the law, allowed that any single interpretation of violation would justify the collective response, and presumed that the deployment of reactive counter-force was the primary question to be resolved. Even in heavily unionized Windsor, many of our police respondents regularly described this approach as "us versus them" policing.

The Sheller-Globe Incident and the New Policy

"It was Mother's Day, as a matter of fact. I recall it was a very nice day" (P5). Up until May of 1987, Sheller-Globe, a Toledo, Ohio-based manufacturer of steering wheels in plants in Indiana, Michigan and Ontario, employed 200 people in its Windsor operation. Following a certain period of stepped-up production (12-16 hour shifts, 7 days per week), workers of the Windsor plant were told that it would close because of declining demand, throwing all 200 out of work. On May 9, three days after this announcement to the workers by management, 18 employees (later joined by Local 195 President Bruce Boyd) barricaded themselves in the plant in a wildcat strike, with some 60 or so keeping a vigil outside the gates. The workers were also joined by New Democratic Party (NDP) legislators Howard McCurdy and Dave Cooke (MPPs) and by City Council Member Donna Champagne. After midnight on May 11, 20-30 police with long batons, helmets and visors entered the plant, peacefully arrested the strikers on charges of trespassing, loaded them into a van, and then formed two lines holding their batons in front of them to escort the van through pickets at the gate. As one police respondent recalls the incident:

> Management [of Sheller Globe] had given us direction and so now we moved and, [laughter] God, they went in there with those big long wooden sticks, they were horribly threatening and we had just acquired new helmets, new blue shiny like you were going to climb into a space ship and they went in with these helmets and these clubs and the media just picked that up and the women were screaming and tying themselves to water coolers. There was a hearing called. The labour community was up in arms like you wouldn't believe … there were, it seems to me, headlines for a week [in the Windsor Star] … And clearly I think that that was really the beginning of what we knew we had to do in terms of developing a policy (P3).

A few months following Sheller-Globe, Windsor police adopted its first formal policy for handling industrial disputes. Although similar policies were already in place in some other police services in Canada, including Hamilton, Vancouver, Winnipeg and the RCMP in British Columbia, there was no provincial requirement or recommendation at this time to develop such a policy. An Ontario provincial standard requiring a labour liaison policy was not introduced until the late 1990s.

The Windsor policy included a number of important points. It specified a preventative and proactive approach. It established labour-liaison officers who were to generate contacts with labour representatives, have face-to-face meetings with representatives of both labour and management and provide them with explicit notification on both law and discretionary allowances on the picket site. The policy combined the command and liaison role in the liaison officer, seen by its advocates as Windsor's unique "stamp." Other aspects of the policy included the minimum deployment of police to the picket site, ongoing education of union and management on both policy and relevant legislation, and the requirement to use minimal force to, above all, keep the peace.

Interpreting the Policy:
Politics as Usual, Strategic Advance, or Inflated Rhetoric?

Both police and labour respondents interpreted the Sheller-Globe incident as a watershed that led to substantial policy change in the policing of labour strikes. The official line and the most frequent interpretation by police and labour interviewees is that the Sheller-Globe action represented a clear break in the Windsor Police Service's approach to labour-management conflict. As one police interviewee put it:

> I think it was Sheller-Globe that really caused us to get moving on the policy because that was a hell of a mess ... that caused ... [the chief] to say, lets get something going here (P3).

Similarly, a labour respondent noted:

> There was a lot more tension [before Sheller-Globe] because you knew that the cops weren't there just to observe as peacekeepers, that they were functioning to assist the employer, whereas now in strikes in recent years, there is a protocol, there was a working relationship with the labour union and the Windsor police and barring the rambos ... there has been a shift in mentality in the Windsor police force from the top down. You can see that the police are friendlier, they'll talk to the picketers. And they'll talk to the company and try to create calm ... they're not confrontational. You see that as a big shift in terms of how far they'll go [before] they arrest anybody (L6).

Yet among both the police and labour respondents, there were also three distinguishable views on the context and impetus of the new policy. Among a number of police and labour respondents, the policy was an outcome of *politics as usual*. It reflected political pressure from the labour community. As one labour respondent stated:

It was Sheller-Globe and the community's response. The community sat there and said "we as the taxpayer, we're paying people to beat people up. Everybody, labour, everybody, saw it as a black eye on the community ... we don't need this, this is the 80s, why are we going out there with sticks and shields" (L7).

The power of the incident of Sheller-Globe to force political change is reflected in the fate of Mayor David Burr, who lost his labour backing: "He's done like Christmas dinner," Local 195 President Bruce Boyd was quoted as saying (Mayne, 1988). CAW Local 444 President Ken Gerard, representing the largest local in the community, also announced he would not support the mayor and, indeed, Burr decided not to seek re-election.

The politics of the policy change were keenly felt by the police, and to some extent, resisted on these grounds:

The whole thing was engineered. We learned later that [CAW President] Bob White was there. Which clearly indicated that it was a set-up. The persons who were sitting in had access to a telephone line and they arranged in advance for photographers to be present. The police were frankly being made dupes of (P6).

Whether set up or not, public pressure pushed the municipal council to publicly question and eventually censure police for being out of touch with Windsor's labour constituency (Council Minutes, 705/87). In presenting Windsor as "a labour town with a labour history," municipal politicians telegraphed to police the significance of labour in the local political context. In so doing they were responding to the substantial and visible political and social roles labour plays in the community. In very clear terms, the municipality asked the police to demonstrate how their approach to labour-management disputes was accommodating to labour.

As a member of the Police Board put it:

I was very much concerned about the relationship of the police to the several constituencies, and that simply came down to the police treating everybody in an even-handed fashion, being sensitive to need and being proactive in achieving those results without [violence?]. "We [the board] simply said this is the way it's going to be" (P6).

While acknowledging the significant role of political pressure, some of our police respondents also saw the new policy as a *strategic advance* in independent police-service delivery. From this perspective, the Sheller-Globe incident provided the opportunity that certain elements within the service were able to use to overcome the overall political conservatism of the police, especially among the rank and file. In their view, labour pressure, municipal politics and conservative, but union-sensitive, police politics effectively cancelled each other out, leaving a policy vacuum which allowed internal reformers within the police and police board to carry the day. A senior police officer involved in initial drafts of the policy stated baldly that it was developed through a canvassing of police knowledge and research of "best practices" in the provincial police community, including the policies of Toronto, Peel Regional, Hamilton-Wentworth, York and the OPP:

> There were parts [of these other policies] that I liked, parts that I didn't particularly like and not only that but we wanted to kind of personalize it, to put our own stamp on it. So I went through and modified their policies, drafted ours, took it to the Chief and he made some further changes and then at a board meeting sometime in 87 … adopted the policy … John Smith [pseudonym] … was on the board and was involved with me and it was passed (P3).

The Police Services Board member referred to above and a handful of officers from the middle ranks were credited with having "masterminded" the reform. Echoing the *Task Force*, one police officer viewed by others within the service as having been an important contributor to the success of the new policy's adoption, argued that the failings of the "traditional" approach were apparent to him as early as the late 60s. During one of his very first assignments with the Windsor Police Force to a strike (at Plasticast), he had questioned an inspector's decision to speak to the management and not to the union, to which the inspector then replied, "get this radical out of here" (P5). He also recalled a conversation with the President of CAW Local 195 in which they both agreed about a particularly nasty strike at Dominion Forge in the 1970s that, "there had to be a better way. This wasn't doing the reputation of the city any good and wasn't really doing anybody any good" (P5). His retrospective account is that an official articulation of police craft development in this area had simply been awaiting the right timing to emerge.

Part of the right timing was that the 1970s and early 1980s were a watershed for policing more generally. Standardization, centralization, call-out times and arrest clearances were no longer taken as unproblematic mechanisms of improved efficiency, and there was a long, slow return to the roots of policing and the "Peelian" principles of crime prevention and proactive community involvement. With the publication of the *Task Force on Police* in 1974, Ontario signalled that it was ready to join in these reforms. *The Task Force* mirrored other documents in the United States (U.S. President's Commission on Law Enforcement and Administration of Justice, 1967; Kelling et. al., 1974) in which bureaucratic, centralized, reactive policing was criticized and an incipient "community policing" was beginning to be articulated.

However, this return to roots was modified on one important point. Unlike the first Peelian police forces, modern policing was now a well-established institution with its own craft knowledge and professional associations. This, plus a cultivated tradition of political independence, allowed police to think themselves better equipped to resist a repeat of nineteenth- and early twentieth-century politicization and patronage. Police agencies now openly serve multiple constituencies, and a multiplicity of roles is required of them. And while this very multiplicity often allows police reform to be blocked as constituencies are played off one another, it also reserves a seedbed for autonomous "craft" development as top-down pulls and bottom-up pressures cancel one another out and leave an actionable space for policy development. As such, we were not surprised to find that the Windsor police were able to cite autonomous professional or craft development as a key factor in the development of the new policy.

A third view of the new policy was also evident in some interviews, although more often expressed implicitly than explicitly, that the change was more rhetorical than a significant break in prior police practices. It is often argued that reforms like community policing are merely rhetorical; that if you penetrate the skin of that rhetoric you will see much continuity and little change in actual behaviour or delivery "on the ground" (Klockars, 1988). We found some evidence in support of this view, to wit, that Sheller-Globe does not represent a clear division between two kinds of philosophies regarding the use of coercion or, more generally, on how labour-industrial conflict should be approached. There are various indications that the formulation of a policy and the development of specific institutional mechanisms and strategies may have reflected changes that had long been practised, albeit without written direction, with much more inconsistency at the field level.

One key issue is the extent to which the police avoided intimidation and sought to maintain a level of neutrality. As one police veteran commented with reference to the 1950s and 1960s, "Our orders were we did not take sides [...] but to keep the peace" (P5). Even during the famous Ford strike in 1945, which had considerable potential for major confrontations, the Windsor police under a pro-labour mayor were reportedly restrained in their actions (Baruth-Walsh and Walsh, 1995). A labour respondent also confirms with reference to a strike in the 1960s that while the police were clearly willing to play the role of protecting management's right to enter property, there were some informal understandings between unions and police:

> If management was coming through [the line], they'd call the police and they'd come down with maybe six or seven squad cars. [Would they talk to you?] Well they would talk to the picket captain, "Tell your guys to get out of the way because you know this is the law." You always held them [management] up fifteen or twenty minutes. They usually got in but there was nothing going on there anyways, they really couldn't do nothing (L3).

And while our younger labour respondents tended to assume that "things were crazier" back in the 1950s and 1960s, some older ones who lived through this period were less certain that police were quick to use force, even arguing that there was some police support and sympathy for the strikers:

> [We] didn't really have too much trouble with the police, we got along really good, well they half-ass supported us because they knew what you were doing, they couldn't say we're with you ... All the picketers thought here comes the fuzz, they're gonna bang heads or something but there wasn't much of that going on – there might be some unruly guys and they'd give them a little tap on the head and quiet them down (L3).

Indeed, there was consensus on both sides that "unruly" union members or troublemakers required police intervention, and that the actions of the few were not characteristic of the pickets *en masse*.

Retired union representatives also agreed with our veteran police respondent in recognizing the 1970s as a time when the police were becoming more supportive of strikers and less confrontational (L4, L5). Accounts of strikes in the early 1980s confirmed that police were continuing to operate in this more tolerant fashion. As one labour respondent put it in describing a 1982 wildcat strike:

> We were in negotiations and there was somewhat of a wildcat. We ended up disabling a truck right in the middle of the driveway coming up to the main gate at Pillette Road, very very disabled and I guess I remember that there was one police car about a half a block away and they basically just sat there and didn't do anything at all, they didn't even get out of their car. People were really pissed off but nothing really came of it – the police presence wasn't all that much (L1).

Thus, while it can be argued that the 1987 policy established a consistency and clarity in approach that was missing under the previous regime, these comments suggest that practices did not undergo a sudden radical shift from coercive to consensual policing.

That being said, the new policy was neither simply rhetorical nor was it merely a continuation of past practices. Certainly, our observations of strike situations confirm that the policy and procedures are implemented in a consistent fashion – with an emphasis on proactive communication, mediation of strike protocols and disputes, and very limited use of force or arrest powers. Interviews with strikers and union representatives also confirm a high level of satisfaction with police actions in strike situations – often viewing the police, as the police like to view themselves, as "peacekeepers." And among both our union and police respondents, there was a clear consensus that substantive changes have occurred.

The impact of a formal policy should not be underestimated. A policy (guidelines of action, Windsor Police Service, 1989) is something which can be pointed at and referred to as the background against which further modifications to prescribed action may occur. A formal written policy is in this way fundamentally different from inchoate practices. It becomes part of the consensus against which further formal commitments and legitimate organizational expression must be measured. Moreover, in a milder form, such a policy validates a particular view of policing and, in this case, the politics in which police may be permitted, and are indeed urged, to speak (cf. Becker, 1984). In addition, what emerged is the notion that police could graduate their response to labour strife. Politics and professional development together allowed police to formally displace immediate responsibility of industrial dispute regulation to the primary participants. The police could also speak in terms of the selective dispensation of professional police expertise, including the use of coercion, by acting in the capacity of senior partners, partnering community resources.

To further understand what compelled this speaking to take place at this time and in this form requires us to take a broader view of the forces underlying the gradual transition in the policing of labour. If professional or craft progress and political opportunities were projected through the policy, these advancements and opportunities reflect deeper trends – trends in industrial relations after Fordism and in the deployment of police resources under neoliberalism.

Windsor Industrial Relations in Broad Context:
Fordism and its Crisis

The archival and interview evidence suggest that labour and community pressure following the Sheller-Globe incident were instrumental in the introduction of the new policy. However, this raises the question as to why the community reaction to Sheller-Globe happened at this juncture. In our view, the answer lies in an understanding of the significant shifts in industrial relations which were occurring in Windsor at the time. Although these shifts are not unique to Windsor, there are certain particular features of the local context which are salient to our understanding of the Windsor history.

In the labour studies literature, the relationship that developed between North American automakers and the United Auto Workers (UAW) after World War II is often presented as the quintessential case of the "Fordist compromise" (Kumar and Meltz, 1992; Russell, 1990). Within the Fordist compromise, employers such as GM and Ford accepted that rewards had to be given to their employees via wages and benefit increases in exchange for productivity gains, while the unions in turn accepted the employer's right to control and transform labour processes to achieve those productivity improvements (Russell, 1990).[8] As Wells (1986) argues, this led to a routinized and bureaucratized relationship between employers, workers and their unions, producing a more predictable collective bargaining process aimed at clarifying wage demands on estimates of productivity gains. While the relationship was still adversarial, conflict resolution was largely ritualized with each party expected to play by the rules. At the same time, workers' rights and wages were tied to narrowly defined job classifications organized within mass-production, Taylorized labour processes. Within this context, labour-management conflict was normalized, routinized, and to some extent, legitimized.

The compromise was also heavily grounded in the governance logic of the Keynesian state. In terms of labour relations, this was first and most clearly expressed in the federal government order-in-council PC 1003 in 1944, providing Canadian labour unions with the legal right to recognition and collective bargaining, along the lines of the Wagner Act in the U.S. (Baragar 1995). Stable funding for unions was also largely achieved through the widespread adoption of the RAND formula. This introduced compulsory dues check-off, one of the direct consequences of the 1945 Ford strike in Windsor (Russell, 1990). Under the auspices of Keynesian economics, this industrial relations protocol and legislation reflected a postwar rapprochement by which community support for strikers as citizens (with legitimate interests and rights to strike) was almost universally accepted. Consequently, during this period workers made substantial gains in wages and benefits, often without the need for lengthy strikes, and auto workers were at the forefront of this development.

These postwar, macro-level developments inform our understanding of the co-operation between labour and employers in the collective bargaining process. As the centre of auto production in Canada, Windsor represented one of the strongest examples of Fordist compromise in Canada and the kinds of relationships that developed between employers and unions within this context, minimized the potential for strike violence and confrontation. At the same time, changes in Fordist industrial relations may also explain why Sheller-Globe became a flashpoint of the repoliticization of industrial relations in the 1980s. Up until the 1970s, collective bargaining negotiations were about contract improvements and it was accepted as legitimate by both parties that some improvements would be achieved. The use of pattern bargaining by the unions involving all three of the major North American producers was also crucial in routinizing and standardizing the collective bargaining process. However, as the Fordist compromise began to crumble in the 1970s, the focus shifted to union concessions. Underlying those concessions was the threat of large-scale job losses, as well as the shift of jobs from the Big Three employers to a growing parts industry (Burawoy, 1985; Russell, 1990). Plants began to close in large numbers in Michigan and Ontario as the Big Three began to subcontract and shift production to lower wage zones in the southern U.S. and maquiladora regions in Mexico and elsewhere (Kopinak, 1996; Swift, 1995). Unemployment rose substantially in Canada and wages stagnated and declined in real terms (Russell, 1990).

With the Reaganite and Thatcherite revolutions in the U.S. and Britain during the 1980s, steps were also taken towards industry deregulation and trade liberalization. One key development was the movement toward the 1989 U.S./Canada Free Trade Agreement (FTA) that, with the inclusion of Mexico, would later become the North American Free Trade Agreement (NAFTA). In the context of these ideologically-informed changes, the UAW and most other U.S. unions accepted concessions in wages, benefits and other key areas like job classifications, in an often vain attempt to prevent plant closures (Kumar, 1993). Rather than maintaining its traditional focus on collective bargaining and contract enforcement through grievance procedures, the UAW also accepted the management effort to reshape labour relations through such management participation programs as quality of work-life programs.

In Canada, the UAW, led by the major locals in Windsor, challenged both political ideology and strategy, and eventually separated from their American parent, forming the CAW in 1984 (Yates, 1990).[9] Once independent, the CAW resisted the clawbacks on Fordist industrial relations, and indeed, also came to define itself as the principal opponent to a related shift away from Keynesian policies towards neo-liberalism and neo-conservatism (Hargrove, 1998; Ginden, 1989; 1995). It became the major private-sector union and one of the strongest forces behind the emerging large-scale Canadian campaign against free trade, defining it as a fatal threat to Canadian jobs and working conditions. Sheller-Globe was important to labour in Windsor in 1987 because it was a clear symbol of the potential Canadian job losses that could result from an increasingly liberalized trade environment. As the major auto-producing city in Canada, Windsor was seen as a key battleground and Sheller-Globe was labour's line in the sand.

Labour's attitude to police tactics developed along the same trajectory. Police intervention had not attracted much interest because the pressure points underlying strike confrontations had been minimized in the past either by labour/management understandings about picket-line protocols, or by the ability of labour to "take care of business" by mobilizing large numbers in those few instances where employers failed to conform. As one labour leader stated, referring to the 1970s, "We never gave much thought to police, it wasn't an issue" (L7). Major employers accepted this convention by halting production during strikes, obviating the critical issue of replacement workers as a major point of confrontation on the picket line. As another explained, "We never really have to worry about the police because there's no way our employer is going to keep the plant going with scabs – the plant is too big, it would just take too many people" (L1).

This protocol was threatened with the emergence of job flight and contracting out, making plant closures a particularly sensitive issue. While the most powerful CAW locals in Windsor, to some significant extent, continued to negotiate in much the same way they had done in the 1960s and 1970s (Ginden, 1989; 1995), job losses associated with increasing subcontracting and capital disinvestment in the Big Three plants awoke the labour movement to the question of how police were interpreting their role.[10] Plant occupations emerged as a tactic to resist job flight, a tactic which the police were ill equipped to manage, but which labour needed to curry for leverage. The urgency of the challenges for labour and the potential for increased picket-line confrontation thus became a strategic question of police loyalty. When labour could no longer count on the ritualization of bargaining under the Fordist compromise and the front pages of the Windsor Star featured a picture of helmeted police with visors and long batons taking action against a few women singing a birthday song, the time was ripe for labour's repoliticization of the police.

Windsor Police in Broad Context: Neoliberalism and Policing Order

If major changes in industrial relations in Windsor can be understood with reference to the crisis and transformation of

Fordism more generally, the crisis in the Keynesian state and the movement towards neoliberalism can account for the *kinds* of policing strategies which have emerged in this context (Jessop, 1994; O'Malley, 1997; O'Malley and Palmer, 1996).[11] Nikolas Rose (1993) has defined neoliberalism as referring to governmental intervention in the name of individual enterprise rather than in the name of social goods. Provisions and guarantees of the welfare state are redefined as mechanisms of dependence, which are reversed through mechanisms of individual, family and community empowerment, also known as "responsibilization" (O'Malley and Palmer, 1996). These mechanisms are introduced to boost the threshold of individual self-governance to self-reliance, and act "at a distance" through preferable intermediaries of volunteer and lay delivery, as can be seen in policies like "workfare." As entrepreneurship and privatization is boosted and individuals responsibilized, so the logic goes, there is a general reduction of the social redistributive infrastructure characteristic of the welfare state. Neoliberalism also introduces managerial restructuring through audits and third-party evaluations in which the emphasis on the public interest or "the social" is replaced, in whole or in part, with an emphasis on market value, consumer choice and taxpayer frugality. On this latter point, our police respondents frequently used the language of efficiency to explain the need for a different approach to policing labour which radically reduced the need for large numbers of uniformed officers.

Many have commented on the tendency of the neoliberal state, stripped of the social infrastructure characteristic of welfare liberalism, to become more autocratic (Hall et al., 1978; Sears, 1999). While much of the redistributive largesse of the neoliberal state is offloaded or trimmed, there are still core areas of the state which remain relatively intact; while individual states deem themselves less capable of directly carrying out accumulation and redistribution, they have buttressed their legitimation and coercive capacities in augmented legal powers, with, for example, more draconian forms of legislation like Ontario's recently passed Safe Streets Act. "More police officers" is a rallying cry of both fiscal conservatives and centre-right liberals alike.

The delivery of services is answerable to the hegemonic discourse of consumer choice, taxpayer interests, user payment, and market value. With regard to public-order policing in particular, responsibilization alongside augmented or expanded legal powers simplifies the criminalization of individuals (criminal responsibility) and the militarization of service delivery (cf. Kraska and Kappeler, 1997; Hills, 1995; de Lint, 1999). In the context of this streamlining of roles, police may be relatively unencumbered by civil constraints once a threshold of restraint is overcome.

But even the coercive arm of the state has been subjected to neoliberal ideology and managerial restructuring. The restructuring, reorganization and reconceptualization of police services themselves in the language of the market and consumer choice, and in the administrative doctrines of the new managerialism follows a counter-tendency. This is to offload traditional service delivery in favour of a co-ordinating or oversight role (rule at a distance) in the community. Privatization and civilianization of service delivery (in community policing) is achieved through discourses and strategies that also serve to distance the police from the immediate threshold of coercive intervention. Instead, police school citizens in self-regulation and provide information and communication services in a way not unlike what was once provided by informal structures of social control. This role dilemma is complicated by the division of commitments in policing to the political community, to administrative or bureaucratic accountability, and to the reigning interpretation of legality.

Policing at a Distance

In the neoliberal state, then, the buttressing of coercion must be reconciled with this distancing of coercive delivery. This is accomplished through what we might call, following Rose and Miller (1992), *policing at a distance*. Under this strategy, police professionalism is not understood so much in tactical delivery, but in tactical oversight (cf. Osborne and Gaebler, 1993). Under community policing, the language of partnering, communication, and co-ordination serves to induct others into the direct provision of security. In as many areas as possible, public police retreat from direct provision to serve instead in a co-ordinating role. Thus, the rhetoric of partnerships, worker empowerment, flattened hierarchies and decentralized command plays up to rank-and-file and trade-craft traditions of decision-making autonomy while also installing a politics of security – via a policing expertise – more deeply into all matters of public interaction.

Evidence of this process[12] is found in Windsor's new policy and in the general trend towards a community-policing approach in industrial relations liaison. In our interviews, we heard time and time again from police respondents that what the new policy called for was communication. The *substance* of that communication is to shift the onus of security delivery onto the parties themselves. Thus, the police according to the policy and to our police respondents, are to communicate lessons on law (i.e., reinforcements on the consequences of breaches of the law) and on the benefits of self-regulation.

Such a policy is indeed consistent with craft development in public-order policing. As D. Waddington (1992) has noted, police control is key in negotiations with organizers or demonstrators. The "rapport" that is developed with union representatives is linked to the positioning of police as granters or deniers of permissions. In their dual position as law enforcement agents and order keepers, police show the parties the "black letter" of what the law permits at the same time as they set out their own reading of what may and may not be done on the picket line, according to their professional discretion.

> The new practice is to explain the law ... we went and talked to them and we brought out the appropriate laws, assaulting a police officer in the execution of his duty, obstructing a highway, obstructing a person's use of property ... we also explained to them that they have a right to stop people ... They [the union reps] would ask us questions, "Can we do this," "Can we do that?" "Can we stop this truck?" ... We developed a rapport (P2).

These lessons in law are set out as give-and-take proposition, as if there is a balance in the law that allows both parties equal opportunity. However, as Turner (1968) has argued, too much predictability may desensitize the public to the felt experiences of the real grievances. Lessons in law promote law-abiding conduct as success criteria, but they may substitute labour standards of successful resolution with police standards. They offer routinization in the place of politicization where politicization may be key to getting a message out.

Lessons on law may also be understood as part of a wider practice in which labour-management conflict is not a question of the public interest, but rather a problem of civil law in the first instance. As has been noted in much of the literature in various contexts (Cruickshank, 1993; Garland, 1996; O'Malley, 1997), empowerment is a strategy of subjectification in which the problem of administration or governing is rhetorically laid open. In this way, it is a strategy in which, after the boundaries of the problem are clearly set, local governance is co-administered.

One police respondent noted that the simple strategy of allowing a token amount of time to stop a truck or car was immeasurable as a carrot to unions: "It gives them a feeling that, well, we've done something. We stopped that truck. And yet there was no violence ..." (P4). Another respondent described how he arrested and jailed an "anti-police" union president and vice-president with 30 other pickets when the two refused to co-operate and then, after a time, took them out of the cell and "explained to them that usually if you co-operate this type of thing shouldn't happen." (P2). He then let the union executive explain to his jailed constituency how he had negotiated the terms of their release:

> It made the union executive look good, that they had negotiated their release ... it made them feel that they had a responsibility that these guys wouldn't cause any future problems. And that particular union and that executive were very co-operative from there on (P2).[13]

We noted earlier that it takes material and rhetorical resources to take action against others, especially where such action promises to be "no-win." Earlier this century, police often characterized pickets as lawbreakers or criminals in order to muster sufficient righteousness to justify such intervention. With police modernization, police professionalism was a ceaseless campaign to effect coercive monopolization in the speed with which the counter-force could be brought to a conflict. Over the decades, the coercive arsenal has become more selective and graduated. Today, a characterization of pickets as clients or constituents or, as put in a RCMP training video, "your neighbours" involved in a civil dispute, re-frames the intervention qualitatively at the same time as it raises the bar at which intervention will be appropriate. Police are organizationally more eager to effect conflict resolution from a distance, through intelligence gathering, surveillance, partnership cultivation, and responsibilization (cf. della Porta and Reiter, 1998). In the first instance, and in the absence of political duress, they are less reactive and less reliant on hard technologies and police presence. This is articulated in the new policy.[14] Both forms of communication, along with hard technologies like videotaping and strategic deployment, in which police were sequestered out of sight in order to avoid being recorded by television cameras and thus be seen as provoking, can be seen as devices by which coercion disciplines at a distance.

With the new policy, and in the context of neoliberal responsibilization and post-Fordist labour practices, the fundamental question is not in what numbers and in what gear police are deployed, but rather when and under what conditions an expenditure of *public* resources is warranted. The policy is designed to compel labour and management to, in effect, see the conflict in routinized or *depoliticized* terms, or as a thing for which recourse to state arbitration is delimited. Even where police liaison officers do their work, they instruct on the new rules of the game, by which each of the parties is informed that they had better be able to show that they have taken adequate steps towards self-regulation. According to our police informants, the courts are also now following this lead – that is, before granting injunctions to restrict pickets, judges are often requiring evidence of some effort by both parties to self-regulate through the negotiation of a strike protocol. This is what is meant by brokering peace "at a distance." In the meantime, police communicate the message that though they prefer to stand back or stay off site, they will be keen to enforce the law and use force when negotiated orders are breached: "We told them that this is a new policy that we were trying to work out and if it didn't work out then the nightsticks and helmets and everything would come out and physical force would be used where necessary, that they would feel the full effect of the law" (P2).

This may further the analyses of della Porta and Reiter (1998) and Wisler and Kriesi (1998). Police will willingly undertake activities in violence reduction, doing so not only by collecting information, negotiation and mediation, but also through "empowering" partners and citing "civilian" jurisdiction. Although they do so making reference to a linear professional development, such "civilization" of the coercive response is rather only selectively suspended according to the uneven politicization of various areas of service delivery. While the privatization or sterilization of public violence is very much part and parcel of the professional motivations of a public police force and can be seen in much of the public-order research, so too is a parallel militarization involving high-tech hardware. It is important to remember here that police are not their own switchmen. Just as they may be happy to leave an "unwinnable war" to others on Monday, the political tide will have them easily taking up coercive work on Tuesday.[15]

For the most part, police practitioners at the administrative level viewed the trend towards the delimitation of public displays of coercion as a natural evolution, as an adaptation of the philosophy of community policing. However, it can and has been argued here that changing industrial relations, governmental logics and local politics continue to reinvent *them*. How far the public police can offload immediate delivery of coercion is a question being confronted today. In the face of regressive changes in labour legislation in Ontario (Labour Relations and Employment Statute Act, 1995) that rescinded a ban against the use of replacement workers, it is unclear whether the police will manage to "keep their distance." In the meantime, there is a clear rise in the use of contract and in-house security to fill the vacuum.[16]

Conclusion

Why did Windsor, a labour town, not institute a community-policing approach to labour-management conflict sooner than it did? In the main there was no felt need among the three principal parties (police, management, and unions) to adopt a new policy, because there was already a sufficient routinization of their representative interests in the response to labour-management conflict. In addition, the more powerful unions in Windsor already enjoyed understandings with management that there would be no attempt to maintain production during strikes. It was not until the development of subcontracting, outsourcing to offshore plants, and the threat of plant closures in the 1980s that this arrangement was challenged and that labour required, at a minimum, symbolic backing of police and local politics. With Sheller-Globe, a precipitating incident was adeptly finessed by labour and local pro-union provincial MPPs as a line in the sand, or as a labour version of "a ditch in which to die" (Waddington, 1993).

Outside of the politics of Windsor, the crisis in Fordism and the rejigging of police delivery might have produced a policy without the rhetoric of responsiveness to labour interests. But even in Windsor, this policy is not a long-standing victory for labour or a less coercive response to industrial disputes. It might be said that coercion is being exercised, but with greater "intelligence." The use of injunctions and of private contract security has increased greatly. In the meantime, police have been encouraged to show the flag of coercion in "high stakes" protest venues, including the Windsor meeting of the OAS in June 2000. Following, and also innovating on, police experience in Vancouver (APEC), Seattle (WTO) and Washington (IMF), Windsor police co-operated with federal and provincial agencies in the transformation of parts of downtown into a "security zone" in which rights and freedoms suffered a "temporary" suspension. Before such events, communications in the form of intelligence on activists are deployed towards the prevention of effective dissent. While the Windsor police established co-operative links and negotiated agreements on protocols with a number of groups involved in the protest, including labour, the RCMP visited the private homes of many of the activists involved in these groups to "interrogate" them. In this context and others (cf. Kraska and Kappeler, 1997), the co-development of paramilitary and community policing is not contradictory; on the contrary, partnering, privatization, and civilianization can coexist nicely with specialist, highly expressive and public coercion. Indeed, it might be argued that in such high-stakes venues the public resources of the host nation is "partnered" or contracted to provide security guarantees for high-powered, transnational stakeholders. That the public police juggle more specialist expertise in the graduation of coercion at some sites and yet see the benefits of offloading delivery at others is to say that the deployment of police authority remains, as ever, sensitized to local and extra-local politics.

Endnotes

*Reprinted with permission of *Canadian Review of Sociology and Anthropology*, 39.1, 2002, pp.1-27.
This research was funded by the University of Windsor Research Board and the Social Science and Humanities Research Council. We would like to thank the anonymous reviewers for their helpful and insightful comments. This manuscript was first submitted in January 2001 and accepted in December 2001.

1   Although organized labour was present at those protests, the major clashes and arrests did not involve labour. In Quebec City, the bulk of the labour movement abided by the police request to stay away from the infamous fence that had been constructed around the conference area. In Windsor, there were no major clashes or arrests during the main, labour-led march. However, as soon as the march and rally were finished and most of the labour participants had left the downtown area, there were significant confrontations between the police and protesters and numerous arrests were made.

2   Strikers and strike captains were also interviewed, as well as police involved in these strikes. The protest organizers, along with the police liaison, were also interviewed. The major protests were the Windsor Days of Action (October 1997) and the OAS Meeting (June 2000).

3   Although Windsor is widely perceived both locally and nationally, to be a labour town with a history of strong union involvement and influence in city and county

politics, the Windsor police were by no means the first to establish a formal policy and structure to deal with labour disputes. A phone survey of police services in Canada found that Hamilton, Winnipeg and Vancouver had established similar policies in the early 1980s. These cities were also known to have strong labour union movements and significant strike activity. Our survey found that Windsor was in the median category of cities making the shift about 14 years ago (median of 15 and mean of 14 years).

4   A wedge is a tight formation of officers, which takes the form of an arrow in order to pierce and divide an opposing mass of pickets, demonstrators, etc.

5   "P#" stands for police respondent while "L#" stands for labour-union respondent.

6   We will refer to the policy that Windsor developed as the "new policy" even though there was no previous written policy. Many of our respondents used the term "new policy" to distinguish both new practices and the written document.

7   According to the police Annual Report of 1991, Windsor's image with regard to labour-management conflict was historically that of a "battleground" (Windsor Police Service, 1991: 11). The Annual Reports (Windsor Police Service, Annual Reports, 1988-1993) also implied that the police had traditionally used a confrontational approach to labour disputes, characterizing their new approach after 1987 as "non-confrontational."

8   In terms of specific collective agreements, the first example of the Fordist compromise is the 1948 UAW/General Motors agreement in which the parties agreed to formulaic wage rules in multi-year contracts that included an annual wage improvement factor tied to average long-term productivity growth and a cost-of-living adjustment tied to the consumer price index (Kumar and Meltz, 1992, p. 53).

9   As the Research Director of the CAW put it, while the anti-concession objectives of the Canadian UAW were, of themselves, modest, they provided another strong reminder that collective bargaining remains at the heart of unionism.

If the auto workers (in Canada), with their reputation for militancy and for being at the leading edge of collective bargaining developments, had fallen in line with their American parent, concessions would not only have been legitimated in Canada but an aura of fatalism would have enveloped them (Ginden, 1989: 81-82).

10 The problems faced by CAW and the other unions were not confined to the auto industry. The year 1987 began with a dispute between a major multinational agribusiness, Archer Daniels Midland (ADM) and the CAW Local 195. In what the union saw as another sign of the times, the company advertised for "temporary production workers" or replacement workers, which was a direct challenge to the local labour movement. Labour responded by mobilizing public support and large numbers of strikers and support pickets, which led to a number of confrontations on the picket lines.

11 As noted, there is a growing body of literature which confirms dramatic changes in policing (O'Malley, 1997; Bayley and Shearing, 1996; Stenson, 1993; Johnston, 1992).

12 Of course, this dilemma between a more coercive enforcement role and more distanced co-ordination role will be expected to work itself out differently across the levels of government or governance and according to the nature of the challenge to post-Fordist accumulation and the neoliberal hegemony. Thus, we might expect that political and industrial crises on a national scale will force the hand of police, and will also be addressed by coercive services more politicized by the national agenda (e.g., the Queen's Park incident). It might be expected that political and industrial crises on a local scale will be politicized more by the local social and political agenda, as illustrated by the Windsor case. The combinatory of marketization and role simplification may also make the public police more vulnerable to external political pressures, including the kinds of political pressure generated by labour in Windsor in 1987.

13 In the meantime, police also educate themselves in a recharacterization of pickets: "The thing that I did come to find almost without exception was how *responsible* those picket captains really were. They had a political agenda too. They had to appear out there that they were going to give the rank and file their money's worth but god, there was so much you could do with those folks when you got them in a room and you started to talk to them and you said: 'Look this isn't going to work for you, it's not going to work for me. I know you've got a political agenda, you're going to want to do this and I can let you do that. Go out there and raise hell and call us what you need to call us but then call it off and let's do this.' And they bought into it every time" (P2, italics added).

14 Acting at a distance, however, the police exercised both trust and distrust in their choice of communications. They had long used and continued to use informants, who were used as a second track or as "insurance." According to a police source, unsolicited information would come to the police very frequently in the major actions, but informants were also "actively cultivated" (P3; cf. Marx, 1974).

15 Learned cultural disgust with public violence, whether generalized across the entire society or taken to hypothesize the evolution of the policing of disorder, would also appear to be of some salience (Marx, 1998).

16 Private police are increasingly used during strikes in Windsor and in Ontario generally. Private security firms like ACCUFAX out of London, Ontario, offer packages of services to companies facing strikes, including trucking, personnel (replacement workers) and security and surveillance services (SN). One police respondent expressed concern about how leading-edge firms go beyond what he understood as their mandate – as in when they double as strikebreakers or carry out some of the production tasks in addition to their security role: "They're licensed for a certain kind of function and should be doing that function ... We've seen an increase [in private security] in the past couple of years ... they're taking a more proactive role" (P8, also 113). That increased

proactivity includes more aggressive videotaping and one incident in which members of the security firm mimicked the public police by wearing tactical-style clothing and arming themselves with collapsible batons (P8).

References

Baragar, F. 1995. "Theory, policy and institutional structure: PC1003 and macroeconomics."
In *Labour Gains, Labour Pains: 50 Years of PC1003*. C. Gonick, P. Phillips and J. Vorst (eds.). Winnipeg: Society for Socialist Studies/Fernwood Publishing.
Baruth-Walsh, M. and M. Walsh. 1995. *Strike: Ninety Days on the Line*. Penumbra Press.
Bayley, D. and C. Shearing. 1996. "The future of policing." *Law and Society Review*, Vol. 30, No. 3, pp. 585-606.
Becker, H. 1984. "Moral entrepreneurs: The creation and enforcement of deviant categories." In *Deviant Behaviour*. D. Kelly (ed.). 2nd ed. New York: St. Martin's Press.
Bercuson, D. 1974. "The Winnipeg general strike." In *On Strike: Six Key Labour Struggles in Canada* – 1919-1949. I. Abella (ed.). Toronto: James Lewis and Samuel.
Brake M. and C. Hale. 1992. *Public Order and Private Lives: The Politics of Law and Order*. London: Routledge.
Brogden, M. 1982. *The Police: Autonomy and Consent*. London and New York: Academic Press.
Burawoy, M. 1985. *The Politics of Production*. London: Verso.
Canadian Police College (CPC). 1981. *The Management of the Police Response to Crisis Situations: The Proceedings of the Tactical Unit Workshop, June 1981*. Ottawa: Canadian Police College.
City of Windsor. 1987. *Council Minutes*. 5 July 1987.
Cruickshank, B. 1993. "Self-Government and Self-Esteem." *Economy & Society*, Vol. 22, No. 3, pp. 329-44.

de Lint, W. 1999. "19th Century disciplinary reform and the prohibition against talking policemen." *Policing & Society*, Vol. 9, No. 1, pp. 33-58.

della Porta, D. and H. Reiter. 1998. "Introduction." In *Policing Protest: The Control of Mass Demonstrations in Western Democracies*. D. della Porta and H. Reiter (eds.). Minneapolis: University of Minnesota Press, pp. 1-34.

Ericson R. and K. Haggerty. 1997. *Policing the Risk Society*. Toronto: University of Toronto Press.

Fielding, N. 1991. *The Police and Social Conflict*. London: Athlone Press.

Fillieule, O. and F. Jobard. 1998. "The policing of protest in France: Toward a model of protest policing." In *Policing Protest: The Control of Mass Demonstrations in Western Democracies*. D. della Porta and H. Reiter (eds.). Minneapolis: University of Minnesota Press.

Garland, D. 1996. "The limits of the sovereign state: Strategies of crime control in contemporary society." *The British Journal of Criminology*, Vol. 36, No. 4, pp. 445-71.

Geary, R. 1985. *Policing Industrial Disputes: 1893-1985*. Cambridge University Press.

Ginden, S. 1989. "Breaking away: The formation of the Canadian Auto Workers." *Studies in Political Economy*, Vol. 29, pp. 63-89.

Ginden, S. 1995. *The Canadian Auto Workers: The Birth and Transformation of a Union*. Toronto: James Lorimer.

Grant, D. and M. Wallace. 1991. "Why do strikes turn violent?" *American Journal of Sociology*, Vol. 96 (March), pp. 1117-50.

Green, S. and S. Mastrofski (eds.). 1988. *Community Policing as Rhetoric and Reality*. New York: Praeger.

Hall, S. et al. 1978. *Policing the Crisis: "Mugging," Law and Order, and the State*. London: MacMillan.

Hargrove, B. 1998. *Labour of Love: The Fight to Create a More Humane Canada*. Toronto: McFarlane, Walter and Ross.

Harring, S. and L. McMullin. 1975. "The Buffalo police 1872-1900: Labor unrest, political power and the creation of the police institution." *Criminal and Social Justice*, Vol. 4, pp. 5-14.

Hills, A. 1995, "Militant tendencies: Paramilitarism in British police." *British Journal of Criminology.* Vol. 35, No. 3, pp. 450-56.

Jaime-Jimenez, O. and F. Reinares, 1998. "The policing of mass demonstrations in Spain: From dictatorship to democracy." In *Policing Protest: The Control of Mass Demonstrations in Western Democracies.* D. della Porta and H. Reiter (eds.). Minneapolis: University of Minnesota Press.

Jamieson, S. 1971. *Times of Trouble: Labour Unrest in Canada.* 1900-1967. Otttawa: Queen's Printer.

Jamieson, S. 1973. *Industrial Relations in Canada.* 2nd ed. Toronto: Macmillan.

Jessop, B. 1994. "Post-Fordism and the state." In *Post-Fordism: A Reader.* A. Amin (ed.). Oxford: Blackwell.

Johnston, L. 1992. *The Rebirth of Private Policing.* London: Routledge and Kegan Paul.

Kelling, G. et al. 1974. *The Kansas City Preventative Patrol Experiment.* Washington, D.C.: Police Foundation.

King, M. 1997. "Policing and public order issues in Canada: Trends for change." *Policing and Society,* Vol. 8, No. 1, pp. 47-76.

Klockars, C. 1988. "The rhetoric of community policing." In *Community Policing: Rhetoric or Reality.* J. Greene and S. Masatrofski (eds.). New York: Praeger.

Kopinak, K. 1996. *Desert Capitalism: Maquiladoras in North America's Western Industrial Corridor.* Tucson: University of Arizona Press.

Kraska, P. and V. Kappeler. 1997. "Militarizing the American police: The rise and normalization of paramilitary units." *Social Problems,* Vol. 44, No. 1.

Kumar, P. 1993. *From Uniformity to Divergence: Industrial Relations in Canada and the United States.* Kingston, Ont.: IRC Press.

Kumar, P. and N. Meltz. 1992. "Industrial relations in the automobile." In *Industrial Relations in Canadian Industry.* R.P. Chaykoowski and A. Verma (eds.). Toronto: Dryden Canada.

Latornell, J. 1993. *Violence on the Picket Line: The Law and Police Response.* Kingston, Ont.: IRC Press.

Lipsky, M. 1968. "Protest as a political resource." *American Political Science Review*, Vol. 62 (Dec.), pp. 1144-58.

Marx, G.T. 1974. "Thoughts on a neglected category of social movement participant: The agent provocateur and the informant." *American Journal of Sociology*, Vol. 80 (Sept.), pp. 402-42.

Marx, G.T. 1998. "Some reflections on the democratic policing of demonstrations." In *Policing Protest: The Control of Mass Demonstrations in Western Democracies*. D. della Porta and H. Reiter (eds.). Minneapolis: University of Minnesota Press.

Mayne, E. 1988. "Sheller-Globe changed labour history." *Windsor Star*, Windsor, Ont. 11 May 1988, p. A4.

McPhail, C., D. Schweingruber and J. McCarthy. 1998. "Policing protest in the U.S.: 1960-1995." In *Policing Protest: The Control of Mass Demonstrations in Western Democracies*. D. della Porta and H. Reiter (eds.). Minneapolis: University of Minnesota Press.

Morgan, J. 1987. *Conflict and Order: The Police and Labour Disputes in England and Wales, 1900-1939*. Oxford: Clarendon.

Murphy, C. 1998. "Policing postmodern Canada." *Canadian Journal of Law and Society*, Vol. 13, No. 2, pp. 1-25.

Olsen, M. 1968. "Perceived legitimacy of social protest actions." *Social Problems*, Vol. 15 (Winter), pp. 297-310.

O'Malley, P. 1992, "Risk, power and crime prevention." *Economy & Society*. Vol. 21, pp. 252-75.

O'Malley, P. 1997. "Policing, politics and post-modernity." *Social & Legal Studies*, Vol. 6, No. 3, pp. 363-81.

O'Malley, P. and B. Palmer. 1996. "Post-Keynesian policing." *Economy & Society*, Vol. 25, No. 2, pp. 137-55.

Ontario Provincial Police (OPP). 1981. *Crowd Control Training*. Archives of Ontario, RG 4-2 63.3.

Ontario Provincial Police (OPP). 1972. *Crowd Control Manual*. OPP: Planning and Research Branch.

Osborne, D. and T. Gaebler. 1993. *Reinventing Government*. New York: Penguin.

Palmer, B. 1992. *Working Class Experience: Rethinking the History of Canadian Labour – 1800-1991*. Toronto: McClelland & Stewart.

Reiner, R. 1998. "Policing protest and disorder in Britain." In *Policing Protest: The Control of Mass Demonstrations in Western Democracies.* D. della Porta and H. Reiter (eds.). Minneapolis: University of Minnesota Press.

Rose, N. 1993. "Government, authority and expertise in advanced liberalism." *Economy & Society*, Vol. 22, No. 3, pp. 283-99.

Rose, N. and P. Miller. 1992. "Political power beyond the state." *The British Journal of Sociology*, Vol. 43, No. 2, pp. 173-201.

Russell, B. 1990. *Back to Work: Labour, State and Industrial Relations in Canada.* Scarborough: Nelson.

Scraton, P. 1985. *The State of the Police: Is Law and Order Out of Control?* London: Pluto Press.

Sears, A. 1999. "The 'lean' state and capitalist restructuring: Toward a theoretical account." *Studies in Political Economy*, Vol. 59, Summer, pp. 91-113.

Shorter, E. and C. Tilly. 1971. "Le déclin de la grève violente en France de 1890 à 1935." *Le mouvement social*, Vol. 79 (July-Sept.), pp. 95-118.

Silver, A. 1966. "The demand for order in civil society: A review of some themes in the history or urban crime, police and riot." In *The Police: Six Sociological Essays.* D Bordua (ed.). New York: Wiley.

Snyder, D. and C. Tilley. 1974. "Hardship and collective violence in France." *American Sociological Review*, Vol. 37 (Oct.), pp. 520-32.

Stenson, K. 1993. "Community policing as a governmental technology." *Economy & Society*, Vol. 22, No. 3, pp. 375-88.

Swift, J. 1995. *Wheels of Fortune: Work and Life in the Age of Falling Expectations.* Toronto: Between the Lines.

Task Force on Policing in Ontario. 1974. *Task Force on Policing in Ontario: The Police are the Public and the Public are the Police.* Toronto: Ontario.

Turner, R.H. 1968. " The public perception of protest." *American Sociological Review*, Vol. 34, pp. 815-31.

Uglow, S. 1988. *Policing Liberal Society.* New York: Oxford University Press.

U.S. President's Commission on Law Enforcement and Administration of Justice. 1967. *The Challenge of Crime in a*

Free Society: A Report. Washington, D.C.: U.S. Government Printing Office.

National Advisory Commission on Criminal Justice Standards and Goals. 1973. *Report on Police.* Washington, D.C.: U.S. Government Printing Office.

Vogler, R. 1991. *Reading the Riot Act.* Milton Keynes: Open University Press.

Waddington, D. 1992. *Contemporary Issues in Public Disorder.* London: Routledge.

Waddington, P. 1993. "Dying in a ditch: The use of police powers in public order." *International Journal of the Sociology of Law*, Vol. 21, pp. 335-53.

Waddington, P. 1994a. *Liberty and Order: Policing Public Order.* London: UCL Press.

Waddington, P. 1994b. "Coercion and accommodation: Policing public order after the Public Order Act." *British Journal of Sociology*, Vol. 45, No. 3, pp. 367-85.

Waddington, P. 1998. "Controlling protest in contemporary historical and comparative perspective." In *Policing Protest: The Control of Mass Demonstrations in Western Democracies.* D. della Porta and H. Reiter (eds.). Minneapolis: University of Minnesota Press.

Wells, D. 1986. "Autoworkers on the firing line." In *On the Job: Confronting the Labour Process in Canada.* C. Heron and R. Storey (eds.). Montreal and Kingston: McGill-Queen's University Press.

Wisler, D. and H. Kriesi. 1998. "Public order, protest cycles, and political process: Two Swiss cities compared." In *Policing Protest: The Control of Mass Demonstrations in Western Democracies.* D. della Porta and H. Reiter (eds.). Minneapolis: University of Minnesota Press.

Windsor and District Labour Council. 1999. *Labour Review.* Windsor, Ont.

Windsor Police Service (WPS). 1989. *Emergency Service Unit Policy and Procedures Manual.* Windsor, Ontario, p. 99.

Windsor Police Service (WPS). 1991. *Annual Report.* Windsor, Ont.

Winter, M. 1998. "Police philosophy and protest policing in the Federal Republic of Germany, 1960-1990." In *Policing*

Protest: The Control of Mass Demonstrations in Western Democracies. D. della Porta and H. Reiter (eds.). Minneapolis: University of Minnesota Press.

Yates, C. 1990. "The internal dynamics of union power: Explaining Canadian autoworker militancy in the 1980s." *Studies in Political Economy*, Vol. 31, pp. 71-105.

14

Interrogating justice: A critical analysis of the police interrogation and its role in the criminal justice process*

James W. Williams

In recent years the Canadian criminal justice system has been plagued by a number of high profile wrongful convictions. While each of these cases has raised serious questions concerning the justice process as a whole, particular attention has been directed towards the police and their ability to satisfy their dual mandate of investigating crime while protecting the interests, rights, and freedoms of the accused. One notable aspect of police operations that has come under increasing scrutiny in this regard is the police interrogation, a practice which is both upheld of police officers as a crucial means of gathering information and disposing of cases, and denounced by civil rights advocates as a serious threat to the standards of fairness and due process. In adopting the police interrogation as its object of study, this paper will argue that each of these characterizations are severely limited, and ultimately, misrepresentative of the more subtle functions of interrogative practices. Specifically, drawing upon the research literature in Britain, the United States, and Canada, the police interrogation will be conceptualized as an interactional medium in which commitments are fashioned to particular criminal identities and renditions of events in a manner that seeks to confirm and legitimate official police narratives. The implications of this constitutive, rather than merely coercive, function of the interrogation will be examined with particular attention to the issues of police accountability, and the limits of legislative reform.

Introduction

The wrongful convictions of Donald Marshall, David Milgaard, and Guy Paul Morin have precipitated a growing crisis of legitimacy within the Canadian criminal justice system. Specifically, public concern has centered on the ability of the justice system to prosecute guilty parties while ensuring the protection of the innocent through the application of the standards of due process. While all stages of the justice process have been subjected to various degrees of public scrutiny, the institution that has received the greatest critical attention is the police. This may be attributed to their highly publicized role in the collection of evidence, the identification of suspects, and the subsequent disposition of criminal cases. One of the most recent episodes of public criticism came with the release of the Kaufman report in which the police were identified as playing a key role in events leading to the wrongful conviction of Guy Paul Morin (Kaufman 1998). As a whole, the report and its recommendations – which feature necessary enhancements to the visibility and accountability of police operations – reflect a growing concern with the susceptibility of the police to both organizational and public pressures to produce successful case outcomes in spite of the potential threats that this expeditiousness may pose to the principles of justice and due process. Similar tendencies have been noted in a number of wrongful conviction cases in Canada (Anderson and Anderson 1998).

In lieu of this undercurrent of public anxiety, the objective of this paper is to engage in a critical analysis of a crucial, yet frequently misunderstood, aspect of police operations – the police interrogation. The importance of such an undertaking stems from the existence of the interrogation as a defining stage in the overall process of case construction and disposition (McConville and Baldwin 1982; McConville, Sanders, and Leng 1991; Baldwin

1993; Marin 1999; Belloni and Hodgson 2000). It represents one of the first points of contact between the police and potential suspects and, thus, serves as a critical forum in which initial information and impressions are exchanged. To the extent that this interaction transpires under conditions of low visibility and is premised upon both a presumption of guilt and the intention of an expeditious outcome, the interrogation emerges as a potential threat to the standards of due process and, subsequently, the attainability of justice within the Canadian criminal justice system.

Based on this critical perspective, the primary objective of this paper is to provide a detailed account of the nature and functions of the police interrogation as a determinative stage in the overall criminal justice process. The uniqueness and sophistication of this analysis will depend upon its conceptualization of the interrogation as part of an extended investigative process organized according to a series of frequently contradictory social, legal, organizational, and occupational norms. This attempt to situate interrogative practices in terms of the overall structure and dynamics of police work stands in direct contrast to the predominant trend within the existing literature to conceive of the interrogation in relatively narrow, technical terms as a methodology designed primarily to elicit confessions and other inculpatory information (Leo 1994). The result of this conceptual delimitation is that it has been evaluated almost exclusively in terms of its relative propensity to produce either true or false positives (Ofshe 1989; Gudjonsson 1992; Gudjonsson and MacKeith 1994; Ofshe and Leo 1997). It is my belief that such a narrow focus belies the varied functions of the interrogation as a crucial dimension of daily police operations, as well as neglects the subtleties of its influence on the entire criminal justice process.

In order to appreciate the nature of this influence, and thus overcome more delimited conceptualizations, it is critical that the definition of the police interrogation be expanded to include not only the legally circumscribed act of active police questioning under conditions of arrest or detention as defined by case law (Watt 1998: 467), but also more informal exchanges between police and suspects prior to the laying of a formal charge. This blurring of the conceptual boundary between police questioning as an informal practice and the interrogation as a legally spatially defined exchange is critical given that these initial interactions are often instrumental in arousing and substantiating initial police suspicions, and thus, in constituting the basic parameters for case construction and disposition. Ultimately, it is in broadening the traditional field of inquiry in this manner that this paper will seek to both refine our understanding of the police interrogation, and explore its implications for accountability, democracy, and due process within the juridical realm.

These stated objectives will be addressed through four stages of analysis. First, the police interrogation and its functions will be defined in terms of the overall context and organization of police work. Specific attention will be paid here to the role of the interrogation in the production and legitimation of police narratives of criminal behaviour, and thus, in the construction of cases in accordance with police "working rules." The second section will then examine the implications of this function for the issues of due process, police accountability, and more generally, wrongful convictions. Having identified the key issues and problems surrounding the police interrogation, the third and fourth sections will attempt to present and critically examine two proposed reforms to interrogative practices: the formal cautioning of suspects prior to questioning as prescribed by *Miranda* in the U.S., the *Police and Criminal Evidence Act* (PACE) in Britain, and the *Charter of Rights and Freedoms* in Canada, and the mandated audio or video-taping of the interrogation itself. Based on the identification of barriers to these reforms, and hence limitations to their effectiveness in practice, the paper will conclude with a brief comment on directions for future research in this area.

Before proceeding, an important proviso is in order. Due to a surprising absence of Canadian research on both the police interrogation in particular and the informal dimensions of the criminal justice system in general, many of the conclusions of this paper are supported by reference to primarily British and, to a lesser extent, American sources. This raises two important issues. First, this paper does not offer an extensive empirical examination of interrogative practices in Canada. Rather, its intention is both to highlight the need for future research in this area and, through a systematic overview of the strengths and limitations of the existing Anglo-American literature, to fashion a well-developed conceptual and theoretical framework according to which this research should proceed. This paper thus constitutes a necessary theoretical first step to a tradition of uniquely Canadian research on the police interrogation.

The reliance upon non-Canadian sources also raises a second issue: that of the generalizability of the conclusions reached in this paper to the Canadian justice system. Clearly there are significant philosophical, organizational, and procedural distinctions in the administration of justice across British, American, and Canadian jurisdictions. The police interrogation is no exception to this as it is governed by fundamentally different rules of evidence and informed by diverse bodies of case law in each juridical context. What is important to keep in mind is that in actual fact these formal provisions provide a fairly myopic and misleading view of the justice process as it operates in practice. This is due to the reality that both interrogations and the general dynamics of case disposition are typically organized according to informal processes, practices, and relationships which bear little relation to formal legal proscriptions – whether in the form of legislation or case law (Ericson 1985; Sharpe 1998). One of the key structural elements of this informal nature of the justice process is the practice of plea-bargaining which is dependent upon the police constructions of cases, complicit and often conciliatory relationships between police, defense attorneys, and prosecutors, organizational demands of efficiency and expeditiousness, and an assumption of guilt on the part of all parties involved. The low visibility and informal nature of these exchanges, and the willingness of the judiciary to accept these expedited case dispositions, ensures that these processes remain largely unaffected by formal rules of evidence and adjudication.

Ultimately, what this suggests is that the issue of generalizability rests upon similarities across the organization of justice work on an operational, rather than formal, level. Not surprisingly, it is in relation to these informal processes that the greatest consistencies are revealed across British, American, and Canadian contexts. This is attributable in large part to the pervasiveness of plea-bargaining in each jurisdiction as an efficient form of case disposition (Ericson 1985; 1993; Kaci and Rush 1988; Fitzgerald 1990; Sharpe 1998), and thus, the dependence of the justice process upon the production and legitimation of police accounts of social reality. Clearly these are accounts which serve to highlight the guilt of the accused, and subsequently, convince all players involved that the best course of action is an expedient, conciliatory, and informal resolution. Given these similarities in the Anglo-American model of justice, and the fact that the interrogation is most frequently brought to bear upon this informal dimension of justice, it is reasonable to conclude that the discussion to follow will be theoretically and substantively relevant to the Canadian context.

Police work and the functions of the interrogation

Perhaps the defining characteristic of the modern police interrogation is its almost universal endorsement by the policing community as a necessary component of any effective investigation (Baldwin 1993; Inbau and Reid 1967; Salhaney 1991; Hess 1997). Based on this conviction, interrogative practices have come to play an irreducible role in the justice process as a means of establishing the culpability of suspects, and subsequently, preparing the cases against them. As Baldwin (1993: 326) argues, "It has now become something of a truism to observe that, in most criminal cases, the crucial stage is the interview at the police station, for it is at that stage that a suspect's fate is as a rule sealed".

Despite this widespread endorsement of the interrogation as a key stage in the justice process, considerable ambiguity and debate surround the specific nature of its functions and effects. Thus, while the most typical rationale involves its technical role in eliciting confessions, providing inculpatory evidence, and generating information pertaining to other crimes (Leo 1994), a number of researchers have indicated that, in actual fact, the interrogation plays a much more limited role in the majority of police investigations (McConville and Baldwin 1981; McConville and Baldwin 1982; Ericson 1993; Bryan 1997). McConville and Baldwin (1982: 169) provide perhaps the strongest articulation of this position arguing that, "The available evidence suggests that, in the total law enforcement picture, the interrogation is comparatively unimportant". The implication here is that most case outcomes are determined by evidence which precedes the interrogation itself – such as forensic data and eyewitness accounts. Nevertheless, despite its apparently limited technical value, the police interrogation continues to be endorsed by the majority of analysts as a key investigative practice, a contradiction which requires a much more subtle, sophisticated, and ultimately, less technical appreciation of its nature and functions.

The starting point for such an alternative approach lies in re-framing the interrogation in relation to the wider structure and context of police work. Specifically, interrogative practices must be viewed as natural extensions of the police activities of case construction and legitimation. This follows from an interpretive approach to policing (Circourel 1976; Sanders 1977; Ericson and Baranek 1982; Ericson 1993; Manning 1977, 1980, 1986, 1988; McConville et al. 1991) which conceives of police work primarily in terms of the production and legitimation of narrative accounts of criminal behaviour, an inherently social process which is itself dependent upon the interpretive work and social interactions of individual police officers under conditions of autonomy and low visibility. It is the relative success of the police in constructing and justifying these accounts, and hence in de-legitimating competing visions, that is believed to be largely determinative of the outcomes of specific cases (Ericson and Baranek 1982; McConville et al. 1991; Ericson 1993). This preliminary narrative work is thus largely constitutive of the power relations between the police and the public. In this respect, the later stages of the justice process come to represent sources of justification and legitimation for the initial accounts developed by the police, rather than autonomous mechanisms of adjudication (Ericson and Baranek 1982; Ericson 1985).

From this perspective on police work, it is reasonable to argue that the police interrogation functions as an integral component of a more general process of account production and legitimation.

This stems from its existence as an interactional medium and dramatic ritual through which police narratives of criminal acts are not only tested, elaborated, and reaffirmed, but also endowed with the organizational and personal commitments of the individuals involved. The result is the conceptualization of interrogations as, "… social encounters fashioned to confirm and legitimate a police narrative" (McConville *et al.* 1991: 327).

It should be noted that an integral part of this process of legitimation is the reconciliation of any lingering ambiguities with the official account of the event. In this way, a narrative is created which highlights the suspect's guilt and selects our mitigating facts and circumstances (McConville and Baldwin 1982). As part of this process of translation, simplification, and naturalization, the suspect's viewpoint is ultimately either ignored or incorporated into the police account through an active process of negotiation and persuasion (McConville *et al.* 1991; Ericson and Baranek 1982). This leads McConville *et al.* (1991: 77) to conclude that, "The interview is not designed to elicit the suspect's own account of the incident, rather the suspect is invited to accede to the officer's view of the case. Where the suspect asserts innocence or introduces evidence which would support a defense, this is generally ignored". A very similar characterization of police activities was offered in a recent court judgment involving the Metro Toronto hold-up squad where the judge ruled that, "…the statement-taking process used by the holdup squad and the members of the York Regional Police Department were designed to both minimize the active involvement of the accused and preclude resort to any independent source of information as to what went on in the statement-taking process" (R. v. Lim: 152). Ultimately then, the interrogative process, drawing upon specific police schemas and theories of suspect culpability, is designed to persuade a suspect to accept a particular, predetermined rendition of events – a narrative account which is based on the excessive simplification of what is, in reality, a complex situation with ambiguous meanings and consequences. In conformity with this underlying logic, the questions asked are not of any true probative value but, "…merely seek to persuade suspects to accept a predetermined version of events" (Baldwin 1993: 341).

While the production of a confession is one specific outcome of this process, of more implicit importance is the commitment that the interrogation fosters, on the part of both the police and the suspect, to the official account of a criminal act. For the police, the performance of the interrogation ritual provides them with an opportunity both to confirm previous suspicions about a case (McConville and Baldwin 1982; McConville *et al.* 1991; Baldwin 1993; Bryan 1997), and actively to incorporate the suspect into the official account through the elicitation of confirmative statements. This latter function is particularly important as it supplies the suspect with what appears to be an authentic subject-position within the police narrative. In this way, the legitimacy of the police account is bolstered as the suspect's involvement in the case is articulated in their own words, rather than those of the detectives. For the suspect, this process usually results in a reluctant identification with the police position – at least to the extent that it is the police account which now becomes the recognized framework according to which the suspect's defense must be organized and articulated. This identification is only accelerated as other possible framings of the events are successively foreclosed through the course of the interrogation.

The end result of this entire process is the legitimation of the organizational narrative and the police actions that were taken in its defense. Once again, this must be seen to conform to the overall logic and structure of police work itself which is premised upon the rendering of the ambiguities and complexities of life events into stabilized, organizationally supported narratives that offer clear lines of organizational action (Manning 1977; 1986; 1988; Ericson 1993). The interrogation thus emerges as a critical sense-making medium through which the unique circumstances of cases may be applied against a background of taken-for-granted assumptions, and thus, converted into fairly routine forms of organizational work (Sudnow 1965; Manning 1986).

Beyond its implications for police narratives as applied in specific cases, there is also a second respect in which the police interrogation fulfills a crucial legitimating function. Following from the position of the police as key representatives of the socio-normative order, and consequently, a critical point at which the boundaries between appropriate and inappropriate behaviour are negotiated, the interrogation may be viewed as a mechanism for both identifying deviations from the status quo, and shaming the individuals who are responsible for this deviation (Hepworth and Turner 1974; McConville and Baldwin 1982). Through this Durkheimian ritual, not only are these social boundaries and norms themselves legitimated and re-produced, but also the position of the police as the irrefutable representatives and arbiters of this normative order. Following this logic, Pepinsky (1970) asserts that.

> The police generally are more strongly motivated by their desire to develop and maintain a stable identity as individuals and as a group than by fear of harm to society at large. The obtaining of confessions specifically and the interrogation process generally serve to create and stabilize this identity by establishing the police as followers and upholders of societal norms. In fact, in this process the police define who does and who does not live up to the norms and by this act seek to define the norms themselves.

Similarly, McConville and Baldwin (1982) conclude that the police interrogation is, "...a vital stage in the process of setting the suspect apart from the rest of the conforming society and, importantly, of setting the police apart from the suspect". A key element of this process is the recognition on the part of the suspects themselves that specific social norms have been improperly violated an act which is intended as both a display of respect for the police, and by extension, a symbolic reaffirmation of dominant social norms and values. This is consistent with the more general characterization of police work as involving the maintenance and re-production of social order, rather than the application of the principles of law (Ericson 1981; 1985; Manning 1977). Once again, within the context of this more general legitimating function, the interrogation emerges as an inherently social, rather than technical, enterprise.

Emerging from this discussion is the notion that the police interrogation may not be reduced to the technical function of eliciting confessions, inculpatory evidence, and/or other case relevant information as part of an overall search for an objective truth (Baldwin 1993). Instead, as a crucial component of the overall context of police work, the interrogation may be seen to function in the production and legitimation of police accounts of criminal behaviour. In this respect, it aids in the translation of the complexities and ambiguities of daily life into the codified narratives which constitute a foundation for both immediate police action, and the subsequent treatment of suspects as they are transformed into cases and processed through the criminal justice system. With this role in the construction of police accounts in mind, Baldwin (1993: 327) asserts that,

> It is evident, therefore, that the idea that police interviewing is, or is becoming, a neutral or objective search for truth cannot be sustained, because any interview inevitably involves exploring with a suspect the details of allegations within a framework of the points that might at a later date need to be proved. Instead of a search for truth, it is much more realistic to see interviews as mechanisms directed towards the construction of proof.

It must be recognized that a fundamental part of this process of production and legitimation is the fostering of commitments to the police account of events through both the manipulation of the suspect's understanding of his actions, and the systematic exclusion of competing accounts. Ultimately then, it is through the interrogative process, as largely a self-fulfilling prophesy, that the police reinforce their commitments to a series of accounts which they themselves have constructed in accordance with the routine demands and structures of their work.

The interrogation and the criminal justice process

While a satisfactory answer has been provided as to the functions of the police interrogation, the implications of interrogative practices for the justice process generally, and the principles of due process in particular, remain to be discussed. In this respect, it becomes crucial to appreciate the relationship between the police interrogation as a means of confirming and legitimating police narratives and the future stages and outcomes of the justice process. The need for such an approach is revealed in the observation by McConville and Baldwin (1982: 174) that,

> It is [interrogations] that, in the majority of cases, colour what happens at latter stages in the criminal process. Indeed, often they determine the outcome of cases at trial.

Questioning provides information classifiable in legally defined ways, resolves doubts, is administratively efficient and fulfills certain psychological needs. Questioning has come to dominate police work and, as a result, police perceptions of reality have come to dominate the criminal process.

Two insights follow from these comments. First, the police interrogation plays an important role in case construction, and subsequently, bears a considerable impact on case outcomes within the more formal stages of the justice process. Secondly, the implications of interrogative strategies for the principles of fairness and due process must be construed in relation to this overall context of criminal justice. It is within this light that more explicit connections may be drawn between the nature and functions of the police interrogation identified above and specific outcomes such as the violation of Charter rights and, in more extreme cases, wrongful convictions.

There are two general ways in which the police interrogation may negatively impact the outcomes of specific cases. First, in a technical sense, interrogations may produce either false confessions, or inculpatory evidence which may be applied in constructing a prosecutorial case against the accused. The potential for each of these outcomes is widely recognized in the literature, and is most commonly attributed to the coercive and manipulative nature of interrogations and the psychological principles upon which they are based (Ofshe 1989; Gudjonsson and MacKeith 1990; Gudjonsson 1992; Wrightsman and Kassin 1993; Gudjonsson and MacKeith 1994; Ofshe and Leo 1997). Nevertheless, despite the deception, coercion, and blatant disregard for Charter rights that are often involved in these types of cases, the direction of the discussion up to this point suggests that the interrogation is likely to play a more subtle role in the justice process. Once again, this is confirmed by the finding that case outcomes are often determined by evidence other than that supplied by the interrogation itself (McConville and Baldwin 1982). Thus, it is problematic to conceive of its impact in these narrow terms.

A second, more sophisticated, view of the police interrogation understands its effects on case outcomes to stem from its role in fostering commitments to false or misleading police narratives. In this respect, the interrogation emerges as an important foundation for processes such as police "tunnel vision" (Kaufman 1998) in which support and justifications are provided for specific police accounts through the systematic exclusion of exculpatory evidence and other possible crime scenarios. The police interrogation is particularly susceptible to these types of effects given its foundation within an assumption of guilt on the part of the police (Baldwin 1993; Ericson 1993). In fact, it is this assumption which explicitly underlies the psychological techniques employed in interrogative settings (Inbau and Reid 1967; Hess 1997). The result of this presumptive logic is that the interrogation is conducted in a manner such that evidence is produced which is ultimately consistent with the initial police hypothesis. The power of police "tunnel vision" which often underlies, motivates, and is ultimately reproduced within this process often means that even neutral or exculpatory information is interpreted in a manner consistent with the overall police narrative (Belloni and Hodgson 2000). This is particularly true in high profile cases in which the police are under extreme pressure to produce publicly recognizable results (Anderson and Anderson 1998).

In this respect, the interrogation is once again identifiable in terms of its operationalization of a series of self-fulfilling prophecies which do not necessarily yield new information or confessions from suspects, but which operate to reinforce police "tunnel vision" and systemic presumptions of guilt (Ericson 1994) through the legitimation of police accounts, and the subsequent foreclosure of other suspects and lines of investigation (McConville and Baldwin 1982; McConville et al. 1991; Baldwin 1993; Ericson 1993; Belloni and Hodgson 2000). It is within the context of these processes that the police interrogation may be understood to impact future stages of the justice process independently of its stated technical functions, and thus, to bear an important responsibility in the production of wrongful convictions and other substantive injustices.

A powerful example of this is provided by the high profile case of Guy Paul Morin who was wrongfully convicted in the sexual assault and murder of his nine-year old neighbour Christine Jessop. What became clear during the public inquiry which followed Morin's exoneration through DNA evidence was the susceptibility of the investigative process to systematic police biases. All efforts were made by investigators in the case to provide evidence which supported the dominant police account, and Morin's place within this narrative, to the neglect of both exculpatory evidence and the pursuit of other suspects. One revelation that was particularly telling was that Morin became a suspect in the case solely on the basis of a statement made by the victim's mother that the neighbour Morin was a "weird-type guy." The only evidence for this was the fact that he was thirty and still lived with his parents, that he played the clarinet, and that he kept honeybees (Kaufman 1998). All interactions which followed this revelation – in particular, interviews with key witnesses as well as the interrogation of Morin himself – were dedicated to providing support for this scripting despite frequently inconsistent and disconfirming evidence.

In terms of exchanges with Morin himself, there were a number of occasions on which his statements were taken out of context and entered into the police account as evidence of his guilt, hence once again revealing the susceptibility of the questioning process to systematic police biases, as well as its propensity to supply confirmations of police accounts in spite of plausible alternatives. For example, Morin's observation during an initial interview that, "[The body] was found across the Ravenshoe Road" (as cited in Kaufman 1998: 794) was interpreted by investigators as evidence that Morin possessed unique knowledge of the murder despite the fact that Ravenshoe Road was a paved east-west route known to local residents yet unfamiliar to the two detectives. In response to this and other statements elicited from Morin, commissioner Kaufman (1998: 799) argued that while officers have a right to investigate hunches and other possible leads in this case,

> ...the comments were 'hard evidence' of nothing. Nothing could be said even remotely to constitute an admission, or a demonstration of knowledge exclusive to the killer. The information in the officers' possession did

not justify any fixed view as to Morin's guilt. However, I find that [the investigators] did 'fix their sights' on Guy Paul Morin – they, themselves, may not have appreciated the extent to which they did so. Subsequent interviews of witnesses... were unduly coloured by their premature, overly fixed views. This, in turn, affected the quality of the interviews they conducted.

Ultimately, this case serves to re-confirm the significance of police interviews and interrogations as critical sites in which support and legitimation are produced for police narratives and accounts. It also demonstrates the potential implications of these processes, particularly when supported by police "tunnel vision," for specific criminal justice outcomes – in this case the wrongful conviction of Guy Paul Morin. Once again, it is the role of the interrogation in producing specific types of accounts which come to dictate the terms in which cases are constructed and disposed of which is relevant, rather than its production of factual elements which are of legal consequence. It is this re-situation of the interrogation in terms of specific police practices, strategies, and objectives which brings us to a final critical issue: the possibilities of reform.

Interrogative practices, the police, and the possibilities of reform

In general, reforms of the police interrogation have been directed to two specific areas: judicial decisions and legislative changes geared to protecting the rights of the accused, and the use of techniques such as audio and video recording to enhance the visibility and accountability of police practices. Focusing first on the former, legislative and judicial reforms have been enacted in a number of countries in response to the concern that police interrogations are conducted in a manner that systematically neglects the constitutional rights of suspects, and thus, the principles of due process. The most noteworthy of these changes have come in the American and British contexts where the *Miranda* decision and the *Police and Criminal Evidence Act* (PACE) have been established to ensure that suspects are unambiguously informed of their rights prior to police questioning. The Canadian equivalent to these judicial safeguards is, of course, the *Canadian Charter of Rights and Freedoms* which, according to Section 24(2), provides for the exclusion of evidence obtained in violation of the Charter rights to silence (Section 7) and to counsel (Section 10b) provided that these violations may be proven to have, "brought the administration of justice into disrepute" (Salhaney 1996; Marin 1999).

While in theory *Miranda*, PACE, and the Charter have represented important steps towards the protection of the rights of the accused, in practice they have been much less successful (Lewis and Allen 1977; Ayling 1984; Ericson 1985; Baldwin 1990; McConville *et al.* 1991; McConville 1992; Baldwin 1993; Moston and Stephenson 1993; Leo and White 1999; Belloni and Hodgson 2000). This failure to bring about significant change in interrogative practices is attributable to a number of different factors. First, suspects often do not appreciate the nature and significance of their rights given both problems with the clarity and adequacy of their communication (Baldwin 1993; Ayling 1984), and their formulation in relatively abstract, legalistic language. These difficulties are only compounded by the frequent presence of language barriers between officers and suspects which interfere with the ability of the accused to both understand and clearly assert their rights (Ainsworth 1993). This very scenario was played out in a 1990 Canadian case in which the accused was led by police to sign an inculpatory statement despite the fact that language difficulties clearly undermined his ability to understand his right to silence and to seek counsel (R. v. Lim).

Another impediment to the efficacy of legislative changes has been the ambiguous and inconsistent nature of legal standards surrounding interrogative practices and due process requirements (Kaci and Rush 1988; Baldwin 1990; Salhaney 1991; Baldwin 1993; Moston and Stephenson 1993). This is attributable to a lack of clarity not only in the law itself, but also in its application as judgments on the admissibility of statements obtained from interrogations tend to be rendered, in British, American, and Canadian judicial contexts, on a case by case basis according to subjective and inconsistent standards (Kaci and Rush 1988; Erison 1985; 1993; Baldwin 1993). Beyond its contribution to a lack of clear guidelines for police conduct in interrogative settings, this trend is indicative of both the enabling structure of law as it applies to police conduct, and the judicial recognition that the police require a certain degree of latitude if they are successfully to fulfill their social responsibilities (Ericson 1993; Sharpe 1998). Each of these factors ultimately serves as a barrier to the development of stricter and more consistent standards for police conduct.

In general, this judicial ambiguity and inconsistency is only exacerbated by a pervasive lack of adequate police training in cautioning procedures and their impact on the admissibility of evidence obtained through the interrogative process (Baldwin 1993), as well as by communication barriers between government agencies and the failure of police departments to allocate responsibility for the implementation of legislative changes (Moore 1992). Focusing once again on the Canadian context, one of the most notable examples of this general lack of procedural knowledge came from the investigation of Paul Bernardo who was charged with the abduction, sexual assault, and murder of two young women in southern Ontario. In this case, the failure of police interviewers to comply with Bernardo's repeated requests for a lawyer resulted in the inadmissibility of all evidence obtained during his first custodial interview. As indicated by a Metro Toronto police report cited in the inquiry that followed his eventual conviction, this failure was attributable to the poor advice of a single officer – Staff Inspector Marrier,

> The interview started and they did not come out of the room for some time. Throughout the interview Bernardo repeated his request to speak to counsel. At some point some considerable time after the start of the interview, the interviewers left the room. There was a discussion about the accused's repeated request for counsel and they were advised that they should continue. There was a mistaken belief, relayed to Detective Irwin by Staff Inspector Marrier, that case law allowed for this scenario until a demand was made by the subject (Campbell 1996: 192).

This oversight resulted in Justice Campbell's conclusion that, "Staff Inspector Marrier, by giving grossly incorrect legal advice to the interview team, undermined that work and effectively ensured that no evidence discovered as a result of the interview could ever be used against Bernardo" (Campbell 1996: 192).

A second major impediment to the success of legal reforms such as *Miranda*, PACE, and the Charter is the "working rules" of the police which are often applied in innovative ways to circumvent legally mandated changes in policy and conduct (Lewis and Allen 1977; McConville *et al.* 1991; McConville 1992; Moore 1992; Ericson 1993; Renke 1996; Leo and White 1999; Belloni and Hodgson 2000). Focusing specifically on the legal rights of suspects, McConville *et al.* (1991: 50) argue that, "The police can adopt numerous ploys to ensure that suspects do not understand their rights, to discourage them from requesting a solicitor, or to encourage them to cancel their request". One specific example of these ploys is a technique referred to as "participating Miranda" (Lewis and Allen 1977) in which *Miranda* warnings are supplied to suspects over an extended period of time within the context of other remarks urging the waiver of rights – i.e. suggestions that a failure to do so may be interpreted as evidence of guilt. A recent review of *Miranda* warnings by Leo and White (1999) confirms that the practices of de-emphasizing the significance of *Miranda* warnings and offering suspects benefits in exchange for waivers continues to the present day throughout the United States. Evidence of threats, inducements, and other police strategies to circumvent constitutional guarantees are also prevalent within Canadian case law (R. v. Cole; R. v. Arp; R. v. Burlingham; R. v. Dawson; R. v. Dutton; R. v. Ballantyne; R. v. Small; R. v. Johns). Perhaps the most egregious of these is the case of R. v. Burlingham in which police attempted to disparage the accused's counsel in order to secure a Charter waiver. The B.C. Court of Appeal strongly condemned this type of police behaviour as a clear violation of the accused's constitutional rights.

"[Section] 10(b) specifically prohibits the police, as they did in this case, from belittling an accused's lawyer with the express goal or effect of undermining the accused's confidence in and relationship with defence counsel. It makes no sense for S. 10(b) of the Charter to provide for the right to retain and instruct counsel if law enforcement authorities are able to undermine either an accused's confidence in his or her lawyer or the solicitor-client relationship" (115).

The police were also cited in this case for offering the accused a deal which expired Monday morning knowing that the accused's counsel would be unavailable during the weekend. This type of manipulation and subversion stands as a clear illustration of what Ericson (1985) refers to as the excessive costs of invoking the law. For Ericson (1985: 71), it is these implicit costs which are responsible for the practical limitations of the Canadian Charter. "To be sure, gains can be made in the individual case, but in the aggregate the costs of legalism are too excessive when weighed against the hope of achieving more justice and some advantage".

Another technique employed by investigators in their efforts to subvert procedural safeguards emerges from the British context where PACE and its attendant *Codes of Practice* require that each individual detained in a police station be assigned a custody officer (McConville 1992). It is the responsibility of these officers, who are independent of the investigation, to make decisions relating to the detention of suspects, to inform suspects of their rights of access to legal advice, and to record all matters relating to suspects in the custody record. Despite this legal requirement, research indicates that it is common for investigators to gain access to suspects without recording their interactions, and with the full support of the custody officer (McConville 1992; Belloni and Hodgson 2000). McConville (1992: 539) provides the following example of this subversive technique in practice,

After he had been booked in by the Custody Officer, and prior to his interrogation, Billy was locked up in cell No. 4. Then a Detective Inspector (D.I.) collected the keys from the Custody Officer, visited Billy in his cell, discussed the call with him and made it clear that he wanted the case dealt with the "easy" way. After the visit, the D.I. returned to the charge room, casually returned the cell keys to the Custody Officer and, in the presence of the Custody Officer, briefed one of the detective constables who was to interview Billy on what had happened and the implications this had for the interrogation".

In most of these cases, the subversive actions undertaken by investigators are justified through appeals to police "working rules" or "working personalities" (Epp 1997). One of the most powerful of these working rules is the principle that departure from legal regulations is both appropriate and situationally justified where there is a genuine belief in the suspect's guilt (Brodeur 1981; McConville 1992; Epp 1997). Of course, this process of legitimation follows from the underlying, and somewhat self-fulfilling, assumption typically held by police officers that they are uniquely qualified to judge the guilt of suspects (Epp 1997). In light of this specialized knowledge, subversive behaviours become viewed as matters of operational necessity (Brodeur 1981) designed to protect the public interest and maintain the social order. This process of rationalization and neutralization is captured once again by McConville (1992: 547) who notes in reference to a specific case that,

> A confession was deemed necessary because the officer thought that without it, the case would fall apart and might not be continued by the Crown Prosecution Service... So far as the officers are concerned, the informal interrogation of Clive is a true moral drama in which right confronts wrong, and the champions of justice take on those bent on attacking the social fabric of society.

This notion of "noble cause" (Kaufman 1998) also played an important role in Morin case where investigators felt justified in applying their working rules to manipulate witness testimony based on the firm conviction that Morin was guilty, and that they were ultimately acting in accordance with the "noble cause" of protecting the best interests of the general public. It is important to keep in mind that these types of violations and subversions are not isolated in nature, nor are they confined to the actions of a few "bad apples," rather, they are consistent with the legal and institutional structures in which the police operate. Thus, they may be more aptly characterized as forms of "structured police deviance" (Hagan and Morden 1981).

Overall then, the success of legal reforms in British, American, and Canadian contexts has been seriously hampered by their failure to take into account the presence and strength of police working rules which constitute an important foundation for investigative practices, and which contribute to the circumvention of legal changes through a variety of innovative strategies. These tendencies, and their resistance to change, are exacerbated by the high degree of autonomy and discretion supplied to police investigators (Manning 1980; Ericson 1981; 1993). As Ericson (1993: 11) notes in reference to the Canadian justice system, "The detective operates under a "visibility cover," so that his decision to ignore a matter can remain unknown to other organizational members, and his decision to construct a matter in a particular way has to be accepted at face value by other organizational members because there are rarely the means or inclinations to do "otherwise". These systemic restrictions on police visibility and accountability are ultimately reinforced within the formal justice system through both the practice of plea bargaining which ensures that police practices are not questioned in open court, and the failure to prosecute instances of police misconduct when they do arise (Lewis and Allen 1977; Doig 1978; Ericson 1985; 1993; Kaci and Rush 1988; Sharpe 1998). These processes are indicative of a fundamental absence of mechanisms designed to bring police behaviour to public view. Once again, the law emerges as an enabling resource, rather than an adequate and viable check on police practices.

In general, what this discussion suggests is that few qualitative changes in police behaviour have been brought about through legislative and judicial mechanisms such as *Miranda*, PACE, and the Charter. Furthermore, the changes that have occurred have tended to involve further reductions in the visibility of police practices as investigators have responded to stricter legislative guidelines through the adoption of more subtle and covert means of obtaining information from suspects (Moston and Stephenson 1993). This trend is particularly dangerous due to the false sense of legitimacy that this accords police practices given their publicly reported compliance with legislative guidelines (Brodeur 1981;

Ericson 1981; 1985; 1993; Sanders and Bridges 1990). Ericson (1993: 144) articulates this very dilemma with specific reference to the interrogation, "Indeed, at this point giving the caution may be useful to the police officer in constructing the appearance that everything proceeded with procedural regularity and that the accused acted voluntarily in condemning himself". Ironically then, existing legislative changes have both forced police practices to become more covert, and consequently less visible to judicial scrutiny, and endowed these practices with greater legitimacy given their implied execution in the spirit of the law. They have thus largely become dramatic rituals of re-assurance (Ericson 1985). In light of this paradox, Sanders and Bridges (1990: 113) conclude,

> Police behaviour has been altered by legal changes, but not in the way intended. Only the manner in which the police secure their goals – putting maximum pressure on the suspects who matter most to them – has changed. Police malpractice has probably not been reduced but it has been made less overt, and hence more difficult to detect and control. In giving the false impression of complete compliance with the law, unduly great faith in the police will now be encouraged.

Ultimately, to the extent that legislative changes neglect the subcultural norms and working rules of the police, they will continue to fail in their attempts to enhance the visibility and accountability of the police generally, and interrogative practices in particular.

A similar series of issues and concerns has faced legislative mandates and policing initiatives requiring all interviews and interrogations of suspects to be either audio- or video-taped. Recently mandated in Britain under PACE as well as various jurisdictions in the United States and Canada, this procedure is based on the logic that recording all contacts with a suspect will yield an unambiguous account which may function to both ensure the protection of the suspect's rights during questioning, and diffuse unfounded challenges to the legality of police actions (Grant 1987; Baldwin 1993; Kaufman 1998; R. v. Barrett; R. v.

Lim; R. v. Coke). Such an objective recording is ultimately viewed by the judiciary as a critical means of eliminating the reasonable doubt that commonly enters into disputes over police questioning. The value of this evidentiary function as clearly expressed in the case of R. v. Coke where it was determined that, "A videotape of the interview would have been of great assistance to determine if the Crown has satisfied its burden. The courts continue to find reasonable doubt where none need be found, but for the failure of the police to ensure an independent objective and impersonal record of the statement taking process is made" (210). Despite its widespread endorsement by both the police and the courts, a number of serious criticisms have been leveled against the video-taping methodology which potentially threaten its viability as a mechanism for police accountability.

First, many researchers have argued that the video-recording is not necessarily representative of the entire history and contexts of exchanges between the suspect and police. As a result, it provides only a limited, and highly de-contextualized, view of police-suspect encounters in any specific case (McConville 1992; Baldwin 1993; Moston and Stephenson 1993; Belloni and Hodgson, 2000). Attesting to these concerns, Baldwin (1993: 328) asserts that, "It is clear... that the tapes can provide only a limited insight into the processes of detention and questioning, and that the meaning to be attached to them is complex and problematic. They can never reveal everything that has happened while a suspect is in custody, since only the 'formal' interview is recorded, and an observer can do no more than make an intuitive assessment of what might have happened off-stage". This analysis leads Baldwin (1993: 328) to conclude that, "The tapes are, then, of limited utility in that they offer no way of examining the social context (or the social 'construction') of interrogation". These same concerns are reiterated by authors such as McConville (1992) and Moston and Stephenson (1993) who similarly argue that a fundamental distinction must be made between the on- and off-camera behaviours of the police, a divergence which once again sacrifices the viability of video-taping as an accountability mechanism. Tentative support for this off-stage dimension of police interrogations in Canada was provided in a 1984 pilot study conducted in Halton Region near Toronto where a number of officers admitted to having conducted informal, "dry run" interviews prior to the official tapings – this despite the existence of strict departmental guidelines prohibiting such behaviour (Grant 1987). In the words of one defense attorney involved in the same project, the implication of such a finding is that, "... the video-statement is nothing but a final performance of a well-rehearsed interview" (Grant, 1987: 51).

Ultimately then, the taping of the formal interview is limited in two specific respects. First, it neglects the prevalence of interviewing and questioning both outside of the police station and prior to the official interview itself (McConville *et al.* 1991; McConville 1992; Moston and Stephenson 1993; Baldwin 1993; Belloni and Hodgson, 2000). The low visibility of police investigators once again compounds and exacerbates this problem. Secondly, the video-taped interrogation is highly de-contextualized in the sense that it mitigates against any appreciation of the ideologies, working rules, and techniques which influence and condition suspect-officer interactions. In a manner similar to *Miranda*, PACE, and the Charter, this reality is particularly problematic in light of the false legitimacy that is bestowed upon police practices given the belief on the part of other actors in the criminal justice system (i.e., lawyers, judges, and jurors) that the video-taped interrogation represents an objective and complete account of police-suspect exchanges (Grant 1987). This very concern was related by another defense counsel interviewed as part of the Halton study, "I have grave doubts about the process. With videotape you have the statement but no equivalent evidence about the pre-statement circumstances. The video-statement acquires its own weight and it becomes difficult to challenge the admissibility at all. Once the Crown has the statement it becomes almost like 'real' evidence" (Grant 1987: 55). This false objectivity becomes particularly problematic in light of the British finding that defense lawyers and the court rarely listen to the audio- and video-recordings of interrogations, relying instead on police summaries (Belloni and Hodgson 2000). The cumulative result of all of this is a fundamentally uncritical view of the police.

Beyond these issues of scope, context, and legitimacy, a second respect in which the video-taping methodology falls short rests, once again, on its fundamental neglect of the working rules of the police and the tendency of these informal rules to overcome and circumvent formal legal proscriptions. In this case, the investigator's belief that strategies of intimidation, manipulation, and deception are a necessary component of effective police work results in his/her innovative use of informal exchanges to influence the suspect's actions and choices in the official interrogation. In some instances, these working beliefs may even lead the officer to act in violation of constitutional safeguards in the full presence of the video-camera. An example of this occurred, once again, in Halton Region in August of 1997 where an investigator, Detective Doug Ford, was recorded assaulting a suspect during a taped interrogation. According to a specific report of the incident, the detective, "… slapped [the suspect] twice in the head, threatened to punch him and then pushed him after saying it was time to 'play hard ball'" (Pron 1997: A4). This matter was further exacerbated by the presence of Inspector Les Graham who allowed the interrogation (which he was observing over closed circuit television) to continue despite his later admission that it was, "'… trampling over the constitutional rights' of the suspect" (Pron 1997: A4). Inspector Graham even considered destroying the tape in order to protect the investigating officer. This incident raises serious questions concerning the value of the video-recording methodology given the failure of interviewers to modify their behaviours, and the likelihood that such actions will be condoned by superior officers based on their beliefs that these devices are necessary in order to secure the conviction of "guilty" suspects. Once again, we are returned to the reality of "noble causes" and "structured police deviance." Ultimately then, due to the dominance of police working rules, video-taping may be seen to provide a means of protecting officers and legitimating their accounts, while offering insufficient safeguards for the rights of the accused. This connection between police working rules and due process is articulated clearly by McConville (1992: 548) who argues,

> For some officers in some situations, structural features of policing legitimate the elevation of "working rules" over formal rules, no matter how much they are enjoined to act "lawfully." Whilst, in the official rhetoric, the video

taping of interrogation might have the dual aims of safeguarding the rights of suspects and protecting police officers, the evidence suggests that it may achieve the latter but at the expense of the former".

Emerging from this general discussion of police cautions and video-taping procedures as two specific attempts that have been made in recent years to reform the interrogative practices of the police is the suggestion that modifications to procedural rules, the organization of the criminal justice process, and the organizational structure and practices of the police are likely to be ineffective in bringing about significant changes in the nature of police work. In many respects, these types of reforms merely represent band-aid solutions for problems which are, in reality, far more systemic in nature. A number of specific explanations have been offered for this recognized inadequacy of previous legislative reforms. First, they have been formulated within the context of a legal system which is not only ambiguous and inconsistent with respect to procedural rules and guidelines, but also largely facilitative of police activities (Ericson and Baranek 1982; Ericson 1993; Belloni and Hodgson 2000). This enabling structure of law was found to coincide with an almost total absence of accountability mechanisms within the judicial process – this given both the tendency of cases to be plea bargained, and hence not subjected to formal review, and the hesitation of the courts to prosecute errant officers. Secondly, the low visibility and high autonomy of police investigators creates conditions of work which are very difficult to police. Thus, while the police are able to demonstrate official compliance with legislative guidelines, problems with visibility make it almost impossible to ensure that these are being satisfied in practice. Finally, these policy reforms have been unsuccessful to the extent that they have failed to take into account not only the resistance offered by police working rules, but also the ability of officers to innovate, and hence, circumvent formal rules. What this suggests is that, in order to be successful, any formal changes to policing policy must take into account the power of the informal dimensions of police work (to which the Halton case stands as an excellent testimonial), and thus, the recognition that all legal proscriptions will inevitably be filtered through the investigator's own rule frameworks and sense of reality (Ericson 1993; Epp 1997; Belloni and Hodgson 2000). With this very dilemma in mind, Ericson (1993: 12) argues that,

> ... legal or administrative rules designed to control detective accounts cannot be viewed as having a direct impact independent of their translation by detectives. Similar to workers in any bureaucracy, detectives will not respond to a new rule aimed at making their task more difficult by a willing commitment to implement it in letter and spirit. Instead, they will assess the rule in the context of the rule frameworks they have already established. They will then develop strategies to avoid the new rule, to implement it with a minimum level of compliance possible, and/or turn it to their advantage in easing their task.

Conclusion

In light of the preceding discussion, any possibilities for reform of the interrogative practices of the police must be grounded within an appreciation of the police interrogation as a specific element within the overall context of police work. Consequently, critical analyses must proceed beyond its manifest technical role in the production of confessions and other incriminating evidence to its function in the legitimation of both police narratives of crime and its control, and societal norms surrounding appropriate and inappropriate behaviour. This shift in focus speaks to the reality that police practices are grounded within, and motivated by, a wider organizational and societal context than is commonly accorded them. It is the failure to appreciate this broader context of police work which accounts for the limited success of both past and present legislative reforms in significantly altering the practice of police interrogations.

Ultimately, it is these conceptual and theoretical insights which must underlie and motivate future research on interrogative practices within the Canadian criminal justice system. Such theoretically informed research is urgently needed in order to examine systematically what appears now as merely isolated anecdotes and case histories. Ideally, this research would take the form of a natural case history which would trace the progression of cases from their initial contact with the police, through the various stages of questioning and interrogation, and finally, to their ultimate disposition within the justice system. Methodologically, this research strategy would combine participant observation, interviews with investigators and suspects, content analysis of written, audio, and video records of interrogations, and archival research of past cases, hence contributing to a comprehensive, triangulated approach. Furthermore, it would need to be attentive to some of the following issues:

* Regional and departmental variations in interrogative practices.
* The impact of crime type and suspect characteristics on both the interrogation and the selection of interrogators.
* The formal and informal training provided to police officers on legal regulations and rules of evidence surrounding interrogations.
* The perceived contribution of the interrogation to the development of specific cases (retrospective).
* The implications of the interrogation for the future disposition of cases (prospective) – i.e., plea-bargaining vs. trial.

Clearly, such a study would involve essential questions of researcher access which may ultimately restrict the methodological depth and scope of the analysis. For example, there is currently some debate as to whether a researcher who observes a police interrogation could be treated as a witness, and thus, compelled to testify in future legal proceedings. Provincial privacy legislation may also come into play in limiting access to both video-recordings and written transcripts of interrogations. Nevertheless, even the most limited study would be of irreducible value as it would contribute at least some empirical form to what is currently an obscure and largely unknown practice. The ultimate hope is that this type of data, informed by the theoretical framework developed within this paper, may provide for a more insightful understanding of the informal dimensions of the justice process, and thus, constitute a meaningful step in the prevention of future miscarriages of justice in Canada.

Endnote

*From the *Canadian Journal of Criminology*, Volume 42 No2 (April 2000).
Reproduced by permission of the *Canadian Journal of Criminology.* Copyright by the Canadian Criminal Justice Association.

Cases cited

R. v. Arp (1995) Doc. Prince George 27932 (B.C.S.C.)
R. v. Ballantyne (1997) Doc. Fort St. John 10929 (B.C.S.C.)
R. v. Barrett (1993) 82 C.C.C. (3d) 266 (Ont. C.A.)
R. v. Burlingham (1995) 97 C.C.C. (3d) 385
R. v. Coke (1996) 4 O.T.C. 210 (Gen. Div.)
R. v. Cole (1989) 77 Nfld. & P.E.I.R. 261
R. v. Dawson (1995) 22 C.C.C. (3d) 181
R. v. Dutton (1996) Doc. Barrie G4488/94 (Ont. Gen. Div.)
R. v. Johns (1998) 123 C.C.C. (3d) 190
R. v. Lim (1990) 1 C.R.R. (2d) 148 (Ont. H.C.J.)
R. v. Small (1998) 123 C.C.C. (3d) 560

References

Ainsworth, Janet E. (1993). In a different register: The pragmatics of powerlessness in police interrogation.   The Yale Law Journal 103: 259-322.
Anderson, Barrie and Dawn Anderson (1998).   Manufacturing Guilt: Wrongful Convictions in Canada. Halifax: Fernwood Publishing.
Ayling, Corey J. (1984). Corroborating confessions: an empirical analysis of legal safeguards against false confessions Wisconsin Law Review 1984(4): 1121-1204.
Baldwin, John (1990). Police interviews on tape. New Law Journal 140: 662-3.

Baldwin, John (1993). Police interview techniques: Establishing truth or proof? British Journal of Criminology 33(3): 325-352.

Belloni, Frank and Jacqueline Hodgson (2000). Criminal Injustice: An Evaluation of the Criminal Justice Process in Britain. London: Macmillan Press.

Brodeur, Jean-Paul (1981). Legitimizing police deviance. In Clifford D. Shearing (ed.), Police Deviance: Its Structure and Control. Toronto: Butterworths.

Bryan, Ian (1997). Interrogation and Confession: A Study of Progress, Process, and Practice. Aldershot: Ashgate-Darmouth.

Campbell, Archie G. (1996). Bernardo Investigation Review: Report of Mr. Justice Archie Campbell. Toronto: Solicitor General and Correctional Services.

Cicourel, Aaron V. (1976). The Social Organization of Policing. London: Heinemann Educational.

Doig, Jameson W. (1978). Police policy behaviour: Patterns of divergence. Policy Studies Journal 7: 436.

Epp, John Arnold (1997). Penetrating police investigative practice post-Morin. University of British Columbia Law Review 31(1): 95-126.

Ericson, Richard V. (1994). The decline of innocence. University of British Columbia Law Review 28: 367-83.

Ericson, Richard V. (1993). Making Crime: A Study of Detective Work, Toronto: University of Toronto Press.

Ericson, Richard V. (1985) Legal inequality. Research in Law, Deviance, and Social Control 7: 33-78.

Ericson, Richard V. (1981) Rules of police deviance. In Clifford D. Shearing (ed.), Police Deviance: Its Structure and Control. Toronto: Butterworth & Co.

Ericson, Richard V. and Patricia Baranek (1982). The Ordering of Justice: A Study of Accused Persons as Dependants in the Criminal Process. Toronto: University of Toronto Press.

Fitzgerald, Oonagh E. (1990). The Guilty Plea and Summary Justice: A Guide for Practitioners. Toronto: Carswell.

Gudjonsson, G. H. (1992). The Psychology of Interrogations, Confessions and Testimony. New York: John Wiley & Sons.

Gudjonsson, G. H. and J. MacKeith (1990). A proven case of false confession: Psychological aspects of the coerced-compliant type. Medicine, Science, and the Law 30: 329-335.

Gudjonsson, G.H. and J. MacKeith (1994). Learning disability and PACE protection during investigative interviewing: A video recorded false confession of a double murder. Journal of Forensic Psychiatry 5: 35-49.

Hagan, John and C. Peter Morden (1981). The police decision to detain: A study of legal labeling and police deviance. In Clifford D. Shearing (ed.). Police Deviance: Its Structure and Control. Toronto: Butterworth & Co.

Hepworth, Mike and Bryan S. Turner (1974). Confessing to murder: Critical notes on the sociology of motivation. British Journal of Law and Society 1(1): 31-49.

Hess, John E. (1997). Interviewing and Interrogation for Law Enforcement. Cincinnati: Anderson Publishing.

Inbau, Fred. E. and John E. Reid (1967). Criminal Interrogation and Confessions. Baltimore: The Williams & Wilkins Company.

Kaci, Judy Hails and George E. Rush (1988). At what price will we obtain confessions. Judicature 71(5): 254-258.

Kaufman, Fred (1998). The Commission on Proceedings Involving Guy Paul Morin. Vol. 2. Toronto: Ontario Ministry of the Attorney General.

Grant, Alan (1987). The Audio-Visual Taping of Police Interview Suspects and Accused Persons by Halton Regional Police Force Ontario, Canada: An Evaluation. Toronto: Law Reform Commission of Canada.

Leo, Richard A. (1994). Police interrogation and social control. Social and Legal Studies 3: 93-120.

Leo, Richard A. and Welsh S. White (1999). Adapting to Miranda: Modern interrogators' strategies for dealing with the obstacles posed by Miranda. Minnesota Law Review 84(2): 397-472.

Lewis, Peter W. and Harry E. Allen (1977). Participating Miranda: An attempt to subvert certain constitutional safeguards. Crime and Delinquency 23(1): 75-80.

Manning, Peter K. (1977). Police Work. Cambridge, Mass.: MIT Press.

Manning, Peter K. (1980). The Narc's Game: Organizational and Informational Limits on Drug Law Enforcement. Cambridge, Mass.: MIT Press.

Manning, Peter K. (1986). Texts as organizational echoes. Human Studies 9(2-3): 287-302.

Manning, Peter K. (1988). Symbolic Communication: Signifying Calls and the Police Response. Cambridge: MIT Press.

Marin, Rene J. (1999). Admissibility of Statements. Ninth Edition. Aurora, ON: Canada Law Book Inc.

McConville, Mike (1992). Videotaping interrogations: Police behaviour on and off camera. Criminal Law Review 1992 (August): 532-548.

McConville, Michael and John Baldwin (1981). Courts, Prosecution, and Conviction. Oxford: Clarendon.

McConville, Michael and John Baldwin (1982). The role of interrogation in crime discovery and conviction. British Journal of Criminology 22: 165-175.

McConville, Michael, Andrew Sanders, and Roger Leng (1991). The Case for the Prosecution. New York: Routledge.

Moore, Kathryn (1992). Police implementation of Supreme Court of Canada Charter decisions: An empirical study. Osgoode Hall Law Journal 30(3): 547-577.

Moston, Stephen and Geoffrey M. Stephenson (1993). The changing face of police interrogation. Journal of Community and Applied Social Psychology 3: 101-115.

Ofshe, Richard J. (1989). Coerced confessions: The logic of seemingly irrational action. Celtic Studies Journal 6: 6-15.

Ofshe, Richard J. and Richard A. Leo (1997). The social psychology of police interrogation: The theory and classification of true and false confessions. Studies in Law, Politics, and Society 16: 189-251.

Pepinsky, Harold E. (1970). A theory of police reaction to Miranda v. Arizona. Crime and Delinquency 16: 379-392.

Pron, Nick (1997). Detective weighed hiding evidence. Toronto Star August 1, 1997: A4.

Renke, Wayne N. (1996). By-passing the tell-tale heart: The right to counsel and the exclusion of evidence. University of British Columbia Law Review 30(1): 99-136.

Salhaney, Roger E. (1991). The Police Manual of Arrest, Seizure, and Interrogation. Fifth Edition. Toronto: Carswell.

Salhaney, Roger E. (1996). The Practical Guide to Evidence in Criminal Cases. Fourth Edition. Toronto: Carswell.

Sanders, William B. (1977). Detective Work: A Study of Criminal Investigations. New York: Free Press.

Sanders, A. and L. Bridges (1990). Access to legal advice and police malpractice. Criminal Law Review 1990 (July): 494-509.

Sharpe, Sybil (1998). Judicial Discretion and Criminal Investigation. London: Sweet & Maxwell.

Sudnow, David (1965). Normal crimes: Sociological features of the penal code in a public defender office. Social Problems 12(3): 255-276.

Watt, David (1998). Watt's Manual of Criminal Evidence. Toronto: Thompson Canada.

Wrightsman, L. and S. Kassin (1993). Confessions in the Courtroom. Newbury Park: Sage Publications.

15

When Police Kill:
The Aftermath*

Richard B. Parent
Simon Verdun-Jones

Introduction

This study examines police use of deadly force and potential deadly force in the Province of British Columbia, Canada, during the period from 1980 to 1994. The analysis is based on a total of 58 separate, documented incidents involving potentially lethal threats to municipal and Royal Canadian Mounted Police Officers within the Province of British Columbia. In 27 of these incidents, the police responded by discharging their firearms and killing a total of 28 people. The remaining 31 cases that were examined concerned incidents in which the police responded with less lethal force.

In addition to an examination of police investigations, Verdict-At-Coroner's-Inquest reports and BC Police Commission data, a total of 34 police officers were interviewed. Eighteen of these officers had been involved in a fatal shooting while the remaining officers had utilised less lethal force during an encounter with a perceived lethal threat. The study reveals the enormous psychological, physical and emotional stresses that police officers experience during a lethal threat. In many instances, these stressors continued to affect the officer long after the lethal threat had been resolved. The study recommends that police personnel within the Province of British Columbia should be given further training in relation to the effects of critical incident stress. This training should include the families and significant others of the police officer involved in a lethal threat.

Police Use of Deadly Force

When police officers use firearms against individuals, it may be assumed that they are using lethal force. Police officers are trained to shoot to kill, contrary to the common notion that their training involves techniques for wounding, rather than killing, their assailants. Firearms training for the police emphasises hitting the target's 'centre of mass' in order to eliminate a potential lethal threat. Officers who discharge a firearm or utilise other forms of potentially deadly force are generally attempting to eliminate a perceived threat. This decision-making process will usually transpire at a time when the individual officer is under considerable stress, thus leaving him or her open to the strong influence of both physiological and psychological factors.

A police officer engaged in a potentially lethal encounter will experience a variety of perceptual alterations. For example, tunnel vision may occur which, in effect, will nullify the officer's peripheral vision. However, the officer may require this vision in order to see other sources of danger, other alternatives to deadly force or to become aware of the presence of innocent bystanders (Geller & Scott, 1992).

Researchers have cited 'time distortions' and 'increased auditory and visual acuity' among the various physiological effects of high-stress confrontations. These physiological changes, collectively known as the 'general adaptive syndrome', are intrinsic within human beings, and function as a survival mechanism. In particular, the so-called 'alarm stage' is an instantaneous, short-term, life-preserving and totally sympathetic nervous system response that occurs when a person consciously or unconsciously perceives a danger-inducing stressor (Murray &

Zentner, 1975). In addition, it has been asserted that stress is a physical and emotional state that, although it is always present in a person, is greatly intensified when an environmental change or threat occurs to which the individual must respond. In fact, an individual's survival depends upon constant negotiation between environmental demands and the person's own adaptive capacities (Murray & Zentner, 1975).

In a modern society, the police are constantly preoccupied with the threat of violence in their day-to-day activities. Skolnick (1966), for example, stated that in reaction police officers develop a 'perceptual shorthand' to identify certain kinds of people as 'symbolic assailants'. These symbolic assailants are individuals who use specific gestures, language and attire that the officer has come to recognise as a prelude to violence. This may also apply to symbolic settings which the officer has come to recognise as harbouring the potential for danger.

The physiological and psychological changes that police officers experience when they are under stress may exert a significant impact in shaping an officer's decision to deploy deadly force. Physical and social settings, including dark or poorly lit places, high crime and violence areas, angry or upset people and non-supportive social structures constitute stress factors that may serve to heighten anxiety. While these factors affect all individuals, police officers are likely to experience particularly high levels of anxiety since they often have little choice as to whether or not to enter a dangerous situation.

Methodology

There have been over 40 separate shooting incidents that have resulted in death by legal intervention within the province of British Columbia since 1980. Municipal police departments were responsible for 16 of these shooting deaths. The database for this research has focused on the period from 1980 to 1994. Specifically, this analysis concerns those incidents in which a firearm was discharged by a member of the police, or in which it would have been legally justified for a member to do so.

In this study, there were three categories of resolution utilized by police to eliminate a perceived deadly threat:

* Those incidents in which a police officer utilised deadly force by way of discharging his/her firearm;
* Those incidents in which a police officer utilised potentially deadly force by discharging his/her firearm but death did not result;
* Those incidents that were resolved without the discharge of a firearm although the police officer would have been justified in using deadly force, as defined within the Criminal Code of Canada.

The data surrounding these three different responses to a perceived lethal threat were gathered from police reports and government documents that include the *BC Police Commission Annual Report on Shots Fired by Police within British Columbia* and the BC Police Commission records pertaining to *Police Honours Night*; recipients of awards for acts of bravery and the BC Coroners Reports regarding the Verdict-At-Coroner's-Inquest.

The Chief Constables of the municipal police departments concerned granted permission to contact those police officers who had resolved a perceived lethal threat by way of discharging their firearm or by other means. (In some instances this protocol could not be implemented as the individual had since terminated his/her employment with the municipal department in question.) The Chief Constables also made available their department records surrounding the incidents of potential or deadly force, including the pertinent details surrounding the police investigation.

Finally, those individual municipal police officers who had discharged their firearms, or who would have been legally justified in discharging their firearms, were contacted and interviewed following the administration of a brief questionnaire. Owing to the relatively small database, it was necessary to interview the maximum number of police officers from the three noted categories identified above. Issues that were explored with these individuals included:

* The situational and perceived stressors during the incident of firearm discharge or perceived lethal threat; e.g. was the officer in a high-crime area, alone, dealing with a potentially dangerous situation?

- The training provided to the officer and the less-than-lethal options available to the officer at the time of the incident.
- The situational factors relevant to the incident.
- To what degree did critical incident stress affect the officer?

The Interview Process

For the purpose of this study, a total of 34 police officers were interviewed. The interviews lasted approximately 45 minutes and were typically scheduled when the officers were working. The vast majority of the interviews occurred within the municipal police stations, in private secluded settings. However, a small number of interviews occurred in public restaurants and in private residences, at the request of the individual officer. The majority of the conversations were taped and supplemental with notes made at the time.

All of the individuals interviewed were caucasian males with the exception of one caucasian female and one oriental male. Two of these 34 individuals are no longer police officers. Both of these individuals left the police force shortly after being involved in a fatal shooting incident. The two officers stated that they left policing as a direct result of their deadly force encounter. During the course of this study, it was discovered that three of the 20 police officers (15%), who were directly involved in a fatal shooting incident, have since left policing to pursue other interests.

The interviews of the 34 police officers were based upon six broad categories of questions. These broad categories included the police officers' background, their preparedness for the lethal threat incident and the actual incident itself. In addition, interview discussions focused upon the events after the incident. The various personal effects that resulted from the incident, including critical incident stress, were discussed and noted. Finally, other issues that were unique to the officer, as well as the nature of the life-threatening specific incident and/or the police shooting, were identified and discussed.

At the start of each interview, the participating subjects were asked in general terms to recall and explain the nature of their life-threatening ordeal. The purpose of the interviews was to obtain additional information that went beyond the scope of the typical police investigative report or the Verdict-At-Coroner's-Inquest report. In this respect, the interviews focused upon the police officer's subjective perception of the incident; namely, how did the perceived lethal threat unfold as viewed through their eyes? Secondly, as they faced the perceived lethal threat, what course of action did they take and why? Included within this framework were the physiological, psychological, physical and emotional issues that relate to critical incident stress and post-shooting effects. These are issues that are traditionally avoided during the police investigation and court process.

Critical Incident Stress and Deadly Force

The richest data was generated during the interviews with the 18 police officers who had actually been involved in a fatal shooting. Without exception, all of these officers indicated that they had, to some degree, been subject to the physiological, psychological, physical and emotional factors that are typically associated with critical incident stress.

The most commonly cited physiological factors experienced by these officers included altered perception of time, as well as visual and auditory distortions. As the incident unfolded, individual officers noted that their deadly force encounter appeared to occur in slow motion. Often their vision was focused upon the perceived threat with a minimal awareness of the events taking place around them. Finally, when shots were fired, they were generally heard as muffled sounds, even though the officers were not wearing ear protection devices:

> We stopped the car and got out. A couple of seconds later a shot rang out. My focus was on the threat. I fired three rounds off at the silhouette and hit the target, one fatal at the head. It was like a scene in a bad movie. It all happened in slow motion. I just knew I got him … it all happened in less than ten seconds. [Cst] 'X' was lucky not to be killed.

In addition to perceptual distortions, the majority of these police officers stated that they experienced a loss of fine motor coordination upon conclusion of their deadly encounter. Typically, their hands would begin to shake or their legs would be subjected to uncontrollable spasms. At the extreme end of the range of physiological effects, one officer indicated that during the course of his deadly encounter he had difficulty controlling his anal sphincter. The fear for his life was so intense that the *general adaptive syndrome* almost overrode the voluntary control of his bowels:

> He was aiming for me and then he shot at me. It went into slow motion from when he fired the first shot. I was amazed that he didn't kill me. I remember thinking I hope that I don't shit myself. I don't want to die here! I'm so close to home.

After the final shooting incident was concluded, the majority of officers interviewed stated that they faced a wide variety of psychological and physical effects that are associated with critical incident stress. The physical effects included a loss of appetite, changes in the pattern of sleep and a marked decrease in their sex drive which resulted in an absence of sexual relations with their spouse or partner. One officer stated, 'My sex life went down the tube, forget about that'. Another police officer reported:

> Your mind says 'You can't cope with this'. Sleep? I'd wake up every night for several months. I would never re-live the incident but my mind would focus on the incident.

Among the psychological effects reported by the officers were depression, guilt, nightmares, flashbacks, a heightened sense of danger and fear. One of the officers related the flashbacks as a:

> [v]ideo going on in your head that you can't control; it just keeps playing the video over and over and over again and you've got no control to turn it off.

Another officer described the after-effects of the shooting in the following manner:

> I dream a lot, now years after the incident. Sometimes they're daytime flashbacks, while I'm working. Every time I pass the exact spot on the freeway where I heard the news report of the [fatal] shooting incident [while I was heading home], I think about it.

One officer reported an overwhelming and uncontrollable emotional state that suddenly caused him to weep and cry for days on end. The officer stated that he felt 'fine' after the fatal shooting incident until some six months later:

> I thought everything was ok, it [the shooting] didn't bother me. I was tough. Then suddenly while I was out shopping with my wife and kids I had to park the car in the shopping centre. I had this urge to cry, I couldn't control it. Once I started I couldn't stop. My wife had to drive us home. It [weeping] lasted for days.

Another police officer stated that, for several months, he possessed an overwhelming fear of being alone:

> You really need somebody after an incident like this. The worst feeling is like losing control. I followed my wife around like a puppy dog. A couple of days after the shooting I went to have a bath. I remember it was the first time that I had been alone since the incident. I got into the bath tub; I was alone and then suddenly I began to be overwhelmed with fear. I can't describe how scared I was. I jumped out of the bath within a few minutes; I had to find my wife! I couldn't be alone; I couldn't cope and felt I was losing control.

The media was identified by most of the police officers as one of the greatest sources of stress immediately after their fatal shooting incidents. This was a consequence of the continuous coverage that surrounded many of the fatal shooting incidents.

Particularly painful was the speculation engaged in by many journalists who were impatient regarding the release of the official police investigation. These journalists would often produce media articles that were written in a negative manner towards the actions of the shooting officer or of the police agency that employed him.

Police agencies will not traditionally divulge the outcome of their investigation until the entire file has been reviewed by independent Crown Counsel regarding the possibility of criminal charges. Typically, the specific details of a police shooting and the subsequent police investigation are first revealed publicly during a Coroner's inquest. It is only upon the conclusion of this painstaking and tedious procedure that the media obtains the full story regarding the fatal police shooting.

Unfortunately, many of the interviewed police officers gave accounts of media distortions and inaccurate journalism that occurred during the waiting period of the Crown review and the Coroner's inquest. These officers stated that the negative slant portrayed in many of the media articles served to intensify their emotional and psychological suffering in relation to the fatal shooting incident.

> The media; I've never had a problem with what we did. We're the good guys and out here to help the public and did a good thing, what we're supposed to do, and now we're getting fucked. I couldn't watch the tv or read the papers; [they were] obvious examples of distortion.

One of the police officers, who was interviewed, stated that he has never spoken to anyone regarding his fatal shooting incident. He related to the event as to the 'death of a child', an event in his life that he described as painful and sad, something that he wished had never happened, and something that he has obviously tried to put behind him. During the interview, this officer produced a file containing over 50 separate newsprint articles surrounding his fatal shooting incident.

The police officer's mother had followed the shooting incident through the local print media. She had clipped and saved all of the printed articles that were related to her son's fatal shooting incident. In conjunction with the 50 plus newsprint articles, the officer kept a 'scrap book' concerning the legal, union and departmental correspondence that were directly related to his shooting incident.

The officer stated that, for the purpose of this interview, he went to his parents' residence and obtained the thick file from the basement of their house. He had always known of the file's existence but could never bring himself to read all of its contents nor could he keep the file at his own residence. This file had not been examined for several years, following the conclusion of the Coroner's inquest into the shooting.

During the course of the interview the officer avoided looking through much of the file. It was obviously painful for him to see its contents and to re-live the memories of his shooting incident. He admitted that he has never been able to bring himself to read most of the print articles within the file. None the less, he displayed a desire to participate in the interview and had exhumed his shooting file so that it could form part of this study.

Upon examining the file, it was apparent that the vast majority of the media articles appeared to originate from two major newspapers. Several of the headline articles that were first published, immediately after the shooting, suggest that the officer acted inappropriately. Some of these headlines are as follows:

'Relatives Want Police Charged in Shooting', 'Were Four Bullets The Only Answer?', 'Police Procedures Deficient', 'Mayor Queries Police Policy', 'Police Training Called Flawed', 'Slain Man's Mother Asks Premier For Probe', 'Police Stay Silent Until Inquiry Done', ' . . . Police Refuse Calls For Details On Shooting', 'Decision On Police Shooting Charges Due'.

The newsprint articles containing the controversial headlines were largely based upon speculation and interviews with the deceased's relatives. During this particular fatal shooting, the media was extremely critical of the police agency and the Chief Constable. The police department stated that they would not provide a detailed account of the shooting incident until both a police investigation and a public Coroner's inquest had been completed. In response to this vacuum of information from police sources, the media portrayed the shooting incident and the police agency in a negative and controversial manner.

Within a few months, the public Coroner's inquest into the shooting was held which, as a result of the independent evidence that was presented, exonerated the police officer for his actions. During the Coroner's inquest, the media coverage was less critical of the officer but continued to be sensational in nature. Some of these newsprint headlines included:

'Said "Stay Back", Then He Died', 'I Would Have Shot Him Too', 'Cops Off Hook in Fatal Shooting', 'Officer Sorry, But Says Forced To Shoot'.

The vast majority of media interest subsided upon conclusion of the Coroner's inquest. Several of the officers who were interviewed added that the Coroner's inquest served as a pivotal point in the process by which they came to terms with the shooting incident. Until the Coroner's inquest, there was a degree of uncertainty regarding the investigative findings of the shooting, regardless of how confident the officer may have been that his conduct had been appropriate.

Only upon the conclusion of this public process of inquiry were many of the officers able to get on with their lives and leave the tragedy of the shooting incident behind them. Even years after the fatal shooting incident had taken place, all of the officers reported that they considered it a significant event in their life, one that they will never forget. In this regard, one police officer stated:

This guy is not gonna fuck-up my life forever. It's completely up to me; whether I cope with this and get on with life. I'm sure I drank too much several times. I think about it every day. If you're gonna give up then it's gonna get to you.

Occasionally, the peers of the officers who were involved in fatal shootings were reported to have exacerbated an already stressful situation. In several instances, it was reported that the peers did not treat their colleagues in the same manner as before the shooting incident. The perception was that these peers would often isolate or ignore the officer. In other cases, the perception was that the peers would provide inappropriate gestures of support. For example, one officer reported that, immediately after his fatal shooting, he was given a mug full of rum and then asked to provide an official statement.

It was also reported that some individuals would make jokes or comments that were particularly hurtful and inappropriate. One officer stated that, after the shooting incident, his peers would frequently remark, 'How are you doing killer?' Two other police officers reported:

> You'd be having a normal conversation and someone would make a stupid ass remark [regarding the shooting]. They'd have a tendency to use black humour. It may be made with good intentions but can be annoying as hell. Wrong thing to say!

> It was a difficult thing to lead into or be asked about. I remember one guy, a locker room comment, 'How's it going killer?' I thought what a stupid thing to say!

Finally, one officer who reported that he had encountered only minimal difficulties in coping with his fatal shooting incident was quick to attribute his experience to 'officer survival' literature. This individual had, prior to the shooting incident, taken a three-day training course regarding 'Street Survival For Police Officers'. This course is almost entirely based upon police activities within the USA but none the less provided necessary information regarding 'what to expect, and what to do, if you are ever involved in a shooting incident'. This police officer largely attributed his successful coping techniques to the course content and course literature that was presented during the three-day session.

> I was married and my wife was four months pregnant. We were home painting when I received the call-out. Things didn't go very well. My spouse saw it on television before I got home. Eventually we were able to hash things through. In 1988 I had been on a 'Street Survival' seminar. I had all of the Calibre Press

handouts; I went downstairs. I went through the book and the material; it really helped.

Critical Incident Stress and Less-Than-Lethal Force

The interviews with the remaining 16 police officers were less profound. These police officers did not utilise deadly force but none the less faced a perceived lethal threat. Once again, all of the officers indicated physiological experiences that included temporal and auditory distortions. However, the critical incident stress experienced by these officers was of a much lesser degree.

All of these individuals stated that they managed to cope with the minor stressors that resulted. None of these officers stated that they were required to take leave from the profession as a consequence of their encounter. Minor psychological effects such as flashbacks and the occasional nightmares occurred.

The nine police officers interviewed, who were recipients of a Police Honours Award, spoke somewhat positively of their life-threatening incident. Many of these officers emphasised that they had acted as officers before them have. However, for some unknown reason, they were acknowledged and rewarded for their conduct. The positive feedback and recognition that they received for their actions appeared to mitigate any of the negative stressors associated with a critical incident. One of the police honours recipients stated:

> I can't believe I got an award for this! I'll never forget when I was standing there during the ceremony, about to get my Chief Constable's award. (I had already received my police honours award.) As I stood there, right beside me was Cst. 'X'. He was involved in a shoot-out and took some real chances, wound up wounding a guy. What he did was *real* bravery. So I get a police honours award from the provincial government for what I did and he got nothing. We both received a Chief Cst's award from our department, yeah, but he's the one who should have got the police honours – not me.

Another police honours award recipient added:

421

Yeah, I guess it wouldn't be politically correct to receive a provincial award recognising bravery after you've killed or wounded someone.

Post-Shooting Effects and Deadly Force

In the months and years since the fatal shooting incident occurred, many of the police officers interviewed reported that they had experienced a variety of personal life changes. These officers directly attributed these changes to their fatal shooting. The police officers who faced a lethal threat, but were able to resolve the incident without using deadly force, did not report these same post-shooting effects.

Several of the police officers, who were involved in a fatal shooting, reported marital or relationship breakdowns shortly after the incident. Often these individuals stated that their relationship with their significant other was 'ok' prior to the shooting. However, when faced with the pressures and stresses that accompanied a fatal shooting, the relationship often crumbled. One officer stated, 'I went through two marriages after the shooting incident'. Another officer reported, 'My marriage ended within a year or two after the shooting. I became distant from my wife and I didn't talk about the shooting incident with her'.

However, there was an equal number of police officers who spoke highly of their spouses or significant others; these were intimate relationships that served to support the police officer during a time of personal crisis. Often these established relationships were strengthened as a result of the shooting incident.

Unfortunately, several of the officers stated that their spouse, significant other or their children suffered personally as a result of their shooting incident. The police officer's fatal shooting frequently became a 'family crisis'. One officer stated, 'My wife needed help [psychological] after what happened to me'. Another officer reported:

Not too many people know this, but as a direct result of my [fatal] shooting, my wife developed an eating disorder. We both know it was in response to me killing the guy. Even though it's been years since the shooting she still suffers with the disorder and a few other things.

In addition to changes in personal relationships, several of the officers interviewed indicated that they became heavy substance abusers shortly after the fatal shooting incident. In conjunction with this substance abuse, some of these individuals reported that they became 'burned out'. These officers would deliberately work long hours and apply for stressful assignments as a means of coping with their traumatic experience. This was also explained as a means of showing to their peers that 'they were ok' as they had *survived* the shooting. In addition, management would be able to see that they could return to even tougher assignments, without any noticeable effect.

In these stressful positions, it was also easier to identify and 'fit in' with their peers. In many instances, the peers within these assignments were described as 'heavy drinkers'. In addition, several of these individuals had also gone through a divorce. One officer stated that he could easily identify with his team members as eight of the officers, within the small section, had also been divorced. However, in hindsight, the officer stated that his new assignment actually perpetuated his stressful lifestyle.

Further personal changes in lifestyle that were directly attributed to the fatal shooting incident, included a change in diet. One officer reported that as a result of the shooting he became a vegetarian:

Thou shall not kill really means thou shall nor murder. I stopped eating meat and never went back to it for ten years. Now I may have the occasional small bit of meat. It's hard to explain why, I don't know exactly why.

Finally, two of the police officers who were interviewed continued to be noticeably affected by the incident even though the deadly force encounter had occurred several years ago. During one interview, as the officer began to re-call how he had faced the threat to his life, his arm started to shake. The shaking continued throughout the interview and was intensified during emotional points in his story. As he spoke of the shooting incident, it was obvious that he could not control the spasms in his arm. However, as the interview came to a close, the officer was able to compose himself emotionally. Upon doing so, his arm ceased shaking.

A second officer was emotionally and psychologically distraught as he recalled his life-threatening encounter that resulted in a fatal shooting. This officer could only discuss the 'technical' aspects of his shooting incident. It appeared that he had not come to terms with the psychological and emotional aspects of his near-death encounter and fatal shooting.

It was later learned that both of these officers had suffered post-traumatic stress to such a degree that they had required extensive counselling and a lengthy time away from the work site. Both of these individuals have since returned to policing and have once again become productive police officers within their organisation. Without hesitation, these individuals volunteered to participate in this study. Both are clearly attempting to come to terms with an incident that has had a profound impact upon their lives.

Summary

A total of 34 police officers, who had faced a lethal threat, were personally interviewed for this study. Most of the individuals interviewed had never spoken to a researcher prior to this study. Twenty-three of the police officers interviewed had discharged their firearm in an attempt to eliminate a perceived lethal threat. As stated, two additional officers were interviewed who did not discharge their weapon but were present when their partner fired a fatal shot. These 25 officers did *not* receive a provincial award for their actions.

In addition, eight police officers who did not use their firearm to resolve a lethal threat were personally interviewed. One additional officer fired his revolver but missed his intended target. These nine officers each received a provincial award for their actions. These officers reported little, if any, negative personal effects as a direct result of their lethal threat incident. In fact, these officers spoke quite positively regarding their lethal threat and the subsequent outcome. Interestingly, these individuals reported minimal psychological and physiological effects as the lethal threat unfolded. This finding may offer some explanation as to why these officers chose non-lethal intervention strategies in comparison to their peers who chose more violent means of dealing with the perceived lethal threat.

This study also revealed that the 18 police officers, who were involved in a fatal shooting, all reported various degrees of physiological, psychological, emotional and physical effects that they attributed directly to the shooting. Significantly, these symptoms were also reported by the two officers who did not pull the trigger but were none the less present when their partner fired the fatal shot. One of these two individuals was so adversely affected by the shooting that he has since left the job. Also noteworthy is that, in the majority of these cases, the individuals involved did not receive any positive public recognition from their police agency regarding the shooting.

Significantly, all 34 of the officers interviewed stated that they were exonerated for their actions in dealing with the lethal threat. All of the officers stated that they were not charged for an offence under the Criminal Code of Canada, nor did they face a disciplinary action as a result of their shooting incident. The police officers involved in the fatal shootings were quick to add that as a result of the Coroner's inquest, their actions were vindicated within a public forum.

Also noteworthy is that all of the officers interviewed stated that they did not face any civil actions as a result of their lethal encounter. In many instances, the media had insinuated that there had been police 'wrong-doings', reporting that criminal, disciplinary or civil actions were imminent against the police officers involved. However, all of the officers spoken to denied any formal repercussions as a result of their shooting incident. Unfortunately, most of these individuals reported personal upheaval and tragedy that they continue to carry with them, several years after the shooting incident. These are consequences that the media failed to report but are nevertheless very real and profound to the officers involved and their families.

Conclusion

This study indicates that police training should address the significant issue of stress management. The interview data revealed the enormous psychological, physical and emotional stresses that police officers experience during a lethal threat. In many instances, these stress factors continued to affect the officer long after the lethal threat had been resolved. Police personnel should be made aware of the potential impact of these factors, before they are placed in a position where they may encounter a lethal threat. Further training in this area may reduce the negative effects of stress when an officer faces a life-threatening situation, thereby allowing the officer to seek alternatives to deadly force.

There is also a need to address the 'survivors' of a deadly force encounter. These individuals require professional counselling and continuing support in their hour of crisis. Significantly, the families of police officers who have been involved in a shooting incident additionally need to be included within this process. This study has discovered that family members are also survivors of a lethal threat and, therefore, require similar counselling and support. Too often, the police officer and his or her family have been left alone to cope with the aftermath of a police shooting. In many instances the outcome has been devastating to both the officer and the members of their family.

Finally, one of the significant findings of this study was that police officers, who were recipients of police honour awards, reported minimal psychological and physiological effects as they faced their lethal threat. This finding may offer some explanation as to why these officers chose non-lethal intervention strategies in comparison to their peers in this study who chose more violent means of dealing with the perceived lethal threat. However, there is clearly a need for further research into this area before any conclusions can be drawn.

*Endnote

Reprinted from, the *Police Journal*, Volume 73 (2000), pp. 241-255, with permission from Vathek Publishing.

References and Bibliography

Alpert, G.P. and Fridell, L.A. (1992) *Police Vehicles and Firearms: Instruments of Deadly Force*. Prospect Heights: Waveland Press.

British Columbia Coroners Act (1993). Victoria: Queen's Printer For British Columbia.

British Columbia Police Commission (1990) *Recommendations of the Committee on the Use of Less Than Lethal Force by Police Officers in British Columbia*. Vancouver, BC, Canada (July).

British Columbia Police Commission (1991) *Provincial Standards For Municipal Police Department in British Columbia*. Ministry of Attorney-General.

British Columbia Police Commission (1994) *A Model Policy and Procedures Manual For Municipal Police Departments in British Columbia*. Ministry of Attorney-General.

Criminal Code of Canada (1994) *Martin's Annual Criminal Code*. Aurora: Canada Law Book, Inc.

Chappell, D. and Graham, L.P. (1985) *Police Use of Deadly Force: Canadian Perspectives*. Toronto, Canada: Centre of Criminology, University of Toronto.

Ellison, K. and Genz, J. (1983) *Stress and the Police Officer*. Springfield, Ill.: Charles C. Thomas.

Federal Bureau of Investigation (1991) *Use of Unauthorized Force By Law Enforcement Personnel: Problems and Solutions*. Quantico: FBI Academy.

Fyfe, J.J. (1986) 'The Split-Second Syndrome and Other Determinants of Police Violence' in A. Campbell and J. Gibbs (eds), *Violent Transactions*. New York: Basil Geberth.

Geller, W. A. and Scott, M.S. (1992) *Deadly Force: What We Know – A Practitioner's Desk Reference on Police-Involved Shootings*. Washington, DC: Police Executive Research Forum.

Geller, W. A. and Toch, H. (eds) (1995) *And Justice For All: Understanding And Controlling Police Abuse of Force*. Washington, DC: Police Executive Research Forum.

International Association of Chiefs of Police (1989) *Use of Force: Concepts and Issues Paper*. Arlington: IACP National Law Enforcement Police Centre.

International Association of Chiefs of Police (1990) *Fear: It Kills; A Collection of Papers for Law Enforcement Survival.* Arlington: IACP National Law Enforcement Police Centre.

Jones, C. (1989) *After the Smoke Clears: Surviving the Police Shooting.* Springfield, Ill.: Charles C. Thomas.

Justice Institute of British Columbia (1992) *Police Use of Force, The 'Comprehensive' Model: Progressive Guidelines for BC Municipal Police Officers.* Vancouver.

Maguire, K. and Pastore, A.L. (eds) (1995) *Sourcebook of Criminal Justice Statistics 1994.* US Department of Justice, Bureau of Justice Statistics. Washington, DC.

Manolias, M. and Hyatt-Williamson, A. (1986) *Study of Post Shooting Experiences in Firearms Officers.* London: Home Office.

Matulia, K.J. (1985) *A Balance of Forces: Model Deadly Force Policy and Procedure*, 2nd edn. Gaithersburg, MD: International Association of Chiefs of Police.

McLaughlin, V. (1992) *Police and the Use of Force: The Savannah Study.* Westport, Ct: Praeger.

Murray, R. and Zentner, J. (1975) *Nursing Concepts for Health Promotion.* Toronto: Prentice-Hall.

National Institute of Justice (1993) *Questions and Answers in Lethal and Non-Lethal Violence.* Quantico: FBI Academy, 13-17.

Noesner, G.W. and Dolan, J.T. (1992) 'First Responder Negotiation Training' (August) *FBI Law Enforcement Bulletin* 1.

Police Services (1993) *Summary Statistics – Police Management Information System 1977-1992.* Ministry of Attorney-General, Province of British Columbia.

Police Services (1994) *Summary Statistics – Police Crime 1984-1993.* Ministry of Attorney-General, Province of British Columbia.

Province (1995) 'Cop-Killer: Stress' (1 October) *The Province* 4.

Royal Canadian Mounted Police Policy and Procedures Manual (1994) Ottawa: Government of Canada.

Schade, T., Bruns, G. and Morrison, G. (1989) 'Armed Confrontations: Police Shooting Performance in Threatening Environments' *American Journal of Police* VIII: 31.

Scharf, P. and Binder, A. (1983) *The Badge and the Bullet – Police Use of Deadly Force*. New York: Praeger Publishers.

Scharf, P., Linninger, R., Marrero, D., Baker, R. and Rice, C. (1978) 'Deadly Force – The Moral Reasoning and Education of Police Officers Faced With The Option of Lethal Legal Violence' *Policy Studies Journal* 7: 450.

Schultz, D.O. and Service, J.G. (1981) *Police Use of Force*. Springfield, Ill.: Charles C. Thomas.

Skolnick, J. and Fyfe, J. (1993) *Above the Law: Police and the Excessive Use of Force*. Toronto: Maxwell MacMillan.

Skolnick, J. (1966) *Justice Without Trial: Law Enforcement in a Democratic Society*. New York: Wiley & Sons, Inc.

Thompson, G.J. (1983) *Verbal Judo: Words for Street Survival*. Springfield, Ill.: Charles C. Thomas.

16

Reflections on the Transnationalization of policing: the Case of the RCMP and Serial Killers*

James Sheptycki

Introduction

Of the perennial questions that lecturers of introductory criminology face surely the most consistent asked regards so-called serial killers. Even the most casual observation of the book titles on offer in the 'criminology' sections of most mainstream book shops will reveal rather grim statistics - all too often nearly one-half of the books on the shelves of such sections are devoted to one subject: bizarre serial sex slayings. This might explain why so many students inquire about the phenomenon, often revealing a macabre curiosity. This subject has been left almost exclusively to pop-criminology (Sheptycki 1993a) and so, with this in mind, I decided it would be worthwhile dedicating some of my research efforts in this direction, if only to have to hand some reasonable answers for my students.

Feminist theorists have long argued that male violence is a primary tactic for the control of women in patriarchal society and, in particular, that the mythology of the serial killer is a powerful weapon of male control and dominance over women (Brownmiller 1976; Hanmer & Saunders 1984; Cameron & Fraser 1987; Caputi 1987; Radford & Russell 1992). The functionality of the myth of the sex slayer for patriarchy overstates the rapaciousness of masculinity and underemphasizes the dimension of chivalry (Sheptycki 1995). This is not to deny that such myths are pervasive or that there is a certain sociological functionality to them. On the contrary, such mythologies can be seen as establishing boundaries between the normal and the abnormal and thus provide an important basis for social ordering; not least for gender ordering. Certain strands of feminist analysis encourage us to view the mythology of the serial killer and the rapist as a way of gender ordering (Soothill & Walby 1991) whereby women's fear of crime is magnified as a result of promulgation, and women are terrorized out of the public domain (Stanko 1985), but this ignores a second side of the process. Broadly speaking, social formations are reinforced by frightening folk devils (Cohen 1972) against which social groups unite, and this dynamic is predicated on the formulation of heroic images to which society can aspire (Erikson 1966).[1] Without the protective hero, whether it be the psychological profiler of the famed FBI Behavioural Sciences Unit or 'Dirty Harry', the folk devil is simply left 'on the loose'. In the case of the serial killer, this would be dysfunctional in the extreme and would approximate the result anticipated by the type of feminist analysis mentioned above (see also Downes & Rock, 1988: 108). The assumption of this paper is that the serial killer is widely understood in our society as a real and present danger and that his status as a premier folk devil virtually guarantees that police resources will be targeted at this type of crime.[2]

This paper is concerned with the way in which police agencies have reacted to the phenomena. It gives an account of how police have gone about being seen to respond to this type of crime and of the technological and organizational innovations that have sprung up as a result. Its special focus is on the role that the Royal Canadian Mounted Police (RCMP) are playing in the transnationalization of policing responses to this type of crime.

Into the Unknown; An Ethnographer Enters the Realm of the 'Manhunters'

In 1995 it seemed impossible to study the police response to this extreme form of violence away from the shadows of these folk devils. In the U.K., the trial of Rosemary West brought to light a gruesome career she shared with her husband Fred West that rivaled all. In Canada the deeds of another husband and wife team, Paul Bernardo and Karla Homulka, were well known. Such cases gain a tremendous amount of media attention, which itself has been conceptualized as an element of the crime problem (Surette 1984). At that time, however, I was more interested to learn about how the police organization itself responded to this type of crime and I got my chance in September of that year.

My initiation into this world proved to be very uncomfortable. I had obtained permission to spend time with officers of the RCMP in order to gain some familiarity with the Violent Crime Linkage Analysis System (ViCLAS), a new development in police computer technology, and my orientation began with a presentation aimed at police managers. I was, in effect, a privileged viewer of a dress rehearsal sitting alone in the front row of a large auditorium while two officers told me about the latest in police investigative techniques. A woman police sergeant from the RCMP spoke first: "We work on the basis that the M.O. [modus operandi] is learned behaviour and, if we can obtain a large enough data base, it might allow us to predict what might happen in a given situation". "However", interjected her male colleague, a member of the Vancouver Police Historical Homicide Squad, "before going on to explain how to use the ViCLAS system itself, we would like to give you some background on this type of crime."

What followed was a slide presentation which began with some multi-coloured bar-charts detailing statistics relating to crime rates in Canada and British Columbia specifically. A series of such slides depicted a general rise in homicide rates, 'sex crimes', and 'abductions.' The viewer was led inexorably to the conclusion that the homicide rate was higher in BC than the rest of Canada and the sexual assault rates were significantly so. Further, while 'solve rates' were showing a declining trend nationally for both homicide and sexual assault, solve rates in BC were consistently lower than the national average. The scope for serial homicide was seen as coming within the rising number of stranger homicides, an increasing proportion of which were remaining unsolved. It was intimated from these data that serial homicide was on the rise in the region. This series of slides ended, punctuated by a slide explaining: "The next part of this presentation moves from abstract numbers to real cases, involving real people and real consequences". The female officer voiced over this slide: "The graphic material that follows is used to grab managers by the short and curlies, because they have not seen this stuff for quite a long time".

The slides in the next sequence were very distressing. They depicted six cases of sexual assault, five of which resulted in the death of the victim. The crimes were extremely violent and horrific. They had been committed in five different cities in Western Canada. All the victims were female, their ages ranged from 3 to 67 and they had suffered the most horrendous attacks. Even now, months later, I am nauseated as I go over my notes and can scarcely bring myself to listen to the taped record. The pictures of the crime scenes were both gruesome and artful, but I withstood this assault by visual-aid. Then the lights went up and the officer from the Historical Homicide Squad switched on a tape recorder. The audio-tape that followed was a 3-minute recording of a 911 call received by police in an unnamed U.S. jurisdiction. A disembodied voice pleaded and screamed for help through the static while a man battered down her door and raped her. This was only the warm-up to the audio portion. Next came 12 vicious minutes of selected highlights from the audio diary of an unnamed American serial killer apprehended in the mid-1980s. In the course of 30 minutes the audience was taken on an emotional roller-coaster ride. The presentation had all of the impact of any of the full-length movie treatments of the subject, and then some.

Ethnographers who work in the police field doubtlessly encounter upsetting situations but it is seldom, I think, that such extreme distress is experienced in a police administration building. Certainly I had come unprepared for the experience. It was only by forcing myself to try and think like a sociologist that I could keep myself from fleeing. I reasoned that this multi-media presentation illustrated that the police themselves capitalized on the functionality of the mythology of the serial killer; in effect they are not cultural dupes, but knowing manipulators of the myth. In this case the manipulation was being used to instill in police managers a sense of mission so that the tedium of data entry on the ViCLAS System would not weaken the resolve to use it.[3] I also asked myself some fairly obvious questions, for example: how had Canadian police officers come to possess these audio-tapes from criminal investigations south of the border? My curiosity in this regard was partly satisfied as the next sequence of slides presented material on a serial rape investigations gleaned from the FBI Law Enforcement Bulletin. A theory of offender psychology, based mainly in a behavioural paradigm, using two studies by the FBI as illustrations, was then related. Next, the facticity of the geographically mobile serial killer was asserted and related to the phenomena of 'linkage blindness' and finally, there was an over-view of the ViCLAS system itself. The entire presentation had taken just over 1 hour.

Linking up the Manhunters – National Developments in Three Countries

Linkage blindness has been put forward as an important organizational short-coming of the police institution in the investigation of all types of serial crime. As one scholar put it:

> Linkage Blindness is the real and ever-present cause of law enforcement's inability to respond to serial murder in a timely and effective manner ... [it can be] defined as the lack of sharing or coordination of investigative information and the lack of adequate networking among law enforcement agencies and law enforcement officers" (Egger 1990: 174).

The genealogy of the term is instructive. It seems to have first entered the lexicon of investigators in the Behavioural Sciences Unit (BSU) of the FBI (later made famous in the film *Silence of the Lambs*) around 1980. In 1981 William French Smith, then U.S. Attorney General, created a Task Force on Violent Crime which was expressly intended to examine ways in which to improve interagency co-operation in such cases. In July 1983 the conceptual model for the National Center for the Analysis of Violent Crime (NCAVC) was first put forward in the U.S.A. This was established in 1984 and located at the FBI training centre in Quantico, Virginia. In 1985 the Violent Criminal Apprehension Program (ViCAP) computer went on-line. In 1986, with funds procured from the National Institute of Justice, a 2-week conference held at Sam Houston State University in Texas produced the *Multi-Agency Investigative Team Manual* (MAIT). The development and interpolation of this concept in the vocabulary of law enforcement gave central (i.e. U.S. federal) control over crimes that were designated to fall under its purview. The NCAVC provided the hub of the infrastructure, ViCAP its communications capability and the MAIT its operations manual.

It was during this period that an intensive effort was made to quantify the size of the problem. Estimates that emerged in the popular press settled on a figure, later disputed as grossly inflated, of about 4000-5000 deaths per annum perpetrated by anything up to 500 serial killers (Jenkins 1994). These law enforcement estimates emerged during a period of intense media coverage of notorious serial murder cases. Henry Lee Lucas was apprehended on 11 June 1983. He was credited with over 360 victims (a number which, again, was later discredited as grossly over-inflated) making him "the most prolific serial killer" (Egger 1990). Lucas received unprecedented media attention, including several televised interviews from prison and a full-length interview in *Penthouse* in 1985. During this period Canada was coming to terms with its own incarnation of this folk devil – Clifford Olsen's case was decided in a British Columbia Court in 1982 amidst a flurry of media coverage, which Canada's *sub judice* rules only partially confounded. In the U.K. Peter Sutcliffe, *aka* the Yorkshire Ripper, was apprehended in January 1981. After a criminal career that lasted more than a decade and which attracted considerable media attention (which was, in part, amplified by police ineptitude and intense campaigning by various feminist organizations) public concern about the issue loomed large indeed.

The American system that emerged in this period was predicated on a centralized model. According to Pierce Brooks, an official at the Justice Department and principal author of the MAIT, the crux of the problem was the lack of a centralized automated computer information and crime analysis system (Brooks *et al.* 1987). It was argued that only a centralized (i.e. federally controlled) system could co-ordinate the process of identifying patterns of a serial homicide, disseminate the necessary information to the appropriate law enforcement agencies and co-ordinate ongoing investigations. A prime example of what such a system could do was the identification of 'signature patterns' in the *modus operandi* of individuals perpetrating serial crimes in a number of different jurisdictions. Thus, ViCAP was put forward in order to overcome what was characterized as a 'systemic myopia.' This programme was originally funded through the Law Enforcement Assistance Administration (LEAA), under the wing of the Integrated Criminal Apprehension Program (ICAP) co-ordinator Robert O. Heck who, incidentally, was one of the principal populizers of serial murder-victim estimates in the 4000-5000 per annum range (Egger 1990; Jenkins 1994).

Canadian police agencies also perceived a problem of systemic myopia and were not far behind in the development of similar systems. Before the end of the decade the Canadian Police Information Centre (CPIC) became operational with its own Major Crimes File system. Belying the generality of its name, this system was limited to serial murder investigations in its first incarnation. As a representative of the RCMP explained in 1988, the system was intended

> to bridge the gaps among record systems maintained by member forces of the Canadian police community and encourage investigators to communicate, to share information and to link major crimes, initially those believed to involve homicide, thereby leading to the rapid apprehension of serial offenders. A crime-portrait computer file, where similarities and patterns are identified, can effectively compare a major crime in Vancouver with one in Montreal and may lead to a specific suspect (quoted in Egger 1990: 196).

However, in contrast to the American system in which the hardware itself was centrally administered, the Canadian model allowed police to employ this software on stand-alone desktop computers *in situ* using standardized data-entry procedures and a hierarchy of regional co-ordinators whose job it is to disseminate the data across the country. This represents a significant difference in organizational philosophy, although in investigative terms the approach is similar.

It might be tempting to ask questions about the relative utility of the centralized versus de-centralized models mentioned above. Such questions miss the more sociological point, that the introduction of information technology into large-scale institutions including police-type agencies tends to reproduce the organizational features of those institutions. As Zuboff (1988) has noted the structure of access to information expresses underlying relations of authority (see especially pp. 392-396). Thus, in the U.S.A. there is an absence of consensus around the general principles of federal, state and local enforcement jurisdiction which historically impeded the development of a strategic architecture for policing. This is compounded by the 'myth' that a multiplicity and diversity of police forces is the best guarantor of freedom through a "healthy system of checks and balances arising out of interagency competition" (Gellner & Morris 1992: 247). This competition is palpable between federal and local levels and even more tangible between federal agencies (see also Fogelson 1977). This has had the consequence of fostering a tendency to 'hoard intelligence' (Gellner & Morris 1992: 248), hence the desire by FBI officials to centralize data-management systems in the context of serial homicide investigation. In contrast, in Canada the RCMP has an undisputed federal mandate for police action as well as functioning as a Provincial police in mandate for police action as well as functioning as a Provincial police in eight out of 10 provinces (Brodeur 1995). At the same time, and unlike the 'continental model', the Canadian system is also highly decentralized with many local level police departments (Mawby 1990) and consequently many local-federal police partnerships where intelligence exchange is formalized and routine. The contrasts between ViCAP and ViCLAS systems are thus understandable in terms of these underlying organizational differences. Some of the literature on the working of electronic communications systems suggests that the more decentralized approach to information management, processing and exchange is the more optimal (Zuboff 1988). However, within policing-type organizations, the relative merits of centralization or decentralization, for a range of issues and functions, is by no means straightforward (Reiss 1995). Within the context of serial homicide investigation there has yet to be a definitive evaluation.

Developments in North America have continued apace, but U.K. police agencies have also had concerns and their own efforts have been no less far-reaching. The most notorious of these concerns has been the criminal career of the Yorkshire Ripper which extended over a decade. Peter William Sutcliffe was first arrested in 1969 for carrying a hammer and was subsequently convicted for 'going equipped for theft'. Later in that year he was accused of attacking a woman in the red-light district of Bradford with a weighted sock but no charges were brought. His career as a serial killer was brought to an end in January 1981 when he was finally arrested and charged with murder. It is interesting to note that the arrest was a relatively simple, even fortuitous, matter of routine law enforcement. Sutcliffe was apprehended as he sat in his car with a prostitute whom two police officers had decided to arrest for soliciting. During the stop it was determined that the license plates on the vehicle were false which led to further enquiries. These lead to the recovery of some tools (specifically a hammer and a screwdriver which had been used as murder weapons) and to Sutcliffe's eventual confession.

The history of this investigation was analysed in great detail in order to glean lessons for future serial murder investigations (Doney 1990). The public record of this particular investigation is revealing of how the police organization responds to this type of crime. In this post-mortem, if one might use that term, it emerged that Sutcliffe had been interviewed by the police on nine separate occasions from 1975 onwards, which was a matter of some considerable embarrassment for the U.K. police. It was pointed out in their defence that the investigation was unprecedented in size. Some 268,000 names were amassed in the investigation, 21,000 people were actually interviewed by police and 31,000 statements were taken. Further, 5.4 million vehicle registration details were screened by the 250 police officers dedicated to the investigation which was calculated to absorb some 5 million hours of police time at a cost of £4 million. A final illustrative statistic, perhaps the most important from the point of view of the Police Department of the Home Office, was that the paper records pertaining to the investigation weighed an estimated 24 tons. This was taken to be indicative of the urgent need to computerize police investigative procedures. It was this investigation, more than any other, that prompted the development of the Home Office Large Major Inquiry System (HOLMES). This system, like the Canadian model described above, depended on the use of information technology and standardized data gathering and formatting to lend an overall national coherence to these types of investigations and, again in contrast to the U.S. model, the hardware itself was not centrally based and administered.

The details that emerged through the inquiry into Sutcliffe's criminal career show that there are two essential characteristics of information technology that are of utility in this sort of criminal investigation. The communication links, afforded by either centralized computerization (along the American model) or through networked computers and the phone/fax interchange (along the Canadian and British models), help to overcome linkage blindness. Computerization also helps to overcome the problems associated with the massive amounts of data that these investigations invariably generate. These two perceived advantages of information technology have made computerization the *sine qua non* of serial murder investigation.

Developments in Canada, the U.S.A. and the U.K. all indicate that information technology was intended to both increase the capacity of police forces to process large quantities of data and to bridge the organizational boundaries between the various police institutions that comprise the 'police community'.[4] Moreover, it is assumed that these developments have relevance in the transnational realm as well. While there is, as yet, little indication that serial murder is a transnational phenomenon, Steven Egger has pointed out that Interpol "is an international network and communication system [already] in place to respond to the transnational character of serial crime" (Egger 1990: 196). Citing the official mission statement of the organization "to facilitate, co-

439

ordinate and encourage international police co-operation as a means for embattling crime", Egger has noted that Interpol is "an increasingly important tool for criminal investigation in the United States to satisfy investigative leads that go beyond the border of this country" and, further, that "the in-place system of this organization is uniquely qualified to provide assistance to investigation of a serial murder with potentially transnational characteristics" (ibid: 196).[5]

Thus, we can see that serial murder has been looked upon by members of the police community as an issue which necessitated the stitching together of the boundaries between their organizations. These institutional boundaries are seen as, all too often, engendering conflict between agencies that, theoretically, ought to operate in concert. Co-ordinated exchange of information is thus the panacea for an organizational problem. As Egger put it:

> where conflict remains between two organizations there may be less of it when an outsider holds an acknowledged monopoly of relevant information. Thus, the ability of these agencies to access and retrieve information from a centralised investigative network may further reduce the conflict between involved agencies (ibid.: 196).

Serial Homicide and Global Police Networks

What becomes apparent in the above analysis is that the FBI has, for almost 20 years, viewed the issue of serial homicide as requiring it to consolidate its institutional mandate for what has been constructed as a federal law enforcement task. At the same time, law enforcement agencies in both the U.K. and Canada have also been pursing similar ends, manufacturing (or reconfiguring) co-ordinated national networks of police officials to pursue investigations into this type of crime. We can also see that at least one police organization (Interpol) has been invoked with regard to establishing a transnational police capability for discovering possible links in serial homicide investigations. However, while this analysis shows something of how this enterprise transgresses geographical and jurisdictional boundaries, it does not illuminate these processes fully. In this section I want to examine further the transnational networking of police officers who have consolidated their role as experts in serial homicide.

In this paper the transnationalization of police work has been described with respect to three interconnected processes: the circulation of knowledge, the exchange of investigative techniques and technology transfer. Together, these three processes can be said to constitute the transnational police response to serial homicide investigation.

Turning first to the circulation of knowledge, we must first take steps to define our understanding of the concept of 'knowledge'; in the sense used here it refers specifically to bureaucratically classified information about crimes, criminals and victims (Ericson 1994). The presentation dress-rehearsal described above used a number of exhibits that are artifacts taken from this knowledge base. Importantly, the audio exhibits were of American origin, giving us an example of the transnational trade in knowledge, but the visual exhibits also transgressed inter-Canadian jurisdictional boundaries, if not national ones, again showing the mobility of such information within police networks. Another illustration of the geographical mobility of police knowledge also became evident during that presentation; it emerged during the discussion of the fifth victim, who had been abducted and murdered during the course of Valentine's Day 1987, that the *modus operandi* of the crime (particularly the method of body disposal) displayed certain common characteristics with several other cases that had taken place over almost 10 years: two in the U.S.A., one in eastern Canada, and a fourth in northern British Columbia. The implication was that a geographically mobile serial killer might have been at work, but this investigation was still ongoing and so the connections between these commonalities had yet to be proved. While such linkage remained indeterminate, this example clearly illustrates the great distances (in both time and space) that knowledge about particular crimes can travel.

The circulation of such knowledge is inextricably tied to the circulation of investigative techniques and expertise. One practical example of the cross-jurisdictional application of techniques is the way Geographical Information Systems (GIS) are being used to map serially related crimes. GIS allow investigating officers to produce maps which display details of crimes, such as locations of abductions, body 'dump sites', and other important places (Rossmo 1994, 1995). Routine activity theory hypothesizes that perpetrators of serially related crime will largely confine their criminal activity within an area bounded by their everyday use of space; this theory of a 'sphere of routine activity' lends such maps a potential investigative utility (see Brantingham & Brantingham 1981 for a general discussion of this approach). Using data from investigations of crimes that are presumed to be serially linked, GIS programmers attempt to construct probability maps of criminals' use of space. One Vancouver City Police officer that I interviewed who does this type of work spends up to 50% of his time on such investigations for other municipal police forces, most of which are in the U.S.A. Indeed, at the time of my interview with him he was working on a series of homicides in San Diego, California. Such an investigation entails the circulation of knowledge within police networks; that is, knowledge crosses jurisdictional boundaries. But it also shows how investigative techniques essential to the generation and manipulation of such knowledge are shared across such boundaries. In order for the knowledge pertaining to a particular crime, or series of crimes, to have investigative utility it must be formatted in accordance with the needs of the investigative technique being brought to bear. Thus, the circulation of knowledge and the exchange of techniques are inextricably linked. In the case of an officer employing the technique of computer mapping, the circulation and exchange are related to a specific investigation.

The ViCLAS system is an example of a permanently linked network in which knowledge circulates and this knowledge depends on the technique of crime profiling. Crime profiling depends on the encapsulation of the facts of specific crimes within a pre-formatted, bureaucratically managed and routinized system of knowledge circulation. These encapsulated facts are a form of police knowledge and, again, the utility of such knowledge depends on a certain technique: crime profiling. The theory brought to bear here is that crime, in this instance serial homicide, is learned behaviour and, as such, each individual crime will bear common traits with other homicides committed by the same person. The technique of crime profiling allows police to discover possible links between crimes separated in time and space that might not be visible otherwise. As the Valentine's Day homicide example mentioned above shows, such common characteristics only *appear* as links; they may, in fact, be an artefact of the application of the technique. Confirmation of any particular hypothetical linkage awaits the successful conclusion of an investigation. This technique is still relatively new and criminologists have, as yet, no precise indication if its efficacy. The spread of this technique between police agencies, however, is ongoing.

Lastly, we can see that the circulation of knowledge and the spread of investigative techniques is dependant on the transfer of technology. GIS technology is finding many applications within police agencies across the developed world, but technology transfer is even more clearly evident in the case of the ViCLAS system. One document that illustrates this technology transfer quite well is a list of participants for a ViCLAS workshop which took place in early 1995. This is summarized in Table 1.

It is apparent from this table that almost one-half of the participants in this workshop were from outside Canada. The extent of participation of European police agencies and other far-flung police organizations indicated in the table appears somewhat limited. However, police officers interviewed at RCMP Headquarters in Vancouver indicated that police agencies in the Netherlands, Belgium, Germany and the U.K. were also interested in acquiring the system, as were police in Australia and New Zealand. Thus, this transnational technology transfer, the attendant exchange of investigative techniques that it entails and, ultimately, the circulation of knowledge about serial homicide that follows from it are well underway. This was a matter of pride for the RCMP, since the software for the ViCLAS system had been designed 'in-house'.

Thus, we can see that technology transfer, the exchange of techniques and the circulation of knowledge combine together to show clearly the interconnectedness of police operations and investigations, irrespective of national or other jurisdictional boundaries. The transnationalization of police work is both product and productive of these linked processes. Interestingly, such processes do not seem especially dependent on any particular institutional forum for police co-operation. Thus, organizations as various as TREVI or 'Friends of TREVI', Interpol or the International Association of Chief Police Officers, and even the most subterranean networks of police officers, are all implicated in these processes of transfer, exchange and circulation.

Some Conclusions and a Postscript

A functional theory of deviance would put forth the proposition that formal agents of social control would seek to establish themselves as highly visible protectors and, further, in the case of extreme folk devils such as the serial killer, would try to maintain an image of themselves as boldly efficacious. Douglas (1987) has argued in the Durkheimian mould, that institutions seek to gain legitimacy by first identifying problems and latterly by showing that a specific set of instituted rules, procedures and practices embodied in the institution that has identified the problem constitute the only reasonable answer to it. Jenkins (1994) has persuasively argued that the development of the FBI's expertise in the domain of the geographically mobile serial killer was instrumental in extending the mandate of the FBI, facilitating the penetration of federal police into local agencies and, further, that the magnification of this particular folk devil was an almost inevitable result. Other scholars (e.g. Egger 1990) have shown that technical advances in crime detection have been instrumental in this process. The utility of these data-handling systems is not incontestable (Lyon 1994) and indeed, has been said to result in 'police inflation' (Ericson & Shering 1986) whereby police "turn the facts of crime into virtues, arguing for more manpower, legal resources and scientific resources in an amplifying spiral" (p.136).

The research undertaken for this paper cannot confirm or refute this latter set of observations. However, it has been able to illuminate the more classical sociological concerns relating to the dialectical and functional relationship between deviance and social control. Specifically, it has shown that these processes need not be thought of as limited in some way to small-scale social orders. Indeed, these processes can and are reproducible in the transnational domain as well. As if to confirm this very point, a

Table 1. ViCLAS workshop 1995; forces attending

Police force represented	Number of officers	Location
Royal Canadian Mounted Police		
	1	St. John's, Newfoundland
	1	Halifax, Nova Scotia
	1	Fredericton, New Brunswick
	5	Ottawa, Ont.
	1	Winnipeg, Manitoba
	1	Regina, Sask.
	2	Edmonton, Alta.
	6	Vancouver, BC
Other Canadian Police Forces		
Quebec Provincial Police	1	Montreal, Que.
Montreal City Police	2	Montreal, Que.
Ontario Provincial Police	3	Orillia, Ont.
Toronto Metro Police	2	Toronto, Ont.
Hamilton City Police	1	Hamilton, Ont.
Vancouver City Police	2	Vancouver, BC.
Niagara Regional Police	1	St. Catharines, Ont.
Police Forces, U.S.A.		
Iowa State Police	1	Des Moines, Iowa
Federal Bureau of Investigation	1	Quantico, Virginia
Minnesota State Police	1	St. Paul, Minnesota
New Jersey State Police	1	Trenton, New Jersey
Washington State Attorney General	1	Seattle, Washington
Police Forces, European		
Netherlands National Police	1	Zoetermeer, Netherlands
Austrian, Ministry of Interior	1	Vienna, Austria
Total	37	

horrific drama unfolded in Western Europe while this paper was being written. In Belgium, the arch folk devil of the serial killer was fused with another equally powerful demon, the paedophile, in the notorious case of Marc Dutroux. As the details of the case became known over the course of 1996, the consequences for police agencies of not responding, and being seen to respond, to such folkdevilry became readily apparent. *The Economist* (26 October 1996) reported in the wake of the storm of protest over the Dutroux scandal "[w]hen 300,000 Belgians took to the streets...they were not just expressing sympathy with the parents of the four girls killed so gruesomely by a paedophile ring". A statement from a spokesperson for the families of the victims made clear what the substantive concern was: "It is our conviction that it was neither fate nor incompetence that botched the investigation into the disappearances, but rather protection and blackmail" (*The Guardian*: 7 March 1997). There remains a widespread conviction throughout Belgium that police and judicial complicity extending to the highest levels of the Belgian criminal justice system resulted in the perpetuation of this series of horrendous crimes. The official Parliamentary enquiry elided the accusations of complicity, instead focusing on what was characterized as a 'catalogue of errors', stating that investigators were slow to get onto the cases, ignored vital evidence, were cold and dismissive towards parents, jealously guarded information and had insufficient resources which were used in a badly co-ordinated and inefficient way (*The Scotsman*: 10 April 1997). In short, the problem was not complicity but incompetence.

However, the consequences of this affair were not limited to Belgium. The very month that the mass demonstrations took place in Brussels an enquiry was quietly launched in Saintes, in the Charentes Marime *departement* of France, into what appeared to be a network distributing pornographic videos involving very young boys and girls, some as young as 6 months old (*The Guardian*: 13 March 1997). The first arrests from this investigation were made in January of 1997, but it was not until March of that year that more than 200 people were detained in a nation-wide operation undertaken by the French *Gendarmerie*. In June of that year, the trial of 71 men involved in this network commenced (*The Independent*: 18 June 1997). Alain Honore,

General Secretary of the French Federation for Health and Social Work, noted as the trial got under way that this network came to light because of publicity given to scandals in other countries: "That opened people's eyes and they started to wonder whether that sort of thing might not be going on here" (*The Times*: 21 June 1997). Significantly, among those detained in the original large-scale operation in March were an unspecified number of French judicial officials. Meanwhile, the trans-European nature of this network was made evident by both Interpol and UNICEF (*The Times*: 21 June 1997). Poland has been identified as the hub for European paedophile networks, producing videos for consumption abroad and functioning as a destination for sex-tourism. That gave further impetus for a tightening-up of linkages for police co-operation throughout the region.

This paper yields some insights into the process of transnationalization as it unfolds within police institutions. Globalization, a process that is said fundamentally to alter the nature of international boundaries, is a concept that has gained widespread usage amongst social scientists, many of whom are seeking to provide empirical evidence about how this process is being experienced by a wide range of people and organizations. An understanding of such processes as they pertain to deviance and social control ought to be of central importance, since the ways of maintaining social order (both practically and symbolically) are central to social life regardless of the territorial boundaries that circumscribe it. As social life is increasingly acted out on a stage that is transnational, so the methods of achieving social order take on a transnational aspect. The empirical evidence presented here shows that the principal method adopted to achieve that end is predicated on the establishment of a technological infrastructure that will facilitate the collection, retrieval and exchange of knowledge (within and between police organizations) about suspect populations and individuals. This paper has characterized this general goal as the product of three specific and inter-related processes: technology transfer, the exchange of investigative techniques and the circulation of knowledge.

We end where we began, however, by noting that while these methods are being adopted across the whole range of police work, as far as it concerns serious criminals such as the serial killer, they take on an added dimension of importance as a symbol of order itself. Such folk devils may be responsible for a relatively small number of crimes, especially in comparison to, say, wife battery (Sheptycki 1993*b*; *Canadian Journal of Criminology* 1995); however, they are a central symbol of disorder and hence remain a central target of the forces of law and order. While development of expertise in this field of criminal investigation is commonly supposed to be the special province of U.S. law enforcement, particularly the FBI, the research that forms the basis of this paper reveals that it is also a preoccupation for many other police agencies, not least the RCMP, and, indeed, that it has taken on a transnational aspect. In the coming years the further development of European police co-operation and even global policing (Sheptycki 1998) will likely ramify this tendency.

Endnotes

*Reprinted from *International Journal of the Sociology of Law,* Vol. 26, Sheptycki: Reflections on the transnationalization of policing; thecase of the RCMP and Serial Killers, pp.17-34, 1998, with permission from Elsevier.
 Research for this paper was made possible by a grant from the British Council of Canada and from the Faculty of Law, University of Edinburgh and was undertaken as a Visiting Research Fellow at Green College, University of British Columbia in 1995. The author is currently an ESRC Junior Research Fellow (Grant Number H524 27 00061 94). I would like to thank the anonymous reviewer of this article and Richard Ericson for their input.

1   The *Collins Dictionary of Sociology* (Harper Collins: Glasgow 1991) defines the term folk devil as "any stereotypical, 'socially constructed' cultural type identified as socially threatening by members of society". Such a cultural type is not a fiction but a stereotype built up on the basis of an ontological *a priori*. In using this term the drama of crime and its control is emphasized, but this in no way suggests that there is no factual basis for the mythology. It merely asserts that the socially constructed

    meaning of the term 'serial killer' has an impact beyond the facts of his existence.

2   Some scholars in the field point out that the stereotype of the serial killer as male is not borne out by the evidence (Hickey 1990, 1991; Kigger 1990). Indeed, there are numerous instances of female serial killers in police case files. However, this particular folk devil is almost always understood as being a white male.

3   The paper version of the ViCLAS Crime Report form is 36 pages long and contains 262 separate question fields. The level of detail required is high, for example the question on types of weapon used includes 12 different types of knife and lists 60 different types of weapon overall. Nor are all the fields of the pre-formatted type; 29 require some form of descriptive analysis, ranging from an account of the victim's lifestyle to a sequencing of events during the attack which requires of the officer that they be "explicit and clinical in your language" and that they "list every event, step by step". The completion of this Report Form could take many hours. Given the prominence of a theory of escalation (whereby offenders begin their careers with relatively minor offences, for example indecent exposure, and gradually move to more serious types of attack) such forms do indeed become very routine as they are to be applied to a very extensive range of offending behaviour.

4   It might be worth stressing here that in many countries there are a large number of police agencies in need of networking in this way. Sam Walker estimated in 1978 that the U.S.A. had approximately 25,000 police agencies (Walker 1978). Belgium might offer an even more extreme example. A report commissioned by the Belgian government in 1987 estimated that the country had over 600 police agencies – this in a country with a land area of just 30,000 square kilometres, scarcely bigger than Vermont and Rhode Island combined. Even in the U.K., which has a relatively homogeneous police system largely, although not exclusively, demarcated by territory alone, linkage blindness is perceived to be a pervasive problem.

5 Interpol is a voluntary system of information exchange between member police forces. National systems such as that developed in Canada and the U.S.A. are, more often, compulsory.

References

Brantingham, P.J. & Brantingham, P.L. (Eds.) (1981) *Environmental Criminology.* Sage: Beverly Hills

Brodeur, J.-P. (1995) Undercover policing in Canada: a study of its consequences. In *Undercover, Police Surveillance in Comparative Perspective.* (C. Fijnaut & G. Marx, Eds). pp 71-102. Kluwer: The Hague.

Brooks, P., Devine, M., Green, T., Hart, B. & Moore, M. (1987) Serial murder; a criminal justice response. *Police Chief* **54**, 37-45.

Brownmiller, S. (1976) *Against Our Will: Men, Women and Rape.* Penguin: Harmondsworth, London.

Cameron, D. & Frazer, E. (1987) *The Lust to Kill.* Polity: Cambridge.

Canadian Journal of Criminology (1995). *'Special Edition; the Violence Against Women Survey'* **35(3).**

Caputi, J. (1987) *The Age of Sex Crime.* The Women's Press: London.

Cohen, S. (1972) *Folk Devils and Moral Panics.* McGibbon and Kee: London.

Douglas, M. (1987) *How Institutions Think.* Routledge and Kegan Paul: London.

Doney, R.H. (1990) The aftermath of the Yorkshire Ripper; the response of the United Kingdom police service. In *Serial Murder, An Elusive Phenomenon* (Egger, S.A., Ed.). Praeger: New York, pp. 95-112.

Downes, D. & Rock, P. (1988) *Understanding Deviance; A Guide to the Sociology of Crime and Rule Breaking*, 2nd Ed. Oxford University Press: Oxford.

Egger, S. (1990) *Serial Murder an Elusive Phenomenon.* Praeger: New York.

Ericson, R. V. (1994) The division of expert knowledge in policing and security. *The British Journal of Sociology* **45**, 149-176.

Ericson, R. V. & Shearing, C. (1986) The scientification of police work. In *The Knowledge Society* (Böhme, G. & Stehr, N., Eds). Reidel: Dordrecht, pp. 129-159.

Erikson, K. (1966) *Wayward Puritans*. Free Press: New York.

Fogelson, R.M. (1977) *Big-City Police*. Harvard University Press: Cambridge, Mass.

Gellner, W. A. & Morris, N. Relations between federal and local police. In *Modern Policing* (Tonry, M. & Morris, N., Eds). University of Chicago Press: Chicago, pp. 231-349.

Hanmer, J. & Saunders, S. (1984) *Well-Founded Fear*. Hutchinson: London.

Hickey, E. (1990) The etiology of victimisation in serial murder: an historical and demographic analysis. In *Serial Murder; An Elusive Phenomenon* (Egger, S.A., Ed.). Praeger: New York.

Hickey, E. (1991) *Serial Murderers and Their Victims*. Brooks Cole/Wadsworth: Monterey, CA, pp. 53-72.

Jenkins, P. (1994) *Using Murder, The Social Construction of Serial Homicide*. Aldine de Gruyter: New York.

Kiger, K. (1990) The darker figure of crime; the serial murder enigma. In *Serial Murder; An Elusive Phenomenon* (Egger, S.A., Ed.). Praeger: New York, pp. 35-52.

Lyon, D. (1994) *The Electronic Eye; The Rise of Surveillance Society*. Policy Press: Cambridge.

Mawby, R. (1990) *Comparitive Policing Issues*. Unwin Hyman: London.

Radford, J. & Russell, D.E.H. (Eds.) (1992) *Fermicide; The Politics of Women Killing*. Open University Press: Buckingham.

Reiss, A.J. (1995) Reflections on policing systems and police co-operation in Europe. In *Comparisons in Policing; An International Perspective* (Brodeur, J.-P., Ed.). Avebury: Aldershot, pp. 228-232.

Rossmo, D.K. (1994) Targeting victims; serial killers and the urban environment. In *Serial and Mass Murder: Theory, Research and Policy* (O'Reilly-Flemming, T. & Egger, S.A., Eds). University of Toronto Press: Toronto, pp. 22-45.

Rossmo, D.K. (1995) *Raptors, stalkers and trappers: hunting patterns of serial killers.* Presentation to the *American Society of Criminology, Boston, November 15, 1995* (unpublished). Available from author.

Sheptycki, J.W.E. (1993*a*) Serial murder; a review of the scholarly literature. *British Journal of Criminology* **33**, 103-108.

Sheptycki, J.W.E. (1993*b*) *Innovations in Policing Domestic Violence.* Avebury: Aldershot.

Sheptycki, J.W.E. (1995) Rapacious Bluebeards and chivalrous knights. New Waverley Paper: Edinburgh. **95(3),** 1-24.

Sheptycki, J.W.E. (1998) The global cops cometh. *The British Journal of Sociology.*

Soothill, K.& Walby, S. (1991) *Sex Crime in the News.* Routledge: London.

Stanko, E.A. (1985) *Intimate Intrusions; Women's Experience of Male Violence.* Routledge and Kegan Paul: London.

Surette, R. (Ed.) (1984) *Justice and the Media.* C.C. Thomas: Springfield Illinois.

Walker, S. (1978) *A Critical History of Police Reform.* Lexington Books: Lexington, Mass.

Zuboff, S. (1988) *In the Age of the Smart Machine; The Future of Work and Power.* Heinemann: Oxford.

17

Police Discretion with Young Offenders[1]

Peter J. Carrington
Jennifer L. Schulenberg

This chapter discusses the main areas of police work with young offenders in which discretion is exercised: the detection of youth crime, clearing youth-related incidents by informal action, referring to alternative measures, or laying a charge, and procedures used to compel the attendance at court of youth who are charged.

Detection of crime can occur in one of two modes. Proactive policing involves police-initiated activities by either an individual officer or the police organization. Proactive mobilization occurs when officers make spontaneous decisions to stop citizens for further investigation, or reflects administrative and supervisory decisions to focus on certain groups of people who are believed to be crime-prone. Reactive policing involves a police response to a specific request by a citizen (e.g. telephoning the police to report a crime). These requests can range from individuals asking for help handling their difficulties, or from community groups requesting a certain level or pattern of service to meet their interests.

Police work predominantly involves reactive policing. Black and Reiss (1970) found that 72% of police-juvenile encounters were citizen-initiated. Similarly, Webster's (1970) findings indicated that less than 20% of police encounters were self-initiated (proactive). More recent findings indicate the same trend but to a lesser degree: approximately 50% (Cordner, 1989) and 53% (Ericson, 1982) of police encounters were reactive and a large proportion of the balance involved administrative work. A study of a large police force in eastern Canada found that even reactive policing involves relatively few calls that relate to crime control (approximately 35%) (Shearing, 1984).

In the reactive situation, a police officer can exercise his or her discretion only after two events have occurred: (i) a decision has been made by either a member of the public (observer, parents, school authorities, etc.) or the victim to call the police, and (ii) the dispatchers have decided this incident warrants sending a patrol car to the scene. The process of dealing with an incident can be broken down into five stages, or decision points (Klinger, 1996). The first stage is gathering initial information and making a decision as to whether further investigation is warranted; i.e. deciding whether the incident involves a criminal violation. In the second stage, investigation results in the identification of the offender(s), or "clearing" the incident. The third stage involves the choice of disposition for each apprehended offender. This can entail the police laying a charge (or referring a recommendation to the Crown to charge in some provinces[2]), with or without a recommendation for post-charge Alternative Measures; referring the youth to pre-charge Alternative Measures or a Youth Justice Committee, or taking informal action. The next decision is whether to make a police (occurrence) report. If the suspect is charged or referred to Alternative Measures, a report must always be completed. However, if an officer chooses to use informal measures to handle the incident it is up to the officer's discretion or departmental policy whether a report is completed. Finally, if charges are (to be) laid, an officer (or officers) make a decision concerning the mode of compelling his or her attendance at court: whether the youth is to be given an appearance notice or summons and released, or taken into custody (arrested); and, if arrested, whether to be released or held for a judicial interim release ("bail") hearing. Thus, officers make three fundamental decisions: (i) whether a youth should be charged or dealt with in other ways; (ii) if not charged, what type of diversion is appropriate (Hornick et al., 1996); or, (iii) if charged, how to compel attendance at court.

Trends over time in the exercise of police discretion

The main statistical indicator of the exercise of police discretion with respect to laying charges is the proportion of young persons apprehended by police who are charged. Carrington (1999) found that the proportion of apprehended young persons charged by police was stable at about 55% during 1977-1983, under the Juvenile Delinquents Act, jumped to approximately 65% after the Young Offenders Act came into force, and remained, with minor variations, at that level until 1996. Figure 1 is based on information from the Uniform Crime Reporting (UCR) Survey, a survey operated by the Canadian Centre for Justice Statistics, a branch of Statistics Canada. It includes all crime recorded by the police in Canada. Figure 1 updates Carrington's analysis to the year 2000, and shows what appears to be a declining trend from 1991 to 2000 (when 59% of young persons apprehended in Canada were charged). The average proportion of apprehended young persons charged from 1986 to 2000 was 64%, which is substantially greater than the average of 55% for the period, 1977-1983.

Looking at the trends over time in separate provinces and territories, Carrington (1999) identified two groups. In one group - Newfoundland, New Brunswick, Quebec, Manitoba, Alberta, British Columbia, and the Yukon - police had exercised a relatively low degree of discretion not to charge under the Juvenile Delinquents Act (charging 50% - 80% of apprehended youth in 1983), and continued to exercise a low degree under the YOA. In the remaining jurisdictions, police had exercised a relatively high degree of discretion under the JDA (charging 25% - 50% of apprehended youth in 1983) but suddenly started to charge higher proportions when the YOA came into effect, so that the amount of discretion exercised approximated that in the first group. The change in Saskatchewan – from an average level of 24% of apprehended youths charged during 1977-1983 to an average level of 67% during 1986-1996 – was the most spectacular, but the

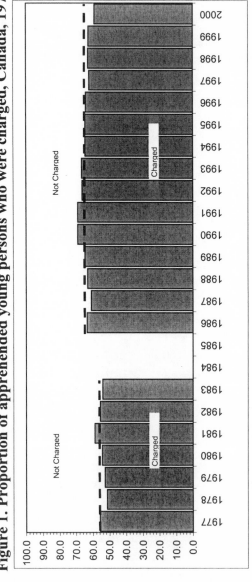

Figure 1. Proportion of apprehended young persons who were charged, Canada, 1977-2000

Sources: 1977-1996: Carrington (1999); 1997-2000: UCR Survey.

second largest increase was in Ontario – from an average level of 34% of apprehended youths charged during 1977-1983 to an average level of 64% during 1986-1996 – and is particularly significant because Ontario accounts for such a large part of the population of Canada. Figure 2 shows the proportion of apprehended youth charged in each province and the Territories in the year 2000.

It appears that one effect of the YOA has been to impose greater uniformity across Canada in the use of discretion concerning the charging of youth. In 1977, there was wide variation among the provinces and territories in the proportions of apprehended youth who were charged: from 23% in Saskatchewan to 84% in New Brunswick. Nine of the eleven jurisdictions (combining the Territories) were more than 10% higher or lower than the national rate of 56%. In effect, the jurisdictions were polarized into low-charging and high-charging regimes, with only two jurisdictions (Alberta and the Territories) close to the national average. Low-charging regimes included - in ascending order of proportion charged – Saskatchewan, Prince Edward Island, Ontario, and British Columbia. The other five provinces charged high proportions of their apprehended youth. In 2000, the range of provincial/territorial proportions charged had narrowed consider-ably: the lowest was 40% in British Columbia, and the highest was 73% in Manitoba. Only four jurisdictions differed by more than 10% from the national rate of 59%: British Columbia and Quebec on the low side, and Manitoba and Ontario on the high side.

Police discretion and the type of offence

The importance of the type, or seriousness, of the offence in the exercise of police discretion has been emphasized by practically every writer on the subject. In Table 1, we present data from the UCR Survey for 2000 to describe the variations in proportions of apprehended young persons charged, by the type of (alleged) offence.Table 1. gives the lie to the truism that the exercise of police discretion is related in a straightforward way to the "seriousness" of the offence. For example, less discretion is exercised with offences against the administration of justice (such

Figure 2. Percentage of apprehended young persons charged, by province, 2000

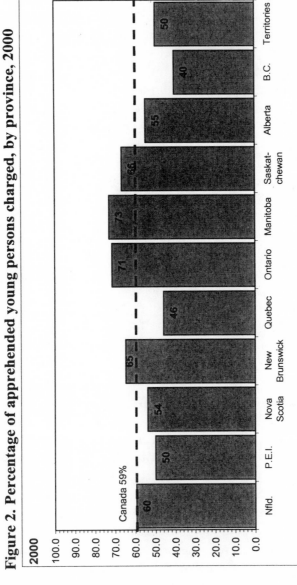

Sources: 1977-1996: Carrington (1999); 1997-2000: UCR Survey.

Table 1. Proportion of apprehended youth charged, by offence, Canada, 2000

Offence category	Percent charged
Homicide and related	100.0
Attempted murder	100.0
Offences against the administration of justice	95.6
Kidnapping	95.3
Robbery	87.4
Possession stolen property	83.6
Abduction	80.0
Criminal code traffic	79.9
Major assault	79.2
Traffic/Import drugs	77.4
Other federal statutes (primarily YOA)	76.3
Impaired driving	76.1
Break and enter	71.1
Sexual assault	67.7
Fraud and related	64.5
Weapons and explosives	62.4
Sexual abuse	55.0
Other criminal code offences	54.3
Theft	52.7
Common assault	52.2
Possession of drugs	47.1
Morals – sexual	46.0
Arson	45.0
Morals - gaming/betting	40.0
Property damage / Mischief	38.1
Public order offences	28.5
Total Violent Crimes	62.7
Total Property Crimes	55.7
Total Other Crimes	63.6
TOTAL – CRIMINAL CODE	58.9

Source: UCR Survey.

as failing to appear for court, or disobeying the conditions of a bail or probation order) than with any other offence except homicide and attempted murder – although administrative offences have no victim and cause no harm, except expense and inconvenience to the justice system. Similarly, a young person apprehended for committing a criminal traffic offence, such as impaired driving, is more likely to be charged than one who is apprehended for sexual assault or burglary (break and enter).

Informal action

When officers decide not to lay (or recommend) a charge, or to recommend alternative measures, they have a choice among several kinds of informal action. They may give an informal or formal warning, involve the parents and/or social services, arrest and question the youth at the police station and release him or her, make a referral to a community-based intervention program, or simply take no action, except possibly to file an occurrence report (Bala, Weiler, et al., 1994). According to Mueller and Heck (1997, p. 116), "a number of criminologists (including Tittle, 1980; Braithwaite, 1989; Sampson and Laub, 1993) have argued that informal sanctions are more influential and cost-effective than formal sanctions that the police can muster in fighting juvenile crime."

Little is known about the use of informal action by police in Canada, or about their screening practices (Hackler & Don, 1990). According to some writers, young offenders are handled informally in circumstances involving less serious crime (Ericson & Haggerty, 1997; Meehan, 1993). There is evidence of less use of informal action since the inception of the YOA (see above; also Carrington 1999; Carrington & Moyer, 1994; Schissel, 1993). Informal warnings have been found to be used more frequently in rural areas or by school resource officers than by regular front-line officers (Hornick et al., 1996), raising the possibility that rural and Youth Officers may use this approach more with youth due to their familiarity with their 'clientele'. British research suggests that the use of informal warnings is largely influenced by the administrative and ideological support within a department (Steer, 1970). Although formal, recorded warnings ("cautions") are used by police in other countries, there is no evidence in the literature that they are currently used in Canada, although caution letters

460

issued by Crowns are used in some provinces as alternative measures (Engler & Crowe, 2000; Task Force, 1996).

Statistical information on the use of informal action and pre-charge diversion by police is available from the Incident-Based Uniform Crime Reporting Survey ("UCR2"), maintained by the Canadian Centre for Justice Statistics. Its drawback is that it is relatively recent, and some police services do not yet participate in it. It began operation in 1988, and by 2001, it covered 59% of recorded incidents in Canada, and 71% of young persons charged.

Figure 3.   Incident clearance status, all UCR2 respondents, 2001

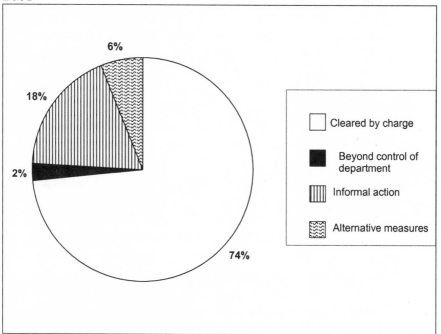

Source: Incident-Based UCR Survey, 2001.

For 2001, the UCR2 covers practically all of the Province of Quebec, much of Ontario (including the OPP and 13 independent municipal police services), and a small number of municipal services in each of the other provinces, except Prince Edward Island. Figure 3 shows the breakdown of clearance statuses of incidents involving at least one apprehended young person, for all respondents to the UCR2 in 2001. Of the 24% of youth-related incidents which were cleared without charge due to police discretion, one-third were diverted to alternative measures, and two-thirds were cleared by informal action.

In 2002, the authors carried out over 200 interviews with more than 300 police officers in 95 police services across Canada, in order to learn more about their exercise of discretion with young offenders.[3] The sample is approximately representative of all police services in Canada – from all provinces and territories, all types of communities, and all types of police service, including independent municipal services, detachments of provincial police services - including the Royal Canadian Mounted Police (RCMP) doing provincial policing under contract - First Nations police services, and police training facilities. The sample included the police services in all of the largest cities in Canada, and a substantial number of police services and detachments in the smallest towns and the most remote rural areas of the country. Over three-quarters (78%) of the police services in our sample indicated that they would usually or always consider using informal action with young persons. Almost two-thirds (62%) of the police forces in our sample make referrals to external agencies for minor and serious offences. These referrals are predominantly to social service agencies, and, in Quebec, to *La Direction de la Protection de la Jeunesse* (DPJ).

Informal warnings generally involve a police officer discussing the young person's behaviour with him or her and the parents, warning them that further law-breaking will result in formal action. As one Canadian policing textbook puts it, "…It is not unusual for an officer to give a stern lecture or a warning to a juvenile, advising of the possible consequences if arrested" (Dantzker & Mitchell, 1998, p. 59). Whether this informal warning is documented varies considerably. A "formal" warning usually involves a police officer entering the incident in the computerized police information system (Records Management System or RMS), or even occasionally having a letter issued to the youth and the parents which alleges the criminal behaviour and the issuance of a warning by police (or by the Crown, on the recommendation of police). The vast majority of police agencies

(93%) in our sample indicated that they use informal warnings with young persons.

In addition, 32% of our sample told us they did use some kind of a formal warning. However, the nature of the formal warning varies considerably between the agencies that answered in the affirmative. For example, in one Ontario police force the youth squad issues the letters and has the young person and parents (or legal guardian) sign the document as well. In other jurisdictions the police will recommend to the Crown to issue a caution letter. Others will make extensive notations in their RMS.

The majority of police agencies (91%) consider parental involvement mandatory when dealing informally with youth-related incidents. Many officers suggest that the effectiveness of informal action is highly dependent on parental involvement. On many occasions, officers indicated that they are better able to assess the situation due to the input of first hand knowledge from the parent(s). In some cases, officers indicated it can have a large impact on their decision-making process if they feel that the young person will face a consequence for their behaviour at home. If an officer feels that the young person's behaviour will be dealt with by Mom or Dad, he or she feels much more comfortable not laying charges or referring to alternative measures: "...Occasionally, the best punishment an officer can provide is to take the juvenile home and release him or her into the custody of the parents" (Dantzker & Mitchell, 1998, p. 59).

Officers in 75% of the police agencies in our sample indicated they will take the young person home, or if absolutely unavoidable, to the police station in order to have the parents take care and control over the young person. In the majority of cases, they deliver the young person directly home. However, in some jurisdictions they may bring the young person to the station as a "higher consequence" (i.e. a more severe sanction), as it inconveniences the parents to have to come to the police station to pick up their child. Further, several officers indicated that having the parents pick the youth up at a police station reinforces the message that the behaviour was criminal and needs to be treated as such, even though they are not proceeding by way of charge or alternative measures: "...If the officer wishes to emphasize the situation, the juvenile is taken to police headquarters and, when it exists, to the Juvenile Unit where the release…requires no further action" (Dantzker & Mitchell, 1998, p. 59). These officers suggest that having the parents come to the police station make them more accountable. They also noted it is much easier to make referrals when the parents and the young person are at the police station.

Use of alternative measures

Rather than using informal action or laying charges, police may choose to recommend a youth for Alternative Measures. Typically, alternative measures are considered appropriate for less serious offences and first offenders. The most common alternative measures programs assigned to youth are community service, an apology, social skills improvement, writing an essay, restitution or compensation, and other activities geared toward the specific young person (Kowalski, 1999). There is considerable jurisdictional variation in the availability of, and procedures for referral to, Alternative Measures programs. As of 1998-99, two jurisdictions (Ontario and Yukon) had exclusively post-charge programs (i.e. required that charges be laid before referral to alternative measures); three (New Brunswick, Manitoba, and Alberta) had exclusively pre-charge programs; and the rest had both modes of referral to alternative measures (Engler & Crowe, 2000). Under both modalities (pre-charge and post-charge), the police may play a large role in referral, assessment and development of a plan, implementing the plan, and in some cases monitoring the youth's compliance with the plan (Hornick et al., 1996), although it is the Crown which has the authority to refer or not refer a youth to AM.

The possibility exists that the availability of alternative measures programs (pre- or post-charge) may lead to the phenomenon known as *net-widening*, in which a measure which is intended to be relatively non-intrusive and to divert people away from other, more intrusive measures, is used with people who would, in its absence, have been dealt with even less intrusively (Lundman, 1993, p. 99). Thus, the use of pre-charge alternative measures with a youth who would, in their absence, have been dealt with by a police warning, is an example of net-widening; as is the use of post-charge alternative measures with a youth who would otherwise not have been charged. Net-widening would also have occurred if a youth's experience in alternative measures, including the process and the assigned "measure", was more intrusive than the court process and disposition which s/he would have experienced if s/he had been processed "formally". It is not always easy to define, let alone measure, "intrusiveness", so whether net-widening has occurred in any particular case is not necessarily clear. Nevertheless, in the aggregate, we see a prima facie case for net-widening if pre-charge AM has been used where otherwise an informal action would have been used, or if post-charge AM is used where otherwise pre-charge AM or informal action would have been used.

Just under one-half (48%) of the police agencies we spoke to indicated they used some form of pre-charge diversion with youth-related incidents. Although almost all the provinces and territories have mandated pre-charge alternative measures, comments made in the interviews suggest that this option is not exercised as often as police believe that it could be. Only 4% of the police forces in our sample have the option of referring youth to an internal (police-run) pre-charge program. In all cases, these programs were run by independent municipal police forces. Of those police agencies in our sample, 15% make pre-charge referrals to an external organization such as John Howard Society or the Boys & Girls Club. All of these types of programs are used by independent municipal forces and tend to be in metropolitan areas. A slightly smaller proportion (9%) of pre-charge referrals are made to a government ministry. One-quarter of the police agencies we spoke to indicated they can divert youths pre-charge to a community-based restorative justice forum. A small percentage of police agencies (12%) reported they use pre-charge diversion by running restorative justice conferences themselves.

Almost all (91%) of our sample indicated that youths were diverted post-charge to alternative measures in their jurisdiction. The majority of officers indicated they did not make any recommendations to the Crown concerning their thoughts on eligibility for post-charge alternative measures. A few stated they *might* tell the Crown Attorney in a private conversation that they would not object to alternative measures. However, the majority of police officers felt that, since the decision rests with the Crown, it was not their place to offer their input. The majority of officers also indicated that, in order for the young person to receive counselling or make reparations for the harm done, they had to charge the young person, since there were no pre-charge alternatives available in their jurisdiction. This finding supports the notion that post-charge alternative measures leads to net-widening.

Procedures used to compel appearance in court

If a formal charge is laid against a young person, police must use their discretion to decide how to ensure that the accused appears in court to answer the charge. The surest method is to arrest the young person and hold him or her in police custody ("pre-trial detention") until the court date. When police detain a young person, they are required to bring him or her before a justice of the peace or judge within 24 hours, or "as soon as possible" thereafter for a judicial interim release hearing (commonly called a "bail" hearing) to decide whether detention until the court date is warranted. Decision-making by the police and by the justice or judge is governed by provisions of the Criminal Code specifying under what conditions detention is permitted.

Young persons incarcerated on remand – that is, while awaiting trial, or during trial – constitute a substantial proportion of all youth incarcerated in Canada. In fiscal 2000/01, remand admissions of young persons accounted for 39% of custodial admissions (Marinelli, 2002). Due to the relatively short stays of remanded youth, they accounted for a smaller, yet still substantial, proportion (22%) of young persons held in custodial facilities on an "average day" in 2000/01 (ibid.).

Studies of bail hearings in youth court have found that judges sometimes stretch the interpretation of the Criminal Code grounds in ordering continued detention for young people, especially for youths who come from unstable or deleterious home situations. Yet, as many writers have pointed out, detention before conviction –that is, of persons presumed innocent – is an undesirable expedient whose use should be minimized, particularly in the case of young persons, who are especially vulnerable to its ill effects (Bala, Hornick, McCall, & Clarke, 1994; Task Force,

1996; Doob & Cesaroni, 2002; Varma, 2002). Unless it is absolutely necessary, pre-trial detention of young persons would appear to be contrary to the intent of the Bail Reform Act (see Law Reform Commission of Canada, 1988), the Young Offenders Act, with its emphasis on minimal interference in the freedom of the young person (Platt, 1991, p. 80), and the United Nations Convention on the Rights of the Child (Task Force, 1996). Also, detention before trial in criminal court has been found by several researchers to increase the probability of conviction and a custodial sentence (Hagan & Morden, 1981; Griffiths & Verdun-Jones, 1994, p. 226).

The only Canadian research which we could find on police decision-making concerning the pre-trial detention specifically of young persons was the study done by Carrington, Moyer and Kopelman (1986, 1988), using data collected when the Juvenile Delinquents Act was still in force. They found that rates of detention at arrest in five major cities in 1981-82 varied widely, from detention of 18% of juveniles arrested in Toronto to 63% in Edmonton. Factors affecting the probability of detention included "legal" variables (the prior record of the juvenile, the seriousness of the offence, and a history of failure to appear for court); a "socio-legal" variable ("lack of community roots"), and "extra-legal" variables (the gender and age of the juvenile, whether s/he had previously been detained, and, in Winnipeg only, whether s/he was an aboriginal).

If the youth is not arrested, attendance at court can be compelled by an Appearance Notice (issued by police and later confirmed by a Justice of the Peace, when the charges are laid), or by a summons issued by a Justice of the Peace when the charges are laid. These documents specify the nature of the charge(s) and the time, date and location of the court at which the young persons is required to attend. It is left up to the young person to comply.

If the youth is arrested, in considering whether continued detention is appropriate, the Criminal Code requires the arresting officer (S. 497) or the Officer In Charge of the police custody facility (S. 498) to assess whether detention is required to:

i.   establish the identity of the person,
ii.   secure or preserve evidence of or relating to the offence,
iii.   prevent the continuation or repetition of the offence or the commission of another offence, or because the officer has reason to believe

(b)   that, if the person is released from custody, the person will fail to attend court....

In making this assessment, the police typically consider the personal history of the accused (any prior breaches, education, family, and employment), the circumstances of the specific charge, and the victim's reaction (Bala, Weiler, et al., 1994). One Canadian study found that an "uncooperative" accused is more likely to be held in custody by the police (Hagan & Morden, 1981).

As an alternative to continued detention, the Criminal Code provides three different methods by which police can release an accused youth from custody. These methods, and the criteria for their use, are the same for young offenders as for adults, and vary in applicability, depending on the seriousness of the alleged offence and whether or not the youth was arrested with a warrant. First, police may release the youth on an Appearance Notice, or with the intention of having a summons issued. Second, they may release the youth by way of a document called a Promise to Appear. Third, the police can release on a Recognizance which requires the suspect to formally acknowledge a debt to the Crown for an amount up to $500 which may or may not require a deposit. The police forces which we interviewed said that a recognizance is rarely or never used with young offenders. The Promise to Appear can be accompanied by an Undertaking, in which the youth agrees to conditions on the release such as limitations on movement or association.

The summons and appearance notice

The summons and appearance notice may be used to compel appearance for less serious offences, which make up the majority of youth-related crimes. They are the only methods of

468

compelling appearance that do not require arresting the young person and bringing him or her back to the police station, although they can also be used to release a youth after arrest and police custody. According to our interviewees, they are rarely used in Canada with young offenders. Almost two-thirds (62%) of the police agencies which we interviewed never use summonses with young persons, or do so rarely. 41% said that they used summonses for minor offences. Only 4% use them with most offences.

When we asked why the summons was not used, or rarely used, with young persons, many officers offered no reason except that it was not the procedure used in their police service. When reasons were given for arresting rather than using summonses with young persons, the main one cited was the need to take him or her to the police station in order to conduct a proper investigation. This would typically involve establishing identity, taking a statement, possibly fingerprinting, possibly notifying the parents, and completion of one or more forms, all of which can be done much more satisfactorily in a police station than in the street or police car. Another reason given for not using summonses was the difficulty of tracking the youth in order to serve the summons (which must be done by an officer in person, not by mail). This reason was cited more often in large metropolitan police services, which deal with significant numbers of transient youth.

When we asked about the use of appearance notices with young persons, none of the police services which we interviewed said that they use them frequently. Their answers universally exhibited a lack of enthusiasm for the appearance notice, as for the summons, as a means of compelling attendance of young persons. As with the summons, the main reason which officers gave for the non-use of appearance notices is the need to arrest and bring the youth to the police station in order to investigate the incident. Another reason cited was that often a youth is apprehended in the company of peers, and it is necessary to arrest in order to separate him or her from the others in order to elicit some degree of co-operation, since youth are generally reluctant to be seen co-operating with police. A third reason for the preference for making the arrest was not stated explicitly, but seems to us to be implicit in officers' views that taking the youth to the police station represents a form of informal action (i.e. an alternative to diversion or charging). It seems that, in some circumstances, arresting the youth and taking him or her to the police station, then releasing without charge, is seen by some officers as more of a "consequence" than releasing at the scene but less than referring to alternative measures or laying a charge. It is, in effect, a form of "formal warning", which may impress the youth with the unacceptability of his or her conduct, without the necessity of subjecting him or her to a formal charge.

Release on a Promise to Appear (PTA)

Many police agencies rely on the Promise to Appear to compel the attendance at court of young persons who have been arrested and taken to the police station. A majority (60%) of police agencies said that they release on a PTA whenever they have taken a youth into custody temporarily, but continued detention is unnecessary. A major reason for this is that the PTA is used in conjunction with an Officer in Charge (OIC) undertaking (discussed below), which imposes conditions on the accused, and which cannot be used with release on a summons or appearance notice.

Release on a PTA with an Officer in Charge Undertaking

Sixty percent of the agencies in our sample said that they use a Promise to Appear with an OIC Undertaking to release young persons who have been arrested and charged. Various conditions are attached, under the authority of S. 499 of the Criminal Code. About one-quarter (26%) of those agencies that use undertakings attach a *no go* condition. This refers to a youth being restricted from going to a certain place or area. This could include places such as donut shops, schools, neighbourhoods, or shopping malls. Just over one-third (36%) of police agencies indicated they commonly attach a *no association* clause to the undertaking. This restricts the youth from coming in contact with certain specified individuals. For example, this clause may be added in cases of assault (to stay away from the victim), gang-related crime (to stay away from fellow gang members), or crimes committed in groups (to separate the co-accused). About one-quarter (24%) of police agencies told us they commonly attach a condition to *keep the peace and be of good behaviour*. The precise meaning of this clause seems to be somewhat contentious. Many officers indicated that it is a very difficult clause to enforce as it is open to almost any interpretation. Officers in 19% of the agencies which we interviewed commonly attach a condition to youth-related undertakings stipulating *no alcohol or drugs*. This condition is commonly attached when the young person committed the crime under the influence of either alcohol or drugs or there is other evidence of substance abuse. Only 2% of the agencies in our sample indicated they commonly attach a condition prohibiting possession of a weapon. Many officers indicated this condition is much more frequently used with adults than with youths.

The *curfew* condition refers to a time limit set for the young person to be at home. The curfew is usually set with specific starting and stopping times, such as dawn to dusk or 7:00 pm to 7:00 am. Some officers said that they do not have the authority to attach a curfew to an Undertaking. The curfew is not specifically authorized by S. 499, although arguably it could be justified under the catch-all S. 499(h): "any other condition…that the officer in charge considers necessary to ensure the safety and security of any victim of or witness to the offence." Another condition that interviewees mentioned is the requirement to *attend school*. In some cases, the youth is committing crimes during school hours, and, upon consultation with the school, officers have discovered the youth is frequently absent. In those circumstances, officers indicated they will attach a condition of attending school. This is not authorized by the Criminal Code, although provincial education legislation may provide the authority.

Many officers seemed to attach considerable significance to the conditions contained in an undertaking. They see these conditions as relatively precise, immediate, enforceable constraints on the young person's future behaviour, and immediate, concrete consequences (sanctions) for the youth's criminal act. These are contrasted with what they see as the remote, delayed, unpredictable, and perhaps inappropriate constraints and sanctions which may (or may not) be imposed eventually by the Youth Court and correctional system.

Detention for a judicial interim release hearing

The final, and most intrusive, option for compelling appearance is detention for a Judicial Interim Release (JIR) hearing. When asked under what circumstances they use pre-trial detention of youth, a large majority of police agencies (82%) answered that they *follow the law* when determining whether a young person will be detained or released. They tended to characterize the decision to detain or release as relatively non-discretionary, determined by the provisions of the Criminal Code, and by the interpretations of the Criminal Code supplied to them in training and by their superiors.

Officers in almost half of the police agencies (46%) in our sample consider detaining a young person who is a *repeat offender*. Some officers indicated this consideration would come into play if the youth had committed the *same* crime previously. However, the clear majority suggested that any lengthy prior record would make them more likely to detain. Although this was not mentioned explicitly, the implicit rationale here seems to be that there is an indication of a propensity to re-offend if released. A special type of repeat offender is one who has a record of *multiple breaches* which can include breaches of probation, undertakings, or bail conditions. Officers in 36% of the police agencies indicated that they considered this as a reason to detain a young person. Similar rationales were provided to those given for detaining a repeat offender. Officers in 26% of the sample mentioned detaining youths who still have charges before the courts. In other words, they were released on a prior offence and have committed another offence before their first court appearance, or during their trial, for the previous offence.

Officers in 28% of our sample of police agencies indicated that they would detain a young person in order to get *bail conditions* at the JIR hearing: that is, in expectation that the youth will be released by the judge or justice of the peace on conditions suggested by the police.

Almost one-quarter of the police agencies indicated they would detain a young person who was intoxicated or *under the influence* of drugs. In several instances, officers indicated they did not have any other place to put the young person, as the parents could not take care and control of the young person, since they were themselves intoxicated, and/or that there were no detoxification facilities for youth in their jurisdiction. This scenario was cited by police in all types of community and in virtually all provinces and territories. In many cases, police expressed great concern about releasing a young person who was intoxicated, on grounds of the youth's own safety. In jurisdictions that have high rates of adolescent drug and alcohol consumption, officers also expressed concern about their own legal liability in releasing an intoxicated young person without parental supervision.

A rationale for detaining a young person which is closely related to intoxication is the *best interests of the youth*. Officers in 20% of the sample of police agencies gave this as a reason for detention. Other circumstances (than intoxication) that would fall under this category would be an officer unable to find a responsible adult, or to make arrangements with social services, to take care and control of a young person. In some provinces and territories, once a young person reaches the age of 14, it can be difficult for the police to have social services place the young person in a foster home if s/he has never been previously placed. Several officers indicated that social services will not take a young person into custody who is over the age of 14.

Several other kinds of reasons for detention of youth were given less frequently. 3% of police agencies indicated they detained a young person *to remove them from prostitution*. Another 3% indicated they detained young persons due to their *attitude*. Finally, 6% of agencies indicated they would detain a young person if the incident was *gang-related*.

The reasons given by police officers for detaining youth fall into three broad categories. The first includes reasons related to law enforcement, narrowly defined, and concern ensuring appearance in court, establishing the identity of the accused, and protecting evidence and witnesses. The second group of reasons could be summarized as "detention for the good of the youth". These include detaining youth who are intoxicated, who do not have a safe or secure home to be released to, and whom social services will not or cannot accommodate, or who are prostitutes. In these circumstances, police find themselves acting, not as law enforcement officials, but as staff of the "only 24-hour emergency service in town".[4] The third type of rationale treats detention as another kind of police disposition – that is, as another in the repertoire of measures which police can take in order to administer a sanction or "meaningful consequence" for a youth's illegal behaviour. This view seems to underlie some officers' statements that they will detain a repeat offender or a youth with multiple breaches, or a youth with a "bad attitude", or a youth in a gang-related incident. A variant of this is the use of detention and the JIR hearing to get judicial bail conditions, in order to impose immediate control on the young person, and, in some cases, to facilitate the work of monitoring programs for high-risk youth, such as the Serious Habitual Offenders Program (SHOP).

Summary

Our discussions with police concerning their use of discretion in decisions whether to arrest, whether to charge, use informal action, or divert, and how to compel appearance at court when a charge is laid, suggest to us that police officers (and police services) tend to see their legal powers as providing, in combination, a multidimensional repertoire of options for "resolving", or disposing of, an incident.

Police officers appear to have two main objectives in deciding upon a disposition for an incident. One is to satisfy the requirements of traditional law enforcement: to investigate the incident, identify and apprehend the perpetrator(s), and assemble the necessary evidence if there is to be a prosecution. Their other, less explicit, objective appears to be to deliver an appropriate sanction, or "consequence", semi-independently of the Youth Court and correctional system. Officers repeatedly stressed the importance of youths' experiencing appropriate consequences for their illegal actions, and many, but by no means all, expressed scepticism about the ability of the courts and correctional system to do so; and therefore, the necessity of their dispensing meaningful consequences. This is not to suggest any impropriety or illegality in the actions of police, but rather to suggest that their own view of the police function in preventing, responding to, and suppressing youth crime is somewhat more expansive than the traditional view of police merely as law enforcement agents. Particularly in metropolitan jurisdictions, police officers tended to contrast unfavourably the perceived remoteness of the Crown and Youth Court, and the cumbersome and slow nature of their proceedings, with their own proximity to the reality of street crime, their own ability to deliver swift sanctions, and their familiarity with the circumstances and needs of individual young offenders.

On the basis of our discussions with police, it is possible to construct a list of the consequences, or sanctions, usually applied by police in dealing with a young person who they believe on reasonable grounds has committed an offence. From least to most severe, these are:

1. Take no further action.
2. Give an informal warning.
3. Involve the parents.
4a Give a formal warning; and/or
4b. Arrest, take to the police station, and release without charge.
5a. Arrest, take to the police station, and refer to pre-charge alternative measures; or
5b. Lay a charge without arrest by way of an appearance notice or summons, then recommend for post-charge alternative measures.
6. Arrest, charge, and release on an appearance notice, a summons, or (more commonly) a PTA without conditions.
7. Arrest, charge, and release on a PTA with conditions on an OIC Undertaking.
8. Arrest, charge, and detain for a JIR hearing.

Apart from these two main objectives – law enforcement and informal sanctioning – a third objective of police action arises from what police see as their crime prevention and social welfare responsibilities – responsibilities which in some cases they would prefer not to assume, but feel that they are forced to do so by the inadequacy of existing social services. On some occasions, police will refer a youth to a diversion program, not as a sanction, but in order to address the youth's perceived needs – whether these needs are directly related to the crime, or are seen as problems with which the youth needs assistance. Furthermore, when a youth has been arrested, an officer may feel, in some circumstances, that it would be irresponsible to release the youth back "out on the street", but is unable to contact the parents, or the parents are unable, unwilling or unsuitable to take custody, and no agency can be found that will take care and control of the youth. Circumstances which are seen as involving a risk to the youth's well-being include intoxication, involvement in prostitution, or a dangerous home environment. In these circumstances, the officer feels constrained to detain the youth; and research on bail hearings suggests that the judge may then approve continued detention, also for welfare reasons (Doob & Cesaroni, 2002, pp. 139-146). In many jurisdictions, police said that this expedient is forced on them by the lack of suitable facilities and agencies for youth.

Notes:

1 Preparation of this chapter was supported by Social Sciences and Humanities Research Council of Canada Standard Research Grant No. 410-2000-0361 and Doctoral Fellowship No. 752-2002-1071.

2 In the "Crown screening" provinces of British Columbia, Quebec, and New Brunswick, when police wish to charge a young person, they make a recommendation to the Crown, which then makes the final decision.

3 Most of the interviews were conducted and analyzed by Schulenberg, as part of her doctoral dissertation at the University of Waterloo.

4 Similar considerations arise at judicial interim release hearings; research on this is reviewed in Doob and Cesaroni, 2002, pp. 139-146.

References

Bala, N., Weiler, R., Copple, P., Smith, R.B., Hornick, J.P., & Paetsch, J.J. (1994). *A Police Reference Manual on Youth and Violence*. Ottawa: Canadian Research Institute for Law and the Family and the Solicitor General of Canada.

Bala, N., Hornick, J.P., McCall, M.L., & Clarke, M.E. (1994). *State Responses to Youth Crime: A Consideration of Principles*. Ottawa: Department of Justice Canada.

Black, D., & Reiss, A.J. Jr. (1970). Police control of juveniles. *American Sociological Review 35*: 63-77.

Braithwaite, J. (1989). *Crime, Shame and Reintegration*. New York: Cambridge University Press.

Carrington, P. J. (1999). Trends in youth crime in Canada, 1977-1996. *Canadian Journal of Criminology 41(1)*: 1-32.

Carrington, P. J., Moyer, S., & Kopelman, F. (1986). *The Determinants of Pre-dispositional Detention and Release under the Juvenile Delinquents Act*. Ottawa: Ministry of the Solicitor General of Canada.

Carrington, P.J., Moyer, S., & Kopelman, F. (1988). Factors affecting pre-dispositional detention and release under the Juvenile Delinquents Act. *Journal of Criminal Justice 16*: 463-476.

Carrington, P.J., & Moyer, S. (1994). Trends in youth crime and police response, pre-and post-YOA. *Canadian Journal of Criminology 36(1)*: 1-28.

Cordner, G. W. (1989). The Police on Patrol. In D.J. Kenny (Ed.) *Police and Policing*. New York, NY: Praeger Publishers.

Dantzker, M.L., & Mitchell, M.P. (1998). *Understanding Today's Police*. Canadian ed. Scarborough, Ont.: Prentice Hall.

Doob, A.N., & Cesaroni, C. (2002). *Youth Crime and the Youth Justice System in Canada*. Toronto: Centre of Criminology, University of Toronto.

Engler, C., & Crowe, S. (2000). Alternative Measures in Canada, 1998-99. *Juristat 20 (6)*. Catalogue No. 85-002. Ottawa: Canadian Centre for Justice Statistics, Statistics Canada.

Ericson, R.V. (1982). *Reproducing Order: A Study of Police Patrol Work*. Toronto: University of Toronto Press.

Ericson, R.V., & Haggerty, K.D. (1997). *Policing the Risk Society*. Toronto: University of Toronto Press.

Griffiths, C.T., & Verdun-Jones, S.N. (1994). *Canadian Criminal Justice*. 2nd ed. Toronto: Harcourt Brace.

Hackler, J., & Don, K. (1990). Estimating system biases: Crime indices that permit comparison across provinces. *Canadian Journal of Criminology 32(2)*: 243-264.

Hagan, J., & Morden, C.P. (1981). The Police Decision to Detain: A Study of Legal Labelling and Police Deviance. In C.D. Shearing, (ed.), *Organizational Police Deviance: Its Structure and Control*. Toronto: Butterworths.

Hornick, J.P., Caputo, T., Hastings, R., Knoll, P.J., Bertrand, L.D., Paetsch, J.J., Stroeder, L., & Maguire, A.O. (1996). *A Police Reference Manual on Crime Prevention and Diversion with Youth*. Cat. No. JS42-75/1996E. Ottawa: Canadian Research Institute of Law and the Family and the Solicitor General Canada.

Klinger, D.A. (1996). Quantifying Law in Police-Citizen Encounters. *Journal of Quantitative Criminology 12(4)*: 391-415.

Kowalski, M. (1999). *Alternative Measures for Youth in Canada. Juristat 19(8)*. Catalogue No. 85-002. Ottawa: Canadian Centre for Justice Statistics, Statistics Canada.

Law Reform Commission of Canada. (1988). *Compelling Appearance, Interim Release and Pre-Trial Detention*. Working Paper No. 57. Ottawa: Law Reform Commission of Canada.

Lundman, R.J. (1993). *Prevention and Control of Juvenile Delinquency*. 2nd ed. New York: Oxford.

Marinelli, J. (2002). Youth Custody and Community Services in Canada, 2000/01. *Juristat 22(8)*. Catalogue No. 85-002. Ottawa: Canadian Centre for Justice Statistics, Statistics Canada.

Meehan, A.J. (1993). Internal Police Records and the Control of Juveniles. *British Journal of Criminology 33(4)*: 504-524.

Mueller, D.G., & Heck, C. (1997). "The Neutral Zone as One Example of Police-Community Problem Solving." In Q.C. Thurman & E.F. McGarrell, (eds.), *Community Policing in a Rural Setting*. Cincinnati, OH: Anderson.

Platt, P. (1991). *A Police Guide to the Young Offenders Act*. Toronto: Butterworths Canada Ltd.

Sampson, R.J., & Laub, J.H. (1993). *Crime in the Making: Pathways and Turning Points through Life.* Cambridge, MA: Harvard University Press.

Schissel, B. (1993). *Social Dimensions of Canadian Youth Justice.* Toronto: Oxford University Press.

Shearing, C.D. (1984). *Dial-A-Cop: A Study of Police Mobilization.* Toronto: Centre of Criminology, University of Toronto.

Steer, D. (1970). *Police Cautions – A Study in the Exercise of Police Discretion.* Oxford: Basil Blackwell.

Task Force on Youth Justice. (1996). *A Review of the Young Offenders Act and the Youth Justice System in Canada.* Ottawa: Report of the Federal-Provincial-Territorial Task Force on Youth Justice for the Standing Committee on Justice and Legal Affairs of the House of Commons.

Tittle, C. R. (1980). *Sanctions and Social Deviance.* New York: Praeger.

Varma, K.N. (2002). Exploring 'youth' in court: An analysis of decision-making in youth court bail hearings. *Canadian Journal of Criminology 44(2)*: 143-164.

Webster, J. (1970). Police task and time study. *Journal of Criminal Law, Criminology, and Police Science 61*: 94-100.

PART V1

THE FUTURE

The Police and the Diverse Society

Challenges

18

The Police and The Diverse Society: Trends and Prospects in the 21st Century

Stephen E. Nancoo

Introduction

Issues having to do with the police and the diverse society profoundly impact on all of us as citizens, taxpayers, practitioners and potential victims. In the twenty-first century, some of the compelling, policing questions we need to address are: What will the crime and societal environment be like in the 21st century? What emerging future conditions are likely to affect policing? How are we to prepare for the future of policing in a diverse society?

Futures Research

For a long time, the arrival of the 21st century has stood for the future and what we shall make of it (Naisbitt and Aburdene, 1990). In preparing for that future, futurists have written a number of studies, some of the most significant include: Toffler (1990); Naisbitt and Aburdene, (1990); Kennedy, (1993) and Sanders 1998). Within recent times, increasing attention is also being paid to the future of policing. In terms of American policing, Tafoya's path-breaking work (1986) employs a Delphi technique that integrates the forecasts of a panel of law enforcement experts.

481

More recently, Bayley (1994) offers a significant comparative analysis and a blueprint for the future of policing as one of society's most basic institutions. Klofas and Stojkovic (1995) take a look at the much broader canvas of the future of crime and justice. In the Canadian context, the most significant works that command our attention are: Loree, (1989), Normandeau and Leighton, (1990); Bayley (1991); Nancoo (1993, 2000).

Even in the best of times, musing about the future is a difficult task in which one could either overlook profound issues or engage in an exercise of pure fantasy. Futurists are certainly restricted by the realization that: the future is neither fixed nor predetermined, the future is not predictable, and individual choices and actions can influence and change the future (Tafoya, 1990).

This chapter will examine **The Police and the Diverse Society: Trends and Prospects in the 21st Century.** First, we will review some of the trends in the external and internal environments and analyze their implications for the future strategic direction of policing. Second, we would explore how as part of the strategic planning process, visioning may influence the outcomes and our conclusions about the future. Defining the police mission and clarifying values become fundamentally important exercises in the context of setting the future, strategic direction of policing the diverse society. Considering these processes, we would trace the emergence of a paradigm shift from the traditional form of policing, and delineate the nature and characteristics of the emerging paradigm of community policing.

Environmental Scanning: Internal and External Trends

In a world where the rate of change is accelerating, monitoring the environment allows one to proactively anticipate and creatively lead and manage the rapidly increasing changes. Environmental scanning provides futurists with a method of identifying future trends that fundamentally influence or alter an organization and its environment. "Environmental scanning is where strategic thinking begins. Because the issues and challenges any organization will face in the future are perking in its environment today, it's important to find ways to see and organize that information now" (Sanders 1998:161). Demographics, aboriginal issues, ethnicity and immigration, economics, political and social forces, organization and management and technology are some of the identified trends that are shaping the future of the diverse Canadian society, policing and police organizations.

Demographics

The aging population: Low fertility and increasing life expectancy trends suggest an aging of the Canadian population. This aging of the population will witness the emergence of a labour force consisting of more women and older Canadians.

Ethnicity and Immigration: Canada encompasses a diversity of racial, ethnic and religious groups, which can be broadly classified as: the aboriginal peoples, charter groups (descendants of British and French and ethnic minorities (visible and non visible minorities).

Aboriginal Peoples: With an average life expectancy that is shorter than the Canadian average and fertility rate about fifty per cent higher than the rest of the population, the Aboriginal population is becoming younger. Aboriginals, who saw a rapid decline of their population from one hundred percent following the arrival of the colonizers, are now increasing in their proportional representation of the Canadian population. With half of the native population living in urban centers, indications are that an increasing number of young native persons will move to urban areas in the future. A serious social issue for all Canadians is the fact that there is currently an over-representation of Aboriginal peoples in prison. "Public inquiries in Alberta, Saskatchewan and Manitoba found that the aboriginal people were more likely than non-Aboriginals to be denied bail, to be held in pre-trial detention, to be charged with multiple offenses, to be given little time with their lawyer and to be incarcerated upon conviction" (Policing in British Columbia Commission of Inquiry, 1994).

Immigrants: The aging of the Canadian population triggered the public policy decision to increase immigration levels, which also saw a dramatic shift in the dominance of source countries for our immigrants. Whereas in the 1960's immigration to Canada consisted of people mainly from the United Kingdom, United States and Europe, changes in immigration laws in 1968 facilitated the arrival of people in Canada from a wider range of countries, especially Asia, Latin America, the Caribbean, and Africa.

The trend toward an increasingly multicultural community as evidenced by the greater diversity of languages, cultures, religions, national and racial origins will likely increase. In his research of Canadian population trends, Samuel (2000:22) notes that the total visible minority population in 1996 was 3.2 million and this is expected to increase to over 8 million by 2016. Another significant trend is that the majority of new Canadians tend to settle in the densely populated metropolitan centers of Toronto, Vancouver, Montreal, Edmonton and Calgary.

The family: The structure of the Canadian family is in a state of flux. Most Canadian families have two incomes, with both spouses working. Projections are that there will be a continuing increase in the number of single parent families, the majority of which will be headed by women.

Technology: The technological revolution is altering social organizations with the explosive growth in computers and computer literacy and advances in artificial intelligence and mass communications. The organization, national and global electronic infrastructures, the information superhighway, will continue to reshape what we do and how we do it.

Globalization: Globalization is a defining feature of the world in which we live. With globalization there is the growth of the information economy, the trend toward electronic commerce, the digitalization of cultural products and the "death of distance". In economic and social terms, we have created a global "ecology" in which events in one part of the global system are felt everywhere, (Canada 2005, pp. 12-13). In the context of policing, with globalization there is transnational crime, cyber crime and borderless crime.

Internal and Other trends: Other significant issues that are impacting on the police in its operations within the diverse Canadian society include a growing demand for police accountability, scarce financial resources, a growth in private policing, the changing nature of crime trends, regionalization of small police services, greater civilianization of personnel and a reorientation of the nature, content and methods of training.

Implications for Policing

Each of the identified environmental trends will have profound implications for the police and the diverse society.
Accompanying the **aging of the population** will be an increase in the fear of crime among the elderly. As a consequence, there will be an increase in non-crime related calls for service from the police. Because of their greater vulnerability, the elderly will increasingly become the targets of incidents of fraud and non-violent offenses.

Mirroring this societal trend, police services are also aging, resulting in the forecast that clusters of police officers will opt for early retirement. As a consequence, police organizations will have an opportunity to increase the recruitment of qualified aboriginals, visible minorities and women, significant groups that are currently underrepresented in policing. This societal and organizational population aging will result in a desirable increase in the number of members of underrepresented groups occupying senior policing positions.

In relation to the **aboriginal people** condition and the implication for policing and police organizations the report, *Closing the Gap* states that there is "an overwhelming desire among aboriginal people for greater control over policing in their communities and for the development of programs tailored to their particular cultures and values" (Policing in British Columbia Commission of Inquiry, 1994). Informed observers have expressed a cautionary note that the traditional model of policing may not meet with the needs and values of aboriginal people (Depew, 1993; Policing in British Columbia Commission of Inquiry, 1994). The public policy conclusions suggest, therefore, a continuation and implementation of the trend towards recognition of aboriginal people right to establish their own policing objectives (Policing in British Columbia Commission of Inquiry, 1994) and the creation of independent, aboriginal policing services.

From a philosophical standpoint, it is expected that aboriginal policing organizations will embrace community policing as the model that is most consistent with their traditions and history (Depew, 1993; Nancoo, 1993, 2000). The future national thrust in aboriginal policing is appropriately captured in the comment: "We believe it is important to establish a good relationship between police forces and aboriginal people. The objectives of our recommendations are to foster the establishment of effective Aboriginal police forces, staffed with officers who will be sensitive to Aboriginal people, and to improve the manner in which non-Aboriginal forces serve Aboriginal people. Such forces, using a community policing approach, will provide services that are culturally appropriate and support the deep commitment to justice that was frequently raised with us by aboriginal presenters" Policing in British Columbia Commission of Inquiry, 1994).

The ethnic, cultural, linguistic, religious and racial diversity occasioned by **immigration** and an increasing number of visible minorities present a great challenge for policing and police organizations. Commissions of Inquiry in various provinces have identified the need for improving race relations between the police and minorities as a priority. Consequently, organizations will have to effectively respond to the greater need for cross-cultural sensitivity and race relations training. There is also the need for strategies by police services that provide for greater participation by minority groups in the policing of our diverse communities. Recognition of this need is manifested in the philosophical commitment to the idea that the police should be representative of the community it serves (*Ontario Police Services Act, 1990*; Policing in British Columbia Commission of Inquiry, 1994) and the establishment of community advisory groups and other mediating mechanisms to facilitate relationships between the police and ethnic communities will continue (Samuel, 1995; Normandeau and Leighton, 1990, Nancoo, 1993 & 2000).

The changing family structure of two working parents and the increasing trend towards single parent families headed predominantly by women suggest a number of challenges for police work and police organizations. The implications for police work are: (1) An increasing number of unsupervised "latch-key kids," creating additional work for the police. (2) The elderly will require a wider range of police services because of fewer offspring caring for the aged. (3) Higher rates of crime against vulnerable groups: women, children and the elderly. (4) An increase in residential break-ins at unoccupied or unsupervised homes is likely. (5) The increase of women in the workforce will probably lead to an increase in crime for women, especially white collar crime (Normandeau and Leighton, 1990; Toronto Police Force Environmental Scan, 2000). Police departments will of necessity have to forge strategic partnerships with other organizations and agencies providing services to victims, vulnerable groups at risk of victimization, and offenders under community supervision.

As **technology** changes, new crimes and new methods of combating crime emerge. For instance, the computer has given rise to computer crime. The computer will greatly facilitate the internationalization of crime leading to increased corporate crime, fraud, and money laundering. On the other hand, the computer also helps in catching conventional criminals; data on criminal styles of operation have provided suspects and led to arrests and convictions in many cases. For an elaboration on the role of technology see Chapter 9 of this book.

Globalization presents special challenges to policing. In order to cope with the new world of transnational[1], borderless crime police services have to think globally and act locally. Greater attempts have to be made to integrate policing efforts and to embark upon transnational policing initiatives to combat transnational crime and acts of terrorism.

In terms of the diverse society, hate crimes are becoming an emerging issue of concern and it is the view of some that action is necessary in order to prevent perpetrators from abusing the information highway with their message of hate. Keeping abreast of technological innovations to prevent and detect crime will motivate police services to provide officers with specialized training as well as enhance the trend towards civilianization with the hiring of experts and specialized consultants. In the recruitment of civilians, police organizations should make every effort to be inclusive by hiring visible minorities and aboriginals.

Vision, Mission and Values: Creating a Desirable Future

Having reviewed environmental trends and their implications for policing, the question of where are we going could be predicated on two differing viewpoints. On the one hand, we could assume that the future will merely be an extension of the past or that we are the mere pawns of an uncertain future. Alternatively we could through deliberate choices attempt to invent or create the desirable future through visioning and strategic planning. Sapp suggests that "what is needed is understanding and planning. Understanding of trends and events that will shape the future is required. Planning is required to effect the changes that are needed to influence the trends and future" (Sapp, 1992, p.196.) Police organizations across Canada have begun the process of developing strategic plans, a trend which is likely to increase as police organizations deliberately engage in the process of strategically thinking about the future (Nancoo, 1995).

Creating a Vision

Visioning starts the strategic planning process because it serves as a driving force in inventing the organization's future. Futurists who begin the strategic planning exercise through an envisioning process believe that critical times demand transformational leaders who will focus on the designing and creating of an ideal, desirable future. Such "leaders look forward to the future. They hold in their minds visions and ideals of what can be done...Leaders breathe life into visions. They communicate their hopes and dreams so others clearly understand and accept them as their own. They show others how their values and interests will be served by the long term vision of the future" (Kouzes and Posner: 1987). Vision answers the important search for meaning among employees and is the fountain of the leader's power and performance.

Progressive chiefs of police and police organizations have begun the process of deliberately engaging in the setting of their own organizational vision statements. The Ontario Provincial Police, Toronto Police Service, Hamilton Police Service, Ottawa

Police Service and Peel Regional Police are cases in point. The Ontario Provincial Government outlined a vision of policing, referred to as the six principles of the *Ontario Police Services Act*. These principles are:

1) The need to ensure the safety and security of all persons and property in Ontario.
2) The importance of safeguarding the fundamental rights guaranteed by the *Canadian Charter of Rights and Freedoms and the Human Rights Code, 1981*.
3) The need for cooperation between the providers of police services and the communities they serve.
4) The importance of respect for victims of crime and understanding of their needs.
5) The need for sensitivity to the pluralistic, multiracial and multicultural character of Ontario society.
6) The need to ensure that police forces are representative of the communities they serve.

Defining the Police Mission

In the 21st century, policing organizations and their stakeholders will have to develop well-defined, focused mission statements. Since there are competing policing strategies, a clear, central mission statement will influence the organization's macro-strategy, resource allocation and style of policing. To illustrate, the mission statement of Hamilton Police Service "is to serve and protect in partnership with the community." Such a mission statement connotes its distinctive model and style of policing. It is different, for example, from the sort of mission statement of an organization beholden to the traditional model of policing as expressed in the case of one police organization "to enforce the laws of the country".

Values

All decisions are based on values and a fundamentally important aspect of the strategic planning process is its emphasis on values. Values are enduring beliefs, or a system of beliefs, that a particular mode of conduct is preferable to an opposite or converse mode of conduct or end-state of existence. Values guide the behaviour of an organization and its employees.

Police organizations are beginning to make explicit their values, which will determine, among other things, the style in which policing will be pursued. With the rapidity of societal change, formulating and publishing these values will provide a useful anchor for policing organizations and personnel.

A number of common themes have emerged among police organizations that have taken the critical step of developing values statements. Some of these commonly shared values among disparate police organizations are to: protect human life as the highest priority, perform duties with the highest ethical standards; share responsibility with the community for improving the quality of life; working in partnership with the community to prevent crime; treat victims of crime with compassion and sensitivity; empower employees; create a professionally, effective and satisfying police service and seek excellence in each activity undertaken.

In creating a vision, defining the mission, clarifying the core organizational values and in formulating strategic plans to effect organizational change, the police service must inform itself of the total quality management and quality leadership approaches. Essentially the total quality management and quality leadership approaches embrace the following fundamental characteristics:

1. Customer/client focus: Everyone in the organization determines who the customer/client is. The analysis of the core competencies that are in the vision, the organization's strengths and weaknesses, opportunities and threats, are an essential part of selecting the customer/client needs that must be served.

2. Total involvement: Everyone works to satisfy the customer/client through continuous improvement processes. Making all managers and employees part of the improvement process increases the acceptance of change.

3. Continuous improvement processes through problem solving and fact based decision-making. A problem-solving approach encourages the use of data to drive decision-making. The emphasis on measurement of customer-client needs and

expectations and the measurement of the capability of meeting those needs form the basis of Total Quality Management (Domb, 1993; Couper and Lobitz, 1991; Nancoo, 1993, 2000).

In the 21st century, the quality movement will of necessity assume new dimensions. The first quality revolution focused on the product. This was followed by the addition of customer and client satisfaction to the quality movement. Quality relationship with employees is the next frontier of an integrated quality movement involving the tripartite components of product/service client/customer and empowered employees in the 21st Century.

Towards a Paradigm Shift in Policing

Consistent with the conclusions emerging from the strategic planning process is an increased recognition in the policing community that a shift from the predominantly traditional form of policing to a new paradigm of policing is necessary. Scholars in both Canada and the United States have underlined the serious shortcomings of the traditional model of policing that continues to be the **modus operandi** of many North American police departments.

On the basis of research over the last 20 years, American scholars have identified the limitations of the traditional model: as "its predominantly reactive stance toward crime control; its nearly exclusive reliance on arrests as a means of reducing crime and controlling disorder; its inability to develop and sustain close working relationships with the community in controlling crime; and its stifling and ultimately unsuccessful methods of bureaucratic control" (Mark Moore, 1994). In the Canadian context, Murphy (1988) observes that "innovation through imitation encourages the tendency to import wholesale from the United States policing philosophies, technologies, and strategies, which in some cases are inappropriate for the Canadian environment."

The strategic planning process with its drive towards creating a vision, defining the police mission scanning the environment and clarifying the values of police services focused attention on the inadequacies of the traditional method of policing. These processes also underlined the need for new approaches to policing and advanced the case for fundamental organizational change to police organizations.

What should the future of policing in the diverse Canadian society be like?

Researchers have observed that a paradigm shift from the traditional form of policing to community policing is developing in the philosophical thinking, strategies and operational practices of a number of pioneering police services. Variously described as community-based policing, community oriented policing and problem-oriented policing, community policing is portrayed as the official morality with respect to policing in Canada (Clairmont, 1992), the most progressive approach to contemporary policing (Normandeau and Leighton, 1990), the dominant ideology and organization mode of progressive policing (Murphy, 1988), a paradigm shift (Nancoo, 1993, 2000) and the new orthodoxy for cops (Eck and Rosenbaum, 1994).

There is growing consensus that community policing will be the operating philosophy of most police organizations in the 21st Century. One could quite legitimately ask why is this the case after only a brief courtship with the American-style 'professional' or "traditional" model of policing?

As more and more police organizations engage in strategic planning, they are coming to the inescapable conclusion that community policing is an idea whose time has indeed come. This is the case of Toronto Police Service, Hamilton Police, Peel Regional Police, Edmonton Police Service, Calgary Police Service, Waterloo Regional Police, Halton Regional Police Service, Ottawa Police Service, Guelph Police Service, Durham Police Service, and Halifax Police Service to identify a few.

In the long term, as we move from strategic planning to strategic leadership-management, and total quality management, police organizations will strive to institutionalize the community policing paradigm. This belief is premised on the view that both total quality management and community policing share the same underlying conceptual frameworks of client focus and client satisfaction, fact-based decision-making and problem solving and widespread employee involvement and participation.

Unlike the United States with its continuing debate on differences between community policing and problem oriented policing, in the Canadian environment problem solving is invariably considered as an integral part of the community policing philosophy. Enlightened police chiefs have given their support to this idea.

The environmental scanning process involves the participation of both the public and the politicians, who have supported the democratic notions of partnerships and accountability, concepts integrally linked to the community policing paradigm.

There is increasing confidence among police organizations because, according to Bayley (1994) Canada has considerable experience with community policing that is readily available within many police organizations. This is especially the case as it applies to rural policing, which as noted by Murphy (1990) "traditional small town police may soon discover that they have all along been slightly ahead of their time."

To some extent as well, Canadian police executives could not be indifferent to the debate on community policing that was taking place in the United States. Without a critical research body, and in light of the close geographical proximity, Canadian policing is inevitably susceptible to the transnational influences of American policing ideas, ideologies and strategies.

It is also important that one should not lose sight of the fact that in embracing community policing, Canadian police chiefs were also attempting to recapture their policing roots. Like many other institutions, Canadian policing was a beneficiary of the British traditions --the traditions of Robert Peel and his principles, and the traditions of such organizations as Metropolitan London Police and the Royal Irish Constabulary -- because of this country's political and institutional connections with Great Britain. These traditions include at least an awareness of Peel's principles one of which articulates the prophetic dictum that the role of the police is "to maintain at all times a relationship with the public that gives reality to the historic tradition that the police are the public and the public are the police; the police being only members of the public who are paid to give full-time attention to duties which are incumbent on every citizen, in the interests of community welfare and existence" (Nancoo, 1993).

To understand the future, it is also necessary for us to understand the past and the present. It is not unexpected therefore that in their attempt to shape their future by an appeal to their historical past, Canadian police organizations are also being pushed by the reformist temper of contemporary times, as evidenced by the community policing recommendations from commissions of inquiries and task forces. For example, Ontario Report on Race Relations and Policing Task Force (1989) and the British Columbia Commission of Inquiry into Policing (1994), both proponents of community policing, were themselves significantly influenced by today's reality of an increasingly diverse society and the reflections of advocacy groups representing various segments of this diverse society.

While the majority of police services proclaim community policing as the most appropriate approach to preventing and solving problems of crime and disorder, this is not always the case in practice. Indeed there are virile pockets of resistance to the idea in some police organizations. Furthermore, the nature of policing, even in the realm of community policing, is significantly different from Peel's conceptualization a century ago. The contemporary conceptualization of community policing involves a wider set of variables in relation to community partnerships, empowered employees and a movement away from the para-military style and structure of police organizations. In short, the realities of policing in many a police organization does not match the rhetoric of community policing espoused by police leaders.

These factors, including attempts at a re-conceptualization, in my view constitute a "re-inventing" of community policing - in a sense paralleling the "reinventing of government" themes now popular in the public administration literature - and consequently my labeling of this movement as **the new paradigm of policing**. Bayley reflected that Canadian policing faces a confrontation of paradigms - reactive containment of crime by the "thin blue line" versus proactive problem solving through the mobilization of community resources. And the widespread public proclamations of police organizations "that we have community policing too" coupled with the demands of advocacy groups allowed one researcher to conclude that "the rise of community policing represents today one of those significant changes **a paradigm shift**" (Nancoo, 1993, 2000).

What augurs well for the future is that some organizations are undertaking fundamental organizational change through their efforts at strategic planning that deliberately seek to establish strategic alliances with the communities in community policing initiatives. For example, Toronto Police Service Beyond 2000 document outlined neighborhood policing as its vision of the future, and many chiefs of police from across Canada well as such organizations as the Ontario Association of Chiefs of Police have come out in support of the idea of community policing. For example, Peel Regional Police noted in its environmental assessment (1994) that in keeping with the mission and values statement, "we are committed to community oriented policing through the practice of problem oriented policing and the development of community partnerships."

The Nature of Community Policing

Community policing is primarily a philosophy of policing. There is remarkable consensus on the philosophical basis of the new paradigm of community policing as evidenced by writers from the United States of America, Canada and Britain (Bayley, 1994; Rosenbaum, 1994; 2000; Peak and Glensor, 1996; Nancoo, 1993, 2000, 2003; Bennett, 1994, Seagrave, 1997; McKenna, 2000; and Griffiths et.al. 2001). Pivotal to this philosophy is the fundamental notion of a co-operative partnership between the police and the public in pursuit of the peace, safety and security of our communities.

The elements of this strategic partnership find expression through consultative and collaborative patterns of partnership behaviours between the police and the community. Organizations involved in the strategic planning and strategic management process are expected to engage in extensive consultations with their communities through focus groups, town hall meetings, surveys, and advisory committees. Collaborative efforts are intended to form strategic alliances with members and agencies of the community in pursuit of the goals of crime prevention and control of crime and disorder.

Given the growing diversity of our population, policing organizations of the future will seek increasingly innovative ways in encouraging citizens to become more involved in, and responsible for policing neighborhoods and communities. Included in this notion of partnership is the democratic principle that while the police should be immune from political interference in its investigations, the police are indeed accountable to the community and its democratic institutions in its policy formulation decision making and implementation processes

To accommodate the changes envisaged by the community policing philosophy, the structures and institutions of policing must be changed. "A police organization that is heavily invested in the professional model of policing - with a centralized hierarchical and bureaucratized command structure - will have difficulty creating an environment that is conducive to community policing strategies and that encourages creative problem solving" (Rosenbaum, 1994:124).

In their book *The Strategic Management of Police Departments*, Moore and Stephens (1991:103) postulate that to change to community policing, "the administrative structure would have to be changed from a functional organization to a geographic one to enable the police to develop the rapport they need with local community groups. The centralized decision-making structure would have to yield to a much flatter, more decentralized style to acknowledge the reality of the organization's dependence on the initiative and discretion of its front-line officers, and to exploit their skills."

In Canada, structural changes and decentralization in police functions are now taking place. For example, in pursuit of community policing the Toronto Police Restructuring Task Force concluded that they will accomplish their goals and strategies by "decentralizing the corporate functions necessary to assist in local problem solving." Ontario Provincial Police, Halton Regional Police, Edmonton Police Service, and Ottawa Police Service are among some of the police organizations that were engaged in restructuring processes.

To accommodate community based policing principles, the following organizational changes are recommended:

More decentralization - management decision-making and routine police operations are moved to a community neighborhood or beat level. Less bureaucracy -- decision making becomes more participatory. Less hierarchical organization -- create fewer ranks and fewer levels of organization (British Columbia Commission of Inquiry into Policing, 1994:C-7).

Canadian policing experience reflects a wide range of implementation programs and tactics in its movement from a primarily reactive and bureaucratic model of policing to a preventive, proactive-reactive, balanced, community based style of policing. It is accepted in the community policing lexicon in Canada that problem solving or problem oriented policing is a critically important strategy in implementing community policing. Problem oriented policing involves a process where problems are systematically defined and researched, then alternative solutions are explored through an interactive process involving both the community and the police.

Unlike conventional policing responses that deal with individual incidents, problem oriented aspect of community policing tends to search for the basic problem that produce the incidents. Problem oriented policing attempts to define common underlying problems that relate to repeated calls for service. "Conventional police response is to the symptoms and not the basic causes of crime, with the result that crime problems remain unresolved and continue to demand police responses. Community policing is aimed at dealing with the whole problem." (Policing in British Columbia Commission of Inquiry).

Toronto Police's elaborate Policing document Vision 2000 provides for community policing arrangement, including provision for structural change and decentralization. For some time now, Toronto Police Service experimented with foot patrols, storefronts and mini stations (Murphy, 1993). Halifax Police Service reorganized into three neigbourhood zones with consultative committees and village constables (Clairmont, 1993). Halton

Regional Police has developed its own style of proactive-reactive policing (Loree, 1993), Hamilton Police introduced differential response while Fredericton has installed a storefront operation. And many small and medium size police services like Sudbury, Sault Ste. Marie, Kitchener, Guelph, and Peterborough, Thunder Bay, Calgary, Halifax, Kingston, Belleville and Victoria have introduced a variety of community policing programs. In addition to the many municipal services, both the OPP and the R.C.M.P. are implementing community policing in small towns in Ontario and various parts of the country.

In Quebec, the Montreal Urban Community Police Service developed a new model of policing in 1996 after five years of analysis, and planning. In its report outlining the new model (Montreal Urban Community Policing, 1996:32) it is stated:

> The Neighbourhood Policing model can improve the quality of life of citizens by favouring the emergence of more dynamic neighbourhood life. Citizen involvement in finding solutions to problems and in projects to counter crime, stimulate social interaction and can reinforce social controls. Geographical responsibility and a service approach will also encourage mobilization of citizens. Finally, the establishment of partnerships with the community and local organizations as well as coordination with other municipal services will facilitate joint actions at all levels.

In Alberta, Edmonton Police Service (Braiden, 1993:211-232; Hornick et. al, 1993: 311-331) has been in the vanguard of the community policing movement in Canada. In its transformation from a traditional to a community-based policing organization, Edmonton Police Service (EPS) initiated a variety of organizational changes during its initial years. Following the identification in 1985 of 21 hot spots in the city, with 81 per cent of the calls in these areas coming from repeat addresses, the EPS introduced The Neighbourhood Foot Patrol based on the principle that policing must be based within the community. The organization also adopted a differential response model that provided for decentralized reporting outlets, problem solving and public involvement. In order to reinforce its commitment to community policing, EPS undertook a planning review and as a consequence developed a new service delivery model in 1995 based on three principles - receiving, responding and reporting (Edmonton Police Service, 1995). Another organizational review in 1998 saw the formulation of seven strategic directions for EPS with a view of reallocating resources to enhance community policing (KPMG, 1998).

The challenge for policing organizations in Canada is to move beyond the individual programs to a service-wide philosophy of community policing.

The Ontario Association of Chiefs of Police sub-committee on Community Policing has developed a model of community policing which states: community policing is not a program; it is a way of doing business – a philosophy. The model provides for five components to community policing. These are: enforcement, community development, police service re-engineering, police learning and problem solving and community-police partnerships. For an explication of the Ontario Community Policing Model, which provides an integrated, service-wide philosophy of community policing, see Chapter 3 in this book.

The importance of community in policing is also reflected in the inter-disciplinary analysis of broad social trends. One of the approaches that is currently in vogue is that advanced by communitarians. The sociologist Amitai Etzioni[2] is one of the key exponents of the communitarianism idea and in the communitarian manifesto it is noted that "our first and foremost purpose is to affirm the moral commitments of parents, young persons, neighbours and citizens...If communities are to function well, most members most of the time must discharge their responsibilities because they are committed to do so, not because they fear lawsuits, penalties or jails" (Etzioni 1993, 266).

Communitarianism emphasizes the need for citizens to fulfill their responsibilities to the community, the importance of duty, blending the strengths of government and market place solutions, the building of partnerships between private and public groups, eliciting the active participation of the community, nurturing civil society. "Communitarians support processes such as problem solving, where neighbourhoods have taken matters into their own hands, closing off streets and creating other physical barriers to disrupt the drug trade, working to overcome problems of homelessness and panhandling...This is where the objectives of communitarians overlap with those of advocates of community problem solving; the recognition that many of the answers to community problems lie not with government, but in the community at large" (Peak and Glensor, 1996:49).

Conclusion: Leadership and the New Policing Paradigm

This chapter identified some of the major trends and challenges for policing and the diverse society in the 21st century. Much is changing in policing, including a change to the community policing paradigm. The success of the police in seriously addressing the challenge of change and the issues that present themselves in the future will depend upon the quality and courage and transformational character of the police leadership. The critical dimension in the successful and acceptable paradigm shift to community policing resides in great measure on the long term, sustained commitment to innovation and change by the police leadership. Quality policing will come from a visionary leadership and the active participation of a trained and empowered workforce in the service of and in partnership with the citizens of a diverse and democratic society. Brann (2001:47) said that "Community policing marks as one of its distinct accomplishments to the contribution it makes to democratic society." The determination to make a significant difference in an environment rife with turbulence and change, problems and pressures, threats and opportunities is the essence of the leadership challenge in the new millennium.

Endnotes

[1] The author was first introduced to the concept of transnationalism, transnational organizations and their impact on nation-states by Dr. Joseph Nye at a graduate seminar at Carleton University in 1973.

[2]I am grateful to Dr. Amitai Etzioni for his elaboration of the communitarian philosophy in our discussion in Manitoba in 2004.

References

Bayley, D. (1991). *Managing the Future: Prospective Issues in Canadian Policing.* Ottawa: Ministry of the Solicitor General of Canada.

Brann, Joseph E. (2001). Community Policing and the Quality of Life. In S.E. Nancoo (Ed.), *Comparative Perspectives on Policing.* Aylmer: Issues and Themes.

Braiden, C. (1993). Community Based Policing: A Process for Change. In J. Chacko and S.E. Nancoo (Eds.), *Community Policing in Canada.* Toronto: Canadian Scholars' Press.

Chacko, James and Stephen E. Nancoo (Eds.). (1993). *Community Policing in Canada.* Toronto: Canadian Scholars' Press.

Clairmont, D. (1993). Community based policing and Organizational Change. In J. Chacko and S.E.Nancoo (Eds.), *Community Policing in Canada.* Toronto: Canadian Scholars' Press.

Couper, D. and Lobitz, S. (1991). *Quality Policing: The Madison Experience.* Washington: Police Executive Research Forum.

Deming, W. E. (1986). *Out of the Crisis.* Mass: MIT.

Depew, R. (1993).Policing Native Communities: Some Principles and Issues in Organizational Theory. In J.Chacko and S.E. Nancoo (Eds.), *Community Policing In Canada* (pp.251-268). Toronto: Canadian Scholars' Press.

Domb, E. (1993). Total Quality Management. In William Bean, *Strategic Planning That Makes Things Happen.*
. Massachusetts: HRD Press.

Edmonton Police Service. (1995). *Community Policing in Edmonton: the vision continues.* Edmonton: Edmonton Police Service.

Etzioni, Amitai. (1993). *The Spirit of Community.* New York: Crown Publishers.

Griffiths, C. T., Parent R. B., Whitelaw, B. (2000). *Community Policing in Canada.* Scarborough: Nelson Thomson

Hornick, J.P., Burrows, B.A., Phillips, D. M. & Leighton, B. (1993). An Impact Evaluation of the Edmonton Neighbourhood Foot Patrol Program. In J. Chacko and S. E. Nancoo (Eds.), *Community Policing in Canada*. Toronto: Canadian Scholars' Press.

KPMG. (1998). *1998 organizational review of the Edmonton Police Service*. Edmonton: Edmonton Police Service.

Kennedy, P. (1993). *Preparing for the twenty-first century*, Toronto: Harper Collins Publishers.

Keohane, R. and Nye, J. (1972). *Transnational Relations and World Politics*. Cambridge, MA: Harvard University Press.

Klofas, J.and Stojkovic S. (Eds.). (1995). *Crime and Justice in the year 2010*. California: Wadsworth Publishing Company.

Kouzes, J .M. and Posner B.Z. (1987). *The Leadership Challenge*. San Francisco: Josey Bass Publishers.

Loree, D. (Ed.). (1989). *Future Issues in Policing*. Ottawa: Canadian Police College.

McKenna, Paul F. (2000). *Foundations of Community Policing in Canada* Scarborough: Prentice Hall Allyn and Bacon Canada.

Moore, M. H. and Stephens, D. W. (1991). *Beyond Command and Control: The Strategic Management of Police Departments*. Washington D.C.: PERF.

Murphy, Chris (1993). The Development, Impact and Implications of Community Policing in Canada. In J. Chacko and S.E. Nancoo (Eds.), *Community Policing in Canada*.

Naisbitt, J. and Aburdene, P. 1990. *Megatrends 2000*, New York: William Morrow.

Nancoo, S E. (1993). The Future: Trends and Issues in Community Policing. In *Community Policing in Canada*. Toronto: Canadian Scholars' Press.

Nancoo, S.E. (1996). *Strategic Planning in Ontario Police Services*. Aylmer: Ontario Police College.

Nancoo, S. E. (Ed.). (2000). *21st Century Canadian Diversity*. Mississauga: Canadian Educators' Press.

Nancoo, S.E. (Ed.). (2001). *Comparative Perspectives in Policing*. Aylmer: Issues and Themes Conference.

Nancoo, S. E. (Ed.). (2002*). Community Policing in Ontario.*
    Aylmer: Issues and Themes Conference.
Normandeau, A. and Leighton, B. (1990). *A Vision of the Future
    of Policing in Canada.* Ottawa: Ministry of the Solicitor
    General of Canada.
Ontario, (1990). *Police Services Act.* Revised Statutes of Ontario.
    Queen's Printer of Ontario.
Ontario Race Relations and Policing Task Force. (1992).*The report
    of the Race Relations and Policing Task Force. Toronto:
    The Task Force.*
Ontario Provincial Police. (1995). *Organizational Review: a
    process and model for change.* Toronto: Queen's Printer.
Palmiotto, Michael J. (2000). *Community Policing.*
    Gaithersburg: Aspen Publishers, Inc.
Peak, Kenneth J. and Glensor, Ronald W. (1996). *Community
    Policing and Problem Solving.* New Jersey: Prentice Hall.
Peel Regional Police Environmental Assessment.
Policing in British Columbia Commission of Inquiry. *Closing
    the Gap.* Victoria: Government of British Columbia.
Rokeach, M. (1973). *The nature of human values.* New York: Free
    Press.
Rosenbaum, D. (Ed.). (1994). *The Challenge of Community
    Policing.* California: Sage Publications.
Sanders, T. Irene. (1998). *Strategic thinking and the new science:
    planning in the midst of chaos, complexity, and change.*
    NY: The Free Press.
Sapp, A. D. (1992). Alternative Futures. In Larry T. Hoover (Ed.),
    Police Management Issues and Perspectives. Washington:
    Police Executive Research Forum.
Seagrave, Jayne. (1997). *Introduction to Policing in Canada.*
    Scarborough: Prentice Hall, Canada.
Tafoya, W. L. (1986). *A delphi forecast of the future of law
    enforcement.* Doctoral Dissertation, University of Maryland
    College. Ann Arbor: University Microfilms International.
Toffler, A. and Toffler. H. (1990). *Powershifts: Knowledge,
    wealth, and violence at the edge of the 21st century.* New
    York: Bantam Books.

503

19

Challenges

Stephen E. Nancoo and Matt Torigian

In this Chapter, some additional, fundamental challenges facing Canadian policing in the 21st Century will be explored. The issues that will be considered are: globalization and transnational policing, national security and terrorism, racial profiling, public policing-private security, and organizational performance measurement. The purpose here is to encourage practitioners, researchers, academics, and students of policing to give thoughtful and empirical consideration to these issues and through research and writing elaborate an agenda for policy makers to deal with these contemporary issues that will confront us well into the future.

Globalization, transnational policing, terrorism and national security

The world of policing in the aftermath of the terrorists attacks in the United States on September 11, 2001[1] has changed significantly. In this section of the chapter, consideration will be given to issues of globalization, transnational policing, terrorism and national security in this dramatically different environment.

Challenges

Globalization and transnational policing

Globalization represents situations where events or activitie "are becoming stretched across the globe such that events, decisions and activities in one part of the world can come to have immediate significance for individuals and communities in quite distant parts of the global system" (Dunleavy 1994: 37). Globalization destroys the isolation traditionally associated with distance. It erodes borders. According to the report *Canada* 2005, *Global Challenges and Opportunities* (1997:25) "these phenomena undermine a traditional source of Canada's security – our geography. New threats are arising from a "borderless world" – environmental degradation, uncontrolled migration, new risks from disease. These threats take particular forms in North America. To an increasing extent, Canada is seen as the 'back-door' to the U.S. for illegal immigration. There is similar traffic in the other direction – illegal immigrants, firearms, drugs, pollution, toxic wastes and even cigarettes. Canada will need to ensure that the openness resulting from globalization...does not threaten the security or quality of life for Canadians."

In the law enforcement community, globalization means that the problems in one country may have roots in another, and that opportunities for organized crime in terms of different jurisdictions are challenges for the law enforcement community (Loeppky, 2003).

Lunney (1998:8) observes that it is instructive to see how crime intelligence annual reports and forecasts have changed in a few years. From focusing mainly on Canadian trends, these reports now discuss the crime threats emanating from all parts of the world, and instead of a monopoly of attention on the drug trade, they now deal with the depredations of economic crimes of all types, identifying sources on distant continents and countries. This has taken place in a very brief period of years. We do not need better evidence that crime is now a global threat, and not merely a national, continental or hemisphere issue.

In coping with the global environment, Lunney (1998:9) advises every police chief in Canada, regardless of the size of the force, to seriously begin to devote a portion of time and attention to the crime threats that exist beyond jurisdictional boundaries. The amount of that time will depend on the size, location and responsibilities of the service. The Commissioner of the RCMP must now be devoting an increasing amount of attention to international crime, and assistance with global peace keeping. For the heads of provincial forces, their direction over criminal intelligence and case management on national and international matters will become an increasingly important priority. The chiefs of the major municipal forces have need to become very familiar with national and international crime trends and events, and must plan to educate themselves and their senior executives on crime in the global environment. Police chiefs must journey overseas to build working affiliations with counterparts which translate into effective conduits for police liaison.

The chief of a city adjacent to a border point will be expected to be knowledgeable about crime conditions across the boundary impacting on the local situation. Chiefs of small towns anywhere in Canada must have access to information which will alert them to external criminal threats, and know how to seek effective assistance. Often it is the citizens of a small city, town or rural area that is seen as the prime victim-in-waiting for a fraudulent international real estate scam, or a car theft ring connected with an off shore syndicate (Lunney, 1998).

In much the same vein the Commissioner of the Ontario Provincial Police, Gwen Boniface (2001) outlined some ways in which law enforcement leaders need to deal with international crime trends in addition to federal government initiatives. These are:

1. Police leaders should first and foremost devote resources to the study and gravity of the problem in their own jurisdictions. A complete and thorough analysis of the problem and its magnitude, will allow police leaders to make more informed decisions concerning methods of dealing with the crime challenge.

2. All police leaders must realize that the criminal element expects law enforcement to be fragmented in relation to their own jurisdictional boundaries. Police agencies must combat this assumption by the willingness to share information nationally and internationally to prevent these crimes.

3. Incumbents within this role, is the need for police leaders to begin thinking about global police information networks, where all of this information can be stored, shared and easily retrieved to reduce continuing global crime trends.

4. Police organizations should also invest time and resources to information technology that will place the policing community on the leading edge of computer advancements, that in effect track and detect international criminal activity, and

5. As a means of addressing both organized crime, and other offences that require expert knowledge, police leaders must continue to either recruit experts into the organization or consult the private sector in contracting out expert services. For example, information technology specialist may be required to assist the police in the investigation of complex computer crimes or money laundering schemes.

All of this points to an emerging scholarly field of transnational policing. The impact of globalization and the increased demands for transnational security has transformed policing in local communities to the extent that police agencies at the national, provincial and local levels are expected to undertake tasks that would enlarge their traditional roles.   In his pioneering work, *Issues in Transnational Policing*, James Sheptycki (2000: 1) notes that transnational policing will be "a crucial concern in the coming years as social life is increasingly lived beyond the parochial conflicts of traditional ways of living".

Terrorism and national security

The tragic events of September 11, 2001 gave a telling and dramatic lesson to the people of the world of the profound impact of globalized crime on individual lives. The Government of Canada in its *Securing an Open Society: National Security Policy*, (2004) states: "the horrific events of September 11, 2001, demonstrated how individuals could exploit such openness to commit acts of terrorism that attempt to undermine the core values of democratic societies. Those events were a stark reminder to

Canadians of the tragic loss of 329 lives aboard Air India flight 182 in 1985."

Margaret Beare (2003) outlines four pieces of legislation which constitute Canada's response to terrorism. These are:

1. Bill C-36, the Omnibus Act to Amend the Criminal Code, The Official Secrets Act, The Canadian Evidence Act, The Proceeds of Crime (money laundering) Act and Other Acts, to Enact Measures Respecting The Registration of Charities, in Order to Combat Terrorism (short title: Anti-terrorism Act) proclaimed into force on December 24, 2001.

2. Bill C-35: An Act to Amend Foreign Missions and International Organization Act was passed by the House of Commons on December 12, 2001.

3. The Public Safety Act (Previously Bill C-55) was introduced on October 31, 2002.

4. The Immigration and Refugee Protection Act, received Royal Assent on November 1, 2001, and implementation on June 28, 2002. It was already in the process of being proclaimed before September 11, however amendments to the Public Safety Act (Bill C-55) could have brought the immigration-related provisions into force sooner than the original June date.

According to Beare (20003:32-37) the perception of security risk has changed since September 11, 2001. Canadians have to be prepared for at least some degree of encroachment on their privacy, and tighter limits on exercise of liberties such as freedom of association and expression of dissent. This means Canadians have to be more aware of the increased powers of the police and other government agencies.

Given the current environment, Beare (2003) offers three policy and research suggestions:

First, along with these enhanced policing powers, we may need to accompany the powers with enhanced oversight. Independent oversight of the RCMP could be considered given its new powers...

Second, new security measures in the future should not be introduced until it has been shown that existing policies and laws are in fact being enforced, and in being enforced, are found to be insufficient. Only then should enhanced powers and greater intrusive measures be introduced. New policies and laws may have unanticipated and adverse consequences while failing to make us safe.

Third, Canada does recognize from time to time that our legislative and policy needs may not be the same as those in the United States. While we clearly must choose when to resist international pressures, the resistance potential should always be considered. We have always valued our multiculturalism and diversity. Nothing has changed since September 11 that ought to make us question this.

Deputy Commissioner of the RCMP, Gary Loeppky (2003) believes that given the global nature of terrorism, to be successful in combating this threat, the sharing of information between police agencies is critical. Towards this end, the RCMP has enunciated an integrated policing philosophy which provides for police agencies working together at the tactical, operational and strategic levels. The concept implicitly extends into "multilateral law enforcement – that is, extensive collaboration with agencies and departments at all levels, community groups, foreign police agencies and even supranational agencies such as the United Nations. It also means integrating with private security firms and other intelligence and enforcement agencies throughout the private and corporate spheres.

Loeppky notes that while there were some types of integrated enforcement teams prior to 9/11, the pace at which their full implementation took place was deeply impacted by the 9/11 aftermath. These integrated teams include:

Integrated Border Enforcement Teams (IBETS) that are mandated to police those areas between the ports of entry to curb transnational criminal activity across the Canadian/US border. Participating in the IBETS are law enforcement agencies of the US and Canada, including various municipal, provincial, state and federal law enforcement agencies and government departments.

Integrated National Security Enforcement Teams (INSET), which is multi-disciplinary and involves such components as intelligence, investigations, proceeds of crime, threat assessment analysis and surveillance. The purpose of INSETS is to increase the capacity for the collection, sharing and analysis of intelligence among partners with respect to targets that are a threat to national security and; create an enhanced investigative capacity to bring such targets to justice. INSETS are made up of representatives of the RCMP, Canada Customs and Revenue Agency, Citizenship and Immigration Canada (CIC), Canadian Security Intelligence Service and provincial and municipal police services.

Integrated Immigration Enforcement Teams (IIETS) which have been mandated to mitigate the threat to Canada by prioritizing outstanding immigrant warrants, apprehending wanted persons and identifying national security threats. Each IIET is jointly operated by personnel from the RCMP and CIC.

Integrated Market Enforcement Teams (IMETS) are intended to strengthen the law enforcement community's ability to detect, investigate and deter capital market fraud by focusing resources on the investigation and prosecution of the most serious corporate frauds and market illegalities (Loeppky, 2003).

In Canada, the fundamental challenge that faces law enforcement and security officials, academics and human rights advocates and government policy makers is how to best balance the fundamental rights of the individual with the collective public good of safety and security in the post-September 11 environment.

National Security

The Government of Canada announced in its, *Securing An Open Society*: Canada's *National Security Policy*, (2004), a strategic framework and action plan designed to ensure that Canada is prepared for and can respond to current and future threats. The Policy contains several measures designed to build a more integrated security system in a way that is consistent with the goals of the policy. The following measures are identified in the policy document:

1. An integrated Threat Assessment Centre will be established to ensure that all threat-related information is brought together, assessed and reaches all who need it in a timely and effective manner.
2. The Government will establish a National Security Advisory Council, which will be made up of security experts external to government.

3. An advisory Cross-Cultural Roundtable on Security, composed of members of Canada's ethno-cultural and religious communities, will be created.
4. The new Department of Public Safety and Emergency Preparedness will be designated as the body responsible for the testing and auditing of federal departments' key security responsibilities and activities.
5. The National Security Policy also identified and elaborated six key security activities – intelligence, emergency planning and management, public health emergencies, transportation security, border security and international security – work together more effectively in meeting the security needs of Canadians.

Racial Profiling

The issue of racial profiling was brought into sharp focus with a series of articles in the *Toronto Star* in 2002 claiming that Toronto Police Service is engaged in racial profiling. The publication of these articles triggered a great deal of debate on the existence or non existence of racial profiling. In response to the Star's articles, the Toronto Police Service initiated a review of the Star's research arguing that the results do not provide evidence of systemic racial profiling being practiced by the Toronto Police Service.

According to Wortley and Tanner (2004:198), "racial profiling is said to exist when the members of certain racial or ethnic groups become subject to greater levels of criminal justice surveillance than others."

In the context of the heightened public debate as a result of the *Toronto Star's* articles, the Ontario Human Rights Commission (OHRC) in 2003 launched an inquiry into the effects of racial profiling on individuals, families, communities and societies as a whole. In its report *Paying the Price: The Human Cost of Racial Profiling,* the OHRC states that "the purpose of its racial profiling inquiry is not to prove or disprove the existence of racial profiling.

It is the Commission's view that previous inquiries have considered this and have found that it does occur" (p.9).

The Report (p.62) argues that "regardless of whether racial profiling can be proven to occur in any given context, the widespread perception among racialized groups that it is occurring is cause for concern" Among its recommendations, the Report (p.68) proposes that "all organizations and institutions entrusted with responsibility for public safety, security and protection should take steps to monitor for and prevent the social phenomenon of racial profiling, and develop or modify their policies, practices, training and public relations activities in this regard."

In a news release (2003), Ontario Association of Chiefs of Police (OACP), indicated that "the report by the OHRC is disappointing. The Commission has implied that police in this province practice a form of racial discrimination, racial profiling. This is unfair to the women and men who put their lives on the line everyday to serve all members of their communities." Both the OACP and Toronto Police Service expressed the view that all police services in Ontario "are working diligently with their local municipal governments, the Ontario Government and community groups to ensure that the police carry out their duties with integrity and professionalism through police recruitment, training and community outreach initiatives."

The Star's articles analyzed data gleaned from the Toronto Police Service's Criminal Information Processing System (CIPS) between 1996-2002. Based on an examination of 483,614 incidents, the Star's analysis concluded that black people are highly overrepresented in certain offence categories and that this pattern of overrepresentation is consistent with the idea that Toronto Police engage in racial profiling. The Star's articles also argued that blacks are treated more harshly after arrest than their white counterparts (Rankin et al., 2002a; 2002b; 2002c).

Wortley (2003: 100) observes that the importance of the racial profiling issue raised by the Star "is not confined to the Toronto area. Indeed, similar 'race/crime' controversies have emerged with respect to the treatment of black people in Nova Scotia and Quebec, the treatment of Asians and South Asians in British Columbia and the treatment of aboriginal people throughout the country."

512

Melchers (2003: 348) argues that the "...belief that police engage in racial profiling undermines public confidence in the police, as well as the credibility of the testimony and evidence submitted by police officers in criminal proceedings...In Toronto (as elsewhere in North America), the issue of racial profiling has become a significant threat to the ability of police to maintain order, ensure public safety, and prosecute those accused of criminal offenses."

Regardless of the validity of the claims of bias, the police is too important an institution for it to function and discharge its duties under a cloud of suspicion of bias and racism. In terms of the way forward, several suggestions at both the strategic and operational levels are worth noting.

At the research level, the *Canadian Journal of Criminology and Criminal Justice* (2003: 44) has made an interesting argument: "Documenting the existence of discrimination is a very tricky business. In addition to the complex statistical challenges, it is important that the research be conducted (1) by individuals who have considerable experience in the area and (2) by individuals who have taken no a priori position with respect to the issue."

Noting that the public must be confused by the claims and counterclaims on the issue of racial profiling, the Journal (2003:44) proposes that "one way of clarifying matters would be through the use of a judicial inquiry, drawing upon a select group of researchers who are clearly impartial. Such a panel could examine the data, collect additional information if necessary, and draw some scientifically valid conclusions. We owe this to the public, to the specific community allegedly affected, to the police."

Police services have made some progress in the hiring of visible minorities and aboriginal people as police officers. It is imperative that police services continue this process of making police organizations more representative of the communities they serve. Police leaders should enrich this process by ensuring that there are diversity plans in place that would address not only the issues of recruitment but also promotions. The proper leading and managing of diversity so that the talents of all policing members of the organizations are used to their fullest potential is necessary. Also, while there is increasing civilianization of police services, police managers should ensure that visible minorities and aboriginals are also hired as members of the civilian staff, an area that has not been properly addressed.

The training of police officers is a critically important area in the effective unbiased delivery of police programs and services. During training at the academy and the field, new police recruits undergo a socialization process. In addition the environment of Canadian policing is changing in significant ways. In Canada and in Canadian policing (Nancoo, 2000), the socio-political environment has witnessed dramatic changes. Some of these changes include demographic changes in terms of race, ethnicity, gender and aging. There are also the impacts of globalization, transnationalization of crime and policing, increase in communications technology and the public policing/private security divide. Police colleges and training institutes in Canada can ignore these changes at their own peril. It is necessary therefore for police colleges and training institutes, the agents of the socialization process, to make determined efforts to hire qualified instructors who are visible minorities and aboriginals. It is foolhardy to continue with the current unrepresentative nature of instructors at police training institutions.

A related issue is the qualifications of instructors hired to instruct at police colleges. While there is a significant increase in the hiring of university and college graduates as new police officers, this has not been the case with the hiring of permanent and seconded instructors at police colleges. The time has indeed come for instructors teaching at police colleges to have, in addition to their practical skills, a university education.

There are initiatives by some police organizations to address the issue of racial profiling. The Ontario Provincial Police has a pilot project that equips cruisers in Toronto and Kenora with in-car digital video cameras. This move allows the OPP to assess allegations of racially motivated police action with objective evidence. On a trial basis, the Kingston Police Service has begun collecting data with respect to the race and ethnicity of citizens stopped and/or searched by police patrol officers. Kingston Police Chief Bill Closs (Kingston Whig Standard: 2003) stated, "we are setting an even higher standard for Kingston Police officers in that they are being asked to acknowledge and understand the existence of unlawful profiling/bias-based policing and the need to prevent

514

it. While my officers and this service have never condoned this practice, publicity generated by the allegations has cast a shadow over the Kingston Police."

Private Security and Public Policing: The foundations of pluralized policing

Canada is entering a new era of policing. The provision of policing services was once considered to be the exclusive domain of governmental organizations operating at the municipal, provincial and national levels. Today, one of the significant transformations in post-modern Canada is the emergence of pluralized policing. With pluralized policing, a significant and increasing share of the demands for safety and security are being provided by private security agencies in addition to the roles being played by public policing and community crime prevention. The re-emergence and ascendancy of private security has altered the traditional thinking of looking at public safety. Reflecting the importance of this development is the fact that the Law Commission of Canada recently published *In Search of Security: The Roles of Public Police and Private Agencies A Discussion Paper*. Written by Dr. George Rigakos, the Commission's first scholar in residence, members of the public are invited to get involved in the public-private policing debate by sending their comments on *In Search of Security*[1] to the Law Commission of Canada.

There is effectively an end to government's monopoly of providing safety and security. This transformation has been described as multilateralized policing (Bayley and Shearing, 2001), pluralized policing (Bayley and Shearing, 1996; Nancoo, 2000), the commodification of policing (Shearing and Stenning, 1983) post modern policing (Stansfield, 1996; Murphy, 1998) and networked policing (Law Reform Commission).

Private security includes a myriad of agencies, services, and products utilized to protect the life and property of residential and commercial clients against crime and disorder. Private security organizations are also providing many of the functions that were once the almost exclusive domain of public policing.

The private security industry has exploded. First, over the last thirty years, the number of individuals employed in private security has outnumbered the actual number of public police officers. According to Statistics Canada "in 1996 there were 59,090 police officers in Canada compared to 82,010 private security officers and private investigators. According to this data, roughly two-thirds of security providers in Canada are employed in the private sector. This figure underestimates the actual number of private security employees because it only includes private security officers and investigators and does not include forensic accountants, insurance investigators or private 'in-house' security officers" (Law Commission of Canada: 10).

Secondly, in addition to the numerical increase of private security personnel, it was also found - based on a 1997 random sample survey – that the private investigation and security services industry generated over \$2 billion in revenue that year and comprised some 2,746 establishments (Law Commission of Canada: 10).

A third indicator of change and growth relates to the types of activities that engage private security firms.

> Private security personnel are now employed in ports, airports, retail shopping centres, commercial complexes and even residential spaces ranging from exclusive gated communities to social housing. All places are places that are publicly accessible.
>
> Alongside street patrols and security guards in shopping centers, there also exists a less visible side of the security industry. More and more private agents handle high stakes investigations such as corporate forensic accounting and insurance fraud detection. In some cases, private businesses prefer to handle infractions internally. This means that infractions are now being dealt with largely outside the purview of the public police and without public scrutiny. In other cases, it is the public police themselves who refer business owners to private firms. As a result, financial management and fraud that was once dealt with criminally and in public is now more likely to be handled privately. (Law Commission of Canada: 11).

A number of reasons have been attributed to the resurgence of private policing. First, it is argued that a security-conscious population perceives a performance gap in the public police delivery of services. That is, the public police do not have the capacity to meet the rising security needs and expectations of the community. This expectation gap is to some extent being met by private security.

Secondly, another powerful influence is the emergence of mass private property. Shearing and Stenning (1983:496) have argued that "to understand the locus of private security it is necessary to examine the changes that have taken place, particularly since the 1950s, in the organization of private property and public space. In North America, many public activities now take place within huge, privately owned facilities, which we call 'mass private property'. Examples include shopping centers with hundreds of individual retail establishments, enormous residential estates with hundreds, if not thousands, of housing units, equally large office, recreational, industrial, and manufacturing complexes, and many university campuses."

In an analysis on Future Trends, Ronald Stansfield (1996: 203) observes that "the transformation of Canada from a modern industrial society into a post modern informational society is having subtle yet profound consequences for policing." He believes that "a key trend in the information era is the expansion of the economic surplus...As more and more space is privatized, this will have a profound effect on police jurisdictions and, consequently on how order is reproduced in the new informational order" (Stansfield 1996: 212).

Public policing and private security need to function within a framework of a democratic society. In this context, we should analyze private security against the touchstone of democratic values and suggest ways this burgeoning phenomenon of private security be made to conform to the expectations of citizens of a democratic society. Three core principles - justice, equity, and accountability – of policing in a democratic society would be highlighted.

In Search of Security advises that "the principle of justice presupposes that policing is carried out in a manner that guarantees the peace of the community and the integrity and humanity of the individual" (Law Commission of Canada:39). The Canadian Charter of Rights and Freedoms also provides basic constitutional safeguards for individuals in their dealings with the police. The Law Commission (p.40) indicates that "public police officers and private security personnel are subject to different standards when they detain an individual. In some cases, private investigators may not be subject to the obligations of informing the accused of his or her right to retain and instruct counsel under section 10(b) of the Charter. When working for a private employer, a private investigator may not be subject to the same standards as a public police officer"

In the sphere of private security there also exists a situation, as pointed out by an Ontario Commission of Inquiry (1997) where security guards exercise powers such as banning individuals from property such as shopping malls. At times no explanation is given and there is no appeal for the penalty that may or may not be deserved. The critical question of parity between the crime and punishment is an important principle of justice.

In terms of the principle of equity, two aspects should be considered. There are (1) the idea of equality of services and (2) the notion of inclusiveness of all members of society. The rise of private security is in part due to the gap in the provision of services provided by the public police, as well as the growth of mass private spaces. Some individuals have the resources to purchase security as a commodity, while many others have to be content with a lower quality of service because of a lack of resources to purchase the equivalent level of service. The dilemma is that those that are at greatest risk, the poor, are least able to afford the benefits of private security systems. When it comes to the idea of inclusiveness and equity, however, it must be noted that women and visible minorities are more likely to find employment in private security than in public policing.

Accountability refers to a process where one is answerable for one's actions and there are also formal channels that members of society could use to file complaints. The Law Commission of Canada (p.40) points out that, "some argue that private security officers are much less accountable for their actions than are public police, especially since private security agencies do not have the equivalent of a public complaint process." Currently, there is not an independent oversight mechanism to hold private security officers and investigators accountable for their actions, nor are there formal channels to which members of a society can file a complaint. "Private security are much less accountable for their actions than are public police because legislation does not establish independent oversight mechanisms that can be used to hold private security responsible" (Law Commission of Canada: 4).

Given the increasing role of private security agencies in the provision of the security needs of the population, it is imperative that policy makers address some of the issues created in this new era of policing. In terms of private security governmental authorities should, as a priority, examine what new regulatory arrangements are necessary to guarantee that private security agencies work within the framework that enhances policing in a democratic society.

It is important that private security agencies become more professional in their outlook and behaviour. Actions necessary to achieve this include:

(1) The establishment of minimum training standards across Canada for individuals employed in private security. As of now only British Columbia requires minimum standards of training.

(2) Given that private security perform many of the functions that public police are involved in, it is important that the regulatory framework for private security be reviewed to reflect contemporary realities.

(3) Because of the large public spaces (mass private property) that private security looks after, consideration should be given to holding private security officers to standards that would guarantee some measure of parity as well as fairness and non-discriminatory behaviour.

(4) Further, given the values of a democratic society, private security should be held accountable for their actions and a regime of oversight mechanisms should be established.

Bayley and Shearing (2001:32) argue "if the public interests of justice, equity of protection, and the quality of service are to be safeguarded, government must audit what security agencies provide and monitor what is going on in a systematic way."

Currently, there is the situation where multinational private security firms work within the Canadian environment. How to make these multinational organizations amenable to national standards is one of the challenges that must be addressed.

In terms of long term change, the fact that we now have a system of "networked policing", "the public private distinction central to the current organization of governance may need to be re-thought. This raises a number of key challenges for reforming the law concerning public police and private security" (Law Commission of Canada: 55).

Organizational Performance Measurement

Organizational Performance Measurement is a critical issue facing police leaders in the 21st Century. Focusing on the performance measurement of public police organizations is important for research, theory and practice. Central questions that need to be addressed are how do we measure the overall effectiveness of police organizations and what are the underlying principles motivating responsible organizational performance (Nancoo, 2001:4).

Police leaders, political officeholders and citizens need to know how their police organizations are performing. Four levels of analyses need to be undertaken in order to provide stakeholders with the necessary information. These include the performance of police services relating to accepted standards; the performance of police organizations relative to other police organizations; the longitudinal organizational performance in terms of the current year vis a vis previous years; and finally the performance of the police service in terms of the expectations of the community.

In the United States of America, police organizations have initiated a number of different approaches to organizational performance measurement. These include:

1. The Commission on Law Enforcement Agency Accreditation Program (CALEA), which includes a large number of standards that must be met by police agencies seeking accreditation. The standards are almost entirely focused on inputs

and processes rather than on outputs or outcomes. The standards require departments to have policies concerning the use of discretion, for example, but the content of those policies is not prescribed. Nor must departments achieve any particular levels of crime solving or citizen satisfaction in order to become accredited. Thus the accreditation standard has limited value for assessing the effectiveness of police agency performance, although they do provide useful guidance for assessing the thoroughness for police administrative practices. Peel Regional Police and Niagara Regional Police are examples of Canadian Police organizations that received accreditation from CALEA.

2. The American Justice Institute developed Police Program Performance Measures (PPPM), a comprehensive system which sets out effectiveness measures that pertain to police performance. This approach sets out a model structure of police objectives with 5 dimensions: crime prevention, crime control, conflict resolution, general service, and police administration. Within these five dimensions, there were 46 specific outcomes that were operationalized into 65 measures. This system has not been widely institutionalized.

3. Mark Moore, David Thatcher, Andrea Dodge, and Tobias Moore in their book *Recognizing Value in Policing: The Challenge of Measuring Police Performance,* outlined seven performance dimensions with associated statistical indicators to evaluate police departments' overall effectiveness. These seven dimensions are: reduce criminal victimization, call offenders to account; reduce fear and enhance personal security; guarantee safety in public space; use financial resources fairly, efficiently and effectively; use force and authority fairly, efficiently and effectively; satisfy customer demands/achieve legitimacy with those policed.

In the United Kingdom, the Police Act 1996 requires all Police Authorities to publish an Annual Policing Plan setting out the priorities, targets and objectives for policing. The Plan must reflect the Government of the United Kingdom Ministerial Priorities. The Local Government Act 1999 requires a Police Authority to produce a Best Value Performance Plan – the Act requiring that all services are reviewed within a 5-year programme of reviews. Jim Barker-McCardle, Assistant Chief Constable of

Kent County Constabulary (2000: 51) indicated that Best Value is a duty to deliver services to clear standards covering both cost and quality – by the most effective, economic and efficient means available. Under this Act the Police Authority must make arrangements to secure continuous improvement in the way its functions are exercised, establishing objectives and performance measures. Each year, a selected number of services must be reviewed and the review findings must be published along with planned improvements, measures and targets in an Annual Performance Plan.

During each review the four "Cs" must be applied: *Challenge* why services are provided in the way they are. *Compare* performers against other similar providers of the service. *Consult* with the users of the service and the local community about the views of each service. *Compete* – can someone else provide that service more competitively?

In the United Kingdom the Police Department is also required to produce Efficiency Plans, an efficiency gain being defined as being made when more or better service is delivered for the same or less cost. The Police Department has to demonstrate that the same level of output of the same quality is achieved for less cost or more outputs and/or output of better quality is achieved for the same cost.

In addition to the Annual Policing Plan, the Efficiency Plan, and the Best Value Performance Plan, Barker-McCardle noted that his department also publishes a Policing Charter for Kent, which sets out the standard of service the police intend to deliver.

In Canada, the Ontario Government instituted a Police Adequacy and Effectiveness Standards Regulation under the Police Services Act. The Adequacy Standards prescribed six core policing areas, necessary to ensure the delivery of adequate and effective police services. These six areas are crime prevention, law enforcement, victim assistance, public order maintenance, emergency response services, and administration and infrastructure. In the case of the Royal Canadian Mounted Police, the Auditor General Office performs comprehensive reviews of this organization and reports to parliament. This is in addition to performance reports conducted by Treasury Board and the organizations own internal reviews. Senior managers of the RCMP also employed the Balanced Scorecard to take the pulse of their organization.

Robert Kaplan and David Norton developed The Balanced Scorecard (1996) in response to what they described as outdated and misleading techniques for evaluating organizational performance. The Balanced Scorecard allows managers to look at the organization from four important perspectives: *Customer perspective*: To achieve our vision, how should we appear to our customers? *Internal perspective*: To satisfy our stakeholders and customers, what must we excel at? *Learning and Growth Perspective:* To achieve our vision, how will we sustain our ability to change and improve? *Financial perspective*: How should we appear to our stakeholders?

In addition to the RCMP, the Ontario Provincial Police used the balanced scorecard approach to measure organizational performance. The Ministry of Municipal Affairs and Housing of Ontario initiated a Municipal Performance Measurement Program, which included a policing dimension.

In spite of these isolated examples, the bottom line however, is that organizational performance measurement in Canadian Policing is an ad hoc, inconsistent and an unsystematic process. There is clear need for police leaders, researchers and policy makers to get together to remedy the situation. In light of the new realities facing policing, certainly an over-arching committee under the auspices of either the Canadian Association of Chiefs of Police or a federal-provincial ministerial committee could look at the issue of police organizations performance measurement and formulate a co-coordinated, coherent and comprehensive plan of action.

Current problems facing policing on issues of police integrity may not be as widespread had there been performance measures at the organizational level in addition to measuring the performance and behaviours of individual officers. In their empirical study, *The Contours of Police Integrity*, Klockars, Ivkovic and Habberfeld (2004: 269) argued that "very different goals and visions of police integrity characterize the individual approach and the occupational or organizational culture approach to the understanding of corruption. The individual approach envisions the police agency of integrity to be one from which all morally defective individual officers have been removed and in which the agency remains vigilant in preventing their entry or emergence. By contrast the occupational or organizational culture approach envisions the police agency of integrity to be one in which the culture of the agency is highly intolerant of corruption."

There is another dimension to their study. Klockars, Ivkovic and Habberfeld (2004: 280) concluded that they were able to "compare agencies with one another in terms of integrity...We were able to identify both agencies of stellar integrity and those whose integrity environments were seriously deficient. This capacity to measure integrity also makes it possible to measure changes in agency integrity over time and across divisions."

In the 21st Century, one of the important challenges facing Canadian policing community is to strive towards excellence in policing. This of necessity requires the establishment of unambiguous organizational performance measurements for the evaluation of police organizations. In order to establish empirically verifiable best practices it is imperative that police organizations move toward the undertaking of comparative police organizational performance measurement.

Endnotes

1. The September 11, 2001 attacks were a series of coordinated terrorist attacks against the United States on September 11, 2001. The attacks involved the hijacking of four commercial airlines. Two aircraft were flown into the Twin Towers of the World Trade Center in New York City; a third aircraft was flown into the Pentagon in Arlington County, Virginia; and the fourth aircraft crashed into a Pennsylvania field, near Shanksville. The attacks are often referred to as September 11 or 9/11. In 2004, the U.S. government commission investigating the attacks officially concluded that the terrorist attacks were conceived and implemented by operatives of the militant al-Quaida organization.

2. This section, public policing-private security, of Chapter 19 relies on the Law Commission of Canada, *In Search of Security: The Roles of Public Police and Private Agencies Discussion Paper*.

References

Bain, R. (2000). Organizational Performance Measurement. The Case of a Municipal Organization. In S. E. Nancoo (Ed.), *Organizational Performance Measurement*. Aylmer: Issues and Themes Conference.

Barker-McCardle, J. (2000). Intelligence-led Policing, Crime Reductions, Performance Management, Regulators, Rat-catchers and Thrusters in S. Nancoo (Ed.), *Organizational Performance Measurement*, pp.43-57. Aylmer: Issues and Themes Conference.

Bayley, D. and Shearing C. (2001). *The New Structure of Policing: Description,Conceptualization and Research Agenda*. Washington DC: National Institute of Justice.

Bayley, D. and Shearing, C. (1996). The Future of Policing. *Law and Society Review*. Vol. 30. pp.585-606.

Beare, Margaret. (2003). Policing with a National Security Agenda http://www.pch.gc.ca/multi/pubs/police/security_e.cfm

Boniface, Gwen. (2001). Police Leaders and the Criminal Justice System in the new millennium. In S.E.Nancoo (Ed.). *Comparative Perspectives in Policing*. Aylmer: Issues and Themes Conference.

Brodeur, Jean-Paul. (1998). *How to recognize good policing*. Thousand Oaks: Sage Publications.

Chan, J.B.L. (2003). *Fair Cop.* Toronto: University of Toronto Press.

Cordner, Gary W., Scarborough, Kathryn E. and Sheehan, Robert. (2004). *Police Administration*. Cincinnati, OH: Anderson Publishing.

Dunleavy, P. (1994). The globalization of public services production: can government be best in the world? *Public Policy and Administration*, (9)(2).

Forcese, Dennis P. (2002). *Police Selected Issues in Canadian*

Law Enforcement. Ottawa:The Golden Dog Press.

Hoover , Larry T. (Ed.), (1996). *Quantifying Quality in Policing*. Washington D.C.: Police Executive Research Forum.

Kaplan, Robert and Norton, David. (1996). *The Balanced Scorecard*. Mass: Harvard University Press.

Klockars, C.B., Ivkovic, S.J & Haberfeld, M.R. (2004). *The Contours of Police Integrity* Thousand Oaks: Sage Publications.

Law Commission of Canada. *In Search of Security: The Roles of Public Police and Private Agencies.*

Loeppky, Gary. (2003). Globalization, Terrorism and Border Crossings. Presentation at Issues and Themes Conference, Aylmer, 2003.

Lunney. R. (1997). Globalization in S. E. Nancoo (Ed.), *21st Century Police Leadership*. Aylmer: Issues and Themes Conference:

Melchers, R. (2003). Do Toronto Police Engage in Racial Profiling? *Canadian Journal of Criminology and Criminal Justice* 45:347-366.

Moore, M., Thatcher D., Dodge A., and Moore.T. (2002). *Recognizing Value in Policing: The Challenge of Measuring Police Performance*. Washington D.C.: Police Executive Research Forum.

Murphy, C. (1998). Policing postmodern Canada. *Canadian Journal of Law and Society*, Vol. 13, No2, pp. 1-25.

Nancoo, S.E. (2000). *21st Century Canadian Diversity*. Mississauga: Canadian Educators' Press.

Nancoo, S.E. (Ed.). (1997). *21st Century Police Leadership*. Aylmer: Issues and Themes Conference.

Nancoo. S. E. (Ed,). (2001). *Organizational Performance Measurement*. Aylmer: Issues and Themes Conference

Nancoo, S.E. (Ed.). (2001a) *Comparative Perspectives in Policing*. Aylmer: Issues and Themes Conference.

O'Neill, M.W., Needle J.A., and Galvin R.T. (1980). Appraising the performance of police agencies: The PPPM (Police Program Performance Measures) System. *Journal of Police Science and Administration*. Vol. 8, No. 3, 253-264.

Rankin, J., Quinn, J., Simmie, S., and Duncanson J. (2002a)

Singled out: An investigation into race and crime. *The Toronto Star*. October 19. A1.

Rankin, J., Quinn, J., Simmie, S., and Duncanson J. (2002b). Police target black drivers. *The Toronto Star*, October 20.

Rankin, J., Quinn, J., Simmie, S., and Duncanson J. (2002c) Black crime rates highest. *The Toronto Star*, October 26. A1.

Rankin, J., Quinn, J., Simmie, S., and Duncanson, J. (2002d). Life and Death on Mean Streets. *The Toronto Star*, October 27 A1.

Shearing C. and Stenning P. (1983). Private Security Implications For Social Control. *Social Problems* 30:493-506.

Sheptycki, J. (Ed.). (2000). *Issues in Transnational Policing*. London: Routledge.

Stansfield, Ronald T. (1996). *Issues in Policing A Canadian Perspective*. Toronto: Thompson Educational Publishers.

Torigian, M.A. (2002). Performance Measures in Policing: An outcome of New Public Management. Unpublished manuscript. University of Western Ontario, Local Government Program.

Wortley, S. (2003). Hidden Intersections: Research on Race, Crime and Criminal Justice in Canada. *Canadian Ethnic Studies* xxxv, no.3: 99-117.

Wortley, S. and Tanner, J. (2003). Data, denials and controversy. The racial profiling debate in Toronto. *Canadian Journal of Criminology and Criminal Justice* 45: 367-390.

Wortley, S. and Tanner J. (2004). Discrimination or "Good" Policing? The Racial Profiling Debate in Canada. In C. Andrews (Ed.), *Our Diverse Citiies*. Metropolis Project, Number 1, Spring 2004.

Notes on Contributors

Professor Carol Agocs is with the Department of Political Science at the University of Western Ontario.

Dr. Peter Carrington is Professor of Sociology at the University of Waterloo, where he has been a faculty member since 1984. Previously, he taught in the Sociology Department of the University of Toronto, where he received his Ph.D. His main teaching and research interests are in the criminal and juvenile systems, social networks, and research methods and statistics. In the past few years, he has been involved in several evaluation studies for the Department of Justice Canada. He is currently doing research on police discretion, criminal and delinquent careers and networks, and the impact of the Youth Criminal Justice Act on the youth justice system in Canada.

Lori A. Cooke-Scott is a former police officer with the City of Dallas Police Department. She holds a master's degree in journalism from the University of North Texas, Denton, and a master's degree in Political Science from McMaster University.

Dr. Willem de Lint is a professor in the Department of Sociology and Anthropology at the University of Windsor. His main areas of research are in policing, political policing, and surveillance and intelligence systems.

Leanne J. Fitch is a sergeant with Fredericton Police and an 18-year police veteran. She holds the Bachelor of Arts and Master of Arts degrees from the University of New Brunswick. She is a part-time lecturer in the Criminology Department at Saint Thomas University. She is an executive member and Newsletter Editor for the Atlantic Women in Law Enforcement Association. In 2003, she was named Officer of the Year for the International Association of Women Police.

Dr. Alan Hall is a professor in the Department of Sociology and Anthropology at the University of Windsor.

Dr. Harish C. Jain is a professor in Michael G. DeGroote School of Business at McMaster University.

Dr. Tammy Landau is a professor in the Department of Justice Studies at Ryerson University.

Dr. Marcel-Eugène LeBeuf is senior research principal at the Community Contact and Aboriginal Policing Services Directorate of the RCMP. He holds a doctorate degree in criminology from the University of Montreal. In his position, he researches and oversees the research direction on organized crime. He has publications on diverse issues as information technologies, social disorder, civilian police officials, community policing and women in policing.

Professor David MacAlister B.A. (S.Fraser), LL.B (Br. Col.), MA (S Fraser), LL.M. (Qu.) is with the School of Criminology at Simon Fraser University.

Julia McLean is a consultant and former researcher with the Canadian Police College.

Professor Ken Menzies did an undergraduate degree in politics and economics at Queens before doing graduate work in sociology in England. He has been teaching at University of Guelph since 1972. He is the author of *Talcott Parsons and the Social Image of Man* and *Sociological Theory in Use*.

Stephen E. Nancoo is an educator and writer. He is the author-editor of *Community Policing in Canada* (with Dr. James Chacko), *Canadian Diversity 2000 and Beyond* (with Dr. Subhas Ramcharan), the *Mass Media and Canadian Diversity* (with Robert Nancoo) and *21st Century Canadian Diversity*. He is a graduate of

Laurentian University and Carleton University. He taught at the University of the West Indies, Carleton University, Ontario Police College, and the Government of Canada Federal Study Centre. He was also a journalist with Thomson Newspapers in Canada and the Caribbean.

Dr. Richard B. Parent is with Delta Police Service.

Jennifer Schulenberg is currently a doctoral candidate in the Department of Sociology at the University of Waterloo. Her research interests are in the sociology of the family, research methodology, juvenile justice, and policing. She is currently the university representative for the Canadian Society of Criminology and on the Membership Committee of the North Central Sociological Association. Her research has been published in several journals including the Canadian Journal of Criminology and Criminal Justice, Canadian Woman Studies, the Sociological Imagination, and a forthcoming report for the Department of Justice on police discretion with young offenders.

Dr. James Sheptycki is a professor at York University. He is the author of *Innovations in Policing Domestic Violence* and *Issues in Transnational Policing*. He is also editor of the journal *Policing and Society*.

Professor Parbudyal Singh is with the School of Business at the University of New Haven.

Dr. David Sunahara is Director of Research at the Canadian Police College. After completing his doctorate in sociology at the University of Alberta, he was employed as a researchers and policy analyst by the Law Enforcement Division of the Alberta Solicitor General. In 1989 he became a civilian member of the Royal Canadian Mounted Police where as a research officer with the Canadian Police College he has conducted a variety of research projects on use of force, ethics, Aboriginal policing and a range of training issues. He also acted as a technical advisor to the Canadian Association of Chiefs of Police (CACP) and sits on the CACP Ethics subcommittee.

Notes on Contributors

Matt Torigian is a superintendent of police with the Waterloo Regional Police Service. He is a member of the Ontario Association of Chiefs of Police sub-committees on Community Policing and Diversity.

Professor Simon Verdun-Jones B.A., M.A. (Cantab), LLM, JSD (Yale) is with the School of Criminology at Simon Fraser University.

Dr. James W. Williams is a professor in the Department of Sociology and Anthropology at the University of Windsor.